What Do We Know About Globalization?

What Do We Know About Globalization?

Issues of Poverty and Income Distribution

Guillermo de la Dehesa

Chairman of the Centre for Economic Policy Research (CEPR)

Blackwell
Publishing

87444832

BLACKWELL PUBLISHING
350 Main Street, Malden, MA 02148-5020, USA
9600 Garsington Road, Oxford OX4 2DQ, UK
550 Swanston Street, Carlton, Victoria 3053, Australia

First published 2007 by Blackwell Publishing Ltd

1   2007

Library of Congress Cataloging-in-Publication Data

Dehesa, Guillermo de la.
What do we known about globalization? : issues of poverty and income
distribution / Guillermo de la Dehesa.
p. cm.
Includes bibliographical references and index.
ISBN 978-1-4051-3669-3 (hardback : alk. paper)
1. Globalization—Economic aspects.   2. Income
distribution.   3. Poverty.   I. Title.

HF1359.D448 2007
339.2—dc22
2007006416

A catalogue record for this title is available from the British Library.
Set in 10.5 on 13 pt Dante
by SNP Best-set Typesetter Ltd, Hong Kong
Printed and bound in Singapore
by Utopia Press Pte Ltd

For further information on
Blackwell Publishing, visit our website:
www.blackwellpublishing.com

Contents

Foreword*

Stanley Fischer

The purpose of Guillermo de la Dehesa's book is summarized by its subtitle: "Issues of Poverty and Income Distribution." In it, he takes on some of the major arguments that rage around the topic of globalization.

Consumer warning: Do not go any further if you are looking for another polemic about globalization and its problems. Do read the book if you want to better understand globalization and its implications, and if you want to know what needs to be done to extend its benefits to countries and people that are not benefiting from it as much as they could.

This is a sober and balanced book. The approach is reasoned, relying heavily on the professional economics literature and on evidence. He starts with technological progress, which is above all else the driver of economic growth. He argues that because scientific and technical advances are generated largely in the richer countries, such progress has an inherent tendency to increase the inequalities between rich and poor countries, and within countries between those who can invent or operate the new technologies, and those who cannot. This argument reflects the consistent empirical finding in the United States that it is primarily the nature of recent technical progress, rather than foreign competition, that has caused income gaps to widen since the 1990s.

* This is a foreword to *What Do We Know About Globalization?: Issues of Poverty and Income Distribution* by Guillermo de la Dehesa. Views expressed are those of the author, and not necessarily of the Bank of Israel.

If economies were closed, the nature of technical progress in one country would not necessarily affect other countries. But in a globalized world, technical progress in one country will affect other countries – and of course, if countries want to benefit not only from access to the markets in other countries, as in export-led growth, but also from gaining access to the newest technologies, they need to open up, that is, to globalize.

If anything, de la Dehesa may concede too much to the opponents of globalization by emphasizing the potential negative impacts of technical progress in one country on other countries. There are also positive impacts, for instance the green revolution. Further, countries not at the technology frontier do not have to invent technology to benefit from technical progress, they just need to import it. That is what China has done, to great effect, and what others can do, including by welcoming foreign direct investment. That is to say, the policy framework in a developing country can have a large impact on the extent to which the country benefits from the potential growth offered by globalization, that is, by integration into the global economy.

After thoroughly reviewing in chapters 1–4 the many forces related to globalization that influence its potential impact on both poverty and inequality, de la Dehesa turns in chapter 5 to discuss the global distribution of income. Here he draws the distinction between the global distribution of income among individuals, no matter what country they live in, and among the average incomes of different countries. Almost certainly the individual distribution of incomes has been becoming more equal in recent years as hundreds of millions of Chinese and Indians have been moving from lower incomes toward the center of the global income distribution. The distribution of average incomes across countries may at the same time have been becoming more unequal, as many small countries, especially in Africa, have been falling behind.

These facts are frequently discussed as if they have major implications for whether globalization is good or bad. That is a trap, because the syllogism: globalization is taking place, some countries have done well during that period, others have not, therefore, globalization is responsible for the distribution of income worsening, is incorrect. He does not fall into that trap: rather, he asks what can be done to make the impact of globalization better – and his answer in the subtitle of the book is that the way to do that is by having more globalization.

He rightly emphasizes first the need to open up to trade. Chapter 7 is titled "More Developing Countries' Access to Developed Countries' Markets," and the initial focus is on the enormous and unjustifiable trade barriers that remain to access for developing countries to industrialized country markets, particularly in agriculture. This is a well-known problem, and the Doha Round of trade negotiations was supposed to make progress in reducing these barriers. But there has so far been dismayingly little progress in that regard. It seems that no amount of calculating the potential gains from freeing up agricultural trade, and no amount of finger-pointing, has made any difference to the willingness of the EU, Japan, and the US substantially to liberalize agricultural trade.

At the same time, de la Dehesa points out that the calculations showing major gains from trade liberalization suggest that about half the benefit will come from the liberalization of South–South trade, from developing countries opening up to each other. Here is an area where developing countries could move ahead, on their own. The problem is that the political economy of trade liberalization is typically perverse: countries that liberalize trade usually think of that as doing a favor to their trading partners, rather than doing good for their own citizens. Nonetheless, here is an area where globalization can be made to work better.

In chapter 8, he emphasizes the potential benefits from welcoming foreign direct investment, particularly as a way of gaining access to foreign technology, and asks what can be done first to encourage FDI, and then to harvest its benefits. In chapter 9 he turns to the growing integration of trade and finance. This is an area that I also believe to be very important, more important than I did just a few years ago. I have been particularly struck in the case of the Israeli economy by the beneficial impact the full opening of the capital account in 1997 seems to have had on FDI, on trade, and on the attitudes of Israeli business-people toward the possibilities offered by the global economy.

After taking up the economics of aid, and the case for increasing it, he turns in his final chapter to the growing importance of migration. As is by now well known, remittances already constitute the largest single source of foreign exchange earnings for several economies. Labor flows are becoming very large, and both their economic and their social impact are rising. Here is another key aspect of globalization. Typically it has many pluses, and key minuses. And typically, de la Dehesa's analysis of the phenomenon is thorough, professional, balanced, and sensible.

To find out what he has to say, read the book!

Introduction

A year ago I published a book entitled *Winners and Losers in Globalization* in which I tried to explain to the economics lay reader, simply but without sacrificing academic rigor, just what globalization really is. I tried to be as objective and instructive as possible because I felt that there was a great deal of confusion surrounding the concept and what it embodied. At best, globalization had become a handy excuse, but it was generally the scapegoat that took the blame whenever things went wrong or whenever there seemed to be no explanation for why something was not going right. It has become sort of like the word "virus," which is used whenever we do not know exactly why someone is ill. Unfortunately, this wide perception, mainly among young people in developed countries, has not changed much since then.

The only important and significant change is an increasing trend of NGOs, which are no longer "against" globalization but in favor of a "better" globalization, in the sense of trying not to leave some poor people and countries behind the potential opportunities that globalization can bring out and establishing some safeguards in the world integration process for short-term capital, for employment and wages and for the environment. The reason why I have decided to embark on this new book has been to deal with two of the fundamental and traditional arguments raised against globalization: that it increases poverty and inequality and also to try to explain how the present process of globalization can be improved, on the one side by deepening it and on the other by helping further those which are left behind it.

1

In my previous book I did not shy away from pointing out the drawbacks of globalization. Globalization, like any change process, although positive overall, entails certain unavoidable, but mainly temporary, negative economic, social, political, and cultural consequences that must be urgently addressed. World-wide terrorism, the global arms race, global drug traffic and the 1.2 million children that are sold or kidnapped every year, to be used as forced labor force or exploited sexually, according to UNICEF, are just four examples, among others, of the dark side of globalization, although, on the other side, there is also a slow but steady process of globalization of democracy and of human rights, not only through governments and international organizations pressure, but also by the action of organizations such as Amnesty International, Transparency International, Oxfam, and other reputed NGOs. The same can be said about the improvement of the environment through the pressure of NGOs such as Greenpeace.

Nevertheless, I also stated that the winners in such a process far outnumbered the losers, that the welfare and living conditions of the vast majority of the world's citizens would improve thanks to globalization, and that efforts would have to be made to develop a safety mechanism to help those who became marginalized or were left out, as they would be the true losers. I hope that with my first book I was able to help people understand this far-reaching and promising process that market economies have been undergoing for several decades now.

In this second book I try to explain with greater precision and detail the causes of inequality, poverty and marginalization, which are unfortunately still prevalent throughout the world, and how, contrary to popular belief, the acceleration of globalization in the last decades tends to reduce the levels of inequality and poverty world-wide but unfortunately not evenly; there is still much to do to reduce this asymmetric distribution of its clear benefits. My thesis, which tries to be underpinned by a substantial amount of theoretical and empirical research, developed by some of the world's top economists, is succinctly the following.

The main source of the world's current vast prosperity is technological progress. In the first 18 centuries of the Christian era, that progress was minimal or at least lower than demographic growth which was also very low. As a result, living conditions throughout the world did not improve or they did so at a snail's pace and with many bumps along the way. The population grew very slowly and nearly everyone in the world, except for a privileged few (mainly nobility), lived in what today would be considered absolute poverty. The world was living under "Malthusian stagnation" where population grows faster than technical progress and output. Following the diffusion of the first Industrial Revolution and the development of modern capitalism (around 1820), a period of growing prosperity began (and continues gathering strength today), making it possible – thanks to the development of new scientific discoveries and the concomitant waves of technological progress – for the twentieth century to become, by far, the most prosperous century in the past two millennia.

Suffice it to say that in the twentieth century the world's real income per inhabitant increased 3.5 times more than it had in the preceding 19 centuries combined. Moreover, this spectacular growth in real per capita GDP was achieved despite the fact that, in just one century, the population grew by 4.5 billion people to close to 6.1 billion in 2000, whereas in the previous 19 centuries it had increased by only 1.3 billion. This means that the population growth in the twentieth century alone was also 3.5 times greater than that achieved in the previous 19 centuries combined. Further proof of this remarkable growth in prosperity is that between 1820 and 2000 life expectancy increased by more than one and a half times, from 26 years to 66 years, while infant mortality fell fourfold, from 200 per thousand to 54 per thousand. Thus, based on the historical experience of the past two centuries, it seems clear that only with scientific and technological progress, coupled with a market economy, can the world prosper as it had in the past century.

Technological progress has facilitated globalization. Indeed, it was a necessary condition, as it made it possible to increasingly lower the costs of production, storage, marketing, distribution, and transport of both goods and ideas, enhancing the flows of trade, capital, technology, and labor, which are the true essence of globalization. However, technological progress was not the only requisite for globalization.

Entrepreneurs who took the risk of exploiting the new opportunities offered by technical progress were a necessary condition as well. But it was also necessary for governments around the world, convinced of its advantages, to allow it or encourage it by gradually liberalizing the flows of goods and services, capital, labor, and technology between countries.

Hence, globalization may have periods of greater advances or declines, depending on whether governments' and lobbies' attitudes toward it are more positive or negative in the light of its short-term consequences. In fact, following the preceding upsurge in globalization, between 1870 and 1913, there was unfortunately another period of retrocession, which started in 1914 and brought about, not only a staunch wave of protectionism, but also lower economic growth, two world wars and a great depression. As a result, the globalization process only began to recover slowly from 1960, finally accelerating from 1980.

However, in addition to being the key factor in improving social well-being, technological progress also tends to cause greater inequality, at least in the short and medium term and, in certain cases, it even stretches out to the long term. Scientific discoveries always come from a certain country or group of countries, generally those with the highest levels of human capital and market size, giving such country or countries a huge productive advantage over the others, as was the case with the United Kingdom in the first Industrial Revolution or the United States in recent decades. Depending on the degree of globalization at any given time, such discoveries take more or less time to be disseminated to other countries through commerce, foreign investment and emigration; accordingly, the absence of globalization can cause the inequality between countries to persist for much longer periods of time.

New technologies are adopted first by those countries that have the human and physical capital needed to copy or assimilate them. They reach the rest of the countries more slowly, in some cases taking many decades to be adopted, either because these countries do not have what it takes to assimilate them or because they are shut off from the rest of the world. As a result, there are almost always certain countries that lag in such advances by more than a century.

Just as technological progress can cause inequality among countries, it can also produce it among the citizens of the same country, including that in which the discovery was made and first developed. This is due to the fact that in each country there are people who, because of their level of income, education, or training, begin to use these new technological discoveries almost immediately, thereby significantly raising their productivity levels. As a result, their salary and income levels are higher than those of their compatriots, who have a lower level of knowledge and take longer to start using them. Thus, the level of income inequality between them grows.

There are other factors that make technological progress generate inequality. First, new technological discoveries and improvements in human capital tend to show growing returns to scale wherever they are applied. In other words, they tend to produce a growing volume of output for each new unit added of factor input, be it physical or human capital. As a result, the productivity and cost advantages achieved by the countries or companies that initiate and develop them tend to grow faster.

Second, such technological developments also tend to give rise to "agglomeration" effects by exploiting "external economies," which generally attract other individuals and specialized companies to the same area or geographical region where these developments are taking place, thereby further accentuating the initial differences in productivity and, particularly, in costs, as the cost savings achieved through the agglomeration of certain specialized economic activities in one specific area is considerable. Lastly, technological developments also give rise to "economies of scale," as major cost savings are generally achieved thanks to the greater size and optimization of the production scale, making such areas or units much more competitive than others that begin to develop such new technologies at a later stage.

In any event, it should be made very clear that, although technological progress produces temporary inequality, its diffusion is accelerating with globalization since the 1980s and, at the same time, is bringing greater absolute prosperity and welfare for nearly everyone compared with their situation prior to its development and implementation, as will be extensively demonstrated throughout this book.

In addition to technological progress, there are other factors that produce inequality between countries. On the one hand, there are structural factors, such as climate and geographical location. Countries located in the tropics, in arid regions, in high mountains or in areas without access to the sea or navigable rivers tend to grow at a substantially slower pace than those located in areas with temperate climates, mild geographical features and natural means of communication and transport. On the other hand, there are exogenous factors, such as demographic growth. The developing countries with the greatest population growth and overpopulation levels need to grow and increase their production of goods and services much more rapidly to be able to raise their per capita income. However, they generally fail to achieve this, and their per capita income tends to drop while their natural resources are overexploited, which in turn leads to very serious nutritional and ecological problems.

Lastly, there are political and institutional endogenous factors which pose some of the most important – if the not the greatest – obstacles to growth of political and institutional character. The absence of a true democracy and a strong civil society, the lack of clearly defined social and economic rules accepted by the population, starting from property rights and adequate judicial and public security systems to defend them, the high level of corruption, the poor quality of public goods and services and the misappropriation of public resources that this entails, as funds are squandered or siphoned off instead of being invested in education, health and such basic services as electricity or drinking water and the lack or weakness of credit and savings institutions are all factors that make it impossible for many countries to emerge from marginalization and poverty.

Nevertheless, contrary to popular opinion, it is precisely through globalization that the inequalities stemming from all the above-mentioned factors would tend slowly to be reduced. Proof of this is the fact that the acceleration of globalization since the 1980s has made it possible to narrow slightly the inequality and firmly the poverty levels in the world, although it must also be said that unfortunately this reduction has not taken place evenly among countries or individuals. The countries which have been able to become more open and global have also managed to grow and reduce their poverty levels the swiftest (although not necessarily their inequality levels, which are growing at least temporarily), whereas other countries, where globalization has taken place at a slower pace, have not been able to improve these levels, and in some cases they have even worsened when globalization has been absent. Moreover, most of the world's inhabitants have experienced a reduction in poverty, thanks to the fact that very populous countries like China and India, which together account for nearly 40 percent of the world's population, have been opening up and globalizing since the 1980s and have also been having great success in eradicating poverty.

Nevertheless, there are some countries that have experienced an increase in poverty levels, mainly in Africa, but also in Latin America, and within countries inequality has been growing in some regions, both in developed and developing countries. Finally, while inequality between the near 200 countries in the world has increased, when weighted by the size of their population, it has been reduced.

There are several reasons why globalization tends to reduce the world's levels of poverty and inequality. On the one hand, as a result of the larger volume of international trade, globalization makes it possible to allocate resources more efficiently given that countries can specialize in producing what they are most competitive at, because they have comparative, absolute or relative, advantages in some products. Also, new technologies are being disseminated more quickly through trade to other countries and peoples, which can improve their knowledge and use of the traded goods and services where these technologies are embodied or have been produced with them.

On the other hand, thanks to greater flows of foreign direct investment, globalization enables companies from developed countries to set up subsidiaries in developing countries to produce at a lower relative cost with respect to productivity. These companies, with very few exceptions, contribute capital and technology to the country in which they are setting up, thus increasing productivity and creating more jobs and exports, which translates into a higher growth rate through higher employment levels, higher salaries, higher skills, and higher income levels.

Lastly, globalization allows for larger migratory flows and, as a result, income levels between countries tend to converge more quickly. This happens not only because of a more efficient allocation of labor and skills with respect to demand, but also because of the remittances the emigrants send home to their country of origin and the knowledge and experience they acquire, which many of them ultimately take back to their home country, making it possible to assimilate new technologies more rapidly.

Thus, the growing process of globalization tends to slowly reduce world inequalities and poverty and, consequently, the developing countries that have managed to open up faster to these flows of goods, services, capital, and technology have prospered more quickly than those that have not. It is therefore necessary for globalization to progress more quickly and with more depth, under world rules agreed among the world's countries. The idea that poor or marginalized people or countries are the "victims of globalization" is an important fallacy. The truth of the matter is that they are mainly "victims of the lack of globalization."

One of the basic conditions for globalization to progress and take root at a good pace is, first, that developed countries (but also many developing countries) must put an end to the scandalous protectionism of their agricultural products and of their labor-intensive goods and services production, which is precisely what most developing countries can export to them. It is estimated that the richer countries' protectionist barriers against these goods, such as textiles, footwear, crafts, toys and clothing, cost developing countries more than $110 billion per year and that their agricultural protectionism costs them another $150 billion a year. That is a total of $260 billion – more than six times the amount of official aid the richer countries contribute to developing countries each year – and that is why we so often hear the leaders of developing nations say that what they want is "more trade than aid."

Second, it is also necessary for the richer countries to drastically reduce the nearly $300 billion they earmark each year for agricultural subsidies. In addition to being a huge strain on their own taxpayers and consumers, these subsidies are also producing a very large amount of un-saleable stocks. Because these stocks are not competitive, they are sold at subsidized dumping prices to the developing countries, causing the national production prices of some countries to collapse (with the only exception of helping net importers of food among least developed countries, which could be helped directly).

Third, it is extremely important for developing countries to continue receiving increasing FDI, among other reasons, because they are going to account in the next forty or so years for almost 90 percent of the world's population and are going to be the future largest markets for developed and developing countries. Since the end of the previous wave of globalization, in 1914, FDI flows to developing countries have been falling as a percentage of total flows, although they have stopped their downward trend in the last few years thanks to the flows received by the large developing countries which have opened up to international trade and FDI.

Lastly, developed countries, most of which have a waning – and dramatically ageing – population, should open their borders to immigration from developing countries, which have serious problems of overpopulation. Not only have migratory flows historically proven that they are the fastest and most direct way to reduce income inequality between countries, but they are also beneficial in helping support the financial situation of most developed countries' public pension and healthcare systems, which are generally unsustainable in the medium or long term.

Developing countries should also substantially reduce their trade and financial protectionism, which is still even more stringent than that of developed countries. This would open the doors for more trade amongst themselves increasing South–South trade and, consequently, producing higher growth rates, thus enabling them to increase their inflows of foreign direct investment. The full liberalization of trade protectionism in the world would increase the world's disposable income by as much as $700 billion a year, which would benefit developed and developing countries alike. This is what I understand by "more globalization."

What is happening with Official Development Aid (ODA), which is essential to helping countries that have been left out in the cold from technological progress and globalization, is also scandalous. Not only has this form of aid fallen by 29 percent in absolute terms and 50 percent in relative terms since the 1990s, but 70 percent of it is granted bilaterally, largely to gain political influence and to boost exports of goods and services from developed countries, which many of the poorer countries neither requested nor needed in the first place. As a result, often, the main result this "tied aid" achieves is to promote corruption and squandering in the recipient countries. What the poorer countries really need in order to avoid being left out of the globalization process altogether is help in developing the public goods and services they need the most: political and social institutions, education, healthcare, drinking water, rural infrastructures, and better sewage systems. There is no private investment in these public goods because, although the social benefits are enormous, the financial returns are scant. Development aid should be earmarked for these public goods and services rather than for meaningless macro-projects that are ultimately never used and only fatten the foreign bank accounts of a few of the recipient country's politicians and bureaucrats.

At the Monterrey Summit in 2002, it was plain to see that the rich countries, having reduced their contribution to development aid substantially as a percentage of GDP during some of their most prosperous years, were not willing to increase it much. This lack of solidarity impedes the saving of numerous human lives each year, lives which are lost to the lack of clean drinking water and terrible pandemics like malaria, AIDS, tuberculosis and diarrhea. Recent studies show that by increasing this aid by $25 billion, i.e. 0.1 percent of the rich countries' GDP, and using it exclusively for healthcare, more than 7.5 million lives could be saved each year. The unwillingness to increase these contributions also makes it impossible to increase the level of education in the poorest countries, which is the best way to reduce their rate of population growth. If the rich countries spend $500 billion each year on arms, they can certainly afford to address these very grave problems of humankind by doubling or tripling their contribution to development aid. Fortunately, in recent years, ODA and other development flows have started to take a promising upward trend mainly for the poorest countries.

In conclusion, there may be still room for a large trade-off between the movements of goods, services, capital, and technology and the movements of people. If all the developed countries do not hurry up and eliminate the trade barriers with the developing countries, if the latter are left without sufficient flows of capital and do not receive more inflows from foreign investment, and if the poorest countries and peoples of the world, who are being left out (some of them because of their own poor quality domestic policies and institutions) from international trade, investment, and technology, do not receive more aid, world income inequality among countries may shoot up producing massive waves of emigration until the mid-twenty-first century from these neglected poor countries to the rich countries, potentially causing widespread violence, terrorism, and even war.

Mass migration will be not only the outcome of increasing income inequality, but also of the increasing population mismatch between developed and developing countries. One need only think that of the 2.65 billion inhabitants that will be added to the world's current population of 6.45 billion, until around the 2050s, all of them will be born in developing countries – and almost 1 billion in the poorest ones – while the developed countries will keep the same population (including an extrapolation of present net immigrant flows), otherwise their population would fall.

This dramatic demographic imbalance, in which rich countries will eventually account for only 13 percent of world's population, can have unforeseeable consequences – all negative – for world peace and security. Only by opening up and globalizing trade, investment, and technology, in substitution for migration, will we avoid a catastrophic situation in the twenty-first century stemming from increased poverty, inequality and, consequently, constant massive waves of unemployed emigrants trying to make it through the rich countries' borders. Therefore, in this sense, contrary to what many believe, what the world needs is more countries joining the present globalization process and increasing the global flows, and before it's too late.

Chapter 1

Technical Progress and Economic Prosperity

The leap of progress achieved by the world in the twentieth century, particularly in the second half, was by far the biggest in history. Until the eighteenth century we had not even vaguely thought about the concept of "progress," and it was not until the nineteenth century that some signs of progress began to appear on the horizon. Finally, in the twentieth century, progress was so spectacular that today it is taken for granted, a given. Today people generally assume that the next generation will live one to two times better than they do in material terms. This is a new sensation that had not been felt in the previous two millennia.

According to one of the best quantitative studies of the world's economic history, carried out by Angus Maddison (2001 and 2003) and covering more than eight centuries, from 1000 to 1820, when the first Industrial Revolution had been consolidated, world real per capita GDP grew only 50 percent, being the net result of the world's population growing almost fourfold, rising from 268.3 million to 1.04 billion inhabitants and world GDP growing 4.5 times. Despite this extremely slow growth for more than eight centuries, it can be considered that the world progressed somewhat, since, in the preceding millennium, that is, between the years 0 and 1000, the world population grew sixfold and GDP grew only 5.9 times; consequently, world real per capita GDP declined slightly.

By contrast, in the 180 years between 1820 and 2000, per capita GDP increased 8.5 times, despite of the population growing almost six-fold, from 1.04 billion in 1820 to 6.1 billion in 2000, meaning that the world's GDP grew 14.5 times. In other words, in the last 180 years there has been eight and a half times more progress in the world, measured by world real per capita GDP growth, than in the preceding 1,820 years, a period ten times longer. These are truly astronomical differences because, in relative terms, per capita income in the past 180 years grew almost 80 times faster than the average for all the preceding 180-year periods.

Other data underpinning this remarkable progress are the life expectancy and infant mortality rates. The increase in the former and the decrease in the latter clearly evidence the improvement in humankind's well-being. In the year 1000 life expectancy was 24 years – exactly the same as that in Egypt and Rome at the beginning of the Christian era. Between 1000 and 1820 – eight centuries – life expectancy had only improved by two years, from 24 to 26. Between 1820 and 2000 it rose to 66 years. That is to say, in these last 180 years it grew 2.5 times, or almost ten times faster than in the preceding two millennia.

In the year 1000 the infant mortality rate was the same as at the beginning of the Christian era: 330 out of every 1,000 infants died before they reached the age of one year. Today the figure stands at 54 out of every 1,000, a sixfold reduction. It should be noted that the population explosion in this past century, which added 4.45 billion inhabitants to the world census, was due exclusively to the increase in the life expectancy rate and the decrease in the infant mortality rate, as the fertility rate has been falling steadily since 1800 and it continues to do so today.

The same can be said about hunger. Trevor Logan (2005) has shown, using the 1888 Cost of Living Survey, that although by conventional income measures, nineteenth-century American and British industrial workers were two to four times as wealthy as poor people in developing countries today, however, today's poor are less hungry than yesterday's more wealthy industrial workers. The reason is that the price of calories has declined dramatically over the last century enhancing the purchasing power of calories. Using the Engel curve implied by the

14

historical calorie elasticities, Logan derives new income estimates for developing countries which yield income estimates that are six to ten times greater than those derived using purchasing power parity of GDP deflators. Thus, according to this new estimate, GDP per capita is undermeasured today.

Another renowned economist, Bradford De Long (2000), has calculated the world's real per capita GDP evolution in the last millennium, reaching very similar staggering conclusions to those of Maddison. In the eleventh, twelfth, and thirteenth centuries the world's real per capita GDP declined. It subsequently improved in the fourteenth and fifteenth centuries, remained stagnant in the sixteenth century, and slightly grew again in the seventeenth and eighteenth centuries. It was not until the nineteenth century that it began to really take off, growing by 230 percent. In the twentieth century it grew by 850 percent, 3.7 times more than in the previous century.

Bearing in mind that the world population in the year 1000 was around 270 million and that it had grown to 900 million by 1800 (3.3 times), in those same eight centuries the world's GDP grew only 3.8 times. Between 1800 and 1900 the world population grew 1.8 times and per capita GDP 2.3 times, meaning that in just one century the world's GDP grew 4.1 times, a little more than it did throughout the whole of the preceding eight centuries. Between 1900 and 2000, the world population went from 1.65 billion to 6.1 billion, i.e., it grew 3.7 times, and per capita GDP grew 8.5 times, meaning that GDP increased 12.2 times, or three times more than in the nineteenth century and almost twice as much as during the preceding nine centuries.

These data clearly show the notable progress of the world's economy in this past century. However, this progress has not been spread out evenly across the countries and regions of the world.

The disparities in per capita GDP growth have broadened, especially following the diffusion of the first Industrial Revolution and the arrival of modern capitalism. More than a thousand years ago, in the year 1000, the average levels of per capita GDP in the world were very similar. Everyone was poor, except for the privileged few who had taken land by force and had become the "nobility." Indeed, today's richest countries – the ones that belong to the OECD – had then a lower per capita GDP than China or India as a result of the economic collapse triggered by the fall of the Roman Empire. Conversely, in 1820, the western European countries, Japan and the main countries resulting from European immigration (i.e. the US, Canada, Australia, and New Zealand) had reached an average per capita GDP that doubled that of the rest of the world.

In 1913 the income level in Europe and the countries resulting from European immigration was already six times that of the rest of the world. In 2000 this difference increased to over seven times. Equally significant is the wide standard deviation in GDP per capita figures: the difference in per capita income between the countries with the highest per capita GDP (i.e. the countries resulting from European immigration and Japan) and those with the lowest per capita income (i.e. Africa), was 19 times in 2000. These differences are measured in terms of purchasing power parities (PPP), based on the purchasing power of each dollar in each country, instead of using the nominal exchange rates of each year (Maddison, 2001).

Between developing countries there are also notable differences. Per capita GDP increased slightly more quickly in Latin America up to 2000 than in eastern Europe and most of Asia and almost twice as quickly as in Africa. Nevertheless, compared with the per capita GDP growth for westerners, all these regions' results have been disappointing.

There have also been significant changes in the specific weight of each of the regions. In the year 1000, Asia (excluding Japan) accounted for more than two-thirds of the world's GDP and western Europe for less than 9 percent. In 1820 the proportions were 56 percent and 24 percent, respectively. In 2000, Asia (excluding Japan) accounted for 30 percent of the world's GDP and western Europe and the countries resulting from European immigration for 46 percent. Between 1820 and 2000, the world's per capita GDP grew by an annual average rate of 1.21 percent. Of this, the per capita GDP of those which today are the OECD countries increased by 1.67 percent annually, while that of the developing countries grew by an annual rate of 0.95 percent. Among

16

the developing countries, per capita GDP growth of Latin America was 1.22 percent, that of eastern Europe and the USSR was 1.06 percent, that of Asia (excluding Japan) was 0.92 percent and that of Africa was 0.67 percent. Among the OECD countries, the per capita GDP of western Europe was 1.51 percent, that of the countries resulting from European immigration was 1.75 percent and that of Japan was 1.93 percent (Maddison, 2001).

However, these changes had already begun as early as the eleventh century, with the slow economic rise of western Europe over the rest of the world. Its ascension began with the city-states in northern Italy, particularly Venice, and their efforts to reactivate Mediterranean commerce. Subsequently, Spain and Portugal opened up the trade routes to America and Asia; however, it was the Low Countries that took the greatest advantage of the opening of these routes, especially those to Asia, which became the economic engine for Europe through its commercial and financial centre, Amsterdam, which retained its dominant position for nearly three centuries until it was superseded by London in the nineteenth century after the first Industrial Revolution.

According to Maddison, by the fourteenth century Europe had already managed to surpass China's per capita income, which had been for some centuries the highest in the world. This was due to the fact that at that time China did not have the appropriate political and social institutions in place and suffered a period of stagnation that was later aggravated by the colonial exploitation resulting from western hegemony over all of Asia, which reached its peak in the eighteenth century.

The completion of the first Industrial Revolution in the nineteenth century led Great Britain to attain world leadership, but later, the arrival of masses of colonists and other immigrants from Europe to North America and with them the introduction of European techniques of production and organization systems turned the United States into the world's leading power by the end of that century.

Japan managed to surpass China, in terms of per capita income, at the beginning of the nineteenth century. The Meiji restoration, in 1868, marked a decisive institutional change for Japanese prosperity, culminating in the second half of the twentieth century when Japan's per capita income overtook western Europe's.

In the case of Latin America, European colonization and subsequent emigration was very similar to that of North America; however, the institutions of Spain and Portugal were less conducive to capitalist development than those of Great Britain. The indigenous population was much greater in size than that of North America but it was excluded from the distribution of land and education. Land was distributed by the crown in the metropolis among nobles and friends, contrary to the settlement by colonists and their families in North America. When independence was achieved in the nineteenth century no major changes were made on the institutional front, where political power rested in the hands of the creole people and indigenous people kept away from the market. Although Latin America managed to grow much faster than Africa and Asia, it was unable to achieve the per capita income levels that its substantial natural resources should have enabled it to reach.

The most serious case is that of Africa, which in 1820 had an even lower per capita income than in the early centuries of the Christian era. The continent later saw very gradual growth, but in the year 2000 its per capita income was still just slightly higher than that of Europe back in 1820. The very slow growth in Africa's well-being was largely due to its tremendous population explosion, which saw growth eight times faster than in Europe.

This view of world economic history, which is much better documented with new quantitative studies and defended by, among others, Angus Maddison (1983, 1995a, 2001, and 2003), Bradford De Long (2000), David Landes (1969 and 1998), and Nicholas Crafts (1983, 1985, 1992, and 1999), refutes previous studies which did not have access to these new statistical sources. These latter studies include those of Bairoch and Levy-Boyer (1981, 1988, and 1992), André Gunder Frank (1998), and Simon Kuznets (1966, 1967, and 1973), who considered that the rise of western Europe over the rest of the developing world did not come until the eighteenth or nineteenth century, that China's per capita income was still higher than that of Europe in 1800 and that the per capita income of India and Japan was only 5 percent below that of China at that time. They also believed that Latin America's per capita income was well above that of North America and that Africa's was only 33 percent lower than Europe's.

In 1776, Adam Smith, based on his analysis of the "price of labor" and other data he had observed, intuitively decided to rank countries according to their per capita income towards the end of the eighteenth century. This classification, which has been confirmed by subsequent data, placed the Low Countries at the top of the list – followed by England, France, the British colonies in North America, Scotland, and Spain and its colonies in America – and ended with China and Bengal.

These opposing views have very important analytical consequences (Maddison, 2001). For those economic historians who did not have access to the new statistical sources, much of the developing countries' lag after 1800 was due to colonial exploitation, and only a minor part of Europe's advance was due to its great scientific and technological progress that led to the Industrial Revolution, as well as to its greater accumulation of capital and better organization and political and economic institutions. More recent economic historians do not deny the role of colonial exploitation and its consequent appropriation of resources and labor from those countries; however, they consider that it was much less significant than estimated by the first group of historians, because Europe had already surpassed Asia's level of well-being four centuries earlier. Most of the growing gap between the two groups of countries was due, after 1820, to the diffusion of the Industrial Revolution in Europe and its substantial impact on productivity and prices.

It is true that the advance of western Europe was accompanied by colonization by violence and the exploitation of other parts of the world; this is a well-documented fact. Europe's colonization of America was fraught with marginalization, conquest and, in many instances, the extermination of native peoples. For three centuries, Europe's contacts with Africa were based on the slave trade. Between the mid-eighteenth century and the nineteenth century, Europe went to war with many Asian countries for the purpose of imposing or maintaining a colonial system and obtaining other commercial benefits. However, it is also true that Europe's development was marked by devastating wars and conflicts, sparked by ruthless competition. Venice clashed with Genoa, Portugal, and Holland; Spain occupied a major part of Italy; the Low Countries fought an 80-year war of independence with Spain and were involved in four wars with England and another four with France to maintain their mercantile and financial supremacy; and Great Britain accumulated over 60 years of war with other European countries between 1688 and 1815.

The new historical view drawn from the new data tends to contradict the theses of Kuznets (1966) and other economic historians and experts on development, who tried to demonstrate that "modern economic growth" had been preceded by a period of "mercantile capitalism" in western Europe, and that this period, in turn, had been preceded by a period of "feudal organization." However, the new data reveal that, during the period of development of the so-called "mercantile capitalism" in Europe, between the twelfth and fifteenth centuries, the pace of economic expansion was not very different from that of preceding centuries and, accordingly, it can be asserted that until the development of "modern capitalism," at the beginning of the nineteenth century, there is no clear distinction between the "feudal system" and "mercantile capitalism" and that the entire preceding period should be classified as "proto-capitalism" (Maddison, 2001).

In the last few years, there has been an increasing interest, by growth theorists and economic historians, to try to find a kind of "unified growth theory" capable of explaining: why the world economy kept under stagnation for most of its history; why technological progress in the preindustrialization era failed to generate economic growth; why the sudden spurt in growth rates of output per capita and population; what was the reason for the transition from Malthusian stagnation to sustained economic growth; what was the source of the dramatic reversal in the positive relation between income per capita and population during most human history; what then triggered the demographic transition; what explains the "great divergence" in income per capita around the world.

Michael Kremer (1993), Lan Pritchett (1997), Oded Galor and Philippe Weil (1999 and 2000), Oded Galor and Omer Moav (2002), Robert Lucas (2002), Gary Hansen and Edward Prescott (2002), Joel Mokyr (2002), Charles Jones (2001 and 2004), Oded Galor and Mountford (2003), and Oded Galor (2004) have tried to explain some of the whys and whats of the history of the world's growth process. Their main findings about the factors which have produced these growth trends and their deviations relate not only to the accumulation of traditional factors of production (labor and capital) but also to the demographic transition (or the decline of population relative to technological growth) to the opening up of the economies, to the development of an adequate institutional framework, and above all, to the increase in education levels and human capital formation and to the fast development of knowledge, ideas, innovation, and thus technological progress. According to Galor and Mountford (2006) the expansion of international trade in the second phase of the Industrial Revolution has played a major role in the timing of demographic transitions across countries and has thereby been a significant determinant of the distribution of world population and a prime cause of the "great divergence" in income per capita across countries in the last two centuries. Their analysis suggests that international trade had an asymmetrical effect on the evolution of industrial and non-industrial economies. While in the first, the gains from trade were directed mainly towards investment in education and growth in output per capita, in the second ones, a significant portion of their gains from trade was channeled towards population growth.

The most important conclusion that can be drawn from the world's economic evolution is that it is progressing basically on the back of the accumulation of physical and human capital, the development of efficient social, economic, and political institutions, the opening-up of countries to global flows of production factors and products and, above all, knowledge, innovation, and technological development. In all the historical booms of the countries of the world all these factors have been present to a greater or lesser degree. This is particularly true of the last two centuries – especially the twentieth century. It was with the culmination of the Industrial Revolution in 1820, coupled with modern capitalism, that the world began to progress much more rapidly than ever before. This acceleration in progress was further fueled by subsequent technological revolutions marked by such inventions as electricity, the telephone, the internal combustion engine, the automobile, the airplane, the television, the computer and, lastly, the Internet.

In other words, world prosperity was achieved primarily through the new waves of technological progress. Without the acceleration in technological development after the first third of the nineteenth century and, particularly, in the second half of the twentieth century, it could not have been possible to attain the levels of per capita income and well-being that most of the world's population enjoys today. As brilliantly explained by William Baumol (2002), the capitalist free-market economy has managed to produce a continuous flow of applied technological innovations because growing competition has forced companies to innovate continually in order to survive. It is a matter of life or death for these companies, but it has paved the way for an ongoing wave of new technological discoveries that have brought about greater prosperity.

Traditionally, and according to the standard theory of industrial organization, it was thought that the innovation rate would decline with greater competition because innovative companies would be increasingly unable to enjoy their monopolistic income flows. However, in recent years it has been empirically proven that this is not so and that there is a positive correlation between competition and innovation. Competition increases the entrepreneur's incentives for, and benefits from, innovation, as innovation enables him to break away from competition, albeit only temporarily, and to achieve greater profits (Aghion, Bloom, Blundell, Griffith, and Howard, 2002).

Each new technology makes it possible to increase productivity and, consequently, salaries, while at the same time making it possible to lower the prices of products and services, with the concomitant increase in real disposable income for all. Technological discoveries in health-care and food services also make it possible to rapidly lower the infant mortality rate and lengthen life expectancy to levels that were unim-aginable just a few decades ago.

However, technological progress is not only the necessary requisite for economic progress in the world and for the globalization process to have taken place. It is also the requisite for there to be greater ine-quality between people and countries, at least in the short and medium term, as will be explained in the next chapter.

It should be noted once again, however, that although per capita GDP, measured in terms of purchasing power, is ten times higher today in the US than in India, after having been only twice as high in the mid-nineteenth century, this does not mean that India has not pro-gressed or, even worse, that the US has progressed at India's expense, as some poorly documented individuals still claim. India has progressed at a rate ten times slower than that of the US but, in the meantime, it has managed to significantly reduce its poverty levels and has consider-ably improved its level of well-being. Both countries have progressed, but the US has done so at a much quicker pace than India until India finally opened up to international trade and capital. As a result, for several years now its annual growth rate has been much higher than that of the US. Today the average worker in Thailand or Tunisia is three times as productive as the average worker in the US in 1900, and the average worker in Argentina or Mexico has five times the produc-tion potential of an American at that time. Today, only 35 percent of the world population has a lower material per capita GDP level than that of the US in 1900 (De Long, 2000).

The reader should also note that, as explained in chapter 5, measur-ing inequality is extremely difficult and complex, as it is practically impossible to ascertain the income distribution for each of the present 6.4 billion individuals in the world, many of whom are not even included in a census and for whom there are no reliable statistics. Indeed, there are often no national systems to monitor income distribution or, when there are such systems, they are often not sufficiently reliable. As the systems to measure the global distribution of income improve and the data become more precise, the results are turning out to be less dramatic than they first seemed and show that inequality is gradually improving as globalization accelerates and new countries open up to it.

Chapter 2
Technical Progress, Poverty, and Inequality

Why does technological progress give rise to inequalities if it is actually the world's most important source of progress and well-being, as shown in the previous chapter? This apparent paradox can be easily explained: unfortunately, although technological progress produces immense benefits to society, they are not enjoyed by all citizens and countries on an equal footing and at the same time.

The Benefits of Technological Progress

On the one hand, technological progress contributes enormously to the development and welfare of the population, as it significantly increases productivity by introducing new technologies that save time and costs associated with production, distribution, transport, and commercialization. On the other hand, technology is one of the pillars of globalization, which, as will be shown later, can also be a powerful tool for reducing inequality. Technology is a necessary condition for globalization, although it is not a sufficient condition; it is also necessary for governments to allow it and encourage it by eliminating the barriers to trade, capital, immigration, and technology itself. New technologies enable the working population and their families to earn higher salaries and income than people who cannot avail themselves of such technologies or are not able to use them.

Technology also empowers the individuals who use or develop it vis-à-vis those who cannot use it or do not know how to create it, as it provides the former with new opportunities to develop themselves and it frees them from their original limitations and discriminations (e.g. location, ethnicity, religion, or sex). Finally, technological development allows people to live longer and better, avoiding or reducing the suffering of illnesses or endemic diseases, reducing pain and increasing performance, improving working conditions, and reducing hunger by finding better ways to feed the increasing population levels.

Technology significantly enhances healthcare, nutrition, and farming and, in the twentieth century, has been decisive in reducing world-wide hunger, lowering the infant mortality rate and increasing life expectancy in almost all countries. Logically, however, its impact has been considerably greater in some countries than others.

Cutler, Deaton, and Lleras-Muney (2006) have studied the fast-falling trends of mortality rates and the fast-increasing trends of life expectancy and find out that mortality rates remain much higher in poor countries with a difference in life expectancy between rich and poor countries of about 30 years. This difference persists despite the remarkable progress in health improvement during the second part of the twentieth century, at least until the HIV/AIDS pandemic. They find a strong correlation between income per capita and mortality rates, a correlation that also exists within countries, where richer, better educated people tend to live longer. According to them, the ultimate determinant of health is the application of scientific advance and technological progress (some of which is induced by income and facilitated by education).

These improvements are supported by specific data. First, the technological revolution in agriculture and cattle-raising was particularly beneficial to the poorer countries. The most powerful revolution has been the biotech revolution, especially genetic modification (GM). The first genetic manipulation involving the recombination of DNA dates back to 1970, and the first one commercially available dates from 1995, although the grafting of plants and cross-breeding of animals have been around and developed for centuries. It was thus that wild plants could be converted into wheat or that wild boars became domesticated pigs. GM is much faster and efficient. Whereas it takes 8 to 12 months to produce a better or stronger plant using grafts, with GM this can be achieved instantaneously. Should one wish, for example, to obtain a plant capable of growing in salty soil, it would only be necessary to isolate a gene of the species that grows in such soil and transfer it directly into the genetic code of other species, without having to wait years crossing successive generations of species. Moreover, GM is much more precise than cross-breeding or grafting.

As everybody knows, sexual reproduction is unpredictable. The union of a strong man and an intelligent woman does not necessarily produce a brilliant, athletic child, as some traits are passed on and others are not. In theory, GM solves this problem by only transferring the desired gene to the plant or animal. Lastly, GM has another advantage in that it allows the transfer of traits between unrelated species. A cactus cannot be crossed with a cereal plant using grafts, but with GM the gene that makes the cactus resistant to drought can be extracted and transferred to a cereal plant that ordinarily requires a lot of water, such as maize (*The Economist*, 2001c).

Crops that are more resistant to viruses and insects and more tolerant to herbicides have been developed in this way and will, in the future, produce protein-rich grains, vegetables enriched with extra vitamins and, in general, foods that are more flavorful, more nutritional and cheaper. As with any technological development, however, just as there are huge benefits, there are also potential dangers. Transferring genes from one species to another could give rise to new allergies. Genetically modified crops could trigger environmental problems; for example, their pollen could drift over to other fields with normal crops and fertilize them. Plants that have been modified against certain types of plague could trigger even fiercer super-plagues or poison other species.

Despite these potential or hypothetical dangers, the use of GM has gradually become more widespread. In 2000, 44 million additional hectares of land were sown with GM seeds – 20 times more than in 1996. In 2004, 81 million additional hectares were sown, almost double that in 2000. At present, most of these GM crops are in the US, where they were discovered and developed, but they are now starting to be used in some European countries, despite strong opposition from non-governmental organizations, and in developing countries, especially in Asia, where China now leads the pack. In total, there are already 17 countries which produce transgenic crops. The reason China has decided to use GM so extensively and so very successfully (it has reduced its production costs drastically and slashed prices of staple foods) is that it still has an authoritarian regime and is not swayed by dissent. As long as consumers in democratic countries continue to have more confidence in the opinions of some NGOs than in those of their health authorities, it will be difficult for this new technology to be disseminated throughout the world, which would be a huge step toward eliminating hunger in many developing countries.

Meanwhile, the solution continues to depend on what other countries do. Japan, for example, is taking giant strides toward improving its traditional grafting technology and producing new, more efficient, and less costly species. In fact, the introduction of crops using new varieties of non-genetically manipulated seeds in developing countries already represents the majority of the total, especially in cereals (*The Economist*, 2001c).

Particularly noteworthy is the fact that, according to the UN's Food and Agricultural Organization (FAO, 2001), the average world-wide production of cereals per hectare rose from 1.2 tons in 1960 to 2.7 tons in 2000. In developing countries it increased from 0.9 tons per hectare to 2.3 tons. The food price index fell from 500 in 1975 to 100 in 2000. Lastly, the average annual caloric intake per inhabitant per day rose from 2,250 in 1960 to 2,800 calories in 2000. In developing countries it rose from 1,900 in 1960 to 2,650 calories in 2000. This underscores just how instrumental new technological discoveries in the field of agriculture have been to improving life, increasing life expectancy, and reducing infant mortality.

Technological progress has been most effective in improving the health of the inhabitants of developing countries. A child born in a developing country today has a life expectancy that is eight years longer than it would have been had the child been born in the 1970s. The

World Bank estimates that the technological progress made in the field of health is responsible for having halved the infant mortality rate between 1960 and 1990. Many illnesses have been eradicated or put in check thanks to new vaccines. Influenza, which killed almost 20 million people between 1918 and 1919, is largely under control today, and smallpox has been eradicated since 1979. Polio, the mumps, whooping cough, rubella, diphtheria, and tetanus are all in check today thanks to vaccines.

Conversely, however, tuberculosis and malaria continue to cause millions of deaths each year, despite the fact that there are adequate treatments and vaccines; unfortunately, they do not reach the people who really need them. The development of antibiotics since the discovery of penicillin in 1928 has made it possible to quickly cure infections that were once lethal.

Oral re-hydration therapy (ORT) has become one of the simplest, cheapest and most effective medical treatments in history. Developed in Bangladesh, it consists of a mixture of sugar and salt dissolved in water to avoid dehydration, and it keeps millions of children from dying of diarrhea each year mostly from drinking unclean water. Before ORT, the most efficient treatment cost $50 per child; with ORT the cost is just 50 cents. The proportion of children in the world who have been inoculated against the six illnesses that can be prevented with vaccines has gone from 5 percent in 1974 to 74 percent in 1998. However, 26 percent is still not receiving these vaccines and, as a result, 30,000 children continue to die each day of illnesses that could be prevented with existing treatments and vaccines (*The Economist*, 2001c).

Nevertheless, technological progress is not beneficial in the same way and at the same time to all countries and to all individuals of the world.

The Effects of Technological Progress on Inequality

Basic research and technological development in the capitalist world in which we live are logically carried out according to market demand.

Those scientists who develop such important scientific and technological tasks, as well as the organizations and companies they work for are not only interested in improving the well-being of humankind. They are also interested in the profitability of such research and findings so that they can continue researching, developing, and improving their new discoveries.

To this end, there is an adequate system to protect intellectual property rights and patents so that these researchers and technologists can benefit, exclusively over a certain number of years, from monopolistic income, without which it would be very difficult for them to raise the funds and secure the equipment needed to do their work. Without this capitalist market system, research and technology would not have been able to make such huge advances during this century, nor would they have had such a favorable impact on economic and social development.

This, of course, means that such research and development is not guided exclusively by the needs of people and of countries. This is particularly true regarding the poorer countries because, among other things, they have little purchasing power, especially at the monopoly prices applied temporarily at the outset and during the years in which the patent is valid. Furthermore, they do not have big enough markets to be profitable. As a result, they tend to be isolated from these processes that are so essential to growth and development. The problem, however, does not lie in market size alone, but also in the relative absence of national researchers and technologists. In the poorer countries the average population has a lower level of schooling and university studies, and even when there are researchers they tend to travel abroad to richer countries where they can hone their knowledge and skills to greater advantage.

As a result of the above, these technological processes are generally concentrated in the richer countries with the best human resources and the largest potential markets. The figures corroborate these assertions. The OECD countries, with only 18 percent of the world population, generate 99 percent of all registered patents. Of the $500 to $600 billion invested in R&D each year, 60 percent comes from private sources. In other words, it is financed by investors and carried out by companies that risk trying to develop new ground-breaking discoveries that will enable them to obtain big profits.

It can therefore be said that the private technology market does not generally cater for the needs of the poorer countries. For example, of the $70 billion plus invested each year in health research, only $300 million is earmarked for AIDS vaccines and $100 million for malaria vaccines, when AIDS causes over three million deaths each year, mostly in Africa, and malaria causes two million deaths each year in the tropics. In 1999, of the 1,238 new medicines developed since the 1990s, only 13 were designed to treat tropical illnesses, mainly because the tropical countries have very little purchasing power.

Patented treatments for AIDS in the wealthy countries cost an average of $10,000 per year. Because the cost of these products is so high, AIDS patients in Africa must either wait until the patents expire – so they can try to get the related generic medicine cheaper – or die. This is where the expression "patents kill" comes from, which is not really fair, because pharmaceutical companies spend on average between $300 million and $500 million to develop a first formula for a treatment and they would certainly not invest that kind of money if the day after discovering the formula, developing it, experimenting, and obtaining authorization from the health authorities – a process that can take up to a whole decade – anybody could just copy it and sell it at a tight margin over the cost of producing it.

Eliminating the patent system would eliminate technological progress in general and would be very detrimental to world growth and welfare. However, there is a powerful argument for applying lower prices to medicines in poorer countries than in richer countries. In 1994, a treaty was signed, whereby countries can circumvent patent protection in the event of a national emergency. In view of the almost exponential growth of AIDS cases in Africa, several pharmaceutical companies, faced with international pressure, have begun to sell treatments for one-tenth of the price they would have charged in richer countries. But this is not enough. In most of the poor countries the patents for the medicines they really need expired long ago. If they cannot get them it is either because the generic medicines are still very expensive or because the country's healthcare system is a disaster – or both.

Some pharmaceutical companies have come up with a new formula to solve this problem. They undertook to deliver licenses to the International Dispensary Association (IDA) to manufacture retroviral medicines to combat AIDS. This foundation then hands the licenses over to world-wide manufacturers of generic medicines so that they can sell them at low prices in the 78 developing countries hardest hit by AIDS. Other manufacturers are willing to follow this initiative for the same type of medicines to combat communicable infectious diseases, while maintaining the traditional patent system for medicines for non-communicable diseases. Finally, some NGOs and wealthy individuals (such as Bill and Melinda Gates) have established funds, which buy these vaccines from the pharma companies at bulk, more reduced prices, and distribute them directly to the people affected by those diseases.

Nevertheless, lower prices for poor countries are not going to wipe out the problem of pharmaceutical research concentrating on illnesses that affect the inhabitants of rich countries. That can only be solved with public funds, and this is where Official Development Aid (ODA) can play a decisive role, as we shall see in chapter 10. A combination of public and private funds can buy vaccines and other medicines from the pharmaceutical companies at price levels which are sufficient to provide incentives to continue investing in research and then they can give them to the poor peoples and countries affected at very low prices. This would be a much better and efficient way to allocate ODA resources to poor countries than that used today by many countries.

Although it may not seem so at first glance, the so-called "digital revolution" is also having a positive impact on poor countries, despite the so-called "digital division." Half the world's inhabitants have never made a telephone call, even though the telephone was discovered almost a century ago. It is also true that, in principle, it does not make any sense to give computers to people who do not have electricity. However, technology is making it possible for this to change in the not-too-distant future. In India inexpensive computers that use batteries that can be recharged manually by turning a crank or by solar power have already been developed.

In Bangladesh, the Grameen Bank has begun to give micro-loans to poor rural families in remote areas to buy mobile phones with which they can make calls to neighboring villages on a charge-per-call basis so that they no longer need to be cut off from the rest of the world. In fact, today more calls are made from rural areas than from urban areas in India, and the bank has become the country's leading supplier of mobile phones and relays. This has also triggered a sort of social revolution, as poor Bengalis could not open an account with the national telephone company because it feared that they would not be able to pay the monthly bill. However, with mobile phones they can purchase prepaid cards and the mobile companies in that country do not need to spend money and time chasing down unpaid bills and, therefore, they can grow more rapidly.

One of the reasons technological development causes inequality is because each new discovery gives the countries or people that invent it, develop it, or are first to apply it a huge initial advantage over the rest of the countries and people of the world. It is very difficult for the countries that later copy and apply the new technology to counter this advantage, and it is practically impossible for those countries that are not able to assimilate and apply the new technology at all because they lack the human and material resources to do so. As a result, they are left behind for years to come. It is in these latter cases that international solidarity and public and private development aid can play a decisive role, albeit not a definitive one, in mitigating this disadvantage by investing in the education and training of the people in these countries and by financing imports of finished products, particularly those that affect health, nutrition, and learning.

Obviously, the better and faster these technology transfer systems work – be it through imports under transfer and training contracts or through direct investment in the country – the sooner the countries that do not produce such technology can begin to enjoy its benefits and avoid being left behind.

Also, the sooner this technology is disseminated throughout the world, the sooner all countries will be able to progress and the greater the pecuniary benefits for the country or countries that produced it and developed it. It is therefore in the interest of all to disseminate such technology as quickly as possible. The problem is that some technologies have huge production or dissemination costs and require substantial capital to be able to launch them. Furthermore, technologies tend to have very long periods to mature and become spread world-wide, which means they can sometimes take several decades to be disseminated.

Even in the country at the so-called technology frontier, that is, the US, the number of years each of the major technologies discovered between 1870 and 2000 took to be disseminated to the majority of the population and companies has been extremely long, albeit being reduced in every new technology.

During that time period there have been three major technological waves. The first – and by far the most important – emerged at the end of the nineteenth century and beginning of the twentieth century and carried on throughout the twentieth century, bringing the discovery of electricity, the telephone, the automobile, aviation and the radio. The second, from the middle of the twentieth century, produced the television, the video, the microwave, and the computer. The third, in the last quarter of the twentieth century brought the personal computer, mobile telephony, and the Internet.

Each new technology has been maturing and disseminating a little faster than the preceding one. The technologies discovered at the end of the nineteenth century matured more slowly than those discovered in the middle of the twentieth century, and these more slowly than those discovered in the last quarter of the twentieth century. The telephone, discovered in 1876, took more than 120 years to reach 94 percent of the US population. The automobile, discovered in 1886, took more than 110 years to be disseminated among 79 percent of the US population. Aviation, discovered in 1902, took nearly 100 years to be fully disseminated in that country. Electricity, discovered in 1873, took more than 80 years to reach 99 percent of the US population. Television, discovered in 1926, was used by 99 percent of the US population in a little over 70 years. Radio, discovered in 1906, is the exception that makes the rule. In only 70 years it had reached 98 percent of the population. The speed with which this discovery was disseminated is due to the lower costs of the systems for transmitting its waves and the lower cost of the devices for its reproduction. The video, discovered in 1958, took a little over 40 years to be used by 79 percent of the American population. The microwave was disseminated more quickly, taking just a little over 35 years to be used by 84 percent of the US population. The personal computer, or PC, was even faster, taking less than 20 years to enter 40 percent of all American homes. The last two technologies, the mobile or cellular telephone and the Internet, were discovered since the 1980s and are being disseminated the most rapidly. The mobile telephone took ten years to reach 25 percent of the population in the US and the Internet has taken less than five years to reach 26 percent of US citizens.

It should be noted that both mobile telephony and the Internet are second-generation technologies, i.e. they are based on previous technologies. Both are based on the telephone and the latter is also based on the computer. This makes it much easier for them to be disseminated than other first-generation technologies, such as electricity, the telephone, the automobile and the computer.

Although all new technologies are initially rejected by the owners and workers of the companies whose technology is being replaced, thereby delaying their implementation, it is interesting to note that the technologies of the first wave were disseminated at a much steadier rate, while those of the second wave, which were disseminated rapidly in the first decades, had a much slower dissemination once they had reached 80 percent of the population. This was the case with both television and radio and will begin to occur with video and the microwave too.

The same will also happen, although to a lesser extent, with the PC, the mobile phone, and the Internet, given that they were preceded by the fixed telephone and the computer, which paved the way for them in advance. These trends are affected by the greater ease with which these technologies are disseminated in urban areas, which have a higher population density, more purchasing power and a lower distribution cost than rural areas, which are farther apart, have a lower population density and higher distribution costs. They are also affected by the fact that dissemination is slower among lower-income families than it is among families that are better off.

So far, we have analyzed the dissemination of technological discoveries in the most advanced country, the US, for which there are more reliable historical statistics. Technological dissemination is slower in developing countries – particularly the poorer ones – than in developed countries. This technological lag is one of the main factors underlying per capita income inequality between the more developed countries and the rest of the world. There are still many countries in the world where the majority of the population does not have electricity, even though this technology has been around for over 100 years. There are even countries where the majority of the population still does not have running water. This means that they are totally marginalized from any type of technology, regardless of when it was disseminated. A recent paper by Chinn and Fairlie (2004) shows that the determinants of the so-called "digital divide" in the use of computers and Internet among countries are: income differentials, which explain most of the differences, physical infrastructure disparities, human capital disparities, and regulatory quality disparities.

When all information technologies are included and their dissemination analyzed, not by individual country but by group of countries, based on their per capita income level the results show that divide (World Bank, 2001b and 2001c). In the previous technological wave, which has the greatest dissemination – fixed telephone and television – the differences between the poorer and richer groups of countries is lower than in the more recent waves. In 2000, the poorest countries, with per capita income of less than $755, had only 85 television sets and 26 telephone lines per 1,000 inhabitants, whereas the richest countries, with per capita income of over $9,266, had 693 television sets and 583 fixed lines per 1,000 inhabitants – 8 times and 22 times more, respectively than in the poorest ones. It is interesting to note how television has had a much broader dissemination than fixed telephones in the poorest countries, despite the fact that the telephone was discovered 50 years before television. There are undoubtedly economic reasons behind this phenomenon, such as the higher cost of distributing telephony services, but there are also political reasons: television is a key factor to political indoctrination.

What is striking is that the differences in the dissemination of new information and telecommunication technologies – mobile phones, personal computers, and the Internet, which have been around for less time – are even greater. In 2000, the poorest countries had only 3 mobile phones per 1,000 inhabitants, whereas the richest countries had 377 per 1,000 inhabitants – 125 times more. In the poorest group of countries there were 4.4 PCs per 1,000 inhabitants, compared with 345.9 in the richest countries group – 79 times more. In the group of richest countries there were 1,980 times more Internet servers per 1,000 inhabitants than in the group of poorest countries: 98.17 versus 0.05. Even the differences between the richest group and the group just below it, the medium-high income group, were also significant. In television sets per 1,000 inhabitants the difference was 3.3 times more; in fixed telephones it was 3.0 times more; in mobile phones it was 2.8 times more; in PCs it was 5.7 times more and in Internet servers it was 20 times more.

By contrast, the differences between the two intermediate groups were not nearly as big. This shows that there is not a linear relationship between per capita income and technological dissemination; in technologies that are more widely disseminated because they have been around longer the technological differences are bigger than they should be based on the differences in per capita income between the countries that invented them, i.e. those with the highest income, and the rest of the countries. The per capita income differences are smaller between the two groups of intermediate countries that copied the technology. The differences in per capita income are also larger between the intermediate groups and the countries with the lowest per capita income. These World Bank data illustrate the importance of the initial advantage of inventors over followers or copiers and the tremendous disadvantage of the poorer countries, which are left behind technologically for a lot longer.

The differences in the dissemination of the more recently introduced knowledge technologies between all the groups of countries are far greater than the differences in per capita income and are much more than proportional even between the richest group and the next one. This shows that the amount of time between discovery and assimilation is much longer at the outset. Other data confirm this important conclusion. The countries with the highest per capita income invest more than twice as much in R&D per inhabitant as the newly industrialized countries, over 35 times more than countries with an intermediate level of per capita income and over 200 times more than the countries with the lowest level of per capita income. This means that the difference in their capacity to generate knowledge is far superior to the difference in their per capita income. Thus, the inequality arising from technological progress is on the rise.

There is also no correlation between the size of the population and the use of new knowledge technologies. For example, in 2001 the US accounted for 26 percent of the world's Internet users, whereas it only has 5 percent of the world population. The European Union of 15 member countries, with just 6.3 percent of the world population, accounted for 21 percent of all users. Asia (excluding Japan) accounted for 30 percent of all users, yet it had 60 percent of the world population. Japan had 8 percent of its users and 2.1 percent of the population, Latin America 3.3 percent and 11.3 percent, respectively and Africa 0.5 percent and 9 percent, respectively. The rest of the world, which included Canada, Oceania, and the Russian Federation and the CIS had 11.3 percent of the users and 11.4 percent of the population.

The technological differences are even significant within countries, spanning decades between different population groups and geographical areas. According to Stephen Roach (2002), there were large differences between ethnic groups within the US. Hispanics use the Internet 3.7 times less than non-Hispanic whites, almost 3.6 times less than Asians and about half as much as African-Americans. In China there were significant differences between the different provinces that have nothing to do with population size. The most developed provinces – Beijing, Guandon, and Shanghai – account for more than 45 percent of all Internet users, despite having a much smaller percentage of the population.

However, in recent decades many developing countries' transition to modern technology has been accelerating through trade, foreign investment, emigration and the new technologies themselves, such as the Internet. The change brought about by the Industrial Revolution spanned several generations in England. The new industrialized countries of south-east Asia have made the technological change in just one generation, and China and India are doing it even faster. The speed with which this change is taking place, while very positive, is proving to have a more traumatic impact on these countries' societies, giving rise to insecurity and discontent among the part of the population that has a harder time assimilating or adapting to change, either because of their level of education or training, or owing to religious or cultural reasons.

A very interesting and recent experience is that of mobile telephones. As most poor countries never had developed fixed-line telephony, they have been able to move directly into mobile telephony, which needs a much lower infrastructure investment and as a consequence mobile telephony is spreading much faster than was estimated. They have been able to jump directly on to the second-generation telephony, shorting out the first one. This experience may be transferable to other technological discoveries.

Today, more people have adopted the Internet and mobile telephony quicker than any other technologies in history. By the end of 2004, 1 billion people were on the internet while the number of mobile phone users reached 1.5 billion.

In short, the problem of growing inequality in per capita income arising from technological progress, which is undoubtedly the most important production factor for economic growth together with human capital, lies in certain of its characteristic features, all of which bear a correlation.

First, R&D investment achieves more than proportionally increasing yields on GDP growth. That is to say, its effect on growth is more than proportional to the accumulated investment: the higher the accumulated investment, the more GDP increases. The new "endogenous" growth models show that the bigger the markets, the greater the inventions and innovations, which speeds up the growth rate and, in turn, makes the markets even bigger. In other words, the proportionally growing yields arise from the high dependence on the size of the technological innovation. Since something only has to be invented once to be able to be applied over and over, and since the fixed R&D costs are easier to amortize the bigger the final market for the invention is, innovative activity tends to increase more than proportionally to the size of the market. As a result, the richest countries can become increasingly richer thanks to their innovative and technological characteristics, which throw them into a virtuous cycle created by the growing size of the market.

Second, scientific and technological activity reveals external agglomeration economies: as investment and production grow they tend to concentrate or agglomerate in a specific center, city or region, and such agglomeration gives rise to substantial cost savings. These savings stem from the fact that the costs of transactions, transport, and production tend to be lower the more concentrated the activity is. For example, if all the research and technological innovation centers are located together, information is disseminated more quickly, the constant personal contact between the scientists and technologists allows new ideas to flow more freely, extremely expensive instruments, such as megacomputers and accelerators, can be shared by various groups of scientists, the latter will feel more drawn to these large centers because they can change from one project or company to another at practically no cost, and so on. These "external economies" make the unit costs of a scientific or technological product lower the more agglomerated its production is.

Third, the productivity of the people who use these new technologies increases sharply, as does their income. However, those who do not use it, either because they lack the training or know-how or because their country does not have a big enough market to be able to implement such technologies, have a lower productivity, lose their jobs because the technologies are implemented in other countries, which makes them more competitive, or they have to resort to lower-paying jobs.

Lastly, each new technology gives the country or company that invented it and developed it first a major advantage over others, either because of the initial costs involved or the lack of the knowledge to copy and use it, which can take many decades to disseminate. Thus, the first movers can have a higher growth rate for a considerable amount of time. Indeed, in some of the less developed countries it can take more than a century for some of these technologies to be applied. As a result, these countries lag behind in this technology and have a lower growth rate.

There is a group of recent econometric models which have been developed in order to explain the impact of technological progress on inequality, using as a paradigm the recent technological wave related to the development of information and communication technologies, the so-called "third industrial revolution" (Hornstein and Krusell, 1996; Greenwood, Hercowitz, and Krusell, 1997; Greenwood and Yorukoglu, 1997; Greenwood and Jovanovic, 1998; Greenwood, 1999; Hornstein, 1999; Hornstein, Krusell, and Violante, 2000). According to these economists, the impact of new technologies on inequality derives from the costs associated with learning and with experience to apply it and to work with it, on the one side, and from the benefits associated with the increase in productivity that derives from its introduction, on the other.

They build their models on four assumptions: first, technological change is associated with the introduction of new goods and in particular with the new technologies embodied in new machines, such as those used now in information technologies; second, adopting these technologies involves a significant cost in terms of learning; third, skilled workers have an advantage at learning over non-skilled workers; fourth, the experience of workers and employees with the existing technologies affects their ability to adopt new technologies.

41

The consequences of these assumptions are the following: first, as adopting these technologies takes time and costs to learn and skilled workers have an advantage at learning them, then there will be an increase in the demand for workers with the skills needed to implement them and for skilled workers in general. Hence, the wages of skilled labor relative to unskilled labor (the so-called skill premium) will rise and income inequality will increase. In their early phases, new technologies will not operate efficiently, due not only to inexperience but also to the fact that their experience in the previous technology reduces their ability to adopt the new one; hence productivity growth tends to stall as the economy makes the costly investment needed if the new technologies are to approach their full potential. As a result, there is a temporary correlation between rapid technological progress, widening wage inequality, and a productivity slowdown in the economies of the countries that introduce them.

Aghion, Howitt, and Violante (1999) go one step further and develop a model to analyze how the speed and the nature of technical change interact with the dynamics of worker's knowledge to determine the returns of unmeasured skills and to shape wage inequality within educational cohorts. They find out that a higher degree of wage inequality is observed within highly educated cohorts. The highest-educated group displays larger within-group inequality than the lowest-educated group. They also find out that the degree of adaptability to the new technological environment is as important as the level of education. For instance, Germany, whose educational system is geared to maintaining high standards for the bottom half of the skill range, has shown a higher degree of adaptability to the new technologies than the US and the UK, and therefore, inequality has risen much less than in the other two countries. Finally, they also found out that the rate of transferability of knowledge and experience by workers from the old to the new technologies plays a major role in the extent of the rise in inequality, if there is not transferability the inequality is mainly between firms and with high transferability is mainly within firms.

Nevertheless, in the long run, everybody will gain. Technological progress, which implies that a unit of labor can eventually produce more output, makes a unit of labor more valuable. Given time, this translates into higher wages and standards of living for all. In the shorter run, skilled workers will do better than unskilled ones, but this disparity will tend to shrink over time for two reasons. First, as technologies mature, the level of skill needed to work them will decline. Firms will substitute away from expensive skilled labor toward cheaper unskilled labor, and the skill premium will tend to decline. Second, young workers will tend to migrate away from low-paying unskilled jobs toward high-paying skilled ones. This tendency will increase the supply of skilled and reduce the amount of unskilled labor , easing the pressure on skill premium. Moreover, the wealthy will do better than the poor in the short run because the introduction of new technologies leads to high profit opportunities for those with the capital to invest in them. Nevertheless, these profit opportunities will shrink over time as the pool of unexploited ideas dries up. As, on average, the old tend to have more capital to invest than the young, the latter will fare worse in the short run than the old, but, in the long run, the rising tide of technological advance will be able to help them as well.

The Need to Speed up Technological Diffusion

There are two ways to consider technology diffusion. One is looking at the spread of science and the other of technology. Science tends to diffuse faster than technology, and within science, academic science diffuses faster than industrial science. Adams, Clemmons, and Stephan (2006) find out that in the US economy, industrial science diffuses 50 percent more rapidly than technology and academic science diffuses even faster. Academic science diffusion between universities and between firms and universities takes, on average, three years. The lag of industrial science diffusion between firms is 3.3 years, compared with 4.8 years in technology for the same companies using the same methodology. Thus, the publication system in science appears to distribute information faster than the patent system. Nevertheless, the speed of science diffusion in the same field varies by a factor of two across industries, depending mainly on the size of firm R&D and science departments.

As regards technology diffusion, a paper by Comin, Hobijn, and Rovito (2006), has tried to assemble new data on the diffusion of about 115 technologies in over 150 countries over the last 200 years called CHAT (Cross-country Historical Adoption of Technology) capturing both the extensive and intensive margins of the diffusion and it has also tried to find some common technology adoption patterns both across countries and over time.

Their main findings are the following: first, once the intensive margin is taken into account, the evolution of the level of the technology in the country does not follow a typical logistic S-shaped pattern. Second, the cross-country dispersion of the level of technology is much larger than the dispersion of income per capita. On average between 3 to 5 times larger and it affects up to 68 percent of the technologies. Third, there are universal leaders and universal followers in technology among countries in the world. That is, the rankings of countries according to the technology adoption level in a given year are highly correlated across technologies and their median is 0.78. Among OECD countries the universality of leadership is weaker and its median is 0.54.

Fourth, there is absolute convergence in 91 percent of the technologies of the CHAT data set. The average speed of convergence is 3.7 percent a year. Thus, half of the distance to the "steady state" is covered in 19 years, which is quite fast. Finally, the speed of convergence of technology across countries has accelerated over time. The median speed of convergence for technologies invented before 1925 has been 2 percent per year. The median speed for convergence for technologies invented between 1925 and 1950 has been 5.5 percent per year (more than twice as fast as before) and for technologies invented after 1950 the median speed of convergence has been 6 percent per year.

As convergence of per capita income depends partly on the degree of international technology diffusion and the absence of it can lead to income divergence if the domestic rate of technological change varies across countries, the right question is the following: what factors could help speed up technological dissemination and its absorption capacity in developing countries?

Education and public investment in basic research are essential; however, public investment in technological end products is not generally effective. This is usually left to private companies, as governments tend to find it difficult ascertaining and trying to pick which technologies will be winners and which ones will be competitive in an open market.

The worst thing a developing country can do is to close its doors to trade, investment, and technology because that also shuts it off from new ideas and innovation. Such has been the case in many countries when the idea of endogenous industrialization has been imposed and, indeed, it is the case today in countries like North Korea. Only a technological leader like the US could try this, and even then it would find it difficult because many of its technological developments have come also from the minds and hands of European and Asian scientists and technologists. Moreover, it needs outside markets in order for its developments to be sufficiently profitable. The opening-up of developing countries is crucial for them to be able to make a rapid transition to modern technologies.

The lack of infrastructure is another major issue, but countries that have a very weak infrastructure should not lose hope. For example, as explained earlier, countries needing a new telephone system need not build a conventional one. They can jump straight into a fiber-optics mobile system. There are many companies that are willing to invest in these new systems in any country, without any cost to the public coffers, provided that they can collect from customers for each call they make. In fact, these companies are even willing to pay large sums of money for a license without requiring that they be granted a monopoly. Historical experience shows that public monopolies in these countries have been very expensive and very inefficient. Unfortunately, however, in the recent study conducted by the International Telecommunications Union, covering 183 countries, only 38 countries had competitive fixed-line telephone markets, 16 had duopolies and the other 129 still had monopolies. When there is competition, service starts to improve, investment rises and prices fall.

Also important is the defense of intellectual property. Many developing countries do not enforce it internally, arguing that they are not producers of technology, while others claim that they can copy it without paying royalties. They are forgetting two things, however. The first is that the companies that own the technology do not want to invest in countries that do not enforce intellectual property laws and allow piracy to go unpunished. The second is that the same countries that do not defend intellectual property also do not stimulate their own innovation and technological development and, as a result, they fall even further behind. Private investment, be it domestic investment to exploit a foreign license or patent or direct foreign investment, is what really encourages innovation and technological development in a developing country. Countries that have pushed for domestic innovation or have required foreign companies established on their soil to do so by creating research or training centers have achieved the best results.

Competition is also a very important factor. In their excellent book, Parente and Prescott (2002) demonstrate how the most significant differences in per capita income in the world arise from the competition policies in place in different countries. Under these policies, countries impose stricter or looser controls on adopting and developing technologies. Most of the time, the limitation on using such technologies is dictated by monopolies that try to capitalize on their privileged, dominant position, often with the help of government officials, thus preventing the introduction of new technologies because they might jeopardize the monopolies' bottom lines.

From this starting point, both authors go on to explain that the reason it was England that developed the first Industrial Revolution and not continental Europe was that the granting of monopolies in Britain had been on the decline in the three centuries leading up to the revolution, as parliament gained greater power vis-à-vis the crown, whereas the absolute monarchies in France and Spain continued to grant monopolies as a basic means of assuring themselves of greater financing; and they only began to reduce them when they realized that they could not compete with Britain's technological prowess after the

Revolution. The same argument explains why, in the fifteenth century, China was unable to embark on a modern economic growth phase, despite the fact that it was one of the technological leaders of the time. The sweeping centralization of power that had once again developed was what kept it from implementing technologies developed between 950 and 1250, the period in which there was much more decentralization. The number of monopolies and the stringent regulation of economic activity increased as power became more centralized, and for six centuries the country was kept from becoming the most advanced country in the world, when it had the infrastructure to achieve it.

The two authors also point out the recent success of the US and Switzerland. Although other countries, such as Canada, Australia, and Brazil, had vast natural resources, it was the high degree of decentralization of the US and Switzerland, through the powers of their states and cantons, respectively, that enabled them to develop the fastest because the latter did not have enough power to avoid the free flow of merchandise throughout the territory, which was initially regulated by the federal government, precluding monopolies from exerting their power. Subsequently, in the twentieth century, the federal government ceased to regulate it, and the US's growth rate declined. A strong, anti-monopolistic policy was later introduced, helping it to recover. Japan's case is similar: the Meiji restoration in 1867 brought about the abolition of all existing monopolies, giving its economy a huge boost. Although power subsequently concentrated excessively in the emperor again, after the Second World War the country was occupied and the American troops did everything they could to keep the power from concentrating in the emperor again, tearing down the existing industrial-bureaucratic complex. Japan experienced the fastest growth in its history until the old conglomerates began to appear again with the help of the public administration.

The obvious conclusion of this study is that developing countries should encourage competition so that they can develop more quickly and prevent the adoption of new technologies from being delayed by the monopolistic interests existing in many of these countries, often with governmental connivance. The quickest way to achieve this is by opening up their economies to trade and foreign investment. According to the authors, the benefits of doing this can be measured not in terms of one or two percentage points but in terms of 1,000 or 2,000 percentage points.

Geographic distance from the country that represents the technology frontier has also a strongly limiting effect on technology diffusion, although the channels of trade, FDI, and direct communication may be alternatives to distance. For instance, the degree of localization of technology diffusion has been declining with the increase in trade and FDI and expansion of the Internet (Keller, 2001a and 2001b).

Another major barrier to the diffusion of technology is the political institution of the country. Some groups of economic agents have a vested interest that is put in jeopardy by the diffusion of the new technology and, although the new technology is socially desirable, to preserve their private benefits, they engage in some kind of lobbying activity with the government to deter the diffusion of the new technology either by forbidding it or taxing it. Thus, barriers raised by lobbies are an important determinant of the speed of diffusion of technologies.

It is important to make a distinction between new technologies that do not have a predecessor technology to replace and new technologies which are the substitutes of an incumbent one. In the first case, rents of the incumbent technologies are not lost and nobody has an incentive to lobby the legislative authority to raise barriers against it making the new one diffuse faster, while in the second, the lobby of producers associated with the old technology may find it beneficial to coordinate in order to reduce its diffusion by lobbying the parliament and government (Krusell and Rios, 1996; Acemoglu and Robinson, 2000).

There is ample empirical evidence that, in countries with a non-democratic effective executive power or a military regime, which are easier to lobby by incumbents and in closed economies, technological diffusion tends to be much slower than in countries with democratic institutions which defend the public interest and that foster openness, competition, and growth (Comin and Hobijn, 2004 and 2005).

Lastly, another necessary requisite to enhance technological investment and to create a high-tech market is to have a financial system capable of investing in it or in financing innovation. Public financing by itself is not enough, but it does help, and the contribution of private capital is essential. In order to attract private funding, two requisites are to be met. First, financial institutions and private investors must be able to earmark a portion, even if it is just a small one, of their total funds to venture and risk capital. Second, there must be a stock market for technological firms, where companies can raise funds by being offered initially to the investors and be quoted and where initial investors can sell their share in them when they consider convenient. The deeper and more liquid the technological stock market the more investors will be attracted by these riskier investments (De la Dehesa, 2002).

Nevertheless, in recent years, some of these technology diffusion trends are changing. Multinational Corporations (MNCs) are the main drivers of technology diffusion, mainly because they are also the main creators of technology and the main investors in R&D. They dominate new patents and often lead innovations in management and organization. Therefore, establishing links with their innovation and production networks can help developing countries to enhance their technological capabilities and to better compete and prosper.

In this context, the way MNCs allocate their R&D activities internationally is very significant. In general, R&D is among the least internationalized functions of MNCs and the one that requires more centralization because of the complex and tacit nature of advanced technical knowledge (Lall, 1979). Traditionally, when R&D internationalization took place both home and host countries were found to be in the developed world, and the only R&D transferred to developing countries was related to adapting products and processes to local conditions. But in the last few years this trend has been changing and MNCs are internationalizing an increasing amount of R&D to developing countries as well.

First, R&D internationalization by MNCs is rising in all key industries and countries through the outsourcing and offshoring of production, processes, and services. Second, R&D internationalization is now growing fastest in some host developing countries, notably in Asia. Third, the drivers of R&D internationalization are changing: the process is no longer driven only by the need for local adaptation or to tap into established knowledge centers. In response to increasing competition, MNCs now relocate segments of R&D so as to access pools of research talent, reduce R&D costs and speed up the process of technology development. Fourth, R&D in some developing countries now grows well beyond local adaptation and involves complex stages of R&D on a par with work undertaken in the developed economies. Fifth, some developing countries are setting up R&D units abroad. In sum, as R&D activities are part of the services, they are going through the same patterns of fragmentation which allow the general trend of service offshoring.

This new trend is going ahead in spite of R&D being less fragmentable than other services, because it involves knowledge that is strategic to the firms, because it often requires dense knowledge exchange between its users and producers within the context of localized clusters and because it tends to have a home country bias due to the fact that R&D activities reflect the linguistic and geographic constraints imposed by person-embodied exchanges and transfers of tacit knowledge (Patel and Pavitt, 2000).

According to the recent World Investment Report (UNCTAD, 2005) the largest 700 MNCs account for a major share of global R&D ($310 billion invested in 2002) and for close to half (46 percent) of the world's total R&D expenditure and for more than two-thirds (69 percent) of the world business investment in R&D (UK DTI, 2004). Over 80 percent of the largest 700 R&D spending firms come from only five countries: United States, Japan, Germany, the UK, and France. Of the top 700 spenders only 24 (3.4 percent) are located in developing countries, 10 come from South Korea, 8 from Taiwan, Province of China, 2 from China, 2 from Brazil, 1 from Hong Kong, and 1 from South Africa.

These top 700 R&D spenders are concentrated in a few industries. More than half (57.2 percent of the total) are in 3 industries: IT hardware (21.7 percent of the total), automotive (18 percent), and pharmaceuticals/biotechnology (17.5 percent). The following most important ones are electronic and electrical (10.4 percent), IT software and computer services (6.3 percent), chemicals (4.8 percent), aerospace and defense (3.9 percent), engineering (2.9 percent), and telecommunications (2.2 percent).

The report shows that there is a rapid increase of R&D spending by these top MNCs in their overseas operations or affiliates. For instance, the US has increased from 10 percent in 1994 to 14 percent in 2002 the relative expenditure in R&D by affiliates in relation to total R&D spending. The same trend is being observed in Japan, Germany, or the UK. According to an UNCTAD survey made in 2004–5, western Europe is the region with a higher degree of internationalization of R&D, with 40 percent, followed by North America, with 23 percent, Japan, with 14 percent and South Korea, with 2 percent. In terms of industries, the highest degree has been achieved by chemicals, with 48 percent, pharmaceuticals (38 percent), electronics (32 percent), automotive (31 percent), and IT hardware (30 percent). Finally, developing countries have almost doubled, in eight years, the share of US parent companies' R&D expenditure, from 7.6 percent of the total in 1994 to 13.5 percent of the total in 2002, of which Asia gets 10 percent of the total, Latin America, 3.2 percent, economies in transition, 0.3 percent, and Africa, 0.1 percent.

As this trend is due to continue, given that its main drivers are real, there is going to be a faster diffusion of R&D to developing countries and one that only a few years ago was not expected. There is, naturally, a very high correlation between FDI relative inflows in developing countries and relative R&D expenditure transfer to them because increasing FDI flows out of developed countries into developing countries are the main drivers of this trend, as will be shown in chapter 8.

Chapter 3
Growth Reducing Exogenous and Structural Factors

There are important factors other than technological progress that have a decisive impact on the less developed countries' lag vis-à-vis the richer countries.

Years ago, Gunnar Myrdal (1972) said, "Poor countries are poor because they are poor." Even earlier, Nicholas Kaldor (1961) said that "Growth rates and output–capital and output–labor ratios are practically constant in the long term both for individual countries and for the world as a whole, therefore, it is practically impossible to achieve convergence in the long term." Time does not seem to be proving them right, as each year there are a number of developing countries that manage to converge, if some only temporarily. However, there are even more cases of countries that do not appear to be capable of ever taking off. These are cases of countries that are gripped by specific structural and exogenous factors that are extremely difficult, but not impossible, to overcome.

Geography

The first factor, which is geographical and determinist, is what Jeffrey Sachs (2001) calls "tropical underdevelopment" in his study on these factors for the Center for International Development at Harvard University and what other economists have dubbed "the latitudinal curse" (Hall and Jones, 1999). One of the most robust pieces of empirical evidence to determine countries' wealth or poverty is that correlating the ecological areas of the earth with per capita income. Of the 30 countries and territories in the world considered by the World Bank as high-income countries, only two very small ones (accounting for 1 percent of the combined population of the 30) – Hong Kong and Singapore – are located in the tropics. The rest are located in temperate areas. Conversely, absolutely all the poorest countries in the world are located in tropical areas. Such is the case of Bolivia, Haiti, Chad, Niger, Mali, Burkina Faso, Uganda, Burundi, the Central African Republic, Zimbabwe, Zambia, Lesotho, Mozambique, and Laos, among a total of 48 (Gallup, Sachs, and Mellinger, 1999).

Another decisive geographic factor affecting countries' income levels is their distance from natural channels of communication, like the sea or navigable rivers. Countries that do not have direct access to the sea or to navigable rivers that enable them to communicate with others are poorer than those that are located near such channels of communication. This means that if a person has the misfortune of being born in an isolated, landlocked tropical country his or her potential for development and well-being is very slim compared with that of a person born in a country by the sea and located in a temperate region (Gallup and Sachs, 1998).

The same holds true within large countries that cover different ecological areas and have poorly communicated interior regions. The subtropical regions of the United States are more backward than the temperate northern regions. For many centuries the tropical north east of Brazil was far behind the more temperate areas of south-eastern Brazil. The temperate areas of northern China are more advanced than the tropical areas of the south east.

Between 1820 and 1992, average annual per capita GDP growth in the non-temperate areas of the world was 0.9 percent, whereas in the temperate regions it was 1.4 percent – half a percentage point higher than in the tropical regions. As a result, the per capita income of the first group, which in 1820 was 68 percent of that of the second group, fell to just 25 percent in 1992. Hence, this factor has clearly been a determining one in the rise in inequality between these two climatic areas of the world.

However, based on the data of Maddison (1995), between 1960 and 1992 both areas grew at the same rate – 2.3 percent – due to the higher growth rate in the tropical regions of Asia, which grew by an annual rate of 2.9 percent. Does this mean that the curse of the tropics is ceasing to stymie growth? According to William Easterly and Ross Levine (2002), who used a sample of 72 countries, both rich and poor, there does not appear to be any reason for geography to affect growth, and, if there is, it is minimal and only indirect. The most important factor for long-term growth is a country's institutions. If they are good, neither an adverse geographic location nor a poor economic policy will diminish long-term growth, although they can affect it in the short run. Only insofar as geography can affect the quality of the institutions would it have any effect at all. The two authors point out that the way in which these countries were colonized has had a much greater influence on their institutions than geography, whose impact has had little or no bearing.

Their viewpoint, which coincides with that of Landes (1998) and that of Acemoglu, Johnson, and Robinson (2001 and 2004) is that the Europeans followed different colonial strategies. In North America, Australia, and New Zealand, the Europeans settled in large numbers with their families, with whom they colonized and worked small tracts of land or engaged in commerce and other services, thus creating institutions to protect private property and control the discretional powers of the governments. In Africa and Latin America, the influx of Europeans was much smaller, large expanses of land were awarded at their discretion to friends and noblemen of the public authorities from the mother country, without the owners actually working them directly, and colonization focused mainly on extracting minerals, crops, and other resources rather than on creating a democratic system with well-defined property rights.

A similar view is argued by Engerman and Sokoloff (2005), who find that the colonization effort by Europeans led some of them to implant ongoing communities who were greatly advantaged over natives in terms of human capital and legal status, resulting in altering the composition of the population in the colony and in situations of extreme inequality. Those American colonies that began with extreme inequality and population heterogeneity are the ones which came to exhibit persistence over time in evolving institutions that restricted access to economic opportunities and generated lower rates of public investment in schools and other infrastructure conducive to growth.

According to Sachs (2001) geography is still the dominant factor. To prove this, he carried out a regression estimation of these countries' growth from 1965 to 1990 using the neoclassical growth model developed by Robert Barro (1991), which takes into account the initial per capita GDP, the initial years of schooling and several economic and institutional policy variables. Another variable was also added to these initial data, measuring the proportion of each country's population that lives in temperate areas. The results of the regression show that temperate areas tend to grow 1.6 percent faster per year than non-temperate areas (i.e. tropical, arid, and mountainous areas). In the long term, this means that temperate areas would have a per capita GDP 2.7 times higher than non-temperate areas. If the same type of regression is carried out addressing the relationship between growth in landlocked areas and growth in coastal areas or areas that have navigable lakes or rivers for communication, it shows that the former have an annual growth rate 0.8 percent lower than the latter. In other words, many countries have two forms of natural disadvantages that cause them to lag behind and suffer poverty and inequality with respect to others.

What is the reason for this apparent tropical underdevelopment? For a long time, many observers asserted that it was due to the period of colonization and exploitation the European powers subjected these areas to and that once they were decolonized they would gradually recover their normal growth rates. However, according to Sachs, this does not appear to have been the case, as practically all the tropical countries were already underdeveloped prior to their colonization at the beginning of the nineteenth century. Tropical Africa was already the area with the lowest standard of living in pre-colonial times, and its late colonization, starting in 1870, improved the precarious situation of some of the countries somewhat, although many others worsened. Unfortunately, the post-colonial period of independence also failed to improve their relative situation. The tropical areas of Latin America did not improve their standard of living at all following their independence starting from 1820. Therefore, the roots of tropical underdevelopment must be deeper, argues Sachs.

Sachs admits, however, that the economic weakness of the tropics has turned into geopolitical weakness and that these countries were subjected to domination by countries with temperate climates because the latter were much stronger economically and, therefore, militarily. In many cases, colonization thwarted these countries' long-term economic growth because of the mother countries' lack of investment in such public goods as education and healthcare or the introduction of political mechanisms of oppression, such as forced labor, the extraction of income through high, coercive taxation and the suppression of all local industry, focusing exclusively on mining and agriculture. In recent times, the dominating countries in the international political arena have shown their lack of solidarity by overlooking many of these countries that were immersed in civil wars that resulted in millions of victims or by refraining from helping them with sufficient aid or by pardoning their debts when they were in a genuinely desperate situation.

Another important but very different explanation was offered by Max Weber (1904), the first person to warn us that modern economic growth is linked to the development of capitalism and that this, in turn, is linked to the European culture and the Protestant ethic. According to the famous sociologist, the advantage enjoyed by temperate countries was of a European nature. However, the spectacular growth of certain temperate areas, such as Japan, Korea, Taiwan, and north-east China has nothing to do with European culture. Also, European colonization has had different results depending on the climate. The temperate Spanish colonies located in southern Latin America – Argentina, Chile, and Uruguay – developed much faster than the colonies in the tropical regions. Southern Brazil, which is more temperate, is more developed than the North. The southern cone and the north of Africa have developed more than the tropical regions of central Africa, even though these regions were also colonized by Europeans.

Since the pioneering work by Max Weber the consequences of religious beliefs (mainly Protestant and Catholic) on economic attitudes and economic growth have been a subject of strong debate as well (Putnam, 1993; La Porta, Lopez de Silanes, Shleifer, and Vishny, 1997; Inglehart, 1999; Landes, 1998; Stulz and Williamson, 2001). One paper (Guiso, Sapienza, and Zingales, 2002) has made an important contribution to the empirical evidence supporting the debate. The authors use the World Values Survey, a representative sample of people in 66 countries, taking into account the religious affiliation of the interviewees, the intensity of their beliefs and their education (religious or not).

Then, they choose seven religion groups: Catholic, Protestant, Jew, Muslim, Hindu, Buddhist, and others and analyze the relations between these groups and six groups of variables: people's attitudes toward cooperation and trust, women, government, legal rules, the market economy and its fairness and thriftiness. They found, on average, that religion tends to be good for development attitudes that are conducive to economic growth, but with the following qualifications: first, religious people are more intolerant and have more conservative views of the role of women in society. Second, these correlations differ depending on whether a specific religion is dominant in a country. Third, these correlations differ across religious denominations.

On average, Christian religions are more positively associated with attitudes that are conducive to economic growth, while Islam is negatively correlated. The ranking between the two main Christian denominations is less clear. Protestants trust others and the legal system more than Catholics and they are less willing to cheat on taxes and accept a bribe with respect to Catholics. By contrast, Catholics support private ownership twice as much as Protestants and are more in favor of competition than any other religious group (including Protestants). The only case in which Protestants seem more pro-market than Catholics is incentives. When asked whether they are willing to accept more income inequality to provide incentives Protestants and Hindus are the only religious groups that favor incentives. These results are consistent with Max Weber's views.

Not only is religion important for economic outcomes but also for culture. Guiso, Sapienza, and Zingales (2006) look at culture and economic outcomes in relation to savings and redistribution. Their finding in the first case is that a 10 percentage point increase in the share of people who think thriftiness is a value to be told to children is linked to a 1.3 percentage point increase in the national saving rate of the country or region where they live. The second, conducted in the US, shows that Catholics, Protestants, and Jewish people have a more negative attitude toward redistribution than those with no religion and that those of African origin or African–Americans are 20 percent more in favor of redistribution than British–Americans. They are followed by Americans of Canadian origin, Hispanics, and American Indians. The most opposed to redistribution are the Japanese–Americans. These attitudes are very highly correlated with their ancestor's time of immigration. British, north Europeans, and Germans were the earlier immigrants, who translated their belief to their children that success is mostly determined by individual actions, which makes government intervention highly undesirable.

Similar conclusions are reached by Tabellini (2005), using the World Values Survey as well, who finds out the importance of culture in the different European regions' economic outcomes. Both GDP per capita and growth are higher in those regions that exhibit higher levels of the "good" cultural values, like trust, beliefs in individual effort, generalized morality, and low obedience, and are lower in those regions or countries which show "bad" cultural values.

Nevertheless, the explanation put forth by Sachs (2001) could still be borne out by the facts, among other reasons because it is easier to produce regressions between geography and growth than between institutions and growth. Sachs maintains that the primary reason for underdevelopment in the tropics lies in these countries' food-production technology and in their healthcare. Generally speaking, countries with temperate climates are food exporters, while tropical countries are importers of food. This is due to the smaller yield per hectare farmed in tropical countries compared with temperate countries. In grain production, for example, the yield in temperate countries is 51 percent higher than in non-temperate countries. There are several factors that make tropical countries' yields so low.

The first is soil erosion. In the ecosystems of the tropics, most of the soil's nutrients, which are in the form of plant matter, are found on top of the soil. When the forest is cleared for ploughing, most of these nutrients are lost and those remaining in the soil tend to be washed away when there are heavy tropical rains. As a result, the soil requires a longer period of time between one crop and the next.

The second is the proliferation of parasites as a result of the broad animal biodiversity. High average temperatures and the absence of winter frosts, which kill these parasites, make it very difficult to eliminate them, both from the plants and from the animals. The third factor is the plants' higher respiration rate as a result of higher temperatures. This reduces their net photosynthesis, which is essential to maintain their metabolic development. Although it may seem paradoxical, the fourth factor is the low availability of, and lack of control over, water. Because of the high temperatures, surface water and water in the plants evaporates very quickly and is not very efficient. Moreover, heavy rains make it difficult to control the use of water, and the excessive humidity makes it very difficult to dry and store crops.

Such high temperatures are also detrimental to productivity. On the one hand, there are more diseases and epidemics and they are harder to cure. What is worse, many of these diseases are transmitted much more easily in tropical climates than in temperate climates. As a result, the infant mortality rate is 52 percent lower in temperate regions than in tropical regions and the life expectancy rate is 8 percent higher in the former than the latter. On the other hand, the torrid heat reduces workers' productivity notably. It is for this reason that Jeffrey Sachs considers the invention of air conditioning the most important factor contributing to the equalization of work productivity between all the countries of the world.

All these factors are interrelated. Low agricultural and cattle-raising productivity has a bearing on malnutrition, which has an impact on resistance to diseases, which turn into epidemics, which affect work productivity, which increases poverty, resulting in higher illiteracy rates, reduced access to medical care, higher infant mortality rates and lower life expectancy rates – in sum, the price of living in the tropics. In two more recent short papers, Sachs (2003a and 2003b) demonstrates how a disease typical of warm and tropical environments, where a key part of the life cycle of the parasite (sporogony) depends on a high ambient temperature, directly affects negatively the level of per capita income even after controlling for the quality of the institutions.

Natural Resources Curse

Some natural resource-rich developing countries tend to create an excessive dependence on their natural resources which generates a lower productive diversification and a lower rate of growth. Resource abundance per se need not do any harm: many countries have abundant natural resources and have managed to outgrow their dependence on them by diversifying their economic activity. That is the case of Canada, Australia, or the US, to name the most important ones. But some developing countries are trapped in their dependency from their large natural resources and suffer from a series of problems provoked by that dependency that reduce or impede their growth potential.

Recent economic growth literature (Auty, 2001; Gylfason and Zoega, 2001; Gylfason, 2004) has shown five channels of transmission from natural resource abundance to slow economic growth. These channels can be described in terms of crowding out: a heavy dependence on natural capital, it is argued, tends to crowd out other types of capital and thereby inhibit economic growth.

The first channel is through the overvaluation of the exchange rate. This channel is known as the "Dutch disease" because this is what happened in the Netherlands after the discovery of natural gas in the North Sea in the late 1950s and early 1960s. But not only did it suffer from overvaluation of its own currency but also from its greater volatility because the prices of raw materials fluctuate a great deal making export earnings unstable and unpredictable and triggering exchange-rate volatility. This exchange-rate instability creates uncertainty that can be harmful to exports and other trade, including foreign investment. Moreover, the natural resource-based industry is able to pay higher wages and also higher interest rates than other exporting and importing competing industries thus making it even more difficult to compete in world markets if the country has centralized wage bargaining where the natural resource-based industry sets the floor to wages. As a result, it tends to reduce the level of exports or bias the composition of exports away from high-tech or high-value-added manufacturing and service exports that are fundamental for potential growth in the long run. The same may happen with FDI, which can be attracted solely by the natural resource impeding diversification, that is, natural capital tends also to crowd out foreign capital.

The Dutch disease channel is operating in many oil and gas exporters. A vivid example is that the Arab countries that are non-oil exporters have achieved, on average, a significant increase in their total exports relative to GDP, while the total exports of Arab oil-producing countries have declined as a proportion of GDP. The same pattern could be applied to FDI, but the results are less clear (Gylfason, 2004).

The second channel is through rent seeking and social capital. Huge natural resources rents, especially in conjunction with ill-defined property rights, lax legal structures and imperfect or missing markets in some developing countries may lead to rampant rent seeking behavior on the part of producers, diverting resources away from socially fruitful economic activity (Auty, 2001). Natural resource-rich countries can be subject to military take-over by neighbors or civil wars can break out, such as Africa's diamond or oil wars which have destroyed lives and social and economic infrastructures and impede the potential growth of the country for many years. There are other more rent-seeking forms such as governments favoring friends or family with privileged access to those resources creating rampant corruption and cronyism which impede economic efficiency and reduce growth. As Sala i Martín and Subramanian (2003) put it: natural resources that are "easy to steal," like oil and mining, turn out to have a very adverse impact growth by triggering corruption chains that end up destroying institutions such as the rule of law.

The third channel operates through education and human capital. Natural resource abundance or intensity may reduce private and public incentives to accumulate human capital due to a high level of non-wage income (dividends, social expending, and low taxes) which may underestimate the long-run value of education. The empirical evidence shows that school enrolment at all levels is inversely related to natural resource abundance or intensity (Gylfason, 2001). Once again, abundant natural capital tends to crowd out human capital.

The fourth channel operates through saving, investment, and physical capital. Natural resource abundance may reduce public and private incentives to save and invest and thereby impede economic growth. When the share of output that accrues to owners of natural resources rises, the demand for capital may fall and lead to lower real interest rates, less saving, and less rapid growth (Gylfason and Zoega, 2001). Not only is the volume of investment what counts but also its quality and efficiency. Governments and individuals who are flush with cash thanks to these resources may tend to invest in unproductive investments and white elephants. An increase in the natural capital share of 20 percentage points goes along with a decrease in the investment ratio of 4 percentage points and a decrease of economic growth of 1 percentage point (Gylfason, 2004).

The final channel operates through money, inflation, and financial capital. Natural capital seems to crowd out financial capital as well because most empirical evidence shows a negative correlation between natural resources dependence and financial depth and maturity. The latter not only depends on natural resources but also, importantly, on inflation, because inflation reflects the opportunity cost of holding cash and other forms of financial capital that grease the wheels of production and exchange. Thus inflation tends to deprive the economic system of the necessary lubrication showing an inverse correlation between inflation, financial depth, and economic growth (Temple, 2000).

In sum, because of these channels and effects, natural-resource abundance tends to be inversely related to economic growth. Gylfason (2004) suggests that an increase of about 10 percentage points in the natural capital share from one country to another is associated with a decrease in per capita growth by 1 percentage point on average. Similar relationships of this kind have been reported in other studies (Sachs and Warner, 1999; Gylfason, Herbertsson, and Zoega 1999).

Population Growth

Another factor that may further inequality among countries is population growth, particularly due to the overpopulation of some developing countries. This factor is partly exogenous and partly endogenously determined: in some cases it can be due to the subjugation of women, owing to religious or other beliefs, and in others it can be attributed to the educational level of women, which, in turn, can be due to various causes, mainly to religious or political factors. The simplest way of comparing inequality among countries or regions is by looking at their relative GDP per capita, which is simply the result of dividing their GDP of a given year by the number of their inhabitants in that year's census. If GDP progresses at a lower rate than the population, GDP per capita will decline. If the opposite is true, it will increase.

Different regions of the world have different incomes per capita depending on the relationship between the population and GDP long-run growth rates. Being the numerator (GDP), the denominator (the population), and the quotient (GDP per capita) since around the 1960s, in Europe, average annual GDP growth has been 3.4 percent, while the average annual growth of the population has been just 0.51 percent. The result is an annual increase in GDP per capita of almost 2.9 percent.

By contrast, in Africa, GDP has grown at a faster pace, 3.6 percent, which is logical considering that its starting point was much lower; however, its population has grown by 2.6 percent, resulting in an average annual GDP per capita growth rate of 1.0 percent. In Latin America, the GDP growth rate has been 4.1 percent, but its population has grown at an average annual rate of 2.4 percent, resulting in an average annual GDP per capita growth rate of 1.7 percent. Lastly, in Asia, the average annual GDP growth rate has been spectacular at

5.5 percent, and the population has grown at a rate of only 2.3 percent, less than in Africa and Latin America. As a result, Asia's average annual GDP per capita grew the fastest of all the regions: 3.7 percent. What this means is that population growth is just as important as GDP growth when it comes to convergence with the developed countries in terms of GDP per capita. Asia was thus able to narrow the gap with developed countries, while Africa and parts of Latin America saw it widen further.

What factors have an impact on population growth rates? One of the most important factors is what is known as "demographic transition," i.e. the significant shift of a society with high fertility and mortality rates to one with low fertility and mortality rates or from one with high fertility and low human capital to another one with low fertility and high human capital (Tamura, 1996; UNFPA, 2002). In this transition, the change in the age structure is more important than population growth itself. If life expectancy increases and parents realize that their children have greater chances of survival the fertility rate will tend to decline and, as the size of the family becomes smaller, there is a greater likelihood that women will join the labor market, thus increasing the working population.

The benefits of demographic transition take time to surface, since in the early phases the number of children and elderly persons grows the fastest. It is only later that the population of working-age persons, that is, the actual workforce and the number of employed persons, begin to rise sharply. The last phase consists of a situation in which, as a result of the constant decline in the fertility rate, the number of elderly persons with respect to people of working age increases, as does the relationship of dependence. These benefits of demographic transition have been a key to the economic success of south-east Asia. In 1950, the fertility rate in the region was six children per fertile woman, and in 2000 it was two. As a result, the population of working-age persons increased from 57 percent of the total population in 1965 to 65 percent in 1995 – four times faster than the number of dependent persons.

It goes without saying that the poorer countries, with their low levels of calorie intake and of labor productivity, their lack of access to public healthcare, and their suffering of large pandemics like AIDS and malaria, have not managed to make this transition or are doing so at a painfully slow pace. Nevertheless, this transition was decisive for the developed countries to achieve better growth and well-being. Why?

First, the investment per child, both at home and in the community, tends to be higher in countries with low fertility rates. Their infant mortality rates thus tend to be much lower and their education levels much higher. It is a question of the old dilemma of quality over quantity: it is much more productive to have few educated and healthy children than to have many that do not survive or are illiterate. As Becker and Lewis (1973) discovered by presuming that children are a normal good, there may be a child-quantity/child-quality trade-off: large families keep living standards low, they choose a large quantity of children, but as parents get richer they demand children of "higher quality" (who are more productive) without necessarily demanding more of them. Nevertheless, the empirical evidence of this trade-off is not conclusive (Angrist, Lavy, and Schlosser, 2005).

Second, this transition usually leads to lower – and even negative – population growth. Therefore, a higher proportion of the population is of working age, which generally increases employment, wages, and the GDP.

Lower population growth places less pressure on fixed resources, such as total farmed area, land, water, and mineral deposits. This makes it possible to invest more in increasing the capital per inhabitant and, consequently, productivity and salaries, rather than investing exclusively in trying to maintain the level of capital per inhabitant, as is the case in countries with higher population growth.

Third, low food productivity reduces the speed at which demographic transition takes place between rural and urban areas. Since fertility rates tend to be much higher in rural areas, the lower rate of development of urban areas slows down the transition and reduces productivity levels.

Fourth, there is a high inverse correlation between the fertility rate and the level of women's education, just as there is an inverse correlation between the level of women's education and the AIDS contagion rate. A higher level of education among women is associated with a greater use of contraceptives and with a lower fertility rate. On the one hand, a higher level of education increases women's economic opportunities and, therefore, it can increase the opportunity cost of children, as measured in terms of the amount of time employed by mothers to have them, feed them, and educate them. If the mother is illiterate and lives in a rural environment, this cost is very low and her fertility rate tends to be higher.

On the other hand, the higher the level of women's education, the lower the infant mortality rate and, consequently, fewer births are necessary to reach the desired number of children. Lastly, educating women can help make the use of contraceptives more effective. Thus, as explained later, most of the development aid that the richer countries pass on to the poorer countries should be earmarked for healthcare and education, the two most efficient tools for eradicating excessive population growth in poor countries. Unfortunately, this is not being done today.

Mention should also be made of another important problem for poor countries with high fertility rates. Since the infant mortality rate is very high, mothers tend to have many children to ensure that at least one of them will survive until the parents get older. Thus, the higher the infant mortality rate, the higher will be the fertility rate, so that the latter exceeds the former. This behavior is absolutely rational: as there is no social security system, the implicit "pension" system, which is also intergenerational, is contained within the same family. Therefore, families must try to ensure that they have a sufficient number of children so that these can take care of the parents when they are no longer able to work because of their health or age.

In short, recent historical experience shows that the countries that have made the fastest demographic transition in the past fifty or so years, such as eastern Asia, have managed to narrow the per capita income inequality gap with the more developed countries.

Chamon and Kremer (2006) have developed an original and interesting analytical model on the link between population and growth.

According to them, the higher the population in advanced economies, the easier it will be for the remaining developing countries to integrate in the world's economy and globalize. In the present globalization wave, the integration success (that is, the capability of becoming rich countries by globalizing) was reached by countries with not very large populations like Japan, Korea, Taiwan Province of China, Hong Kong, Thailand and Malaysia. But now, two hugely populated countries, China and India, have the opportunity of becoming rich in a few decades by (as Japan and Korea previously did) selling what they can manufacture or produce and becoming more and more technologically sophisticated in what they export. If they succeed, then there will be almost 2.4 billion more people in advanced countries, so it will be easier for the rest of developing countries to export to them and integrate fully into the world's economy.

Other Structural Factors

There is also another group of "force majeure" natural factors, which although not directly dependent on a country's population, also have an impact on per capita GDP inequality in the world. The first is that developing countries tend to be the hardest hit by natural disasters. It has been a long-term constant that developing countries, especially their most densely populated areas, are particularly susceptible to the effects of natural disasters. According to the World Bank (2001), between 1990 and 1998, 94 percent of the 568 major natural disasters and more than 97 percent of all deaths related to such disasters occurred in developing countries.

In Bangladesh alone, during that short period of time three storms, four floods, two cyclones, and a tsunami took the lives of 400,000 people and caused damage to another 42 million. The same can be said about the recent tsunami that killed dozens of millions inhabitants and devastated parts of Indonesia, Malaysia, Thailand, and Sri Lanka. In Latin America and the Caribbean, the great natural disasters associated with "El Niño," hurricanes "Mitch," "George," and "Emily," the landslides caused by heavy rains in Venezuela and Central America and the "Quindío" earthquake, took thousands of lives and caused billions of dollars in damages. The list goes on and on, with the floods on the Yang Tse River in China, the "Monsoons" in Bangladesh, the droughts in the southern cone of Africa, the earthquakes in Turkey and Iran, and cyclone "Orissa" in India, to name but a few.

Statistical research reveals that the inhabitants of the countries with the lowest GDP per capita are four times more likely to die as a result of a natural disaster than those with a higher per capita income.

There are several reasons for this unfortunate paradox (World Bank, 2001). Firstly, poor people and communities cannot afford to pay the higher prices required to live in areas that are better protected from natural disasters and, moreover, they mostly live crammed into precarious poor-quality dwellings. This is why the poorer communities have such a high likelihood of being located in areas that are vulnerable to inclement weather conditions and seismic activity and to suffer the loss of their dwellings. For example, during the same period 1990–8, the profiles of the natural disasters in Peru and Japan are very similar. However, the average number of victims in Peru was 2,900 whereas in Japan it was 63.

Second, the average cost of natural disasters in proportion to GDP is 20 times higher in developing countries than in developed countries; hence developing countries use up their already scant budgetary funds for education, healthcare and social assistance, making the poor poorer still. Moreover, the disasters have a direct impact on these people's most important asset – labor – because, in addition to leaving them homeless, they often leave them with disabilities and deaths, preventing them from working or earning a living, and this sinks them further into the quagmire of poverty. Lastly, unlike in developed countries, these people do not have any insurance to cover the losses arising from these disasters.

Another very important factor contributing to these inequalities is the fact that military conflicts and civil wars seem to take place overwhelmingly in the poorest countries. There is also a tremendous difference between developing and developed countries in the percentage of expenses incurred as a result of military conflicts and civil wars (especially the latter, as they have become the predominant form of military conflict in developing countries) given that, between 1987 and 1997, more than 85 percent of all armed conflicts took place within their national borders. During that period there were 14 in Africa, 14 in Asia, and one in Europe. Unfortunately, 90 percent of the victims in these wars were civilians. The civil wars in Cambodia, Angola, the Democratic Republic of the Congo, and the Sudan have been particularly bloody, with over seven million dead, mostly civilians (World Bank, 2001).

Not even children are spared. They, too, are forced to take up arms, and even if they manage to survive they bear psychological scars for the rest of their lives that prevent them from getting an education and a job that pays. These wars paralyze economies because they destroy physical, social, and human capital, reduce investment, divert almost all spending to non-productive activities and drive the more skilled laborers to emigrate. It is calculated that, on average, the GDP falls 2 percent during each year of civil war with respect to what it would have been had there not been a conflict.

It goes without saying that countries, whether developed or developing, which produce and export arms and the mafias that trade in arms are the only ones who benefit from these tragic wars. Indeed, they often participate in these wars, either directly or indirectly by encouraging them, and it is incomprehensible that there is nothing the United Nations can do to stop them. This is an aberration, and it is unforgivable for an international community that prides itself on being democratic and a defender of the right of all citizens to live in peace and prosperity.

Chapter 4
Growth Reducing Endogenous Factors

There is another group of factors that are not exogenous to developing countries and that also give rise to inequality: the policies and institutions that these countries have developed as independent, sovereign states or that they have, to a certain degree, inherited from their colonizers. Such policies and institutions have enabled some of these countries to succeed in taking off and converging with the more developed countries while others have failed to do so.

The first factor within this group is the countries' level of democracy and freedom, as well as the quality of their political, legal, judicial, social, and economic institutions, as these determine how private and public resources are to be collected and distributed in each country and how the funds saved by private individuals are to be invested. This depends, on the one hand, on each country's degree of democracy and institutional development and, on the other, on the know-how of its leaders and governing classes: both are generally very closely related.

For example, in the case of a dictatorship with little or no freedom and a high level of corruption, it is very likely that budgetary resources will be collected through taxes, which will not be paid by the people and companies that should be paying them. The taxes that are collected will then typically be routed to bank accounts held by the dictator and his cronies outside the country or invested in unproductive resources, such as arms and security, buildings to be used by the dictator, the state television and other propagandistic media, and so on, rather than in education, drinkable water, electricity, and basic infrastructures, which are necessary for any developing country to advance and improve its per capita income. Moreover, in a corrupt dictatorship neither property rights nor the judicial institutions in charge of defending them are upheld, so private funds are not invested or are channeled out of the country.

Conversely, at the other end of the spectrum, in the case of a democratic country with respected and respectable political and social institutions and a high level of freedom, there are more guarantees that public resources will be collected more equitably and invested so as to achieve a better economic and social return and that private funds will be allocated more efficiently.

All the empirical studies on the correlation between politico-economic freedom and development reveal very high indices of correlation. The Fraser Institute's 2001 annual report on economic freedom in the world, covering 123 countries, shows that the countries with the lowest ranking are also the poorest. Guinea Bissau, Myanmar, and the Congo have the least freedom and are also the poorest. Cuba and North Korea are not included in the study because there are no available data on them; however, they have even fewer freedoms than the three countries mentioned above. Although freedom is a necessary condition for an economy to prosper, it is not a fully sufficient condition. Other important factors also come into play, some of which are structural and have already been discussed in earlier chapters. Nevertheless, freedom is a decisive condition, since it contributes directly to ensuring a more efficient, democratic running of any economy. A distinction should also be made between political freedom and economic freedom. The optimum situation would be to have them both; however, some countries (e.g. India), despite being democracies, have not had such good growth results as China, which is not a democracy. The difference between China and India is that since 1979 China has enjoyed much greater economic freedom than India with its over-bureaucratic society.

Nobel laureate in economics Douglass North (2000) addressed this issue simply when he said, "How do we account for the persistence of poverty in the midst of plenty? If we know the sources of plenty, why don't poor countries simply adopt policies that make for plenty? . . . We must create incentives for people to invest in more efficient technology, increase their skills, and organize efficient markets." Alexander Gerschenkron maintained the same line of thought years earlier (1962) when he asserted that the more backward countries should set up appropriate social and economic institutions to encourage investment and the adoption of new technologies.

However, as demonstrated by experts in growth and development theory, things are not as simple as they seem. There are still today paradoxes that are hard to explain. For instance, the Lucas paradox (1990), which asks why, with increasing capital flows between countries, capital is not flowing from rich into poor countries, where, by being scarcer, its price and yield are higher? Or the Becker paradox (1982) which asks how, with the reduction in inequalities in the world in terms of life expectancy, there has not been a greater convergence of education levels between countries? Many of the reasons for these paradoxes have to do with political and institutional factors, which Hall and Jones (1999) refer to as "social infrastructure."

Growth and development theories are hard to compare and contrast empirically. As pointed out by Daniel Cohen and Marcelo Soto (2002), the traditional factors behind growth generation have lost weighting when empirically accounted for their relative contribution. Physical capital does not have the spill-over effects anticipated in all production sectors; foreign capital does not flow to the countries that need it the most. Human capital seems to contribute less than expected to growth, or at least sufficiently to explain the wide gap between poor countries and rich countries. Only the total factor productivity or "Solow's residual" seems to have a major impact.

Cohen and Soto do not give up hope, however, and believe that, little by little, a virtuous circle is forming in poor developing countries. If these countries can continue to increase their life expectancy rates, this increase will provide an impulse to their education levels, allowing for an improvement in human capital accumulation and, ultimately, for an increase in the prices of their non-traded goods, thus attracting more foreign investment.

Education

Of all the policies that have been correlated with the level of per capita income, education is the one with the highest index. Robert Barro (1991) proves that, by measuring the level of human capital in a large number of countries based on primary and secondary schooling rates, the higher these rates are the more skilled and productive are its workers, the higher is its absorption of advanced technology from developed countries and the greater the country's long-term growth and the lower its fertility and infant mortality rates, as the amount of human and physical capital per head tends to increase as more importance is placed on improving children's education and health than on the number of children. In further research made with Lee (Barro and Lee, 1993, 1996, and 2000) both economists have made another step by measuring education attainment across countries because using merely enrolment ratios or literacy rates does not adequately measure the aggregate stock of human capital available as an input to production.

They find out that educational attainment has improved in the decade up to 2000 in all regions in the world except in the transition countries in the 1990s. For the 23 developed countries, the average years of schooling for persons aged 25 and over have increased from 9.3 years in 1990 to 9.8 years in 2000. For 73 developing countries the average years of attainment grew by 23 percent from 4.0 years in 1990 to 4.9 years in 2000, while in the transition economies they have remained at the level of 10 years. Among developing countries, sub-Saharan Africa and Middle East/North Africa showed the strongest progress growing by about 35 percent from 2.8 years to 3.8 years and from 3.8 years to 5.1 years respectively.

Thus, although developing countries have advanced faster their levels are still rather low. In 2000, 37 percent of their population 25 and over had no formal schooling and only 27 percent had some secondary education. In the case of women, the "gender ratio," that is the ratio of female to male attainment, expressed as a percentage, increased in most developing countries from 63 percent in 1990 to 70 percent in 2000 for the population aged 25 and over. Nevertheless their levels in Middle East/North Africa and South Asia, of 68 percent and 53 percent respectively, are still very low compared to those in Latin America and the transition countries, where the gender ratio is 90 percent and 100 percent respectively.

Further, the social and economic return on investing in human capital is the highest of all. According to the World Bank (1991), for every one-year increase in the average number of years of schooling of the workforce in developing countries, GDP long-term growth increases at an annual rate of 9 percent. This is also the case with the first three years of schooling; i.e. the difference between having no education at all and having completed the first three years is a 27 percent increase in GDP over the next three years. The additional return on a fourth year of schooling drops to 4 percent growth per year; i.e. GDP grows by 12 percent over the next three years. The same applies to developed countries. Marcelo Soto (2002) has reviewed more recently the marginal product returns of years of schooling, using neo-classical and endogenous growth models, and finds out that the marginal product of an extra year of schooling ranges from 7 to 10 percent, and if physical capital is allowed to increase as a response of human capital, as predicted by both models, the long-term effect of an additional year of schooling rises to 12 to 16 percent.

Education and training improve an individual's ability to assimilate and use information. They help him to know himself better, as well as the world around him. They enhance his mind by broadening his experience and enable him to take better decisions as a provider, consumer and, in general, as a citizen. By building his self-esteem, creativity and innovative capacity, his chances of getting ahead personally and socially are much greater. In macroeconomic terms, all of this means increased productivity, growth, and well-being.

The economic booms experienced by Japan, Chile, and Korea are a very clear example of success resulting primarily from having invested heavily in education. In Japan, with the restoration of the Meiji Era in 1868, under Emperor Mutsuhito, education was given an enormous push. In 1868, only 15 percent of the Japanese population knew how to read and write. By 1907, primary education was universal, free and obligatory, reaching 90 percent of the population (in Spain, for example, it reached only 25 percent at the beginning of the twentieth century) and secondary education had grown tenfold. For many decades now the literacy rate in Chile has been higher than in many developed countries, including, among others, Spain. Between 1910 and 1940, Korea invested significantly in education and agricultural and industrial technical training with the help of foreign technicians and engineers. From 1945 the country started to focus on higher education and sent tens of thousands of students to foreign universities, today, Korea has reached a higher income per capita than some European countries and it has developed a high level technology.

Of course, investing in education is not all that attractive to politicians because the budgetary strain is immediate, whereas the positive results are always longer-term. Politicians, who generally have to be re-elected every four years, prefer other investments – particularly in physical infrastructures – with results that are tangible in the shorter term, preferably before they run for re-election. They would rather not allocate money to an investment that is intangible and whose benefits will be reaped by a later generation of politicians that may not even belong to the same political party. This is one of the problems with today's democracies: they tend to focus on the short term and are only guided by the immediate results of surveys that do not always correspond with what the country and its citizens really need. In any event, it has been proven that dictatorial regimes invest much less in education, as the last thing a dictator wants is well-educated citizens who realize that they are worse off than the citizens of other, democratic regimes. The only exception left today that proves the rule is Cuba.

The good news is that over the past century, access to education has increased enormously, illiteracy has fallen dramatically and a higher proportion of people are completing primary, secondary, and tertiary education than ever before. But huge problems remain. About 115 million children of primary school age are not currently enrolled in school. Some 264 million children of secondary school age are not currently enrolled. Large educational disparities exist within and between countries. The quality of schooling is often very low. Moreover, demographic projections suggest that developing countries will have 80 million more children of primary and secondary school age by 2025, an increase of 6 percent to 1.9 billion.

Millions of children have access to schooling but do not attend. One explanation is that their families value more the time these children spend in other activities, such as performing work for income or looking after other smaller children so that other household members are free to work in market activities. A troubled household economic situation is often more of a deterrent to school enrolment than lack of access to school. Another explanation is that education competes for scarce national resources with many other worthy projects, such as building roads, finding water, or providing medical care. Unfortunately, organized interest groups may also divert funding from education to their own causes. When social crises, such as crime, unemployment, or civil war demand the time and resources of government, citizens may support channeling resources to them. The short-term horizon of politicians is another deterrent to funding long-term activities such as education. Finally, discrimination may inhibit educational participation, particularly for girls and for linguistic, religious, and ethnic minorities. Besides some religious beliefs, verbal and physical abuse, a lack of functional, secure toilets for girls, and long distances between home and school can deter parents from sending daughters to school. Girls' education may also be seen as a low priority if they leave their parents' household upon marriage (Cohen and Bloom, 2005).

Schooling rates in the world are published by UNESCO (2000). The primary schooling rate for males in OECD countries is 11 percentage points higher than that for developing countries; the difference with respect to females is 16 points. These rates are 15 and 21 points higher, respectively, if we exclude China and India, two of the developing countries with the highest rates. Noteworthy among the developing countries for its extremely low rates is sub-Saharan Africa: 35 percentage points lower than the OECD countries with respect to males and 43 points lower for females. Also noteworthy is the case of the Arab countries, where the difference in rates between males and females is higher than the rest of the developing world, except for sub-Saharan Africa, where Islam is also the predominant religion. It should therefore come as no surprise that these two regions are the ones with the highest fertility rates in the world. The same does not hold true in Latin America or Asia, which are not Islamic and whose schooling rates do not vary significantly between males and females.

Logically, the differences between developed countries and developing countries are even greater at the secondary schooling and higher education levels. At the secondary level the difference is 25 percentage points for males and 36 points for females. The differences at the higher education level are 38 percentage points for males and 49 for females. Noteworthy, however, are the differences in secondary schooling and higher education between North America and Europe: nine and eight percentage points in secondary schooling and 34 and 46 points in higher education for males and females, respectively.

There are enormous divergences throughout the world in illiteracy rates relating to both income and sex. In the countries with the lowest income per capita, the rate is 44 percent for females and 24 percent for males, aged 15 and over. In medium- to low-income countries, the rate is 22 percent for females and 13 percent for males. In medium- to high-income countries the rate is 15 percent for females and 12 percent for males. Lastly, in high-income countries the rate is practically zero for both females and males. On the one hand, it can be observed that it takes a growing marginal effort to reduce illiteracy, which underscores the enormous return on the investment made to reduce illiteracy in poor countries. On the other hand, there is a much smaller difference than would be determined by income level between countries with a medium- to high-income level and those with a medium- to low-income level. This suggests that there must be other factors reducing the difference so much in the former, such as the urban proportion of the population, especially where big countries are concerned, or religion.

Also noteworthy is the high level of illiteracy among females, an insurmountable barrier for a country's development since it goes hand in hand with very high fertility and infant mortality rates and a very low productivity rate.

Another interesting aspect of the level of education in the different regions is the relative weight of public and private education. There is not a great difference between what is spent on state education in developed countries and in developing countries in terms of percentage of GDP. The world total is 4.8 percent, that of the OECD countries is 5.1 percent and that of developing countries is 3.8 percent. Obviously, in developed countries, which have more budgetary resources, given the higher volume of their GDP, the percentage earmarked for education has a lower (4 to 7 percentage points) relative weight within total expenditure than in developing countries. At the high end of the spectrum are, paradoxically, the United States, Europe and sub-Saharan Africa with 5.5 percent, 5.3 percent and 5.6 percent of GDP, respectively. This apparent paradox is due to the fact that the percentage of private education in developed countries is very high, while it is generally very low in developing countries and almost non-existent in sub-Saharan Africa.

This paradox leads us to another very important aspect of education: quality. Having a high rate of schooling is not enough if the quality of the education offered is poor. Most studies of the economic aspects of education focus on school attainment or the quantity of education, because it is easier to measure and readily tracked over time. But it distorts policies and potentially may lead to bad decisions. The policy challenges that are facing most countries and mainly developing countries are those which have to do with quality, rather than quantity. Higher quality translates into higher earnings for individuals over their lifetime. Moreover, a society with a more educated labor force can also expect faster economic growth even if returns may not be discernible for many years. The research done by Eric Hanushek (2005) shows that a radical improvement of quality in primary and secondary education in year 2005, that takes 10 years to accomplish, will increase annual GDP growth by close to 7 percent in 2040 and a reform that takes 30 years to be accomplished will increase it by 4 percent in 2040.

Therefore, the faster it is done the better the returns and the easier to cover its full costs.

Quality should be defined as measured language, mathematics, and science skills, which in turn reflect a variety of factors such as family inputs, health, and schooling. Of these, existing research suggests that the clearest way to improvement lies in strengthening schools. The way to measure it is by recurrent evaluations and tests of students to show their progress over time, although these evaluations frequently focus on inputs to the system rather than on student achievements and outcomes because it is less expensive.

Public education in the United States is of poorer quality than private education, especially at secondary and higher education levels, than, for example, in Europe, Japan, or Korea. A survey conducted in the United States in the 1980s showed that, among students aged 21 to 25 in public colleges and universities, 20 percent had not attained an eighth-grade reading level and 35 percent could not answer questions on relatively simple quantitative problems. These aptitudes are higher in Europe and Japan. The countries of the Far East have improved the quality of their education notably by increasing the amount of schoolwork rather than the budget for education. For example, in Japan, China, and Korea children go to school 240 days a year and, on top of this, families spend an additional 20 percent on private supplemental classes. In Europe, children go to school 210 to 220 days a year, while in the United States they attend school 180 days per year. Conversely, private university education in the United States is far superior to that in Europe and even more so with respect to Japan and Korea. Nevertheless, almost 50 percent of the PhDs awarded in mathematics and engineering from those universities go to Asian students, particularly to students from China, Taiwan, India, Japan, and Korea.

The Asian countries' educational success illustrates that *how much* is spent on education is not as important as *how* it is spent. In eastern Asia 3 percent of GDP is spent on education – less than in other developing countries, which spend an average of 4 percent, and much less than Africa, where education spending averages 5 percent, and the OECD countries, whose spending on education is slightly higher than that of Africa. However, the students of China, Korea, Taiwan, India, and Japan are better than those of the rest of the world.

How did they achieve this? First of all, their family surroundings have been much more propitious for education. Mothers force their children to do their homework and help them with it at home. Second, their companies and governments are much more demanding when hiring workers and they pay a premium to get the best. Third, the number of students per classroom and teacher is higher than in western countries. While this is apparently negative from the standpoint of educational quality, it enables them to pay their teachers better salaries and, although they have fewer teachers, the ones they have are very good and dedicated. Fourth, these teachers not only teach each child to read and write correctly, but they also make them work number problems out in their head. Calculators are prohibited until the children are able to perform all operations mentally.

Higher education in the Far East has also been exemplary. Since primary education benefits the society as a whole and higher education basically benefits the person who receives it, in these countries (except Singapore) students must pay for their own studies, and the revenues are used to grant scholarships and aid to outstanding poor students. In view of the cost of attending the university, many students go into debt to pay for their studies. As a result, not only do they need to study hard, but they must also choose their degree carefully – normally a technical degree – so that they can get a job that pays well enough to repay their loans. This explains why there are more than three million university students in technical schools in this group of countries, many of whom will emigrate to the West. It also explains why in some countries, such as Korea, almost 70 percent of the population between the ages of 19 and 25 studies for a university degree.

In short, the developing countries that made a commitment to educate their citizens at the expense of other, less productive, investments managed to grow faster than the developed countries and were able to converge in terms of per capita income, not only because they were able to increase their productivity and GDP (the numerator of the ratio), but also because they were thus able to reduce their population growth rate (the denominator). As a result, since the 1960s they have doubled their per capita income faster than the developed countries, despite having fewer natural resources and physical capital. Europe has doubled it every 40 years, the United States every 30 years, whereas Japan has been able to double it every 20 years, India every 15 years, and China and Korea every 9 years.

This is the reason why major donors have increased their Official Development Aid for education in general and for primary education in particular, since 1990. Donor commitments for education reached in 2003 US$6.7 billion – more than double the amount in real terms committed just six years earlier. Commitments for primary education have risen even faster, quadrupling to US$1.9 billion between 1990 and 2003. To these figures we have to add private foundations; NGOs and other charities provide another US$1 billion annually for primary education, totaling US$2.9 billion annually.

Nevertheless, this amount is not enough to meet the Millennium Development Goal of achieving universal primary education by 2015. The Millennium Project has calculated a figure between US$7 and 17 billion per year to achieve it. But much depends also on the actions taking by developing countries themselves to improve the quality of education.

Healthcare

In recent years, some economists have changed the way that they think about health. Traditionally, social epidemiologists argued that it is socio-economic status, including income, that is the primary determinant of health, not healthcare. Now some reputed economists are challenging this idea. For instance, Amartya Sen (1999) has successfully pressed the importance of recognizing aspects of well-being beyond real income and argued that health should be the primary claim on our attention. The same can be said about Jeffrey Sachs and his Commission on Macroeconomics and Health (2002a) where he argued that health is a necessary, and perhaps even a sufficient, condition for economic growth in the poorest countries. Still, there is a heated debate between the role of nutrition and health in development.

Robert Fogel (2000 and 2005), the Nobel Prize-winning economic historian, has made a major contribution to understanding the role of nutrition in health and in development. His main argument is the following: the escape from hunger and premature death of poor people is based on eating more, but that is only possible if more food is produced and this in turn is only possible by being bigger and stronger to work, which in turn is only possible if they or their parents eat more. That is called the "nutritional trap." People could not work to produce food because they were too weak and they were weak because they could not produce food to be stronger (Deaton, 2005). The synergistic improvement of health and living standards was referred to by Fogel and Costa (1997) as the "techno-physio evolution": "A synergism between technological and physiological improvements that is biological, but not genetic, rapid, culturally transmitted and not necessarily stable."

When food supply is low, people cannot be large, because large bodies are simply too large to survive, given that they use up too many calories in resting and maintenance, leaving nothing for work. Our ancestors could manage to survive and procreate because they were much smaller than we are, but they lived shorter lives than we do. The issue is to find out the process by which they have been able to escape from hunger and premature death and turned into the large, long-lived animals that we are today. According to Fogel, using the case of England since the eighteenth century, the fact of being bigger and stronger can account for around half of the growth in national income in Britain since 1790. It has been able to enlarge longevity and reduce morbidity including that from non-infectious diseases. Therefore, the synergy between nutrition, size and weight has been the key element of the historical great escape from hunger and death. That means that poor nutrition remains an impediment to health in much of the world today.

Deaton and Subramanian (1996) and Deaton (2005) have some doubts about the ability of the nutritional trap, by itself, to have long-lasting effects in today's world. In modern economies, even very poor ones, the trap cannot be binding, given that the 2,000 calories that can provide the means to escape from the trap can be bought with only a fraction of the daily wage. For them, nutritional traps are much easier to understand once diseases are given their proper place in the theory. Diseases interact with nutrition and each reinforces the other. Malnutrition affects the immune system, so that people who do not have enough to eat are more likely to succumb to infectious diseases. At the same time, disease prevents the absorption of nutrients so that, even when food is obtainable, through own cultivation or in exchange for work, it cannot be turned into nutrition. It was most probably the removal of human waste from the drinking water that permitted nutrition to do its work on the human body, making us all bigger and stronger and enhancing the efficiency of labor, particularly in manual occupations.

It is more difficult to prove the link between economic growth and health as made by Easterly (1999), without taking into account the role of disease and its prevention (Deaton, 2005). Sometimes their correlation is positive but at other times is not. While it is hard to imagine the absence of a correlation between health and income in the very long run, the relationship can vanish for substantial periods of time. If economic growth reliably improved nutrition in poor countries now and if nutrition is the primary barrier to health, then we should let health look after itself. But if causation runs the other way, as argued by Sachs, or if growth by itself is no guarantee of health improvement in the medium run, then some sort of public action in the provision of health is required to turn economic growth into health improvements. Economic growth frequently needs help to guarantee an improvement in population health.

Therefore, another fundamental aspect of growth and per capita income is investment in healthcare. Without investments in potable water, the lack of which is the leading cause of death in poor countries, especially among children, or to fight malaria, tuberculosis, and AIDS, sickness and death are weakening and destroying the workforces of poor countries, and this has a very major impact on productivity and

GDP. Nevertheless, in many developing countries not enough funds are earmarked for these investments. Sometimes this is due to an inability to collect the funds; other times it is due to rampant corruption in some of these countries, as a result of which the funds are diverted for the benefit of a handful of politicians or government officials.

There are large public and private spending differences on health-care among the countries of the world. As explained in chapter 3, the poor and very poor countries are located in the tropics and remote areas and are the ones hit hardest by disease and major epidemics. They are also the ones that devote the smallest dollar amounts to healthcare; the amounts are much lower than would be expected based on their income per inhabitant vis-à-vis the medium-, medium- to high-, and high-income countries. According to the World Bank (2002) the countries with the highest income per capita devote 135 times more in dollar terms than the poor and poorest countries, even though their income per capita is only (and no less than) 20 times higher. Medium- to high-income countries allocate 13 times more in dollar terms than the poor and very poor countries, even though their income is six times higher, and medium-income countries earmark five times more than the poor and poorest countries, while their income per head is only three times higher. These differences are smaller, however, taking into account total expenditure (i.e. including domestic private spending and international aid), as private spending is almost twice as high as public spending.

As a consequence, the devastation that diseases cause to the people of these countries, especially in sub-Saharan Africa, is huge. AIDS, which produces 2.6 million deaths each year, of which 2.1 million are in Africa, is causing an annual loss of 89,819 years of productive life. Deaths from diarrhea exceed 2 million a year and cause the loss of over 62,000 years of productive life. Tuberculosis claims 1.7 million lives each year and the loss of 33,300 years of productive life. Lastly, malaria causes over 1 million deaths annually and the loss of 45,000 years of productive life. Africa, which suffers 80 percent of all deaths from AIDS and 87 percent of all deaths from malaria, followed by south-east Asia, which suffers 44 percent of all deaths from tuberculosis, are the two regions most affected by these fatal diseases. Diarrhea is more evenly spread between Africa and Asia, but Africa suffers more cases (World Bank, 2002).

The problem is that all these terrible epidemics are on the rise rather than coming under control. For example, between 1995 and 1999, the number of cases of tuberculosis increased by nearly half a million in Africa and by a quarter of a million in south-east Asia – and they are expected to grow at an even faster rate between 2000 and 2005. By 2005 it is estimated that they will have reached ten million people: four million in Asia and 3.2 million in Africa. The situation with AIDS is even more alarming. Of the 40 million people affected worldwide, 28.5 million live in Africa, only one million of which receive treatment. As a result, according to the projections in the report issued by the UN (2002), there will be 68 million AIDS deaths by the mid-2020s – there have been 24.8 million deaths since the 1980s – unless there is a radical change in the treatment of this disease. In 2001, there were five million new cases of AIDS and three million deaths, of which almost 600,000 were children under the age of 15.

Paradoxically, however, investment in healthcare offers a high return in these countries. A recent study by Gupta, Clements, and Tiongson (1998) reveals that for each percentage point increase in healthcare investment the infant mortality rate falls by two percentage points among poor families and that an increase of 0.4 percentage point of GDP in healthcare spending reduces the infant mortality rate by 5 deaths for every 1,000. Jeffrey Sachs (2001 and 2002a) reached similar conclusions.

The main problem facing these poor countries is that healthcare spending is not being correctly distributed to the poor. In most cases, the poorest 20 percent is allocated less expenditure per family than the richest 20 percent, and in some cases spending is not progressive because the poorest 20 percent is not allocated a higher percentage than the richest 20 percent, taking into account the difference in income between the two groups. In other words, the poor are clearly neglected when it comes to distributing healthcare spending. At the same time, advantage is not being taken of the high return on each dollar spent on healthcare. The return is much higher when it is aimed at the poorest, as the rich are able to afford private healthcare. Poverty is more closely linked to infant mortality than inequality is. Therefore, healthcare spending offers a more than proportional return when it is used on poor families.

Other major aspects include, on the one hand, the combination of spending on education and healthcare. When women receive primary education the infant mortality rate drops drastically. On the other hand, the urbanization of the rural population also reduces infant mortality more than proportionally, as rural areas usually lack minimum-standard healthcare centers to take care of the local people, who tend to be the poorest – hence the non-progressive nature of healthcare spending in these countries.

It is absolutely shameful to see how so many people continue to die in such countries when there are treatments for these diseases. Treatments for malaria, diarrhea, and tuberculosis have been around since the nineteenth century, and the diseases are treated successfully in developed countries. Yet, more than a century later, the treatments are still not reaching these poor countries. Later in this book, in the chapter on the OECD countries' Official Development Aid (chapter 10), I will address in greater detail the causes of this scandal, which illustrates the manifest lack of international solidarity and the neglect of the rest of the world toward these countries and the poorest people in low-income countries.

Institutions

Among the economists specializing in growth and development following the trail blazed by Nobel Prize winner historian Douglass North (1981 and 1990; and North and Thomas, 1973), there is a great deal of literature that underscores the growing importance of institutions in economic development. According to North (1990), "Institutions are the rules of the game in society or more formally, are the humanly devised constraints that shape human interaction" which "in consequence they structure incentives in human exchange, whether political, social or economic." Recent work by Hall and Jones (1999), Acemoglu, Jonson, and Robinson (2001 and 2004), Acemoglu (2003), Rodrik, Subramanian, and Trebbi (2002), Rodrik and Subramanian (2003), and Easterly and Levine (2002), contributes significantly to this viewpoint and demonstrates the importance of institutions over other factors that have been studied in greater depth, such as international trade, integration, economic policies, and geography.

As pointed out in chapter 3, Easterly and Levine believe that the quality of institutions is the determinant factor for an economy to achieve long-term growth, even more important than geography and economic policy. If institutions are quality institutions, poor geographical location and erroneous economic policies become minor elements in achieving high long-term growth. Having said this, geography can have negative effects on the quality of institutions, but Easterly and Levine consider that previous colonization has a greater influence on institutions than geographical location.

Rodrik, Subramanian, and Trebbi reached similar conclusions empirically, demonstrating that institutions are the single most important factor determining the difference in income between countries and that the most important for increasing incomes is finding the right institutional preconditions rather than trying to micromanage outcomes. Institutions are more important than geographical location, i.e. the climate, physical geography, natural resources, tropical diseases and access to natural communication routes, contrary to the findings of Diamond (1997) Gallup, Sachs, and Mellinger (1998) and Sachs (2001). They also consider it to be a more important factor than openness and foreign trade in order to achieve changes in productivity and growth, contrary to the conclusions of Frankel and Romer (1999) and Sachs and Warner (1995). The problem, when analyzing all these factors, is that there are problems of endogeneity and reverse causality between them. Both integration with the rest of the world and the quality of institutions are endogenous in that they conform with each other and with the country's geography and income level, as well.

Geography, the most exogenous factor of all, has a direct effect on income levels through agricultural production and the infant mortality rate. However, it can also have an indirect effect on integration in world markets because of distance and on the quality of institutions because of the poor endowment of natural resources and other production factors that tend to cause extreme inequalities, making it possible for power to be concentrated in the hands of small groups of elites. The same thing happens, paradoxically, in countries that have a single very important natural resource. This is what is known as "the curse of resources" as was demonstrated in the previous chapter.

Integration with markets and institutions lies in endogenous factors and, therefore, it is very hard to demonstrate their causality. Increased trade and integration can be due to higher levels of productivity or income or to higher-quality institutions. The latter can be the result of higher levels of income or greater trade integration, as openness tends to improve the level of institutions. Despite these difficulties, the three economists demonstrate that institutions play a much more important role than integration and geography. In all cases, the levels of the rule of law and the protection of property rights show a positive correlation with income and growth, whereas integration and geography show regressions that are sometimes negative and sometimes weaker. The quality of institutions also has a positive impact on integration and vice versa, demonstrating that integration has a positive effect on income, thus giving rise to higher-quality institutions, and finally, geography also has an indirect effect on the quality of institutions.

A similar view is expressed by Edison (2003) who, looking at the relationship between policies and institutions, finds out that institutions have a strong and significant effect on per capita GDP growth and that part of this impact reflects the role of institutions in enhancing the sustainability of policies. Sound policies need to be supported and sustained by good institutions, while weak institutions may reduce the chance that good policies will be adopted or may undermine policy effectiveness. In other words, the bottom line is not that policies are unimportant but that their influence on economic performance is already reflected in the strength of institutions.

McArthur and Sachs (2001) in their response to Acemoglu, Johnson, and Robinson (2001) and using a regression analysis based on similar data and expanding the sample of countries analyzed, end up by confirming that both institutions and geography-related health variables such as malaria incidence of life expectancy at birth are strongly linked to gross national product per capita and that the evidence presented by Acemoglu et al. is likely to be limited by the inherently small sample of ex-colonies and the limited dispersion of those countries, which were mainly concentrated in tropical zones. Similar arguments are developed by Sachs (2003a and 2003b) who argues that of course institutions matter but not for everything, given that the role of geography and resource endowments should not be underestimated. He thinks that it is a common mistake to believe and a weak argument to make that geography equals determinism. Even if good health is important to development, not all malarial regions are condemned to poverty, and landlocked regions may be burdened by high transport costs but not necessarily condemned to poverty. Rather, special investments targeted to fight malaria and to construct roads, rail, communications, and other transport facilities may help to initiate a self-sustaining growth. The same can be achieved though migration, yet the international system denies that option, and regional integration, by breaking the barriers that limit the size of markets.

Acemoglu, Johnson, and Robinson (2004; Acemoglu and Robinson, 2006) insist on the idea and bring evidence to it, that institutions are the fundamental cause of long-run growth. Their main arguments are: first, economic institutions matter for economic growth because they shape the incentives of key economic actors in society and in particular they influence investments in physical and human capital and technology as well as the organization of production. Although they recognize that cultural and geographical factors may also matter for economic performance, differences in economic institutions are the major source of cross-country differences in economic growth and prosperity, by affecting not only potential growth, but also wealth, human and physical capital distribution (one case in point is that of North and South Korea). Second, economic institutions are endogenous, since they are determined by collective choices of the society, in large part for their economic consequences. As there are always different preferences in society about economic institutions because they affect the distribution of resources, there is typically a conflict of interest among various groups of individuals whose outcome is determined by their relative political power. Thus political power shapes economic institutions and this is the reason why they are endogenous.

Third, why may the exercise of political power lead to economic inefficiencies and even to poverty? Because there are commitment problems inherent in the use of political power. Those wielding political power tend to use it in their best interests, creating a problem between efficiency and distribution, because credible compensating transfers cannot be made to offset the distributional consequences of any particular set of economic institutions. The elite may pursue inefficient policies to extract revenue from other groups to reduce their demand for productive factors, thus inherently benefiting from changes in factor prices, and to empoverish other groups competing for political power. That elite preference for inefficient policies translates into inefficient economic institutions and the elite may manipulate economic institutions in order to further increase their income or rent extraction (Acemoglu, 2006). Fourth, the distribution of political power in society is also endogenous. Political institutions also determine the incentives and constraints in the political sphere and can give birth to a democracy, an autocracy, or a dictatorship, thus, they determined the "de jure political power."

Fifth, however, the distribution of resources (physical and human capital stocks) determines the "de facto political power" which may impose itself over the "de jure political power." Sixth, political institutions are also endogenous, because the distribution of political power determines the evolution of political institutions. Political institutions allocate "de jure political power," and those who hold "de facto political power" try to influence the evolution of political institutions to maintain those political institutions which maintain them in power, making political institutions very persistent, and difficult to change the status quo.

In sum, the two major sources of political power: political institutions which determine the "de jure political power," and the distribution of resources, which determines the "de facto political power" determine the choice of economic institutions and influence the future evolution of political institutions. Economic institutions, in their turn, determine economic outcomes including the aggregate rate of growth of the economy and the future distribution of resources.

Amartya Sen (1999 and 2000) shows also the important role played by institutions in development. He considers that all countries that are independent, hold elections regularly, have opposition parties that fulfill their duty to criticize the government, and allow the press to question freely the "wisdom" of their leaders without censure are democratic countries. This means that institutions born of a liberal democracy that observes not only political freedom, but also essential civil liberties, such as personal freedom, freedom of religion, freedom to associate, and freedom of the press, are an excellent foundation for growth and development.

What is very important for the development of quality institutions is that there seems to be strong evidence about how globalization and openness tend to help improve the level of governance, of institutional quality, and of democracy (Hamilton, 2002; Bonaglia, Braga de Macedo, and Bussolo, 2001). They show that trade policy, competition by foreign producers and institutional investors and openness-related differences in institution-building costs and benefits are the three major transmission mechanisms through which openness strongly reduces corruption levels in the long run. Nevertheless, in the short run and mainly for some very poor countries, domestic policies may be more valuable than pursuing globalization at all costs, because reducing trade barriers may not bring immediately positive corruption reductions. After controlling for many cross-country differences, the influence of openness on corruption is close to one-third of that exercised by development. They also deal with the issue of reverse causality (a corrupt bureaucracy may induce a lower degree of international integration by erecting discretionary barriers) by demonstrating that it is openness that directly affects corruption and not vice versa.

Giavazzi and Tabellini (2004) find positive feedback effects between political and economic liberalizations. But the timing of events indicates that causality is more likely to run from political to economic liberalizations, rather than vice versa. They also find that the sequence of both reforms matters. Countries that first liberalize and then become democracies do much better than countries that pursue the opposite sequence in almost all dimensions.

Rigobon and Rodrik (2004) find similar long-term results of openness although with a more mixed and complex causality. They estimate the interrelationships among economic institutions, political institutions, openness and income levels and they find that democracy and the rule of law are both good for economic performance, but the latter has a much stronger positive impact on incomes. Openness, measured as the proportion of trade on GDP, tends to have a negative impact on income levels and democracy but a positive effect on the rule of law. On the other hand, higher income produces greater openness and better institutions, although these effects are not very strong, and the rule of law and democracy tend to be mutually reinforcing. Then, openness tends to improve the rule of law, which eventually increases incomes and reinforces democracy and both end up by improving economic and political institutions, which help to increase development.

Democracy can be a very important factor conducive to growth. Rober Barro (1999) has shown for a panel study of over 100 countries, democratic institutions provide a check on governmental power and thereby limit the potential of public officials to amass personal wealth and to carry out unpopular policies, but more democracy encourages rich-to-poor redistributions of income and may enhance the power of interest groups. Growth is initially increasing in an index of electoral rights, but the relation may turn negative once a certain amount of rights have been attained. That is, in the worst dictatorships an increase in democracy tends to stimulate growth, but after a certain accumulation of rights a further increase may impair growth if the concern for social and redistribution is intensified and become "too democratic."

Tavares and Wacziarg (2001) introduce a new methodology to examine the empirical relationship between democracy and economic growth, looking not only to its direct but also indirect effects on variables that in turn determine growth. Their results show, on the one hand, that democracy fosters growth by improving the accumulation of human capital and, less robustly, by lowering income inequality. On the other hand, democracy hinders growth by reducing the rate of physical capital accumulation and, less robustly, by raising the ratio of government consumption to GDP. Democratic institutions are responsive to the demands of the poor by expanding access to education and lowering income inequality but do so at the expense of physical capital accumulation.

In a recent paper, Persson and Tabellini (2006), in a similar vein to Giavazzi and Tabellini, find out that democracy is, in general, positively correlated with growth, but it depends, in a subtle way, on the details of democratic reforms. On the one hand, democratic and economic liberalizations in isolation each induce growth accelerations, but countries liberalizing their economy before extending political rights do better than those carrying out the opposite sequence. However, new presidential democracies tend to grow faster than new parliamentary democracies, which have more difficulty achieving proper fiscal and trade reforms. Finally, it is very important to distinguish between expected and actual political reforms: expectations of regime change have an independent effect on growth, and taking expectations into account helps identify a stronger growth effect of democracy.

Finally, Glaeser, La Porta, Lopez de Silanes, and Shleifer (2004) think otherwise about institutions and growth. They ask themselves if institutions cause growth (as found out by North, Acemoglu, et al. etc.) or, alternatively, if growth and human capital accumulation lead to better institutions (as supported originally by Lipset and followed by Djankov et al. and Barro). Their view is much closer to the second. They find that human capital is a more basic source of growth than are the institutions and that poor countries get out of poverty through good policies, often pursued by dictators and then subsequently, improve their political institutions. This line of work seems to accord well with the experiences of South Korea, Taiwan, and China.

Among all these institutional aspects, mention should first be made of the existence of a rule of law that guarantees the right to private property and social justice and is respected by all citizens. If there is not a clear and real rule of law, i.e. one that is observed, it is nearly impossible to have a stable, prosperous state.

The protection of private property is of utmost importance within this rule of law. Hernando De Soto (2000), in his excellent book, *The Mystery of Capital: Why Capitalism Triumphs in the West and Fails Everywhere Else*, carries out a statistical study in which he tries to quantify the extralegal property wealth of the poor throughout the world, estimated at US$9.3 trillion. In 1996 this figure was almost equal to the value of all the companies listed on the major stock exchanges of the 20 most developed countries, more than 20 times the total foreign investment in developing countries, more than 46 times the World Bank's total loans since the 1970s, and 93 times more than the development aid granted since its inception. The problem lies in the fact that this amazing amount of wealth cannot be moved; it lies there, "dead," because its owners do not hold the legally registered property deeds. They are extralegal possessions that are transferred about in the world of informal economy; however, the transfer of these assets is only valid in small local circles, each of which has its own ways and customs. As a result, the owners cannot use their modest properties as collateral for loans to invest in productive activities. Since there are no mortgages, there is no construction. Since there is no way to get credit for industrial and commercial activities, there is also no banking system. In short, the possibility of using the properties to obtain credit and carry on productive activities is practically non-existent.

It is incredible to think that such an important opportunity to prosper could be lost because something as basic as the legal acknowledgment of property rights was not developed. The current president of Brazil, Luiz Ignácio "Lula" da Silva, has taken the intelligent decision to grant property rights to those living in *favelas* situated, for the most part, on public land. This will enable these people to make improvements to the assets or perhaps use them as collateral for a mortgage loan. Until now they only occupied them illegally. Some countries, however, not only refuse to take similar measures but have introduced tighter restrictions, from prohibiting the sale of land to taxing land at rates so high that it is impossible to pay the taxes. Some countries in which property can be registered have minimum registration periods, which run from three to seven years.

Not only is it important to mobilize the property of each citizen in the market, but also to develop a financial market that enables him, on the one hand, to take out insurance against general risks, catastrophes, life, etc. and, on the other, to obtain financing to develop a project or business. However, it is precisely the financial market that most needs clear game rules and solid institutions in order to be able to operate. It needs an adequate bankruptcy law, it needs there to be a bank that can foreclose on bad debts, and it needs a central bank that supervises, inspects, and penalizes banks that do not operate with total transparency and that do not play by the rules of the game, in addition to serving as a lender of last resort, etc.

Financial development is a key factor to generate growth. Different financial development indices as a percentage GDP are linked to the levels of income per capita in different groups of countries. Not only are the differences between them important, but there is also empirical evidence that the countries with the greatest financial development grow up to twice as fast as those that lack financial development (Levine, 1997 and 2000; Levine and Zervos, 1998). There is also empirical evidence that financial development promotes creativity and technological development and that, contrary to popular belief, it benefits the poorest above all (Dollar and Kraay, 2000). A novel experiment developed in the poorer countries since the 1990s has confirmed these ideas. The main evidence has been contributed by the so-called "micro-finance" or "micro-loans," originally invented by Professor Yunus in Bangladesh through its Grameen Bank. These loans were first granted exclusively to the poorest women (in an Islamic country!), who, working in small groups, with joint liability, use them to produce farm products or crafts that they later could sell in local markets. The debtors of Grameen Bank also become its shareholders. The success of this experiment has been so overwhelming that in just a few years it has spread throughout the developing world.

Other fundamental institutions include those that monitor and defend competition. What really constrain market opportunities and economic activity are the transaction costs arising from the lack of adequate information and transparency, the problems of defining and enforcing property rights and compliance with contracts, the barriers to entry for new competitors or to exit for existing ones, and openness to international competition. Competition is the driving force and incentive for institutional and economic change.

In the markets of goods and services, the key element of competition is that all competitors should be able to sell their goods and services freely, wherever they want and for however much they want, provided that they do not take advantage of a situation of market dominance. Such competition increases efficiency (i.e. productivity), as it encourages competitors to reduce costs, innovate, reduce excess capacity, and organize themselves more efficiently. Increased productivity is, in turn, the long-term growth driver, fueled by technological progress, which as we have seen earlier, is reinforced by protecting intellectual property rights, trade, foreign direct investment, licenses and the creation of joint ventures. In the markets of production factors, labor, and capital, competition helps to ensure that the two factors are assigned with greater efficiency and productivity. In the case of labor it is necessary to try to defend the rights of all workers equally, regardless of their condition, gender, and classification. This means that the rights of association, organization, collective bargaining and strike, as well as health and safety conditions in the workplace, minimum work age, minimum wage, severance pay, unemployment pay, and disability pay are fundamental rights, even though the remuneration will logically be small at the outset.

However, it is also important to avoid making the regulation of this market too rigid and fastidious, as has happened in Europe. Otherwise, there will be discrimination among employees, excessive government intervention, solving conflicts will be slow and costly, and it will be difficult to mobilize workers, all of which reduces the efficiency and productivity of this factor, which is so crucial to development. In capital markets competition between financial institutions and the transparency of the information on their activities and solvency are fundamental issues. On the one hand, they reduce the cost of the other more important resource in the production activity and, on the other hand, they ensure that customers and investors do not lose out. It is also necessary to make sure that excessive financial crises do not arise, jeopardizing savings and intermediation capabilities and payment systems.

The *World Competitiveness Yearbook* (2000) asserts that the higher the per capita income and the longer such institutions have been running, the higher the efficiency of the institutions that defend competition. In developed countries the institutions that defend competition have been running for an average of 27 years, compared with 10 years in some developing countries, and the former are 40 percent more efficient than the latter. Also, as explained above, the best way to increase competition is by opening up to international trade and investment. The higher the volume of imports as a percentage of GDP, the lower the margin between prices and costs will be. This benefits not only consumers but also producers who use them as inputs or consumables. Openness is also a fundamental tool for pressuring governments into eliminating institutional barriers to competition in domestic markets faster, as these barriers reduce a country's ability to compete abroad. To reduce the short-term adverse effects of such openness on the domestic economy and the costs of adjustment, it is necessary to make the product and production factor markets more flexible.

It is also essential that there be solid, experienced institutions to defend competition in order to efficiently implement a privatization policy. Historical experience has shown that when state-run companies provide public services they are generally less efficient than private companies. The most important objective, when privatizing companies, is not to generate money to pour into the public coffers with the short-term view of filling in budgetary holes, as many politicians who are in power for four or eight years seem to think. The objective must be to open the service up to competition so that it will be more efficient and less costly for users and so that more jobs will be created and more investment generated in the country. The price at which a public service is sold is the present value of future profit flows, discounted at a specific interest rate. In most cases, the only thing that is being done is to advance a future inflow of public funds. The private buyer is interested in acquiring the service because he feels that he can achieve more profits than the discounted future profits, because he believes that he can run the business more efficiently and bring the service to a greater number of users. If there are no clear rules on the conditions under which the public service is to be transferred and the service is not opened up to other competitors, the only thing that happens is that the public monopoly becomes a private one and the buyer gets rich.

This has been the case in some developing countries where the telephone or electricity service has been privatized for the sole purpose of raising short-term public funds. As a result, in the longer run everyone comes out losing – except the buyer, who, in addition, is generally a national, as it is not desirable to allow strategic assets to fall into the hands of foreigners (as if nationals are necessarily better managers than foreigners, when the opposite tends to be true in these cases). The end result is that these countries fail to achieve a significant initial investment in foreign currency, the knock-on investment of the foreign company's suppliers setting up in their country, the creation of new jobs, improved efficiency or a reduction in the cost of the service.

As was shown earlier about education, the mere existence of institutions is not enough – they must also be of good quality in order to fulfill their role efficiently. There is a high correlation between the quality of political and administrative institutions and economic growth (World Bank, 2002). The quality of these institutions is partially determined by the existence of fundamental checks and balances of public powers. The first is a judicial power independent from political power. It has been conclusively proven that greater judicial independence means better protection of property rights. However, in addition to being independent, justice must be efficient. If judicial procedures are too many in number or too complex in form (especially if they are written), if they are very slow and if, as a result of the foregoing, they are very expensive, most citizens, especially the poorest ones, will be unable to avail themselves of justice and will therefore be defenseless. The second is the media. Freedom of the press is highly and positively correlated with the private ownership thereof. The greater the percentage of the media in the hands of the state, the less freedom there is. Moreover, the state's efficiency improves notably with freedom of the press.

The third is the degree of economic openness. The more economic freedom and openness and the greater the weight of international transactions as a percentage of GDP, the greater is the validity of the rule of law and the greater is the state's efficiency as well. The reason for this is obvious. In most cases, international transactions place a sort of filter and limit on what the state can do to its citizens with impunity, as these transactions involve international rules, which must be followed because, otherwise, they would considerably reduce the country's economic growth potential through its exterior sector.

Corruption is another institutional ill in most countries. It does exist in all societies, at all stages of economic growth and under different political and economic regimes. But its degree of intensity is what makes the difference in its negative effects on growth. Countries with a high level of corruption tend to grow more slowly because their political, economic, and social institutions do not work or, just as bad, they are not of high enough quality, or because there is not an adequate system of checks and balances to protect the civil society from government power. Corruption is one of the worst scourges for many developing countries, as it involves enormous costs in order to carry on private activities and, in general, for the legal protection of the citizens, who are subject to all manner of impediments and limitations on their activities but cannot resort to ordinary courts to defend themselves for fear of jeopardizing their livelihood – or even their lives.

Corruption is also like a regressive tax in that it affects the smallest companies much more negatively than the larger ones (at a ratio of 8 to 1.5) and the poorest citizens much more than the wealthier ones (4 to 1.5). Corruption causes the countries that most suffer or exercise it to receive smaller flows of foreign investment, because investors fear that they will be subjected to a flagrant lack of legal protection or even out-and-out blackmail by the authorities of that country. Corruption also bears an additional cost in that corrupt governments, rather than authorizing smaller, less expensive works that are much more necessary, will always have an incentive for contracting major infrastructure works and imports, even though the country does not need them, so that they can extort more in a smaller number of projects (World Bank, 2002).

Corruption depends, first, on the degree of the state's intervention in the economy (Shleifer, 1993). The more the state intervenes, the more corruption there is. There is a positive correlation between the number of formalities imposed by public authorities and the corruption index. The problem is that there is also a positive relationship between the countries with the lowest per capita income and those with the highest number of administrative formalities, which are tantamount to extralegal taxes but which, because they are regressive, affect the poorest the most. Second, it depends on how the public administration's civil servants are hired. If they are hand-picked from amongst the family and friends of the politicians in power, the levels of corruption and delays in bureaucratic formalities tend to be much greater than if they are hired objectively on the basis of their personal merits. There are still some poor countries where civil servant posts are auctioned off, in which case it is assumed that the winning bidders will benefit from the extraordinary revenues they extort from their fellow citizens.

Of course, in order for a civil servant to be corrupt there must be someone, a company or an individual, that corrupts him, either by bowing to his corrupt demands or by making him a corrupt offer. It all boils down to supply and demand. The causes of the demand for corruption are, as we saw in the preceding paragraph, policies that basically arise from the lack of democratic institutions, a high degree of state intervention and the hand-picking of civil servants. The causes of the offer of corruption are economic. As long as the extra cost of corruption can be passed on to consumers it will be more easily accepted. Problems only arise if the cost is too high or if it is not certain that, once the price has been paid, the desired public service, be it a formality, a concession, a sale, etc., can be obtained.

In order to try to eliminate or reduce corruption between companies from wealthier countries when dealing with developing countries, the OECD has taken two very important steps. On the one hand, a code of ethics has been established for international companies that trade or have contracts with such countries. On the other hand, two fundamental changes have been made to the legislation of the OECD countries. The first one has to do with taxes. It is prohibited by law for these companies to deduct from their taxes in their country of origin payments made to politicians, civil servants, or citizens of those countries in order to be able to operate in them. Just why such deductions were allowed in most of the OECD countries in the first place is incomprehensible. The second one is of a criminal nature. Corruptors can also be tried in their country of origin for crimes of corruption, not just in the destination country, as was the case previously.

In many developing countries there are "informal" institutions that replace or sometimes supplement those established legally, allowing the markets to operate and many citizens to benefit from the existence of such "informal" markets. These institutions are based on social norms and customs that make up the culture of the country and have developed spontaneously because there were no legal regulations on which to base contracts. The institutions are based essentially on the premise that the people interacting in such markets will always act in a predictable manner and in accordance with customs and that they will fulfill their commitments because, otherwise, they would be punished socially, damaging their reputation and trustworthiness. These institutions often exist in poor, isolated countries in which informal institutions are the only way to make the local or regional markets work. However, the "informal" nature of these institutions can prove to be an obstacle when trying to develop markets, as is the case when the closed social networks using them, whether local communities, classes, castes, tribes, or clans, restrict the volume and scope of potential transactions, preventing other more numerous groups or new outside participants from accessing the markets.

The establishment of formal institutions and contracts in these countries is a major challenge for their leaders, as historical experience shows that the new formal rules in place do not take into account traditional social norms and customs and do not ordinarily produce the desired results. They can thus find themselves in a situation where the benefits achieved are scant, and yet the same institutions that made the markets work before have been destroyed. The solution in these cases is, on the one hand, to supplement the existing informal institutions with new ones to be used exclusively for international trade and trade with larger companies, until the number and cultural diversity of the participants reaches a majority and then, and only then, the old ones should be slowly replaced with the new ones. On the other hand, it is important that the new formal institutions avoid establishing regulatory barriers that are excessively onerous, as this only creates greater incentives for informal economic activity, as has been the case in some of the developing countries in Africa.

A new area of research on the role of institutions in growth is that undertaken by Philippe Aghion (2002), Acemoglu, Johnson, and Robinson (2001), and Acemoglu, Aghion, and Zilibotti (2002), among other economists, in which they combine new theories on endogenous growth with new microeconomic and industrial organization theories to analyze the institutional changes needed as a country develops and converges with the technological frontier. In the early stages of development an incentive-based institutional policy should be implemented to encourage investment leading to growth. In other words, there should be more room to maneuver to allow for state intervention, subsidies for investment, production, and exports, low-interest loans and so on with a view to achieving growth based on a greater accumulation of physical and human capital. This type of growth can be achieved with rigid institutions and state intervention. Such was the case of certain European countries during the second half of the nineteenth century, the Latin American countries in the 1970s and, most notably, Japan and South Korea after the Second World War.

As a country converges with the technological frontier, the growth strategy should be focused on openness, selection and innovation rather than capital accumulation. Under this strategy of innovation-based growth it is necessary to choose the best managers and companies and the best scientists and technologists. Whereas in the first strategy the economy does not need to be open, in the second strategy it must be open. In the first strategy emphasis should be placed on primary education, secondary education, and vocational training; in the second emphasis should be placed on higher education and research. While in the first strategy vertical integration is advisable, in the second it is preferable to focus only on innovation and to subcontract most of the other activities. Countries that fail to go from one strategy to the next and from one level of institution to another, remaining in the investment-based growth strategy, eventually become stagnant.

Finally, there is growing debate around the influence of politics on economic outcomes and the relationship between the size and strength of states or governments and development. Since the pioneering work by Douglass North (1981 and 1990) a large body of work in economics highlights the benefits of "limited government" because, as he argued, the politically determined structure of property rights need not maximize the efficiency or the growth potential of the economy; instead, it strives to maximize the returns to the rulers or politically strong groups, thus it is better to have an efficient system that reduces transaction costs and encourages economic. While a structure of property rights that limits potential expropriation by rulers and encourages investment by citizens increases economic growth, rulers will typically attempt to increase their share of revenues by taxation or expropriation. Therefore, this view suggests that limited government and constraints on power of the state to tax will stimulate growth.

Nevertheless, although there are numerous examples of disastrous economic performances under self-interested political elites and rulers with few checks and balances, many successful growth experiences, notably in east Asia, have also taken place under the auspices of strong states. Examples of success under strong authoritarian regimes like South Korea under General Park or China under Teng Tsiao Ping are well known. Moreover, in contrast to the implications of the simple form of this limited government view, government revenues as a fraction of GDP appear to be higher in richer countries and in societies that are generally considered to have more constrained governments. Governments in advanced economies are able to raise higher tax revenues and play a more important role in the economy than authoritarian rulers in poor countries (Acemoglu, 2005).

This is the reason why many political scientists, especially in the context of African politics, view the main barrier to economic development not as the strength of the state but as the state capacity, power or monopoly over violence or to face the resistance posed by chiefs, landlords, bosses, rich peasants, clan leaders, etc. (Herbst, 2000). Thus "weak states," they argue, have a limited capacity to tax, regulate, and play a development role and in many poor countries there is the need for more state not less.

According to Acemoglu (2005) both excessively weak and strong states create distortions in the allocation of resources and consequently are likely to act as impediments to economic development. While strong states tend to impose high taxes or extract high private rents for the ruler, discouraging investment and entrepreneurial effort by citizens, weak states fail to invest in needed public goods such as infrastructures, roads, or legal rules for contract enforcement. They under-invest in public goods because self-interested political elites undertake investments only when they expect future private rewards, and when the state is weak, they can appropriate fewer rewards in the future because states are politically weak when rulers can be replaced easily. Thus, as the state takes actions that are important for the efficient functioning of the economy, it is necessarily an organization of society that provides the right incentives to the self-interested agents controlling the state and this is only possible through a balanced distribution of political power between state and society and between the investments by the citizens and those controlling the state. The problem is that the strength of the state in many less developed nations is not limited by the power of citizens but by other privileged social groups, such as tribal chiefs or wealthy landowners.

Artadi and Sala i Martín (2003) have tried to find out the real causes of the lower economic growth in Africa since decolonization in 1960, given that between 1960 and 1980 per capita GDP increased slightly from $1,500 to about $2,000, then it stagnated at this very low level ever since, what they call "the economic tragedy of the twentieth century." Using the Sala i Martín, Dopplehofer, and Miller (2003) determinants of economic growth, they confirm the relevance of the factors enumerated in this and previous chapters, by finding out that the main factors explaining such a slow growth are: low level of investment but expensive investments goods, low levels and quality of education, poor health, adverse geography, closed economies, too much public expenditure, and too many military conflicts.

Chapter 5
The World Distribution of Income

Economists use five main concepts – convergence, extreme and absolute poverty, relative poverty and inequality – when discussing the world-wide distribution of income. It is worthwhile clarifying each of these terms, how they are measured and their scope, as they can be confusing and some times misused, not only by the opponents of globalization but also sometimes in the past by highly credible national and international institutions, such as the United Nations.

Estimating the world distribution of income is no easy task since it is nearly impossible to know the income of every individual on the planet. For this reason, economists who specialize in this field try to use many different statistical approximations, different sources and different surveys to arrive at as reliable a figure as possible. There are three major issues related to how to measure income distribution.

The first is whether it should be measured comparing countries or comparing individuals. Some economists have confined themselves to analyzing world distribution of income by comparing each country's average per capita income figures and they show that the world's income distribution is becoming more unequal, but, as will be shown later, this measurement system has a major shortcoming in that countries' population figures vary wildly (from less than 500,000 to more than 1 billion people) and therefore, when analyzing the world's distribution of income, it is more convenient to weight countries by population, giving every individual in the world equal weight; in this case the world's income distribution is becoming more equal. When testing growth theories and convergence, on the contrary, it makes more sense to treat countries equally. Finally, when analyzing inequality it makes sense to look both at world personal inequality and to between-country and within-country inequality as well.

The second measurement issue is whether income should be compared among countries and individuals using actual exchange rates or PPP (purchasing power parity) exchange rates. When incomes in different countries are compared using actual exchange rates, the evidence shows that world income distribution is more unequal than by using PPP exchange rates. The use of actual exchange rates has some drawbacks: first, they are affected by capital flows and monetary policy and they tend to be rather volatile. Second, they fail to reflect the different price levels of every country. Third, they do not reflect the large amount of non-monetary exchange in developing countries (barter) or cash payment for services that are not subject to international competition. By contrast, PPP exchange rates are better suited for comparing developed and developing countries' per capita incomes, but they also have a drawback: historical series are more difficult to compare than using actual exchange rates because comprehensive estimates of PPP incomes for developing countries, based on actual data of prices of comparable goods and services, go back only to the 1970s.

The third measurement issue is whether to use national consumption surveys or national accounts consumption statistics. Surveys tend to estimate a higher rate of poverty and inequality than national accounts. Surveys tend to have more problems of design, sample selection, and execution than national statistics but, unfortunately, the latter tend to be less accurate in developing countries than in developed countries. Most of the discrepancy between both estimates is probably due to the fact that, as people improve their incomes, they are less likely to respond accurately to the surveys. As a result the ratio of survey consumption to national-accounts consumption tends to be highest in poorest countries and goes down as countries grow richer.

Convergence

The first concept is convergence or real convergence. Convergence is one of the results of applying Robert Solow's (1956) and Trevor Swan's (1956) neoclassical growth models, which are based on the assumption that, since marginal returns on capital accumulation tend to decrease in the long term, countries with higher initial capital stocks tend to have a lower long-term growth rate than those countries with a lower initial capital stock and, therefore, the two will tend to converge toward similar per capita income levels at some point in the very distant future (the "steady state").

Empirical studies carried out on this convergence (called "beta" or absolute convergence) by Robert Barro and Xavier Sala i Martín (1995) show that, in reality, only partial convergence occurs. "Beta convergence" occurs when the per capita income (or product) in poor countries tends to grow much faster than that of rich countries in the long term. Some countries with lower initial capital stock and low per capita income have managed to converge with richer countries, but the vast majority have not. Nevertheless, it is important to emphasize that the principal common factor of those countries, which achieved greater beta convergence, is greater openness of their economies to international markets and globalization. For example, there was strong "beta convergence" between 1870 and 1913 – the greatest period of globalization in history – fundamentally due to considerable international migration, which tended to even out wage differences between countries, as shown by Jeffrey Sachs and Andrew Warner (1995).

There is also another form of neoclassical convergence, known as "sigma convergence"; i.e. the gradual reduction, over the long run, in the dispersion of per capita income between countries (the long-term reduction of the logarithm of per capita product or income) even in periods which experienced some "beta convergence." However, what empirical studies have mostly confirmed is the existence of "conditional convergence" that occurs between countries, which despite their different initial capital stock and per capita income, tend to have similar demographic, savings, and schooling rates and similar political and institutional structures (all factors which determine a country's "steady state"). According to Barro and Sala i Martín (1995), these countries tend to converge toward their own "steady state" at a pace inversely proportional to their distance from it, as has occurred with European Union member countries and the US states. This "conditional convergence" is, nevertheless, quite slow, since it tends to improve by 2 percent per year, on average.

There is also another convergence trend, called "convergence clubs" found out by Dany Quah (1996), which take place when neighboring countries or those with strong commercial links tend to converge toward each other but not with respect to other groups of richer countries. Quah estimates that inter-country income distribution, which was unimodal for a long time, has become bimodal, with the emergence of two "twin peaks" where income levels of relatively rich countries and those of relatively poor countries gravitate within each group, although the divergence between them persists or widens. It is as if there were two different "stable or steady states" (using Solow's terminology): one for relatively rich countries with high average income and another for relatively poor countries with low average income.

However, Dany Quah's (1996) findings are somehow contradicted by Sala i Martín (2002a), who shows that, while there were two convergence groups or "twin peaks" in 1970, since income distribution was fundamentally grouped in a poor country peak (which alternated between one and two dollars, i.e. between the two fundamental thresholds of absolute poverty) and a rich country peak of approximately US$9,000, neither peak occurs at present. Since 1970, the two peaks have been converging toward a global middle class. This difference in findings apparently lies in the fact that Quah used country aggregate data while Sala i Martín used personal per capita income data, aggregated in five income brackets.

Although the previous period of greatest globalization (1870–1913) enabled unconditional convergence to be achieved, the current period (1950–2002) has still not fully attained it, since mass migration between the poorest and richest countries has yet to match that attained in the first period (over 100 million people migrated between 1870 and 1913), although there is still hope that it will be attained gradually over the next few decades if the current globalization process continues and if (as is more likely) the huge disparities in population growth persist between rich countries and some poor countries. The United Nations Population Prospects (2005) estimate that more than 100 percent of the 3.1 billion increase in world population by the 2050s will occur in developing countries, as the population of developed countries will fall over the same period.

The main problem with convergence studies is that they have very little to say about world distribution of income since they are only interested in how countries converge on each other in terms of per capita income, rather than how global income is distributed among individuals within each country, group of countries, or the world. The other aim of convergence studies is to analyze the success or failure of specific countries in terms of their macroeconomic and microeconomic policies, their institutional framework and their culture. As Robert Barro (1997) shows, real convergence is not synonymous with better distribution of income. Despite convergence, distribution can worsen for two main reasons: first, shocks or perturbations can affect the income of individual countries or groups of countries, tending to increase the dispersion of per capita income; second, a country's internal income distribution can worsen even if the country is converging, which is the case of China and India today, which has a knock-on effect on world distribution of income.

Absolute Poverty and Extreme Poverty

The second concept is poverty. There are three degrees of poverty: the first is extreme poverty which is measured by the number of people getting an income of less than one dollar a day, which means that they cannot meet basic needs for survival. They are chronically hungry, unable to get healthcare, they lack safe drinking water and sanitation, cannot afford education for their children, and perhaps lack rudimentary shelter. The second concept is absolute poverty defined as those people that live on less than two dollars a day, who meet the basic needs but just barely. The third is relative poverty, defined by household income level below a given proportion of the national average. These dollars are accounted in terms of their current purchasing power since, logically, the purchasing power of a dollar spent in India or sub-Saharan Africa is much higher than that of a dollar spent in Germany or the US. While the price of homogenous tradable goods (i.e. those which are exported, imported, or compete with imports) tends to be similar worldwide (excluding transport and insurance costs), the prices of many services and non-tradable goods, which still account for the majority of goods produced by economies, show very significant differences between countries as they tend to be much lower in poorer countries, where wages are much lower and such goods and services are usually very labor-intensive, making the purchasing power of one dollar greater in these countries.

In the first case, extreme poverty, measured as the number of people living on less than one dollar per day, fell from 1.4 billion in 1970 to 1.183 billion in 1987, increasing slightly to 1.2 billion in 1998 according to a study by the World Bank (2000). Bourguignon and Morrison (2002) estimate that the number of people in absolute poverty fell about 100 million between 1980 and 1992 (end point of their analysis) and Chen and Ravallion (2002) estimate that there was a further fall of about another 100 million between 1993 and 1998. In relative terms, absolute poverty has declined significantly as a percentage of the total world population, simply because the latter grew substantially in the same period from 1970 to 1998. In 1970, 40 percent of the world's population was living in absolute poverty, compared with just 24 percent in 1998. The United Nations' most important Millennium Goal is to bring it down to 14 percent by 2015.

Extreme poverty declined most in eastern and southern Asia, especially China and India, due to the greater openness of their economies to globalization, while it declined more slowly or remained stable in Latin America and increased in sub-Saharan Africa.

111

From a historical point of view, extreme poverty has increased in the last two centuries, mainly due to the world-wide population explosion, which has been many times greater than all previous population explosions put together but it has been falling in relative terms. In 1800 the world population was 900 million, by 1900 it was 1.6 billion and it is currently 6.4 billion; therefore, extreme poverty in relative terms, i.e. as a percentage of the total world population, has fallen dramatically. According to economic historians, in 1800, 60 percent of the world population lived on less than one 1998 US dollar per day, compared with 24 percent currently, according to the World Bank. The world average per capita income in 1800 was US$650 (in today's dollars), i.e. less than two dollars per day, whereas currently only 45 percent of the world's population lives on such a meager sum, according to World Bank estimates.

The World Bank (2000) has also estimated absolute poverty, that is, the number of people living with less than two US dollars a day. Its estimate shows that it has increased from 2.2 billion people in 1970 to 2.8 billion people in 1998, an increase of 600 hundred million. That more than compensates for the fall in extreme poverty.

The obvious conclusion to these facts is that, however they are measured, world poverty levels are still economically, socially and morally unacceptable and their reduction should be the main political priority of all governments, international organizations and non-governmental organizations world-wide.

Nevertheless, some recent studies carried out by Surjit Bhalla (2002) and Xavier Sala i Martín (2002b) have criticized previous poverty measurements and estimates made by the World Bank.

Sala i Martín uses a model originally developed by Deininger and Squire (1996) which estimates five income levels (quintiles) per country and year, in countries where there are accurate studies on the Gini coefficient. However, the problem with this methodology is that it assumes that all individuals within a quintile have the same level of income and, therefore, underestimates the level of inequality in each of the five quintiles although it does not make clear how intra-quintile income distribution will perform over time (i.e. if it will improve or worsen) and it also underestimates absolute poverty levels as it places each quintile above or below the chosen poverty threshold, where it is highly likely that only some of the individuals in the quintile below the threshold will have an income level truly below the aforementioned threshold. Thus, in a more recent analysis, Sala i Martín (2002b) goes a step further in working out per capita income distribution within each quintile by using a density function of the core 100 income distribution observations per country and per year, which gives a more individualized result.

His study applies the same five individualized quintiles of annual income to 97 countries between 1970 and 1998 and then integrates them in order to build an estimate of the world distribution of income. The data from the 97 countries is then supplemented by data from a further 28 countries where there are insufficient statistics to establish the five income quintiles, thus giving a data group of 125 countries, which represents approximately 90 percent of the world's population.

Sala i Martín's main conclusions are as follows: first, contrary to the findings of the World Bank, extreme and absolute poverty (whether measured in terms of less than one or two dollars of daily income) has declined considerably in the last few decades, especially since 1976. The total number of people living on less than one dollar per day fell by 234 million between 1976 and 1998 and the number of people living on less than two dollars per day fell by more than 450 million in the same period. Nevertheless, absolute poverty keeps being still significant and unacceptable, as in 1998 there were still more than 350 million people living on less than one dollar per day and almost one billion people living on less than two dollars per day.

Second, there is significant disparity in regional extreme and absolute poverty levels since the bulk of the reductions took place in Asia. In Latin America, there was a decline in poverty during the period in question but it was mainly concentrated in the 1970s, with little or no improvement thereafter. Africa, however, suffered a sharp increase in extreme and absolute poverty, in both absolute and relative terms (an increase of 175 million people living on less than one dollar per day and 227 million people living on less than two dollars per day); its percentage of the world's population living on less than a dollar per day rose from 22 percent to 44 percent in the period 1970 to 1998 and the percentage of those living on less than two dollars per day rose from 53 percent to 64 percent. As a result of such disparity, in 1970, 11 percent of the world's poor lived in Africa and 76 percent in Asia but by 1998, 66 percent of the world's poor lived in Africa and only 15 percent in Asia. The main reason for this disparity lies in the different growth rates; while Asian economies grew steadily over this period, the African ones did not grow at all.

Surjit Bhalla (2002) reached similar conclusions using the same methodology and the same poverty line of $1.08 per day, indicating that in 1999, the number of extreme poor was 400 million lower than previously estimated by the World Bank, i.e. 766 million rather than 1.15 billion. Similarly, extreme poverty measured as a percentage of the world's population was only 14 percent in 1999 (rather than 23 percent) and it fell to 13.1 percent in 2000. This means that poverty fell 25 percentage points, from 37.4 percent in 1985 to 13.1 percent in 2000, contrasting with the World Bank's estimates of a 10 percentage point fall from 33 percent in 1985 to 23 percent in 1999, i.e. since globalization started to accelerate. These completely different results meant that Millennium Development Goals of reducing extreme poverty to 14 percent by 2015 had already been achieved by 1999.

Therefore, there are significant differences between the findings of the World Bank and those of Sala i Martín and Bhalla regarding extreme and absolute poverty evolution. Extreme and absolute poverty figures calculated by Sala i Martín and Bhalla are much lower than those of the World Bank, which estimated that in 1998 there were 1.2 billion people living on less than a dollar per day and 2.8 billion living on less than two dollars per day.

Relative Poverty

The third concept is relative poverty, which is measured according to average consumption expenditure per country. Shaohua Chen and

Martin Ravallion (2001) measured relative poverty as the percentage of the population living on less than a third of the average national consumption expenditure in 1993 and showed that the percentage fell from 36.3 percent in 1987 to 32.1 percent in 1998.

However, using the same methodology, Bhalla shows that, contrary to Chen and Ravallion's World Bank findings, both absolute poverty and relative poverty have been significantly reduced since the 1980s. The World Bank poverty level data are based on applying some unpublished data on exchange rates, in terms of purchasing power parity, to consumption expenditure, but only for 1993. Bhalla applies the official annual exchange rate series (World Development Indicators) published by the World Bank, based on purchasing power, to income as a whole. The difference between the exchange rates is minimal as consumption expenditure represents two-thirds of income in most poor countries. The only difference is that the World Bank exchange rate data are only available for 1993 and understates the progress in poverty reduction subsequently achieved in China and India, because, for example, the exchange rate (applied solely to consumption expenditure) estimated for southern Asia is 18.5 percent lower than the official published figure and the sub-Saharan Africa figure is 5.2 percent higher than the official published figure. This makes sub-Saharan Africa 23 percent richer than southern Asia. Sala i Martín achieved similar results, showing a rather greater reduction in relative poverty.

Inequality

The fourth concept is inequality in income distribution, which can have three different measures: between individuals in the same country, between countries, and between individuals globally. Simon Kuznets (1955 and 1962) found out that personal inequality varies in a systematic way along a country's development path. He noted that among the low-income countries income distribution was more unequal in the relatively richer of them, while among the high-income countries, the income distribution was more unequal in the relatively poorer countries in the group. Based on this evidence, he suggested that in early stages of development rising income per capita leads to a worsening of inequality, while in the late stages of development rising income per capita leads to an improvement in the distribution of income. This came to be known as the "Kuznets curve," an inverted U-shaped relationship between income per capita and personal income inequality.

Although early empirical studies supported this hypothesis, they show serious data problems. The construction of a comprehensive data set on income inequality by Deininger and Squire (1996 and 1998) enables researchers to reject the validity of the curve. Various complex measures are used to measure inequality (the Gini coefficient, the Theil index and the Atkinson index are the most common) but all three have their advantages and their drawbacks. Although economists tend to prefer the Gini coefficient, the Theil index is more convenient for decomposition of the sources of inequality. Both equal zero when income is evenly distributed and rise as income distribution becomes more unequal.

When comparing per capita income inequality between countries, different results are obtained, depending on whether the income is compared using current exchange rates converted to dollars or weighting the exchange rate by the purchasing power of the income in each country (using the price of comparable or homogeneous goods and services in each country in the latter case).

Measuring inequality by purchasing-power weighted per capita income is much closer to reality and is also more objective and more reliable, as current exchange rates are affected by each country's short-term capital movements and monetary policy. Furthermore, exchange rates do not reflect the large volume of auto-consumption and barter, which exists in most developing countries. Despite this, incomprehensibly (considering it has qualified economists), the United Nations Development Program Annual Report (UNDP, 1999) continues year after year to use nominal current exchange rates without weighting for purchasing power, which means that the results are less reliable or even false. Xavier Sala i Martín (2002a) shows that the conclusions of the 1999 Annual Report, which asserts that in 1960 the richest 20 percent of people living in rich countries had 30 times more income than the poorest 20 percent of people in poor countries, and that the gap widened to a multiple of 60 in 1990 and 74 in 1997, are false. Using Summers and Heston's (1998) purchasing-power-adjusted per capita income series, Sala i Martín concludes that, on the contrary, the income gap was 11.3 times in 1960, rose to 15.9 times in 1990 and fell to 15.09 times in 1997 – i.e. the income gap started to narrow as of 1990, when globalization accelerated.

When comparing per capita income by country, the results depend on whether or not the population of the respective countries is taken into account. Naturally, weighting by population gives a much more realistic measurement of the world distribution of income because, while inequality measurements within each country refer to individuals, inter-country measurements are purely on a per-country basis, without taking into account whether the country is very small (e.g. Luxembourg or Singapore) or very large (China or India, which together represent almost 40 percent of the world's population).

Xavier Sala i Martín (2002a) uses the following revealing example: let us assume that five billion people live in poor countries which are not growing and the remaining one billion live in rich growing countries. The apparently logical conclusion is that inter-country per capita income inequality is growing. Let us now suppose that one billion of the aforementioned five billion people live in a very poor country which experiences faster growth than richer countries and whose per capita income is converging with that of the richer countries. Let us also assume that the inequality within this country is gradually increasing at the same time. Given that the country with one billion inhabitants is just one of a 150-country sample, the result is that per capita income inequality is rising. However, the per capita income of one billion people has improved by converging with that of rich countries.

The problem is that, instead of comparing the evolution of per capita GDP variance with the evolution of intra-country inequality, the per capita GDP variance needs to be weighted by population by adding the intra-country inequality evolution using five income quintiles for each country and a density function of the income distribution within each of the five quintiles. If the latter comparison is made, Sala i Martín shows, by way of the Gini coefficient, that the inequality in global per capita GDP fell by more than 7 percent between 1978 and 1998 and that inequality in inter-country per capita GDP ceased to widen in the 1980s and improved in the 1990s. The fundamental reason for this lies in the distribution of per capita income between countries and not within each country, since China and India, which represent 40 percent of the world's population, have considerably improved their per capita income levels since the 1980s. However, they have both experienced increased inequality in their internal income distribution over the same period, due fundamentally to their extremely rapid growth, focused much more in urban and coastal areas than in rural and interior areas.

Studies by other economists, including Schultz (1998) Melchior, Telle, and Wiig (2000), and Dowrick and Akmal (2001), have reached the same conclusion despite using only the per capita GDP variance weighted by population rather than the per capita GDP variance within each country. T. Paul Schultz was the first to discover that world-wide per capita income inequality has been falling since 1975. Bhalla's (2002) recent study fully confirms the trend in inequality reduction shown by Sala i Martín. Using a new methodology, Bhalla incorporates the Lorenz curve using a pioneering study by Kakwani (1980), which enables the curve to be parameterized to generate an estimate for each percentile of the population. When only four observations are available, the fifth quintile is derived from these four. The results of the basic equation are filtered though a Simple Accounting Procedure (SAP) by way of an iterative process in order to repeatedly estimate each quintile based on existing distribution data.

By contrast, another study by Robert Wade (2001b) concerning these four ways of measuring inequality reached the conclusion that, since the early 1980s, inter-country inequality has increased, except where GDP is measured in terms of purchasing power and countries are weighted by population, in which case it has remained almost the same.

The World Bank 2000 report included two papers by its staff economists, which also contradicted findings that show that inequality fell or rose slightly in the 1990s. The first study, by Branko Milanovic (2002), covers 85 percent of the world population between 1988 and 1993, and shows that the Gini coefficient worsened by 0.4 points, from 0.62 in 1988 to 0.66 in 1993, i.e. 5.6 percent worse. The second study, by Yuri Dikhanov and Michael Ward (2000), found that the Gini coefficient worsened from 0.63 to 0.67 over the same period, i.e. 6 percent worse, and also that the percentage of world income held by the poorest 10 percent fell by 27 percent while that of the richest 10 percent grew 8 percent. However, both studies have two significant limitations: first, they were both carried out over a period of only five years (1988–93) and, second, both used country surveys rather than national accounting data or a mixture of both.

Another recent survey by François Bourguignon and Christian Morrison (2002) covering the period 1820–1993 used the Theil index to show that world interpersonal inequality grew sharply following the culmination of the first Industrial Revolution and the first period of globalization, from 0.55 in 1820 to 0.80 in 1914. From 1914 to 1950 it remained more or less constant at around 0.80 as the Great Depression had a very negative effect on rich countries and, after falling in the period from the Second World War until the early 1960s, began to rise again, reaching 0.87 in 1993. In other words, inequality grew 58 percent over the period of two centuries.

Nevertheless, using the same index, Xavier Sala i Martín (2002a), although he has achieved similar results for inequality evolution up until the period 1978–1998, thereafter shows that inequality fell over this period due mainly to greater income convergence between countries. The difference between the two studies is based on the fact that Bourguignon and Morrison used a different country sample, they also grouped supposedly similar countries together instead of using individual country data and, lastly, they used a different method to calculate the income quintiles within each country.

Sala i Martín (2002a) extended his study by using other indices to measure income distribution. First, he used the Atkinson index to show that global inequality has fallen almost 12 percent since the 1980s, although it has remained constant recently. Sala i Martín also used indices, which can be broken down into the two measures of inequality: inter-country and intra-country. With the Theil index, he showed that global inequality has fallen but that intra-country inequality has increased slightly. He also used several other measurements, including mean logarithmic deviation and the square of the coefficient of variation, which gave similar results. The mean logarithmic deviation showed that global inequality fell by almost 14 percent between 1980 and 1992, due entirely to the inter-country inequality since intra-country inequality grew over the same period. Between 1978 and 1998, the inter-country index fell from 0.67 to 0.51 and the intra-country index grew from 0.18 to 0.23, i.e. the improvement in the first index more than offset the decline in the second. Measuring the square of the coefficient of variation showed a greater fall in global inequality since the intra-country index remained constant but the inter-country index fell to a greater extent.

Finally, Sala i Martín in a more recent study (2002b) subsequently admitted that his aforementioned study slightly underestimated global inequality since, when the five income quintiles per country are used in his new study, the reduction in inequality in the 1980s and 1990s is slightly lower. The reason for this is that in the previous study (2002a), it was assumed that all individuals within a quintile had the same income whereas in the later study (2002b), the differential within each quintile was adjusted using a density function for each country. This increased the income disparity within each quintile and each country, making global inequality greater by increasing the intra-country component but, at the same time, making the inter-country inequality component smaller. The Gini coefficient fell by 5 percent, the logarithmic variance by 7 percent, the square of the coefficient of variation by 9.6 percent, the Theil coefficient by 10 percent and the mean logarithmic deviation by 13 percent. These new results do not in any way alter the conclusions concerning inequality reduction since the 1980s, but they do show that the reduction was slightly lower.

The impact of these new findings is that, whereas World Bank studies state that the bulk of global inequality (between 75 percent and 88 percent according to the various indices) is a result of per capita income inequality between countries and not within countries, according to Sala i Martín's recent study, since relative inequality within each country is not only greater but is growing and gaining in importance, the percentage of inter-country inequality is lower, falling to between 51 percent and 66 percent.

Intra-country inequality tends to be much higher in the English-speaking countries (excluding Canada), Latin America, and Africa than in continental Europe and Asia. Different cultural and religious roots are a significant factor in the differing inequality levels but technological development also plays a fundamental role, as do the differences in demographic growth rates, the geographic location of the population, political systems (true or nominal democracy, dictatorship, etc.), healthcare and education levels, the degree of development of institutions and civil society, as we shall see in the next few chapters.

A book by Bhalla (2002) shows that the acceleration of globalization since the 1980s has reduced global inequality, although this improvement is not well distributed between countries as the two countries with the highest populations, China and India (together representing around 40 percent of the total world population), have made the biggest contribution to reducing inequality. In spite of this, he reached two conclusions: that inequality is lower nowadays, first, because developing countries as a whole have grown more quickly than developed countries and, second, if the poor individual is considered, rather than the poor country, then income growth in poor countries has not only been faster than in rich countries but has also been faster than at any previous time in history. In fact, he shows that between 1980 and 2000, the relative income of the poorest individuals grew much faster; for every 10 percent increase in world income, that of poor individuals grew 15.8 percent, reflecting the massive improvement in China and India since the 1980s as both countries embraced globalization.

Bhalla, using the SAP, Gini coefficient and national accounting data in his empirical study, found that inequality fell during the 1980s and 1990s and that today, the Gini index is 65.1 (the lowest since 1910), after reaching 66.4 in 1960 and 69.3 in 1973.

Bhalla's analysis (2002) is very similar to that of Bourguignon and Morrison (2001). Both use national accounting data and the Gini coefficient but Bhalla's SAP is more disaggregated as it includes percentiles for each country and is cleaner. However, the two studies cover different periods; he covers 1950–2000 while Bourguignon and Morrison cover 1820–1992, meaning the two only overlap in the period 1950–92. Bourguignon and Morrison estimate that, in this period, inequality grew from 64 in 1950 to 65.7 in 1980 and then remained steady at around 65.7, while Bhalla estimates that inequality rose to 69.3 in 1973 and subsequently fell, reaching 65.1 in 2000. Nevertheless, the Gini coefficient according to him is always greater throughout the overlap period.

Between 1960 and 2000, inequality fell further in developing countries which account for 80 percent of the world's population, than in developed countries; it fell almost seven percentage points in developing countries and only one percentage point in developed countries. However, the developed countries are still more egalitarian, despite the fact that their internal inequality has increased greatly in recent years. Internal inequality also increased, slightly in southern Asia and sub-Saharan Africa and more particularly in eastern Europe, with an increase of 11 percentage points due to the collapse of communist regimes and the subsequent seizing of state assets by groups linked to the former *nomenklatura*.

Sala i Martín has also modified the results of the evolution of the average income gap between the richest 20 percent and the poorest 20 percent of the world population; the gap grew from a multiple of 40 in 1970 to 45 in 1980, falling to 41 in 1990 and then to 39 in 1998. The gap between per capita income of those people located in the highest income distribution quintile compared to the lowest quintile fell the least, remaining constant at ten times between 1970 and 1980, falling to 9.2 times in 1990 and 8.6 times in 1998.

Finally, in a recent paper, Angus Deaton (2005) following previous work by Ravallion (2001 and 2003) has analyzed the discrepancies between those different studies to measure poverty, that is, those which are based on household surveys, internationally comparable according to the Living Standards Measuring Study (LSMS) of the World Bank, and those which are based on internationally comparable national accounts using purchasing power parity exchange rates. According to the direct measurement through household surveys (as used by World Bank) growth among the poor of the world has been sluggish compared with average growth rates of the countries where they live. Therefore, the number of the world's poor has fallen very slowly.

According to national accounts data based on Deininger and Squire (1996) and using Penn World Tables combined with inequality measures, growth has been, at least on average, good for the poor and there has been a very rapid reduction of world poverty levels in the countries which have grown faster, mostly due to their greater openness to the rest of the world economies. If the surveys are going to be accepted, growth in the world is a good deal slower than indicated from the results of the national accounts studies. If the national accounts are to be accepted, then the World Bank official poverty numbers are clearly overstated.

According to Deaton's paper, based on 557 survey-based estimates of mean consumption for 127 countries between 1979 and 2000, consumption estimated from surveys is typically lower than consumption coming from national accounts; the average ratio is 0.86. Income measured in the surveys is, on average, larger than consumption in surveys but lower than national accounts and much less than GDP. Survey income is less than 60 percent of national accounts GDP, on average. His conclusions are the following: first, both systems have measurement problems. The surveys system tends to understate mean consumption and overstate the fraction of people in poverty, given that the rich households tend to be less cooperative with the survey than poor people. The national accounts system, probably for political reasons, tends to understate consumption in the poorest countries and to overstate the rate of growth of average consumption, both over time in poor countries and at a moment of time between poor and rich countries and the growth rate of GDP.

Second, although using national accounts to complement surveys in measuring poverty makes sense, it gives a poor measure of poverty, for three reasons: first, national accounts are designed to generate estimates of macroeconomic aggregates, not estimates of poverty. They are designed to track money not people. Second, the differences in the coverage of both systems means that, even if everything were perfectly measured, it would not be correct to apply inequality or distributional measures, which are derived from surveys that measure one thing, to means that are derived from national accounts, which measure another, and hence it is perfectly possible for the poor to do less well than the average, without any increase in measured inequality. Third, it is a fact that neither mean consumption nor its distribution are measured accurately, either by surveys or national accounts because these measures are of dubious quality for most poor countries, they are noisy to say the least.

Therefore, Deaton thinks that the downward bias in measure of consumption from surveys tends to bias up the World Bank poverty estimates and that the national accounts tend to bias down the rate of poverty decline. Nevertheless, against the view of Sala i Martín and Bhalla, he states that there is no choice but to continue using the surveys, because only they provide direct measures of the living standards of the poor. This debate is still open, but it is difficult not to take into account the now extensive work done by those economists who have used national account statistics as a complement to contradict the result of the surveys done under the World Bank research units. But still, most of the discrepancy between the survey and the national account estimates is probably due to the fact that, as people get better off, they are less likely to respond accurately or at all to surveys. As a result, as countries get richer, the ratio of survey consumption to national account consumption tends to fall while it is highest among the poorest countries.

In any case, we should be aware of the substantial difficulties in comparing income distribution data across countries. Countries differ in the concept measured (income versus consumption), the measure of income (gross versus net), the unit of observation (individuals versus households) and the coverage of the survey (national versus sub-national).

In sum, in the worst case, the true poverty and inequality figures may lie somewhere between the extremes suggested by the two methodologies, the World Bank's estimates being too pessimistic and the others too optimistic. But it is important to continue doing research about these discrepancies and finding a wider consensus about the true estimates.

However, what is more important is to reject once for all this ridiculous idea that global capitalism is making progress at the expense of the poor and that globalization tends to increase poverty and inequality. Two vivid examples prove that it is totally wrong: on the one hand, the poorest and slowest-growing countries in the world are mainly located in sub-Saharan Africa. How can it be plausibly claimed that these countries are the victims of globalization? That would be an odd conclusion, given that these economies are so comparatively isolated from the rest of the world economy by force of history, circumstance and, to a large extent, the policies of their own and other governments. Sub-Saharan Africa suffers not from globalization but for the lack of it.

On the other hand, China, India, and other developing countries in Asia are showing how great the benefits of integration and globalization can be. They cannot be considered as good examples of free-market capitalism, but have consciously chosen to seize the opportunities afforded by the global economy. Nevertheless, there are marked result differences in both countries. While China, since the 1980s, has been able to reduce the number of people living on less than one dollar a day, adjusted to reflect purchasing power, by 400 million, India has dropped the number of absolute poor by 70 million. One of the reasons for this divergence is that India has had a much a higher birth rate, but it is not enough to explain why, against mainstream development theory and empirical work, a full democracy does worse than an authoritarian regime in reducing poverty. Another reason is that democracies tend to have a shorter time horizon and have a bias toward direct methods to tackle poverty, such as subsidies and handouts, which in the long run are less effective than investing in education, infrastructures to achieve higher growth and employment rates. Finally, there is the issue of India's multi-ethnicity, multilingual and multi-religious fragmentation, in which all groups tend to use beggar-thy-neighbor politics, plus a peculiar relationship between caste and class. In states where caste and class have merged, as in Kerala, the results are as good, or even better, than in China. But, in the long run to have a well established democracy is a huge advantage over China (*The Economist*, 2004 and 2005).

Chapter 6
Globalization and Inequality

Inequality is a hugely complex subject. Although there is a general consensus in developed countries that poverty must be eradicated because it is economically inefficient, socially undesirable, and morally intolerable, the same level of consensus does not exist in relation to inequality. There is a clear consensus in society, at least in more advanced countries, that high inequality in income, wealth, and opportunity distribution is unjust and that every effort should be made to improve the lot of those who are most disadvantaged. However, there is much less agreement in society on the achievement of total equality or, at least, a fair distribution of income. Therefore, policies which promote equality should always tend to have broad support from society as a whole in order to be successful.

There are several economic reasons for this. First, inequality sometimes increases because the income of the poor falls compared with that of the rich, and sometimes because the income of the rich increases more quickly than that of the poor. The latter reason is more frequent, as is happening in the US at present. During the Great Depression, which was a genuine disaster for world growth, equality improved greatly for the simple reason that stock market rallies tend to increase inequality since they benefit the owners of capital (i.e. investors) versus wage earners, whereas inequality declines during stock market slumps for the opposite reason. In the Great Depression, the decline in the income of the rich due to the stock market crash was even greater than the decline in the income of the wage earners who lost their jobs.

Second, a total war on inequality may have negative effects on growth by removing incentives for citizens to innovate and work harder. Third, there are economic policies that seek greater equality in the long term but have negative effects in the short term, such as anti-inflation policies, which require a temporary increase in interest rates, or structural reforms which can trigger a temporary rise in unemployment. Finally, the opposite can also happen; there are policies that seek equality in the short and medium term, but which have a negative effect on the well-being of future generations. For example, over-generous pensions today may make it necessary to reduce pensions in the future if the fertility rate falls and life expectancy rises, producing a rapid ageing of the population.

There is increasing consensus that policies, which reduce inequality, should be long-term policies based on investment in human capital, education, health, and solid and efficient institutions, rather than generous short-term policies to reduce inequality, which may soon have to be reversed due to a shortage of budgetary resources. The reason for this broad consensus is that those policies do not only improve equality – they also improve growth. The problem is that, in democratic countries, political cycles tend to last between four and eight years and politicians do not tend to look very far ahead, preferring short-term results with a view to re-election; therefore, they give priority to physical infrastructures and to increasing the benefits of the welfare state over investments in education, training, health, and structural reforms.

Generally speaking, there is a broad consensus in almost all societies that achieving equal opportunities for all citizens is a social objective worth fighting for, but actually attaining it is a very difficult and controversial task. This is one of the factors that distinguishes the US and EU social and welfare models. The United States seriously attempts to achieve equal opportunities for all citizens via education and health, although it has only partly succeeded. However, since it is fundamentally a meritocracy, once citizens have had access to equal opportunities, there is generally little compassion or sympathy, or (with exceptions) any willingness to help those who have not or could not take advantage of their opportunity and remain on the margins of society. Except in cases of innate physical or mental incapacity, these persons on the margin tend to be considered essentially as "voluntary losers."

Unfortunately, this US social model is now under increasing critique because equality of opportunity and social mobility have been fading away and inequality has been rising since the late 1970s. For instance, since 1979, accumulated income of households in the lowest 20 percent by earnings has only grown 6.4 percent, while that of households in the top 20 percent grew by 70 percent and that of the top 1 percent by earnings grew by 184 percent. In 2001, the top 1 percent of households earned 20 percent of all income and held 33.4 percent of all net worth (*The Economist*, 2005). Since the early 1970s, social mobility has been falling for two consecutive generations. For instance, 42 percent of those born in the poorest 20 percent ended up where they started, another 24 percent moved up slightly to the next-bottom and only 6 percent made it to the top 20 percent.

Conversely, in the EU, which is based on a much older and more stratified society (and in which it is more difficult to obtain equality of opportunity and social climbing), society is much more willing to help the unemployed or marginalized ex post. Americans prefer to make a greater effort ex ante, whereas Europeans are more willing to do so ex-post. The US model is obviously tougher from a social standpoint but it also tends to be more efficient and cheaper than the EU model. Therefore, the US has less concern for – and even less interest in – the need to achieve greater equality ex post, whereas the EU tries to reduce inequality, mainly via more progressive direct income taxes and more generous systems of social security and unemployment benefits. In any case, generally speaking, citizens world-wide tend to worry more about absolute levels of living standards, which include poverty, rather than relative levels of inequality, unless the latter are unfortunately very high, as is still the case in many developing and a few developed countries.

Empirical studies illustrate that both excessive inequality and excessive equality have a negative impact on economic development. This is the main problem that affected communist countries, where the alleged total (but nevertheless high) social equality did not provide sufficient incentives for citizens to be more enterprising and hard working and attempt to improve their situation relative to the rest. Now that they have managed to escape this situation, they are faced with the problem of the sharpest rise in inequality in recent history since the privatization of the assets of the former all-powerful state was irregular and not very transparent in some cases and simply corrupt in other cases; these public assets often ended in the hands of a few who, to make matters worse, were often former members of the old *nomenklatura*, because they had asymmetric information in their favor.

In general, the levels of inequality within a country are influenced by many factors, ranging from historical to cultural and religious ones. Non-Islamic Asian countries tend to be much more egalitarian than countries in Africa and Latin America. Protestant countries in the north of Europe, excluding the UK, are much more egalitarian than the countries in the south of Europe, which are mainly Catholic. In any case, history and empirical evidence have demonstrated that more egalitarian countries have had greater political and economic stability than the more unequal countries, and they have also had stronger long-term growth.

The fundamental problem lies in how to tackle the issue of inequality. In the final analysis, absolute equality can only be achieved through coercion, if not through political violence, and past experience demonstrates that absolute equality is not economically efficient due to the lack of incentives, and that countries that achieve it grow increasingly slowly and ultimately become impoverished. The most common method in developed countries is progressive taxation of income. The problem with this method is that the richest, who fundamentally live off the capital they have accumulated because they are enterprising or have inherited wealth, manage to avoid paying these taxes by engaging the help of expert advisors who look for legislative errors or loopholes, or by corrupting civil servants, or by taking their wealth to other countries; consequently, it is mainly wage earners at any level and owners of fixed and immobile assets who mostly pay taxes.

This phenomenon is increasingly common since, as economies become more open, high net-worth individuals, large companies, and capital become more mobile and tend to settle in countries with low taxes or in tax havens, whereas the majority of wage earners have neither the means nor the opportunity to do the same, so that tax becomes regressive rather than progressive, as originally planned. Therefore, governments are increasingly seeking alternative sources of income via taxes on spending or even on financial transactions.

Experience shows that the redistributive effects of policies based on progressive and increasingly complex and opaque tax systems have proven less equitable than policies based on the use of the expenditure side of the government budget, especially when directed at education and healthcare in the long term. The countries that have achieved the best results are those which, on the revenue side, have achieved a taxation system that is simple, transparent and easy to collect and administer, with reasonable marginal rates and, on the expenditure side, have prioritized more productive budgetary expenses by drastically cutting military spending, excess spending in the public sector, and generous handouts to inefficient public companies. Privatization of such companies, when conducted in a proper, transparent and competitive way (rather than quickly and arbitrarily, to raise funds in the short term), within a competitive framework in order to achieve a better, more efficient productive apparatus, provides excellent results.

The best way to reduce inequality is undoubtedly to cut it at the root, by reducing or compensating for the disadvantages, which the poorest or most marginalized people suffer from birth, by providing the highest-quality healthcare and education opportunities. This is not easy to achieve in developed countries and even less so in developing countries, where budgetary resources are scarce. However, those developing countries that have made greater efforts in this respect, such as countries in south-east Asia and, to a more limited extent, China, have achieved greater social and economic results than the rest.

Nevertheless, the issue of reducing inequality is very complex. As Alesina and Angeletos (2005) have shown, there is a dilemma: on the one hand, a small government is not able to redistribute and to correct enough for market inequalities and injustices and, on the other, a bigger government will increase the probability of corruption and rent-seeking and, thus, of adding inequality. In many developing countries public spending toward the poor is often mis-targeted and creates pockets of corruption and favoritism, and sometimes certain lobbies come out as big winners at the expense of the truly needy. Nevertheless, even well intended policy makers would resist calls for cutting these programs because they perceive that the cost of corruption is worth paying, because it is the only way to, at least partially, improve the condition of the poor.

The problem then is that the willingness to accommodate some corruption in the present may lead to a vicious circle where high levels of government intervention, market inefficiency and corruption are self-sustained in perpetuity and jeopardize the long-run effectiveness of well intended policies. The reason for achieving this political equilibrium is that both the individuals who have a sufficiently high advantage in rent-seeking prefer a bigger government and the poor, who benefit from redistribution, prefer high tax and large government even at the cost of more government resources dissipated by corruption. This is what has happened and is happening in various populist regimes in Latin America, which are supported by a paradoxical coalition between the poor, who benefit from redistribution and the rich insiders who benefit from corruption.

Globalization and Inequality: Theoretical Models

There are various theoretical analyses that explain how globalization can have a positive or negative impact on inequality between countries.

The first is derived from Solow–Ramsey-type neoclassical growth models, which are based on two assumptions. The first assumption is that all countries end up having access to the dominant technology, which provides exogenous improvement, albeit with a considerable delay in some cases. The second assumption is that there are decreasing returns on production, that is that the rates of return on the production factors that can be accumulated, especially capital, tend to fall as these factors become more abundant and are accumulated to a greater extent. Therefore, there is a certain convergence in the long term, between the income levels of more developed countries with greater capital accumulation and less developed countries with lesser capital accumulation. This is the line of research of the Barro (1991), Mankiw, Romer, and Weil (1992), Parente and Prescott (1994), and Mankiw (1995) models. On the basis of these assumptions, the differences in economic policies, savings rates, technological development, and institutions do not lead to greater differences in growth rates in the long term, but they do lead to differences in capital and income per worker.

The second theory, based on the same type of model, acknowledges that there are notable differences in the levels of technology between countries and that it is the diffusion of technology from the more developed to the less developed countries, i.e. globalization, that keeps world-wide distribution of income stable and determines how political, institutional and economic differences are translated into differences in income per capita between countries. This line of argument includes the models of Grossman and Helpman (1991), Coe and Helpman (1995), Howitt (2000), Aghion and Howitt (1998), Eaton and Kortum (1999), Barro and Sala i Martín (1997), Krusell, Ohanian, Rios-Rull, and Violante (2000), and Acemoglu and Zilibotti (2001).

The third theory is based on the model developed by Acemoglu and Ventura (2001), which introduces a new variable: international trade. Both illustrate that, even in the absence of diminishing returns on production and technological spill-over, international trade leads to a stable world income distribution. This is because countries that accumulate capital faster than average experience a decline in export prices and, therefore, in the barter terms of trade, thus reducing the rate of return to capital and thereby discouraging its accumulation. At the same time, there is an increase in demand for products and in the marginal return to capital in the rest of the world, which promotes accumulation. Naturally, a certain degree of specialization is required for the barter terms of trade to fall since, if all domestic and foreign products were perfectly interchangeable, other countries would have no demand whatsoever for their products and the accumulation of capital would not affect the fall in their barter terms of trade.

Thus, this model includes the positive element of globalization, through international trade, to achieve a greater degree of equality and convergence in the long term, in the same way as the previous model introduced it by means of the diffusion and "externalities" of technology, which are reinforced by international trade and investment. In the end, as Ventura (2005) stresses in his recent paper, using a general world equilibrium model in which different regions of the world are treated as parts of a single whole, that economic growth in the world economy is determined by a tension between diminishing returns and market-size effects on capital accumulation, where trade frictions of various sorts determine the shape of the world income distribution and its dynamics.

The fourth model is the Lucas (2000) model, a variation on the neoclassical model, which determines that the disparities in income in the twentieth century will tend to disappear sooner or later, as greater opening of economies, the implementation by less developed countries of best practices in politics and institutions, and the progress of globalization lead these countries to achieve the universal or dominant technology predicted by Solow. Therefore, increasing equality may be achieved between all the countries in the world in the twenty-first century. This prediction is based on the simple idea that, since 1800, countries that have begun to develop have commenced at increasingly rapid rates and, therefore, a country that begins to develop in the early twenty-first century will quickly achieve 12 percent growth, compared to growth of only 7 percent achieved by such countries in the early twentieth century. Every country is equally likely to join the "growth club," with a probability ratio of between 0.01 and 0.03 over time.

Finally, the "endogenous growth" models, initially developed by Romer (1986), Lucas (1988), Rebelo (1991), and Grossman and Helpman (1991), are based on different suppositions and reach more pessimistic conclusions (although Lucas subsequently went back to a much more optimistic neoclassical model, as described above). These models consider, on the one hand, that technical progress is endogenous rather than exogenous, i.e. that it depends on competitive policies that encourage greater investment in education, training, and research and development, improved taxation of the production factors, and opening economies up to foreign capital and international trade. On the other hand, the accumulation of physical and human capital, considered as a combination of the two, tends to generate increasing returns rather than decreasing returns; therefore, long-term growth can be explained almost entirely by capital accumulation, without resorting to the "Solow residual" or technical progress. Finally, scientific and technical knowledge not only produces "externalities" which benefit the other production factors, but it is also the factor that generates the greatest rising marginal returns. The conclusion is that the long-term convergence of growth and income is much more difficult, since countries that start off with less physical and human capital and a lower level of technology will find difficulties in catching up with the most developed countries.

A model by Crafts and Venables (2001) adds elements of the "new economic geography" and "new trade theory" to the foregoing endogenous growth models to better explain the impact of globalization on world income convergence and distribution. The elements of new economic geography (Fujita, Krugman, and Venables, 2001) include not only the "first nature" of geographical location in terms of latitude, relief, and natural means of transport, but also the geographical "second nature" of the spatial interaction between economic agents, which determine agglomeration effects of external and scale economies that lead to increasing returns and, as regards new trade theory (Krugman, 1991a and 1991b), they include the "gravity models" (see below) and the nature of current international trade based on imperfect markets or oligopolies, in which companies' returns rise to scale. The essence of globalization is that it changes these spatial interactions and international trade patterns by reducing transport costs.

Both economists start from the basic idea that there are two factors which shape a country's production structure and income level. The first is its internal capacity, which depends on its endowment of production factors, knowledge, qualifications, and social infrastructure. The second is its relationship with other countries or regions, in other words, its geography, in terms of its access to world markets and the supply of goods, services, production factors, and knowledge. Traditional models are based on constant scale returns and the endowment of production factors, and they establish that trade liberalization enables countries to fully exploit their comparative advantages and this trade replaces factor mobility, such as emigration and capital movements, since the liberalization reduces price differences in those production factors between countries.

The Crafts and Venables model is also based on the endowment of factors, but it involves increasing scale returns and the location theory; in other words, companies will tend to locate where they are closest to their potential markets and the supply of inputs for their production. The locations with the best access to markets will attract a disproportionately high number of productive companies, with which they will be able to maintain higher productivity and higher salaries than locations with less access to those markets. The greater labor and financial mobility there is, the more those higher salaries will attract workers and capital, producing a causal accumulation process, which will lead to strong spatial concentration of productive activity. The lower the transport costs are, the higher the factor mobility and thus, the greater the tendency toward spatial agglomeration in a very small number of locations (Krugman, 1991a and 1991b).

The movement of labor is a necessary but insufficient condition for agglomeration given that a large part of the demand for production comes not from end consumers but from companies, since there are intermediate inputs needed for final production; therefore, many companies are located near to where they can be supplied with these inputs. In other words, downstream companies will locate where they can boost their upstream market and upstream companies will locate where they can increase their supply and cut the prices of their intermediate goods. This interaction can also create a process of casual accumulation and of concentration in clusters of associated industrial activities (Venables, 1996). As Alfred Marshall (1890) first pointed out, this concentration leads to strong external economies due to the cost savings derived from the greater ease of hiring specialized workers and of spreading technology among companies that are located together. In other words, by increasingly reducing the cost of transport, trade and capital movements, globalization can lead to an agglomeration of companies, economic activity and, consequently, income in some countries which initially had a larger market, or in industrial clusters in certain preferred locations, at the expense of other less suitable locations, thus producing situations of divergence (Krugman and Venables, 1995).

Under these premises, several models have tried to illustrate that new communication and information technologies will enable the distance to be reduced, and that the centripetal forces which lead to agglomeration will gradually become centrifugal forces and enable goods and services to be produced in developing countries, far from the large markets, taking advantage of lower labor and land costs; in this way, globalization would lead to convergence rather than divergence. The model of Baldwin and Martin (1999) is one such model.

Crafts and Venables' response is that, to date, this has only been applied to some IT services (which can be decentralized at great distances) in particular to India and China, and to light manufactures, as has already occurred to many developing countries, in particular in south-east Asia. In other cases, distance continues to act as a fundamental barrier, as the empirical evidence gathered by the two economists demonstrates: this evidence illustrates that, if the distance increases from 1,000 kilometers to 8,000 kilometers, trade flows, direct investments, and investments in technology tend to fall significantly. Trade may fall by 93 percent (Venables, 2001), portfolio investments by 85 percent (Portes and Rey, 1999), foreign direct investment by 42 percent (Di Mauro, 2000), and technology flows by only 5 percent (Keller, 2002).

In any case, even in these last models, the possibility of greater convergence is not totally ruled out, as new technologies increasingly cut the costs of transporting ideas and innovation, and globalization, via trade and foreign direct investment, disseminates technology more quickly, as illustrated by the recent empirical evidence of a steady reduction in inequality among countries since the 1980s.

How Does Inequality Affect Growth?

The impact of greater inequality on growth is theoretically indeterminate since it is relatively easy to think of cases where it could be either beneficial or damaging (Arjona, Ladaique, and Pearson, 2001) and the same can be said about social protection and redistribution. On the one hand, economic growth theory tells us that, in a closed economy, the greater the amount of savings, the lower is the cost of capital and the greater is the rate of investment and hence the highest is the rate of growth. Because the rich have a higher savings rate than the poor, because the propensity to save is higher from profits than from wage income, it follows that the more unequally national income is distributed, the greater will be the aggregate savings rate and hence the greater will be the investment and the growth rate (Lewis, 1954; Kaldor, 1956, 1957; Cass and Stiglitz, 1969). In this theoretical case, income redistribution will retard growth. Similarly, if the wage distribution is artificially compressed, by minimum wage legislation or centralized wage bargaining, it will result in a reduction of the incentive to invest in those qualifications which would qualify someone for high-productivity jobs. But, in an open economy, the situation changes because savings can be found elsewhere, provided they can be attracted by having competitive and profitable productive activities or higher interest rate yielding debt instruments, because of its lower level of savings.

Nevertheless, high inequality tends to be bad for growth in the real world. First, financial markets tend to suffer from well-known failures when it comes to financing investments by those individuals without assets other than their own labor. Hence, capital markets may not make funds available to poorer households even when rates of return (both private and social) are high, because there is no asset that can be reclaimed and seized by a bank or other financial institution in the event of a non-performing loan. Thus, a wide income distribution may be associated with lower lending and investment, due to the poor credit constraints and rationing, than in an economy with a narrower distribution of final income and end up with a lower rate of growth.

Moreover, as human capital accumulation becomes an even more important factor than physical capital for economic growth, if the poor cannot borrow to invest in their education the end result can be a lower rate of growth (Saint Paul and Verdier, 1992; Galor and Zeira, 1993; Perotti, 1993; Piketty, 1997; Galor and Moav, 2004). As Aghion, Caroli, and Garcia Peñalosa (1999) put it, there is no trade-off between inequality and growth but both feed on each other, for two reasons: human capital formation and political and macroeconomic stability, two key elements for faster growth, tend to be much higher in more equal than in more unequal economies.

Second, inequality is detrimental to the security of property rights, which is an essential element of growth and development. Glaeser, Scheinkman, and Shleifer (2002) base this finding in that inequality enables the rich to subvert the political, regulatory, and legal institutions of society to their own benefit. If one person is sufficiently richer than another and courts are corruptible, the legal system will be in favor of the rich not the just, as happened in the US during the gilded age or in Russia in the 1990s, or in some developing countries now. The reaction of the have-nots may be to redistribute from the haves through violence, jeopardizing even more property rights, so that it deters investment by the rich.

Third, a wide income distribution may cause social and political unrest, which in turn tend to discourage economic activity and to slow growth. This argument has been used mainly in the case of Latin America to draw a link between inequality and radical shifts in government policy and even in the form of government. The consequences may include support for confiscatory policies, including uncompensated land reform, excessive regulation and even tolerance of corruption.

Fourth, inequality can also lead to tolerance of socially disruptive behavior in the form of widespread crime, wildcat strikes or riots, insecurity or even in its most extreme form of support for insurgency, separatist movements, and tolerance of drug gangs (Perotti, 1992, 1994, and 1996).

Redistribution policies may also have two side-effects on economic growth. On the one side, if benefit systems discourage people from working, the amount of labor supplied in the economy is lowered, so reducing the level of output and, in some cases, the level of capital investment and growth. If social provisions discourage people from saving, then, unless public saving rises by an equivalent amount, there is a reduction in the capital available for reinvestment. Moreover, the taxes necessary to finance social protection may reduce the return to innovation (Mirrlees, 1971). An important example of this trend has been the generous universality of the Scandinavian welfare state system, which tended to "politicize" the return to economic activity, and so encouraged people to pursue material gain through the political process rather than through economic activity, with a loss of entrepreneurship and innovation (Lindbeck, 1975).

On the other hand, in a situation of scarce or absent private insurance markets where individuals face borrowing constraints a system of social security allows people to get insurance against risks, which the private sector finds difficult to pool and manage, such as sickness or unemployment. Moreover, having such a public insurance enables individuals to take more risks in their economic behavior and become more entrepreneurial. In that case, assuming that there is a positive relationship between the riskiness of a project and its expected rate of return, the insurance provided by public protection may foster growth.

There are other reasons why social protection can be good for growth. First, it leads to a more cohesive society, better able to take difficult political and economic decisions, such as promoting structural adjustment and reforms, because it prevents a group of people or a class to fall far behind and leave the market economy, causing a permanent loss of output. The same can be said about keeping children out of poverty, which will tend to have long-term benefits on their social and intellectual development and will induce long-term growth.

Second, social protection can be considered as a social investment or a productive factor through the so-called "employment-oriented social policies" which alter the balance between active and passive social expenditures. Active policies look at increasing the employment of the beneficiaries of the expenditure instead of passive policies, which are pure transfers of consumption from one group in society to another, either in the form of cash or services. If active policies succeed in increasing the quantity of labor supplied in the economy they will promote growth; thus, the more active spending there is in the total social expenditure the more positive are the effects going to be on growth.

It is very important to stress that the relationship between social protection and growth cannot be dissociated from the link between inequality and social protection. In other words, more social protection may reduce growth but voters decide on the level of social protection according to the level of inequality in the country. The reason is the following: the median voter makes an assessment of potential gains in personal or household income from voting for redistribution. Unless income is completely evenly distributed, the median voter will always have an income less than the mean income of the country, thus, the more the mean income exceeds that of the median voter, the more likely will the median voter be to believe that the financial rewards from redistribution can exceed any loss of income due to a reduced economic activity. Empirical tests by Persson and Tabellini (1994) and by Alesina and Rodrik (1994), Milanovic (1999), and Kristov, Lindert, and McLelland (1992) tend to show that, in democracies, a wider income distribution and a bigger gap between rich and poor tends to lead to slower growth because voters tend to favor more redistribution which in turn has the side-effect of slowing growth. Naturally, in many developing countries democracies are often only formal and in some cases absent, so there is no way to prove this important link.

But while the theory seems to be clear, there is not yet a full consensus among economists about the tested empirical effects of income inequality and social protection on growth. In the 1980s and early 1990s, some of them found out that income inequality is bad for growth and social protection good for growth (Cashin, 1994; Perotti, 1992 and 1994; Castles and Dowrick, 1990) but later others like Atkinson (1999) and Gwartney, Lawson, and Holcombe (1998) found the contrary. In the last decade a growing consensus has been built around the positive relationship of social protection and growth and the negative relationship between inequality and growth (Perotti, 1996) or about the positive relationship of "active spending" on growth (Arjona, Ladaique, and Pearson, 2001) but there are others who still find evidence to the contrary (Forbes, 2000).

Banerjee and Duflo (2000) find it very difficult to find cross-country evidence of inequality and growth because there are many stable relationships in the data that do not fit very well with the linear models that have been used to interpret the data, thus the most fruitful approaches are those which take the inherent non-linearities present in the data very seriously. Finally, in a recent book, Elhanan Helpman (2004) argues that his tentative conclusion is that inequality slows growth. Although the research in this area is not fully conclusive he argues, with limited confidence, that inequality within a country slows growth, but without being very sure yet about the channels through which this happens.

Globalization and Inequality at the End of the Nineteenth Century

Two events distinguish the late nineteenth-century period of globalization from that of the late twentieth century. First, a decline in inequality seems to have been significant and pervasive in the poor, industrial late comers in the late nineteenth-century sample. Second, mass migration appears to have had a more important effect than trade on inequality in the late nineteenth century (Williamson, 2000).

142

In the last major globalization process – between 1870 and 1914 – the rapid and profound opening-up of economies had very little to do with the increase in inequality between countries that continued in that period; conversely, globalization in general was a fundamental factor in the convergence of income between countries world-wide, especially due to the great migration flows in that period (O'Rourke and Williamson, 1999; O'Rourke, 2001).

This period of globalization was characterized by a sharp decline in transport costs, a considerable increase in international trade, massive emigration from the Old World to the New World (especially to the US) and large flows of capital in the same direction. Transatlantic maritime transport costs fell by 70 percent between 1840 and 1870 and by a further 45 percent between 1870 and 1913, and railway transport costs fell even faster. The increase in trade and the reduction in barriers to importation significantly narrowed commodity price differentials (Williamson, 2000). For example, the price of wheat in Liverpool was 58 percent higher than in Chicago in 1870, 18 percent higher in 1895 and only 16 percent higher in 1913 (Harley, 1980). The difference in cotton prices between London and Bombay fell from 57 percent in 1873 to 20 percent in 1913, the difference in jute prices between London and Calcutta went from 35 percent to 4 percent in the same period, and the difference in rice prices between London and Rangoon shrank from 93 percent to 26 percent (Collins, 1996).

There were enormous flows of capital from the "center" to the "periphery" in that period. The capital stock invested by the United Kingdom in other countries in 1870 represented 17 percent of the country's total financial wealth and 33 percent in 1913. In certain peak years, the UK's investment flows amounted to very high percentages of its GDP: 7.7 percent in 1872, 6.9 percent in 1888 and 8.7 percent in 1911. Germany's current account had a 4 percent surplus in 1880 and Japan's had a 5 percent surplus (O'Rourke and Williamson, 1999).

The same can be said for the recipient countries. In 1910, net foreign debt as a percentage of total domestic investment amounted to 37 percent in Canada, 70 percent in Argentina and 75 percent in Mexico; 35 percent of total cash flows in this period was accounted for by foreign direct investment (Dunning, 1993), 62.8 percent of which was invested in developing countries: 32.7 percent in Latin America, 6.4 percent in Africa and 20.9 percent in Asia (7 percent in China). The majority of these investments were in infrastructure: 70 percent in railways and municipal water, sewage, and telephone systems; railways alone accounted for 41 percent (Feis, 1930).

Over 60 million Europeans migrated to the New World between 1870 and 1913 and over 100 million people migrated worldwide. The immigration rates in some countries were huge: in the 1880s, for every 1,000 inhabitants, 291.8 in Argentina were immigrants, 167.6 in Canada, 118.4 in Cuba and 102 in the US. Logically, the rate of emigration from Europe was also very high: for every 1,000 inhabitants, 141.7 emigrated from Ireland, 107.7 from Italy and 95.2 from Norway. Although emigration was initially from the richest countries in Europe, the majority originated in the poorest countries in southern and eastern Europe; in other words, from the poorest countries in Europe to the richest countries in the New World (Baldwin and Martin, 1999).

All these globalization factors, in particular emigration, contributed to reducing the inequality in income between the two worlds. The well-known Heckscher and Ohlin (1933) theorem on the tendency for the price of production factors to equalize in the long run as their international mobility and integration increases, either directly or via international trade, seems to have worked in this period by reducing differences in income, since this is shaped by the greater productivity in countries where the ratio between capital and labor, and between skilled and unskilled labor, is greater.

The huge capital flows from the countries in which capital was most abundant to the countries in which it was scarcest and the massive flows of comparatively more skilled workers from the countries where they were more abundant to those where they were less abundant equalized the price of both production factors in both worlds and, consequently, brought about greater income equality between the two. The same can be said about land prices, which increased incredibly sharply in the Americas (250 percent in the US) and in Australia (400 percent) in that period, yet fell in the UK and France; therefore, the ratio between salaries of unskilled urban employees and the returns on farmland rose in Europe, where it was initially low, and fell in the Americas and Australia, where it was initially high, leading to a convergence of prices and returns on tilled land in relation to wages.

The reason for this convergence lies not only in higher flows of the two fundamental production factors (capital and labor) via foreign investment and emigration, but also in the higher volume of international trade between the two worlds since the prices of both factors were equalized on both sides due to the export of land-intensive commodities and foodstuffs from the New World to the Old in exchange for the export from the latter to the former of labor-intensive manufactured goods.

In other words, trade replaces the movements of capital, labor (which is not very mobile) and land (immobile) with the movement of products made by those factors. As illustrated by the studies carried out by O'Rourke and Williamson (1996 and 1999) and Taylor and Williamson (1997), the massive capital flows and migration largely explain the convergence between countries (up to 70 percent in the case of migration), while trade was more significant in intra-country income distribution.

The price convergence of the production factors reduced inequality between the two worlds, but did not eliminate it within either of them. The landowners – the richest Europeans – together with the new entrepreneurs of the Industrial Revolution lost the workers who emigrated to the New World, which increased the ratio between wages and returns on land in the Old World, which in turn made income distribution in Europe more equal. Conversely, the massive immigration in the Americas reduced that ratio there, which caused inequality to increase, particularly in countries where land ownership was very concentrated, as in Latin America. However, inequality increased much less in North America, where land distribution was based on family farms inherited from the colonization of the land on which the families that had occupied it worked directly and not land which the landowners had obtained due to decisions made by overseas or national metropolises (as happened in Latin America) or had occupied as

145

colonists, which meant that they did not work directly on the farms, but used sharecroppers and laborers.

Studies carried out, for the same period on income distribution and inequality are very partial and incomplete due to the lack of reliable data. Williamson (1997) invented an alternative technique for measuring inequality on the basis of the ratio of an unqualified employee's salary with a worker's average production per hour, in other words, between the income of the poorest and the weighted average of all the prices of the production factors, from the salaries of the most highly qualified to returns on capital and land. Williamson's results illustrate that inequality fell sharply in the poorest countries in Europe such as Sweden, Norway, Denmark, and Italy, remained stable in the richest countries such as the UK, France, and Germany and in the countries which participated least in the globalization process, and increased irregularly in the New World, for example in the US, Australia, Latin America, and Asia.

This historical evidence illustrates not only that the rise in inter-country inequality in this period was not due to globalization, but also that if the latter had not taken place, inequality would have increased to a greater extent.

Current Globalization and Inequality

The Heckscher–Ohlin theorem on the equalization of production factor prices seems to have worked in the context of globalization at the end of the nineteenth century, when trade was dominated by the exchange of land-intensive foodstuffs from the Americas, Africa, and Asia for labor-intensive manufactures from Europe, and when there were major flows of capital and emigrants from Europe to the other continents, especially the Americas (O'Rourke and Williamson, 1999).

The situation is very different in the current globalization process. On the one hand, international intra-industrial or intra-company trade – i.e. trade within companies of the same sector or between a parent company and its foreign subsidiaries, or even among its subsidiaries – is increasingly important due to the resurgence of multinational companies. Capital flows are lower in relative terms than in the previous globalization wave and they take place predominantly between developed countries (although developing countries' share is growing much faster in the last years) and migratory flows are also lower. On the other hand, the dominant production factors are the abundance of skilled labor as compared to unskilled labor, the capital–product ratio, and the fact that the two dominant regions are the North and South, as opposed to Europe versus the Americas or the center versus the periphery.

After globalization and market integration were halted in 1914, the world entered a "dark age" of strong protectionism during which there were two world wars and the Great Depression. It was not until after the Second World War that an attempt was resumed to gradually return to the pre-1914 levels of globalization and to recover from the tremendous losses in growth and well-being experienced in the forty-plus years of the "dark age." Globalization has accelerated gradually, in particular since the 1980s, but it has not yet fully regained its 1914 levels in some key aspects, such as emigration, which is fundamental to equalizing income in the long term and to reducing inequality.

With regard to the integration of the product markets, there has also been a sharp fall in rail, road, and air transport costs, whereas maritime transport costs have remained stable or risen (Hummels, 1999). However, the liberalization and reduction of barriers to the trade of manufactures is much greater than in 1913. Average industrial tariffs are much lower now, with some notable exceptions, such as the UK, China, and India. Moreover, the industrial tariffs are much higher in developing countries than in developed countries, while in 1913 the opposite was the case. Other sectors, such as agriculture and foodstuffs, are much more protected by the developed countries than they were in 1913. Agricultural protection in these countries has boosted the prices received by farmers by 60 percent in Japan, 40 percent in Europe and 20 percent in the US (Coppel and Durand, 1999). Non-tariff barriers are also greater than in 1913.

147

The integration of capital markets derived from direct investment flows is more significant now than at the end of the previous period of globalization. Foreign direct investment represented 35 percent of the stock of long-term debt in 1913, and now exceeds 50 percent. The stock of foreign direct investment amounted to 9 percent of world GDP in 1913 and now exceeds 20 percent (UNCTAD, 2002a), although most of this is due to flows between developed countries. In 1914, 62.8 percent of the stock of foreign direct investment was located in developing countries, compared to only 33 percent today; the remaining 66 percent is located in the developed countries (UNCTAD, 2002b). The rest of capital flows is much more significant today than it was in 1913, particularly when compared with portfolio investment and debt, although its distribution is still biased toward developed countries, and the stock currently located in developing countries is lower than in 1913 (Obsfeld and Taylor, 2001).

The composition of these capital flows is very different from those in 1913. It is now concentrated in industry and services, whereas it was previously focused on the primary sector and infrastructure. In 1914, 55 percent of the stock of foreign direct investment was concentrated in the primary sector (agriculture and mining), 20 percent in railways, 15 percent in manufacturing, and 10 percent in services, trade, and banking (Dunning, 1993). In the 1990s, 6 percent of the stock of foreign direct investment from the European Union went to the primary sector, 31.5 percent to manufacturing and 63 percent to services (Baldwin and Martín, 1999). The composition of portfolio flows has also changed significantly. At the end of the nineteenth century, the majority of flows were in the form of bonds, whereas they are now almost equally divided between bank loans, bonds and equities (World Bank, 2000).

Another very significant factor is that gross capital flows are now much greater than net capital flows; this is clear evidence of the importance and relative weighting of short-term capital movements (Bordo, Eichengreen, and Kim, 1998). Lastly, the majority of foreign direct investment flows correspond to multinationals that operate in the countries of origin and destination of the flows, whereas they were previously used by institutions and companies in the center to do business with the periphery.

Finally, the integration of labor markets – the key production factor in improving inter-country income distribution via migration – is much less intense than it was in the previous period of globalization. The United Nations calculated that the world stock of immigrants represented 2.5 percent of the world population, whereas in 1911 it exceeded 7.5 percent. For example, immigrants then represented 14.5 percent of the population in the US and 22 percent in Canada, compared with 8.5 percent in the US and 11 percent in Canada today. In the European Union, they account for 5 percent of the population, with considerable disparity between countries: 10 percent in Germany, 12 percent in Belgium, 8 percent in Austria and 4 percent in Spain. The two European countries with the highest proportion of immigrants are Luxembourg (40 percent) and Switzerland (17 percent). The actual annual immigration flows amount to 1.1 million in the US (0.4 percent of the total population) and 1.2 million in the EU (0.35 percent of the total population).

In this new process of globalization, the Heckscher–Ohlin model illustrates that inequality would tend to increase in the North since skilled workers benefit to the detriment of unskilled workers, who must compete with immigrants and imported labor-intensive products.

Nevertheless, empirical evidence in the sixty or so years of the present globalization process shows that the growing integration of developing countries with the world's economy has been a clear route for them to move from poverty to prosperity by starting to export traditional goods and later becoming more and more specialized in higher technology goods and services. Japan exported cheap goods after the Second World War and later moved on to more technologically sophisticated products. When Japan became rich, Korea, Taiwan Province of China, Hong Kong, and Singapore replaced Japan as low wage exporters and when they moved into more technologically sophisticated goods, Thailand and Malaysia filled the same niche. Now China and India are exactly following the same process in manufactured goods and in services. As these countries become more advanced, their success will improve the export opportunities for the remaining developing countries, which will exploit their new opportunity. For instance, when China becomes rich, a billion more people will live in toy-importing countries and a billion fewer in toy-exporting countries, opening up opportunities for other countries to fill this niche. Therefore, that global integration trend may allow for most of the world to grow faster and for many developing countries to converge with rich countries. But of course convergence depends also on other factors such as initial conditions, the quality of institutions, demographic trends, and migration trends (Chamon and Kremer, 2006).

According to the IMF (2000) two different pictures come out of the late twentieth-century globalization as regards prosperity and convergence among the world economies: one in terms of GDP per capita growth rates and the other in terms of GDP per capita growth combined with the size of a country's population.

The first picture is negative: 75 percent of developing countries recorded slower per capita income growth than in industrial countries over the period 1970–98, and per capita income fell in 32 countries and only 7 developing countries grew fast enough to reduce substantially the income gap with the industrial countries as a group. The second picture is positive, less than 10 percent of the developing world's population lives in countries where average income declined, while 70 percent of the world's population lives in countries where income growth exceeded that of industrial countries. This more positive outcome mainly reflects strong economic growth in China in particular and also in India, which together account for 50 percent of the population in developing countries and which had per capita growth rates of 7 percent and 2.5 percent respectively, over the period.

An even better third picture also emerges when examining the growth performance over a shorter timeframe. During the period 1993–8, 14 developing countries, double that for the whole period, converged rapidly toward the industrial countries despite the financial crisis that occurred in Asia, Russia, and Latin America. Conversely, per capita income fell in only 23 developing countries, versus 32 in the whole period. The improved performance in these countries partly reflects stronger domestic policies and for some of these countries, a more supportive external environment, mainly more open trade. This more recent trend gives some hope for the future of convergence in this second phase of globalization.

Finally, another positive factor coming out of the present wave of globalization (and in a similar fashion to the previous one) is the large process of the world's disinflation since the 1990s, which is helping to increase the purchasing power of many citizens and mainly those with lower incomes (Rogoff, 2003, 2004) (Chen, Imbs, and Scott, 2004) which also helps to reduce inequality and helps central banks to keep inflation well controlled (Razin and Loungani, 2005).

Intra-country Inequality

As mentioned in the previous chapter, in the mid-1950s, Simon Kuznets (1955, 1962) showed that inequality within a country correlates with the level of development via an inverted U-shaped bell curve (the Kuznets curve). As economies develop, inequality increases until it reaches a peak, and then it starts to decrease. This theory was supported by subsequent empirical evidence (Ahluwalia, 1976; Jain, 1975; Anand and Kanbur, 1993). However, Li, Squire, and Zou (1998) later found contrary evidence using a sample of 49 countries, since they illustrated that inequality tended to be relatively stable over time and that there was no clear evidence for Kuznets' assertion.

A study by Cornia and Kiiski (2001) using WIDER broader database (which includes 73 countries) reinforces the above thesis that intra-country inequality has remained constant in the very long term (1950–2000), but it also illustrated that this inequality has varied significantly in recent decades, falling between 1950 and 1970 and rising again since 1980. Bhalla (2002) later reached the same conclusion, pointing out that intra-country inequality has only deteriorated since the 1980s.

The results of other studies on intra-country inequality diverge considerably. The study by Freeman and Oostendorp (2000), for the

International Labor Organization (ILO) showed that wage dispersion fell in rich and medium- to high-income countries in the 1980s and 1990s and rose in average-income countries, including the European former communist countries; in other words, they refute the theory. Burniaux, Dang, Fore, Forster, Mira D'Ercole, and Oxley (1998), on the other hand, illustrated that inequality increased in the OECD countries, with the exception of Denmark, Canada, and France, due to the increase in workers' wage bands, which supports the Heckscher–Ohlin thesis. Lindert and Williamson (2001) demonstrated that both studies could be compatible since wage dispersion can fall at the same time as income dispersion between workers rises if there is higher unemployment and a reduction in working hours.

The results are mixed in developing countries. Inequality has been falling slowly in Latin America, although it has risen recently in some countries due to their financial crises, and it has increased slightly in Africa and more sharply in China and India; therefore, in population-weighted terms, total inequality has increased (Lindert and Williamson, 2001).

However, this global tendency toward greater inequality illustrated by the studies cited above can by no means be attributed to globalization itself since there are many other factors which have had a greater effect – particularly the impact of the strong technological development in the developed countries and the strong regional growth of some major developing countries, most notably China and India, where growth has been unevenly distributed between the inland and rural regions, which have grown more slowly, and the coastal and manufacturing regions, which have grown more quickly. In other countries, inequality has increased due to the collapse of communism and the difficult transition to democracy, or due to demographic trends (the case of Africa) or to unequal developments in education.

Other studies have focused more specifically on the impact of opening up economies, that is, of globalization, on intra-country income distribution. Higgins and Williamson (1999) have performed regression analyses between the opening up of economies and inequality and provide some negative (though small) coefficients; in other words, globalization reduces intra-country inequality, but not very significantly. Spilimbergo, Londoño, and Székely (1999) used the data series of Deininger and Squire (1996) and showed that the opening-up of economies tends to increase inequality in developed countries with a higher proportion of skilled workers, which is consistent with the theory, and tends to reduce inequality in countries with greater stocks of capital and land, which is not consistent with the Heckscher–Ohlin model. All these discrepancies seem to depend on the choice of indicator used to illustrate the opening-up of economies.

Recent studies on intra-country inequality, for example those by Sala i Martín (2002a and 2002b) and by Bhalla (2002), which were discussed in detail in the previous chapter, show that inequality has increased in recent years, mainly because countries with large populations, such as China and India, which represent a large percentage of the world's developing country population, have undergone sharp growth that has not been equally distributed among the whole population since certain regions have grown more quickly than others. Urban areas have grown more quickly than rural areas and coastal areas have grown more quickly than inland areas. In any case, this phenomenon will undoubtedly be temporary until growth is expanding to all areas and regions or population is slowly moving to the faster growth areas.

Inter-country Inequality

Empirical studies carried out on inter-country inequality show a more positive impact of globalization on reducing this inequality. Emigration has been the pillar of globalization, creating a greater tendency toward income equality between countries. The huge migratory movements from 1870 to 1914 – in which nearly 100 million people emigrated from one country to another, 60 million of them Europeans going to the Americas – made a decisive contribution to reducing income inequality between countries. However, there has been much less migration in recent decades, if we consider that 6.6 percent of the world population emigrated in the previous period of globalization (i.e. 100 million out of an average total population of 1,500 million). It is calculated that another 100 million people have emigrated since the 1980s, but this represents only 1.8 percent of the average total population of 5,500 million.

This lower emigration rate may be a clear symptom of greater income convergence between countries, as pointed out by Straubhaar (1988), since one of the greatest causes of emigration is wage and income differentials between countries. The greater convergence of incomes between countries has been boosted particularly by the strong worldwide growth in trade and foreign direct investment, which has not only enabled greater investment and job creation in developing countries, but also led to greater diffusion of technology, as confirmed by Coe and Helpman (1995) and Keller (2001b).

However, as illustrated by Sala i Martín and Bhalla, inequality between individuals rather than countries is the important factor for studies into the impact of globalization on inequality. It is important to know what has happened to the poorest 20 percent in the world, not those in China or the US. A poor person in Bangladesh has more in common with a poor person in Mozambique than with a poor person in the US. Until a few years ago, for statistical convenience and simplicity, each individual country was taken as the unit of analysis. The results of this "easy" method showed that inequality has increased. But this is not the correct way to measure inequality since the patterns of change in inter-country inequality are consistent with either an increase or a decrease in inequality. It all depends on where the change took place within global distribution. If incomes in the poorest economies rise faster than in the rich countries and there is not a significant overlap in distributions, individual inequality world-wide will tend to improve. The lack of data has prevented analyses from being carried out on groups of individuals as well as groups of countries.

The most recent studies show clearly that inter-country inequality has fallen significantly since the 1980s. Sala i Martín (2002a and 2002b) and Bhalla (2002) point to significant reductions in inequality, in contrast with the results of the Bourguignon and Morrison (2002) study, which estimates that inequality increased from 0.650 in 1970 to 0.657 in 1992. According to Sala i Martín, who, like Bourguignon and Morrison, uses the Gini coefficient, inter-country inequality fell from 0.67 in 1976 to 0.51 in 1998, while the intra-country coefficient rose from 0.18 to 0.23. Naturally, since the reduction in inequality is much greater between countries than within each country, the total inequality coefficient has been reduced significantly. In order to cross-check his results, Sala i Martín also used other indices to measure the inequality of income distribution, such as those used by Theil, Atkinson, and others. The reduction of inter-country inequality shown by these indices fluctuates between 7 percent and 14 percent.

Bhalla also used the Gini coefficient and concluded that inequality reached 0.693 in 1973 and then fell to 0.657 in 1980 and to 0.651 in 2000, the lowest level since 1910. Similar conclusions had previously been reached by Schultz (1998), Melchior, Telle, and Wiig (2000), and Dowrick and Akmal (2001).

If Bourguignon and Morrison had extended their study to the year 2000, it is very likely that they would have noted a significant reduction in inequality due to the acceleration of globalization. In any case, this reduction was achieved without any massive migratory movements, unlike the previous globalization process between 1870 and 1913, in which nearly 100 million people emigrated to other countries, thereby reducing inequality between countries; this has given the globalization factor a greater weighting in recent years and has led to the hope that, when migration increases greatly in the coming decades (see final chapter), inter-country inequality may fall much more sharply.

In a recent paper, Stanley Fischer (2003) asks the right question after showing how between 1980 and 2000 (the period of acceleration of globalization) inter-country inequality has increased, if every country is taken as one point in the correlation between growth of GDP per head and GDP per head in 1980. On average, the rich countries are getting richer faster than the poor countries. Therefore, the correlation is very low, showing an upward-sloping pattern of points instead of a markedly downward-sloping pattern. If, on the contrary, the same correlation is done weighting every country by its population, the pattern becomes downward-sloping showing that poor people, rather than poor countries, have benefited from the increase in globalization reducing their GDP per head gap with the rich countries. The reason for this different outcome is due to the fact that two of the poorest and most populated countries in the world, China and India, have been growing at a much faster rate than the rich countries.

His right question is not whether globalization is a good thing, but why some countries and in the case of Africa, almost the entire sub-Saharan region, combined severely limited economic opening and integration with dismal economic performance. The explanation given by Fischer is very similar to the one advanced in this book. Both rich and poor countries are part of the blame. The first ones by maintaining trade restrictions for the goods and services that poor countries can export to them and by reducing the amount of foreign aid, both in nominal and real volumes, to the poor countries, during a large part of this period. The second ones by maintaining even higher restrictions to trade with other poor countries and not developing the right economic and political institutions to attract foreign direct investment. Therefore, more globalization is needed to try to improve the dismal growth rate situation of some of the poorest countries and regions, which have been left out of its acceleration in the last two decades. This very important issue is going to be addressed in the following chapters.

Finally, there is also a widespread misconception about globalization reducing world labor standards. The argument assumes that standards increase costs of production sufficiently to impose a competitive disadvantage on producers with higher standards. Initially the proposition was that bad standards in developing countries would drive out good standards in advanced economies and that it would result in a race to the bottom in standards of "social dumping."

This argument ignores the ways in which a country can maintain standards in the face of competition. First, part of the cost will fall on workers, who prefer higher standards. A mandated increase in benefits will shift the supply of labor (making it more attractive for workers) and the demand for labor (raising costs) where the schedules are measured with respect to wages only. The extent to which the cost falls on employers or workers is an issue of incidence comparable to that of incidence of taxes. Second, some standards that raise short-term costs to firms may have greater benefits than costs for an economy in the long run. Child labor laws, requiring children to attend school and the like, increase human capital formation at the expense of higher costs of production for firms that employ children. Some health and safety regulations, which reduce injuries and even deaths, may also pay for themselves at the national level, although not at the firm level.

Third, given the different goods produced between advanced countries and developed countries, it is more plausible to worry that bad standards in some developing countries might drive out good standards in other developing countries. Finally, with flexible exchange rates, economies can adjust to different standards through fluctuations in exchange rates. That is, countries may choose the standards that they want. But, the real fact is that labor standards have risen with globalization in developed countries as well as in developing countries, which keep signing up to ILO conventions, committing them to improve their standards (Freeman, 2003). Moreover, Maskus (2003) finds that labor standards are positively correlated with export performance in east Asia.

Chapter 7

More Developing Countries' Access to Developed Countries' Markets

Previous chapters discussed how the integration of developing countries into the global markets tends to provide faster growth and to reduce the world's poverty and, sometimes, the world's inequality. However, the high import barriers in developed countries and in most developing countries prevent exporters in developing countries from taking advantage of that integration, thus precluding them from becoming more global and growing faster (IMF and World Bank, 2002).

The developed countries' barriers against products from developing countries are one of the major economic obstacles to world development at the start of the new millennium since they only benefit a few interest groups at the expense of most citizens, in both developing and developed countries. The average import tariff in developed countries is less than 5 percent for imports from all countries, but it goes up to 14.50 percent for products from the poorest countries (i.e. those which live on under one dollar/day), 14.15 percent for those coming from poor countries (under two dollars/day) and 6.50 percent for low-income countries' exports (over two dollars/day) and, consequently, rich countries are clearly discriminating against trade with the poorer countries.

Different calculations show that eliminating all the world's trade barriers would provide a gain of $254 billion per year in world's welfare, of which $108 billion would revert to developing countries (Anderson, Dimaran, Francois, Hertel, Hoekman, and Martin, 2000). Another study calculated $355 billion by 2015 which, adjusted for growth, would be $265 billion at the present time (World Bank, 2002). These are very spectacular figures when compared with the $70 billion per year that developed countries give as official development aid to developing countries. The World Bank estimates that the faster growth attained by reducing world-wide trade barriers would decrease the number of people living on less than 1 dollar per day by over 13 percent in 2015 and enable the Millennium poverty objectives to be attained (World Bank, 2002).

Successive rounds of multilateral trade negotiations have managed to reduce average tariff levels, but there is still considerable scope for improvement. The least developed countries have higher average tariffs (17.9 percent) than developing countries (14 percent) and than developed countries (5 percent). However, exports from developing countries face higher barriers than those from developed countries because: (1) in addition to tariffs, there are many other barriers, such as specific tariffs, contingents and quotas, rules of origin costs, and technical and environmental standards; (2) average tariffs do not reflect the impact of the dispersion, especially the maximum tariffs (i.e. over 15 percent) and escalating tariffs (i.e. which increase depending on how processed the import is, so as to increase effective protection); and (3) the uncertainty about applying the tariffs, which are often discretionary since they are subject to the interpretation of complex standards and procedures.

Average protection, measured by the average equivalent effective ad valorem tariff applied to bilateral trade flows among countries, is observed to be higher in developing and medium-income countries than in developed countries. Since trade between developing countries represents 40 percent of the total, that protection is also very negative. Protection in the European Union is biased against imports from medium-income countries, whereas in the US it is more biased against imports from less developed countries, and all countries apply the highest protection on agricultural trade. One of the Uruguay Round's successes was that it converted the quantitative restrictions and other non-tariff barriers into tariffs, thereby increasing transparency – but at the expense of slightly increasing effective protection. Another success was that it froze the infamous Multifiber Agreement, which has finally expired in January 2005, within a large opposition by developed countries' manufacturers albeit having had a large term of 10 years to adapt to its expected disappearance, but the fact is that developed countries have barely reduced their barriers in this area waiting for the last minute, thus breaching the agreement. In any case, those equivalent "ad valorem" tariffs do not include the effect of internal or export subsidies, which will be discussed later on.

The problem is not the developed countries' average tariffs (which are low) but the major dispersion behind those averages. Between 6 percent and 14 percent of the developed countries' average tariffs include peak tariffs up to or even over 100 percent. These peaks are centered on textiles and clothing in Canada and the US, and agricultural products in Japan and the EU. If a 15 percent cap were set on those tariffs, the barriers against textile and clothing imports would fall by 20 percent in the US and by 59 percent in the case of imports from China. If the same cap were set in the EU for agricultural imports, average protection would fall 50 percent to 60 percent.

It so happens that those peak tariffs are applied to products in which developing countries have a comparative advantage, i.e. agricultural produce and labor-intensive industrial products. In the latter case, protection creates considerable problems because it penalizes countries that want to develop technologically in order to rise out of poverty. Tariff barriers against commodities and primary products are relatively low, but they are substantially higher in the case of low-tech, labor-intensive products, processed foods and light industrial products. Barriers to medium-tech products (e.g. auto spare parts) were subsequently reduced and they are very low for high-tech products (Cernat, Laird, and Turrini, 2002).

This leads to really shocking situations. In the US, tariff revenues on imports from Bangladesh match those on imports from France, which are twelve times larger (Gresser, 2002). The policy of escalating tariffs has the same effects since they progressively penalize more processed imports from developing countries.

Another type of protection is the so-called "contingent protection" implemented via antidumping cases, i.e. in cases in which it appears that an exporting country is selling a good in a foreign country below cost or below the price in the country of origin. Since 1995, over 2,000 cases have been initiated, two-thirds by developing countries, and nearly 60 percent of them against products from other developing countries. This system has three risks: (1) it may be used to further the ends of economic interest groups; (2) it may endanger the non-discriminatory application of trade policies; and (3) the deterrent effect of an antidumping investigation tends to go considerably further than the exporter in question.

Finally, there is also non-tariff protection imposed by mainly developed countries, based on technical and regulatory barriers and standards, where developing countries are ill prepared to deal with them. Although standards and regulations for products and processes are vital for attaining reasonable levels of quality, safety, compatibility, and health, they are very often hijacked by lobbies, especially when the standard-setting processes are not transparent. Developing countries state that over 50 percent of their potential exports of fresh and processed fish, meat, fruit, and vegetables to the EU do not take place due to inability to comply with EU standards (OECD, 2001b). A recent survey of civil servants in developing countries showed that they believed that minimum standards and other technical requirements posed greater barriers to agricultural exports than did transport and insurance costs, tariffs, and quotas (Henson, Loader, Swinbank, and Lux, 2000).

Most developing countries have preferential access to developed countries' markets in a wide range of products through generalized systems of preferences (GSP) and bilateral or regional agreements. However, the benefits of many of those schemes for developing countries are very small. The GSP scheme in the US excludes textiles, clothing, and footwear and imposes a maximum of $100 million of exports per product and country. The benefits are not fixed but may be changed unilaterally. In fact, GSP have often been withdrawn when developing countries started to export successfully (Özden and Reinhardt, 2002). The preference margins are considerably more limited on products which developed countries classify as "sensitive." The competitive advantage they offer is low and the graduation mechanisms for a specific country and product mean that some exports are not selected for preferential treatment, so there is no incentive to invest in anticipation of those expected benefits.

Preferential systems mean that rules of origin are supervised so as to avoid mere trans-shipments without providing additional local value, thereby reducing the incentives to adopt such systems. An example is where the soles, insoles, and the laces of shoes must be made in the exporting country. Consequently, only one-third of potential imports into the EU from developing countries under GSP finally manage to enter the EU due to its harsh rules of origin. There is ample empirical evidence that those problems reduce the incentives for some developing countries to liberalize trade, thus often perpetuating the anti-export bias in their trade systems (Özden and Reinhardt, 2002).

However, in recent years, reinforced generalized regional preference schemes have been developed, especially for sub-Saharan Africa, and some developed countries have granted substantial reductions in tariffs and contingents to the least developed countries. Noteworthy is the EU "EBA" initiative (Everything but Arms) to eliminate trade barriers to 49 poor countries and the US "AGAO" (African Growth and Opportunity) program. The former does not include sugar, bananas, and rice, which will be gradually liberalized, and the latter includes reverse preferences to force developing countries to use US textiles, strict rules of origin and requirements of proof that child labor was not used and that internationally recognized labor rights were protected; to date, only 15 African countries have used this program and just four (Gabon, Lesotho, Nigeria, and South Africa) represent 85 percent of imports under the program.

At the G8 summit in Kananaskis, the Canadian government announced that it would extend free access to its market (except for milk, chicken, and eggs) to all the least developed countries. A recent study showed that if those schemes were adopted by all developed countries, the poorest countries' exports would increase by $2.5 billion (+11 percent) and enable them to diversify their export structures and, consequently, boost growth and lower poverty (Bacchetta and Bora, 2002).

Trade Barriers to Textiles and Clothing

Since textile and clothing production often requires only simple technology and is intensive in unskilled labor, many developing countries have a major comparative advantage in those two sectors, and this is clearly evident in foreign trade statistics. In the mid-1960s, developing countries accounted for 15 percent of world-wide textile exports and just below 25 percent of world-wide clothing exports. In 1998, those percentages had increased to 50 percent and 70 percent, respectively, with a combined volume of $213 billion, which has kept growing since the late 1990s. However, sub-Saharan Africa contributed less than 2 percent of that figure and a volume of only $3.5 billion. In some countries, those exports were the main export revenue source. For example, textiles account for 51 percent of Pakistan's goods exports and clothing for 50 percent of Sri Lanka's; textiles and clothing represent 83 percent of Bangladesh's exports and 87 percent of Cambodia's.

That huge growth was attained despite high quantitative restrictions and import tariffs imposed by developed countries through the Multi-fiber Agreement (MFA). This agreement was based on bilateral quotas between importers (mainly developed countries) and exporters (mostly developing countries). Importing countries had to lift their quotas by 6 percent per year but, in general, the quota increase was smaller for countries that already exported and greater for new countries. The average equivalence of those quotas as export taxes and as effective import tariffs, in 1997, were generally much higher in the US and Canada than in Japan and the EU. Nevertheless, the dispersion of the quotas and of their equivalents in taxes or tariffs was considerable, so the most competitive countries (China, Bangladesh, and India) face much tougher quotas than the least competitive. For example, the equivalent tax on T-shirts from China is 300 percent.

The Agreement on Textiles and Clothing (ATC) reached in the Uruguay Round established that those quotas had to be phased out in ten years either through integration or elimination by 2005, and quotas that had not been phased out (a three-year safeguard clause was established for imports from certain countries that could be seriously detrimental to domestic industry) would have to increase at a greater pace, by 16 percent in the first phase and 25 percent in the last phase.

Although the quota increase and the integration process have been fulfilled, few of the restrictions had actually been eliminated before its term expired in 2005, with the exception of Norway. The US, Canada and the EU still had most of their quotas in place. The US has eliminated 13 out of a total of 750, Canada 29 out of 295 and the EU 14 out of 219; consequently, the rest have been finally phased out just before the deadline in 2005, but some have been introduced again recently.

In addition to the fact that the quotas were phased out at the last minute, the tariffs on those products are still very high: over 10 percent on average and with considerable dispersion, since the peaks reach nearly 30 percent. Nevertheless, developing countries also have high effective tariffs (16 percent on average); the largest exporting countries, such as ASEAN, India, and China, have the highest tariffs (20 percent to 33 percent on textiles and 30 percent to 35 percent on clothing). The same occurs in Mexico and South Africa.

Those restrictions are a considerable burden on many developing countries and on some developed countries, too (IMF and World Bank, 2002). In accordance with the GTAP (Global Trade Analysis Project) model, it was calculated that the combined effect of quotas and tariffs on developing countries' income is about $24 billion per year and the loss of export revenues is a further $40 billion per year. For developed countries, the loss of income is half that amount and the loss of export revenues is similar. The sub-Saharan countries are especially hard hit since, if textile and clothing trade were fully liberalized, their cotton exports would increase by over $130 million in 1997 terms. The high tariffs in the developing countries also impose very high costs in terms of income and export revenues since textile and clothing trade between developing countries represents half of their textile exports and 20 percent of their clothing exports.

Simulations were also carried out to ascertain the effect on employment in developing countries of not liberalizing the textile and clothing trade by developed countries. The conclusion is that liberalization would increase employment in those countries by about 27 million jobs. Each job maintained in the developed countries by that protection costs 35 jobs in developing countries and the effect is concentrated on the poorest people in those countries. Moreover, the poorest families in developed countries suffer most from that protection since they have to pay considerably more for basic necessities because tariffs and quotas are higher on cotton and synthetic textiles and clothing than on wool or silk products. The existence of quotas means, first, that importers mark up higher margins on products with quotas and second, that exporters have incentives to export their more expensive products.

Trade Barriers to Agricultural Products

Although the obstacles to textiles, clothing, and footwear are high and they are now being reduced with the end of the MFA, those for agricultural imports from developing countries are even higher. This is a major scandal in today's increasingly global world, because there is no justification whatsoever for this situation, which has a very negative impact on developing countries since agriculture still accounts, on average, for 50 percent of their employment, 27 percent of their exports, and 27 percent of their GDP. That effect is even more negative in the poorest countries, where those percentages are even higher. While textile and footwear protection is aimed at protecting developed countries' unskilled workers (i.e. the poorest people in developed countries), by contrast, agricultural protection is aimed at protecting the richest farmers in developed countries from competition from the poorest farmers in developing countries, that is, the agriculture protection effect is clearly regressive and perverse.

The OECD countries' agriculture has traditionally been sheltered from all types of competition; in fact, it was not until the Uruguay Round in 1994 that it entered the GATT negotiations as a sector. At the end of that round, it was agreed to open trade in agricultural products subject to the following: contingents and quotas were converted into tariffs; average tariffs were to be reduced by 36 percent in six years from 1986 to 1992; all tariffs were to be reduced by a minimum of 15 percent; tariff contingencies were to be introduced to guarantee a minimum degree of market access at the end of the period; export subsidies would decline by 36 percent in value and by 21 percent in volume for each product in six years; and national subsidies would be reduced by 20 percent in the six-year period from 1986 to 1992, except for subsidies under 5 percent, those related to development or technical progress and those aimed at reducing production.

However, those commitments included very protectionist safeguard clauses, which enabled those countries to automatically impose additional tariffs if imports increased rapidly or prices declined too much.

Despite the expectations raised by the Uruguay Round, liberalization has been very limited. First, the chosen baseline period (1986–92) was one with exceptionally high protection levels. Second, national protection was allowed to increase in some products. Third, "dirty tariffication" has been widely used on products considered to be sensitive; this involves inflating the difference between national and international prices, thereby increasing the calculated equivalent tariff (Hathaway and Ingco, 1996). Some studies show that, despite the Uruguay Round, average protection has actually increased (Nogués, 2000).

In the Millennium Round, which commenced recently in Doha, trade ministers acknowledged those distortions and undertook to substantially improve market access for agricultural products, further reduce export subsidies with a view to eliminating them, and considerably reduce national subsidies that distort trade. Finally, in the Doha meeting in Hong Kong at the end of 2005, an agreement was reached to eliminate export subsidies by developed countries.

The fact is that OECD countries' agriculture continues to be heavily protected and to receive disproportionate government aid. Import tariffs and export subsidies are still the main mechanisms to protect and support market prices. In 2001, 68 percent of agricultural production in OECD countries was protected from imports and their exports were subsidized. The total value of both mechanisms was $145 billion per year, i.e. 63 percent of the aid received by the agricultural sector (OECD, 2002). Direct export subsidies have been decreasing, in compliance with the Uruguay Round commitments, and now account for only about $6.5 billion, but there are other indirect export subsidies (export credit, food aid, and state-owned trading companies).

Agricultural subsidies in the OECD countries totaled $311 billion in 2001, i.e. 1.3 percent of their GDP and 33 percent of their total agricultural revenues (OECD, 2002). The average prices received by farmers in OECD countries were 31 percent higher than international border prices. The dispersion in these figures is enormous. For example, in the EU, consumers pay a premium of 160 percent over the international price for sugar, 126 percent for butter and lamb, 100 percent for rice, 88 percent for powdered milk, 83 percent for bananas, 62 percent for cheese, 57 percent for beef, and 52 percent for corn (European Commission, 2000).

Of these $311 billion, the EU allocates most aid and protection in absolute terms ($93 billion), followed by the US ($49 billion), Japan ($47 billion), and Korea ($16.8 billion). However, in relative terms, Switzerland, Norway, Korea, Japan, and Iceland provide the most aid: between 59 percent and 69 percent of their total agriculture revenues, compared with 35 percent in the EU as a whole (OECD, 2001c). Their protection is also very high: average prices received by farmers in OECD countries are 1.3 times higher than international border prices, with the consequent burden on consumers in those countries.

Those figures do not include President Bush's decision (under the Farm Security and Rural Investment Act of 2002 – FSRIA) to increase aid by $41 billion between 2002 and 2007, i.e. 21 percent more than that established in the Farm Act of 1996, bringing US subsidies relatively into line with those of the EU.

These shocking agricultural aid figures cannot be justified in economic terms and they have a doubly perverse social effect – on citizens of OECD countries, who pay for them directly and on citizens in developing countries, who suffer from them directly and indirectly. Almost nobody gains and almost everybody loses.

First, that aid represents a very high cost for taxpayers in OECD countries, especially for the poor, who pay the bulk of VAT because consumption accounts for a larger share of their disposable income and VAT is the main tax that finances the national budgets. Second, the high food prices imposed on all consumers in those countries falls disproportionately on the poorest consumers, who also spend a larger proportion of their income on food, and disproportionately benefits farmers, particularly the biggest farmers, who receive over 70 percent of total aid. Of the 887,000 farmers who receive subsidies in the EU, 721,081 receive less than €5,000 per year and 1,095 receive more than €150,000, of whom 374 collect between €200,000 and €300,000, 112 collect between €300,000 and €400,000, and 40 collect over €400,000 per year. That aid is an opaque and diabolical mechanism for transferring income from the poor to the rich in all the OECD countries (OECD, 2001a).

For example, the EU spends 46 percent (45 billion euros) of its budget on agriculture to subsidizing 3.4 percent of the working population (farmers) or 12 percent of the total population (i.e. including farmers' families and contracted wage earners). In 1999, each farmer in the EU received an average of $17,000 per year, compared with an average of $11,000 in the OECD countries; nevertheless, that was not the largest amount paid to each farmer since Norway pays $33,000, Switzerland $32,000, Japan $26,000, and the US (after the recent increase established by President Bush) nearly $20,000 per farmer. It is worth recalling that average income per capita in the world is only $5,170 and that 4.51 billion people (74.4 percent of the worldwide population) live on less than $730 per year (World Bank, 2002).

Third, that aid imposes very high costs on farmers in developing countries: it reduces the income of producers and exporters of agricultural products in those countries, particularly the poorest countries,

where agricultural production and exports account for a larger proportion of GDP, and especially tropical and subtropical countries, whose
exports suffer from even higher trade barriers. Moreover, production
aid in the OECD countries causes huge surpluses of produce (grains,
meat, milk, butter, beetroot sugar, etc.) that have to be exported (actually dumped) to developing countries at large subsidies, depressing the
prices of these products in those countries and ruining many of their
farmers, although this does benefit consumers in those countries. The
only exception is that poorest net food importing countries benefit
from these export subsidies. In short, most of the world's citizens lose
out, especially the poorest in the developed world and in developing
countries, where they are much more numerous. Consequently, this
is one of the greatest economic and social scandals in the world today,
and it is incomprehensible in societies that claim to be the most
democratic.

Admittedly, developing countries are also very protectionist with
regard to agricultural products. If anything, this exacerbates the
problem. Nevertheless, those barriers have fallen faster than in
the developed countries since the 1980s, especially in the two largest
countries, India and China (the latter due to its recent entry into
the WTO).

The IMF has developed a static analysis of the cost of agricultural
protection and aid for developing and developed countries, calculated
in terms of the loss in consumer income and export revenues (IMF and
World Bank, 2002). The figures are huge – $506 billion per year. The
absolute cost is greater for developed countries ($359 billion or 70
percent of the total cost) as they include some of the world's largest
food exporters, such as Australia, Canada, and New Zealand. The cost
to developing countries is $147 billion, i.e. the other 30 percent.
However, the relative cost is much greater for developing countries
since, at current exchange rates, their aggregate GDP is one-quarter of
the aggregate GDP of the developed countries, so the effect is quite the
opposite: 62 percent of the relative cost is borne by developing countries and the other 38 percent by the OECD countries. Additionally,
taking into account the relative weighting of agriculture in GDP for

each group of countries, the relative cost for developing countries is even greater, as agriculture accounts for only 2 percent of the developed countries' GDP, whereas in developing countries it averages 15 percent, and reaches 24 percent in the poorest countries.

The protection figures above are averages. In fact, the developing countries' vital exports face higher tariffs and tougher quotas; accordingly, liberalization of trade in agricultural products benefits developing countries to a greater extent. For example, Brazil's soy bean exports have suffered an increase in estimated protection by OECD countries, from an equivalent of 4.5 percent of its total agricultural revenues in 1997 to 23.1 percent in 2000. Equivalent protection against sugar exports was 48.9 percent of total agricultural revenue in 2000 in the case of the EU and 47.1 percent in the case of the US. The same situation occurs in natural orange juice exports, which are subject to a tariff of $8.32 per liter on entering the US, i.e. 50 percent of the price. Argentina's meat exports face an "ad valorem" tariff of 174.9 percent on entering the European Union, and its exports to Japan bear a tariff of 195 percent on dairy products and 282 percent on vegetable oil. An OECD study (2001c) has calculated average, protective tariffs for "in-quota," "over-quota," and "out-quota" agricultural imports by its country members. The average tariffs are striking, ranging anything between 100 percent and 155 percent for in-quota products, between 121 percent and 546 percent for over-quota products, and between 29 percent and 129 percent for out-quota products.

Protective tariffs and national aid in OECD countries increase price stability in the protected markets but they simultaneously destabilize prices in world markets by limiting the percentage of world supply and demand that is most price-sensitive. Developing countries suffer most from this instability as they have fewer resources available to smooth income–expenditure flows. Liberalizing agricultural trade would reduce price instability of these products in the world markets by two-thirds (Tyers and Anderson, 1992).

Nevertheless, liberalizing world agricultural trade would also involve sizeable adjustment costs for developing countries. Eliminating only aid and subsidies in developed countries would have a negative effect on these countries, with the exception of Argentina, Brazil, and India, for two main reasons; first, because of variations in the real terms of trade (i.e. the relative price of each agricultural export in relation to that of each agricultural import), as the prices of the most subsidized products would increase for developing countries, which are net importers of these products, and farmers in developed countries would switch to other crops; and, second, because of intrinsic problems (related to climate and land) faced by developing countries in substituting their agricultural imports from developed countries, which would have increased in price following the elimination of export subsidies.

For this reason, it is vital that the reduction of agricultural protection and the elimination of export subsidies in developed countries be accompanied by a simultaneous reduction in protective tariffs in developing countries, as this would create a net transfer of income to developing country consumers while at the same time reducing protection to developed countries, meaning that farmers' income in developing countries would also be improved. In other words, in general, farmers in developing countries would benefit more than those in developed countries as they face greater barriers on their principal exports, while consumers in developed countries would benefit much more (due to the lower cost of subsidies and the lower price of imports) than those in developing countries, which are net importers of the products most subsidized by developed countries; therefore, the elimination of subsidies and protection in both groups needs to be simultaneous (IMF and World Bank, 2002).

In conclusion, reference should be made to analyses, which have tried to calculate the effect in terms of improved income and welfare. First, Brown, Deardoff, and Stern (2001) calculated that a further 33 percent reduction in total tariffs (on goods and services) in the Millennium Round would give a one-off increase in global welfare of approximately $600 billion, compared to the $75 billion increase achieved by the Uruguay Round. The bulk of this improvement would come from the reduction in agricultural protection since, while the average protective tariffs on industrial products have fallen from 40 percent to 4 percent in the last 50 years, tariffs on agricultural products have remained at 40 percent. The improvement would be much greater if the same percentage of agricultural aid, which amounts to $300 billion (roughly the GDP of sub-Saharan Africa), were eliminated.

The joint study by the IMF and the World Bank (2002) extensively quoted in this chapter, concerning the liberalization of trade in agricultural produce, textiles, and clothing, i.e. removal of protective tariffs, quotas, and subsidies (which have the biggest impact on developing countries), has calculated that total liberalization of agricultural trade would reduce the loss of income and export revenues – i.e. increase disposable income – by $566 billion per year, whereas liberalizing trade in textiles and clothing would reduce the loss of income and export revenues by $136 billion per year, i.e. a total of more than $700 billion a year for all countries.

The Doha Development Agenda

There is at present an interesting debate about the efficiency of the Multilateral Trade Organizations, the GATT and the WTO, to liberalize trade. In two papers, Andrew Rose (2002a and 2002b) shows that these organizations have not fulfilled their tasks of reducing protection and increasing trade. In his first paper, using a "gravity model" of bilateral merchandise trade and a large IMF panel data set covering 175 countries over 50 years, Rose does not find sufficient evidence of positive significant effects of GATT/WTO membership on encouraging trade, while the GSP does not seem to have a strong effect either although being associated with an approximate doubling of trade. The gravity model shows that bilateral trade cannot be linked to membership in WTO or its predecessor the GATT. Thus, the explanation of trade growing faster than income for many years must have had other candidates such as higher rates of productivity in tradable goods, falling transport costs, regional trade associations and integrations, converging tastes, growing international liquidity, and changing endowments.

In his second paper Rose uses 68 measures of trade policy and trade liberalization to ask if membership in these organizations is associated with more liberal trade policy and finds out that almost no measures of trade policy are significantly correlated with GATT or WTO membership. For instance, India has been a founding member of GATT since 1948 and by 1987 its tariff revenues still reached 53 percent of import values! Comparable tariff data exist for 91 countries in 1987, at which time 89 countries had lower tariffs than India, 23 of these 89 countries were not members of GATT and they had tariff rates averaging 15.7 percent and GATT members collected tariffs averaged 11.4 percent. The only exception to this negative rule is that WTO members tend to have slightly more freedom as judged by the Heritage Foundation's index of economic freedom.

Subramanian and Wei (2003) also using a gravity trade model disagree partially with Rose's findings. They show that the GATT/WTO have done an excellent job of promoting trade wherever it was designed to do so and correspondingly failed to promote trade wherever the designed rules militated against it. The WTO has served to increase industrial country imports by about 68 percent through successive rounds of tariff liberalization, but it has partially failed to increase imports of developing countries because they were exempted from the basic GATT/WTO mission of progressively lowering import barriers under the so-called principle of Special and Differential Treatment (SDT).

Luckily, given that industrial countries have accounted for nearly two-thirds of global imports during the period 1950–2000, the positive impact on global trade has been substantial, creating an additional 44 percent worth of current world trade. They stress that the above does not imply that developing countries have not benefited from WTO membership. A distinction needs to be made between developing country WTO members as exporters and importers. Their results suggest that there has been limited impact of WTO membership on developing country imports, but the positive impact of WTO membership on industrial country imports meant that imports from developing countries (namely, developing country exports) also increased significantly, about one-third.

Nevertheless, WTO permissiveness toward developing countries has changed since the Uruguay Round. The good news is that new

173

members are significantly different from old members in that membership in WTO for the former group is associated with an increase in imports close to 30 percent relative to non-members. The bad news is that the Uruguay Round has had little effect on the old members, who continue to be no more open than non-WTO members even in the aftermath of the Round. SDT of developing countries is still alive and well for old members. Finally, another item of bad news is that WTO membership in sectors with high protection in the industrial countries (food, clothing, and footwear) has had no impact on trade.

The new Millennium Round launched at Doha in November 2001 was after all aiming at opening markets in order to foster growth and alleviate poverty in the developing world, but the strong disagreement at the next meeting in Cancun provoked almost a collapse of the multilateral trade negotiations, notwithstanding the positive emergence of the G90 and the G22.

Before Cancun, public opinions were focusing on the interpretation of the TRIPs agreement on the enforcement of intellectual property rights for medicines. The possibility to take measures (compulsory licenses and production of generic drugs) to protect health in case of diseases such as AIDS had been reaffirmed in Doha, and the translation of this position in terms of specific policies independently from the outcome of Cancun has been a major achievement in economic terms and from the moral point of view (Bell, Devarajan, and Gersbach, 2003). But there are a series of other key issues incorporated in the Doha agenda on which progress has been delayed following Cancun (Fontagné, 2003).

Some implementation related issues have been raised by the unbalanced deal concluded in Marrakech. The developing world considers that developed economies have not fulfilled their commitment concerning the pace of liberalization in labor intensive industries, such as the implementation of the Agreement on Textiles and Clothing (ATC) whereas their own commitments, especially in intellectual property, were disproportionate. The next item is agriculture. The ambiguous formulation regarding "reductions of, with a view to phasing out, all forms of export subsidies" is only part of the problem. Market access, as well as "distorting domestic policies" (meaning domestic subsidies), are also key issues. Moreover, the negotiation on services, on market access for non-agricultural products and the sensitive Singapore subjects are still at stake.

The Doha agenda is also taking into consideration, for the first time, the specific needs of least developed countries (LDCs). On the one side, the target of quota-free market access for products originating from LDCs is endorsed at the declaration; as well the importance of provisions regarding SDT for LDCs is reaffirmed. The problem with these countries is that if market access is favorable to their growth, then liberalizing imports in the developed countries on a multilateral basis will erode the margin of preference conceded to them and will reduce their relative access to these markets. Moreover, if less distorting domestic agricultural subsidies in developed countries increases world prices of food products, then LDC, which are net importers of food will be adversely affected through a negative terms of trade effect, that is, their import prices will go up faster than their export prices and they will be net losers (Fontagné, 2003).

Improving market access is still an "unfinished business" according to the WTO. Despite low average levels of protection, as I mentioned earlier, agriculture and labor intensive industries carry a much higher level of protection than the average and the dispersion of tariffs within sectors can be very large too, due to tariff peaks. Thus, a uniform duty equal to the mean tariff would be welfare improving and less easy to be captured by vested interests. On top of this, a large variety of non-tariff instruments are used to protect markets which make it even more difficult to measure protection.

The simple average of "bound tariffs," that is, the upper limit for applied tariffs, on which the importing country has made a commitment, is 5.2 percent for Canada, 4.1 percent for the EU, 3.9 percent for the US and 3.5 percent for Japan. In agriculture, the simple average bound rates are estimated to be 19.5 percent for the EU, 11.7 percent for Japan, 5.5 percent for the US, and 4.6 percent for Canada, according to the OECD, but the World Bank estimates are higher: 20 percent, 29.7 percent, 9 percent, and 8.8 percent respectively. The new database on trade barriers developed by the ITC (UCTAD/WTO) in collaboration with CEPII (Bouet, Bureau, Decreux, and Jean, 2001) shows that Canada (6.7 percent) and Japan (10.7 percent) are more protected than the EU (3.9 percent) and the US (4.1 percent).

Developing countries are even more protective of their markets. The simple average of bound tariffs for industrial products oscillates, for instance, between 17 percent and 31 percent. The estimated simple average of tariffs for agriculture oscillates between 80 percent and 120 percent according to the OECD and 101 percent and 105 percent according to the World Bank.

According to the WTO, there are 10.5 percent of tariff lines with applied most favored nation (MFN) duties above 15 percent (the threshold corresponding to the international definition of tariff peaks) in Canada, 1.7 percent in the EU, 4.3 percent in the US, and 3.3 percent in Japan. In total there are more than 1,000 HS6 positions affected by tariff peaks in these four economies (Hoekman, Ng, and Olarreaga, 2001). These tariff peaks are concentrated in sugar, tobacco, cereals, fruit and vegetables, and fish products, as well as in footwear and clothing. LDC countries are the most severely affected. Their share of affected exports is much larger than the developing world average: 15 percent as opposed to 8 percent on the US market and 30 percent as opposed to 12 percent on Canada.

In addition to tariffs, quotas have been steadily maintained under ATC, because the industrial countries have liberalized very slowly and choose the less sensitive products first. This lack of market access might be an explanation of the poor performance of LDC in world trade since the 1970s. While the share of developing countries as a whole in world exports rose from one-quarter to one-third, the share of LDCS declined from 1.9 percent to 0.5 percent (IMF–WB, 2002).

Moreover, there are a large number of protective measures applied at the border (TBT and SPS) to avoid allogenic species, predators, and diseases that must be notified to the WTO. On the basis of notifications less than one-quarter of the product categories identified at the HS6 level of the nomenclature are traded free of any barrier. Conversely, the remaining products accounting for 88 percent of world merchandise trade do face at least one measure justified on environmental grounds in one market and 13 percent of world trade is effectively affected by such measures (Fontagné and Pajot, 2002). Food products are the most affected especially fish, meat, and other animal products. While the share of LDC exports of products potentially affected by these measures is below the world average, their share of directly affected exports (40 percent) is much higher than the average.

A key achievement of the Uruguay Round has been to extend multilateral discipline to domestic support in the farming sector as well as to export subsidies. The so-called "boxes" characterize what is prohibited, allowed or to be phased out. Even if the amount of domestic support granted to farmers has hardly decreased in the OECD a slight reduction of domestic distortions has been observed. But, the associated increase in agricultural output in the OECD countries, due to this support, combined with reduced imports by rich countries, is estimated to flatten world prices at the expense of developing countries (Watkins, 2003).

What should be the multilateral formula to liberalize agriculture and industrial products' present protection? It would require very simple liberalization schemes. Concerning market access for products, there are 146 WTO members negotiating on thousands of products. Under such circumstances any means for simplifying negotiations would be preferred by them. This is why a "formula approach" consisting in the systematic compression of tariffs based on simple arithmetic approaches should be chosen. There are two contending formulas at this round.

On the one hand, there is the "Swiss formula" (proposed by Switzerland in the Tokyo Round in the 1970s, but not supported for Switzerland in the current agriculture negotiations) which produces much steeper cuts on higher tariffs, because the target tariff depends non-linearly on the initial tariff. On the other hand there is the linear approach of the Uruguay Round, which applies the same percentage reductions no matter what the starting tariff rate is. Supporters of the Swiss method say that it is needed to deal with the tariff peaks. Supporters of the linear formula say that it is more simple and flexible. The present draft proposal, called the "banded approach," is a compromise between the linear Uruguay Round and the harmonizing Swiss formula. It envisages a Uruguay Round approach that is applied in bands with steeper cuts at higher levels, making it a kind of harmonizing formula but with flexibility. Thus, actual cuts can vary around the averages so long as they are above the minimums set for each product ("tariff line"). This approach is also intended toward reducing tariff peaks and tariff escalation.

This formula approach apparently fits well with the objectives of the Doha Development Agenda (DDA) by strongly reducing tariff peaks, by offering better access to LDC exports in agriculture and labor intensive manufactures, by largely opening other developing countries' markets that remain highly protected and thus stimulating South–South trade, by offering different coefficients of reductions for developed and developing countries, respecting the spirit of the SDT and for different coefficients for trade in manufactures and food products to match obvious political economy constraints (Fontagné, 2003).

Nevertheless, the two latter supposed advantages contradict the objective of making agricultural markets more open or of enhancing South–South trade. The key issue here is the erosion of preferences and thus a breakdown of developing countries into sub-groups may be necessary. Any non-linear formula approach will have two effects: first, to eradicate the remaining peaks faced by LDC exporters and second to erode the margin of preference these LDCs have been granted. The net effect could be negative for them (Ianchovichina, Mattoo, and Olarreaga, 2001). While free access for peak products limited to LDC would lead to an 11 percent increase in their total exports, the extension of free access to other developing countries would halve such a benefit and a further reduction of the MFN duty of 5 percent would result in such benefits disappearing for LDC countries (Hoekman, Ng, and Olarreaga, 2002).

The remaining developing countries are in a different situation: they are not covered by recent initiatives in favor of poor countries (ACP, GSP, AGOA, and EBA), and they do not benefit from such a preferential access. These countries should therefore strongly lobby in favor of a non-linear formula (Fontagné, 2003).

The expected results of the Doha Round have been calculated using computable general equilibrium models (CGE) deconstructing the benefits of the various items in the Doha agenda. On the basis of a linear reduction of tariffs of 50 percent for industrial and food products, in border measures for services, in export subsidies and in domestic support, Francois, van Meijl, and van Tongeren (2003) find that liberalization at the border in agriculture (27 percent of world gains) leads to larger gains than market access for non-agriculture products (16 percent) and even less for services (11 percent).

A recent analysis by Anderson, Martin, and van der Mensbrugghe (2005), using the latest GTAP and the World Bank LINKAGE model, shows that moving to free merchandise trade would boost real incomes in sub-Saharan Africa proportionally more than in other developing countries or high-income countries, despite a terms-of-trade loss in parts of the region. Net farm incomes would rise substantially, alleviating rural poverty. A Doha partial liberalization would be the more positive the more developing countries themselves cut tariffs, particularly on agricultural imports.

But the striking result of the Francois et al. analysis is that a reduction in domestic supports only secures 4 percent of total gains, while the most favored by the domestic support reduction are the same developed countries. Therefore, tariff reductions matter much more for the developing world than domestic support cuts of developed countries. Reductions in domestic support alone will produce a very limited welfare gain at the world level, resulting in a welfare gain for the EU and Japan, and a loss elsewhere, in particular in LDC and ACP countries. In contrast, a reduction in border protection alone would lead to larger gains at the world level, shared among all country groups, with the exception of the former Soviet Union. Nevertheless, there are limits to these computations. First, as was argued before, preferential access is generally associated with the enforcement of rules of origin for exported products, hindering LDCs from taking full advantage of their preferences; and second, trade preferences without MFN access for products of interest to other developing countries will not benefit the majority of the world's poor, since most of them live outside LDC (Hoekman, 2003).

But there is also some concern about OECD tariff reductions translating into worsening export performance for the LDC, provoking larger erosion to their trade preferences. Francois, Hoekman, and Manchin (2005) confirm that trade preferences are underutilized because administrative barriers and burdens (estimated to be at least 4 percent on average) reduce the magnitude of the erosion costs significantly, even under a full elimination of OECD tariffs and hence full MFN liberalization-based preference erosion, and that the erosion problem is primarily bilateral rather than a WTO-based concern. Finally, trade liberalization has to be combined with aid to those countries which will have difficulty competing in world markets in order to alleviate their level of poverty. Trade liberalization is a necessary condition for growth, but there are other factors that need to be tackled such as the enhancement and development of quality institutions, education, health, and domestic savings, which need the help of aid to be accelerated.

Anderson and Valenzuela (2005), using the GTAP database (Hertel, 1997) and the GTAP–AGR model of the global economy (Keeney and Hertel, 2005) have found out: first, full global globalization of goods and services trade would raise net farm income in all six developing country regions, and more than it would raise non-agricultural value added. Second, global liberalization would not raise net farm incomes in each and every developing country; Bangladesh, India, the Philippines, and Russia would be exceptions because of their high agricultural protection rates in the GTAP database. Third, developed countries' agricultural protectionist policies depress agricultural value added in developing countries, notwithstanding their tariff preferences to numerous low-income countries, while several large developing countries (Bangladesh, India, China, and Indonesia) help rather than harm agricultural relative to non-agricultural value added, with the harm from their own non-agricultural policies being more than offset by help from their own agricultural policies. In sum, a multilateral move to global free trade would be good for developing country farmers.

Hoekman (2004) argues that simplicity and determination will help in achieving a final deal at the Doha round of the WTO. For instance, no matter which system is finally chosen to reduce tariffs, the ultimate goal should be the complete removal of tariffs on goods that are of export interest to developing countries. It would be a good decision to eliminate all of them by 2015, the target date for the achievement of the Millennium Development Goals. The quick elimination of agricultural export subsidies and the decoupling of domestic subsidies should be the second goal. Stronger disciplines in antidumping should be the third. Strong reductions or the elimination of the external levels of reciprocal preferences (PTAs) and non reciprocal preferences (MFNs) are also essential. The best way should be to agree on a single preferential rate equal to zero. Given their erosion effect on actual preferences enjoyed by the least developed countries by eliminating them, those countries affected should be subsidized directly with aid. Developing countries should also lower their own barriers as a trade-off to encourage South–South trade which is increasing fast. This could be achieved by eliminating the difference between their bound and applied rates, as the OECD members are doing.

Unfortunately, the most recent meeting of the Doha Round in Hong Kong has not met the expectations. Results have been rather poor. The only important agreement has been the decision, by OECD countries, to eliminate progressively and in parallel all of their forms of export subsidies, including those that have an equivalent effect (as food aid, state trading, and export credits) before 2013, and to eliminate most of them before 2011. But, first, the amount of these subsidies is small, only around $5 billion; second, this long-term deadline is still subject to the end result of other parallel negotiations about modalities and about potential agreements about their access to non-agricultural markets in developing countries; third, the EU and the US are going to maintain their national subsidies to agriculture, and fourth, the cotton negotiation, so important to some African countries did not reach a final agreement. A second positive but disputed step has been to give the 50 least developed countries a duty-free and quota-free market access on 97 percent of import lines by the EU, Japan, and the US, by 2008, but their value, already small, will decline as most favored nation tariffs decline.

Nevertheless, hope should not be lost yet. Given that the fast-track authority by the US Congress to the US government to negotiate trade agreements ends in the middle of 2007, a major effort should already be made before the next agreed negotiating deadline (April 30, 2006) to try to continue negotiating a trade-off between agricultural and some high labor content manufacturing protection, by the OECD countries, against industrial and manufacturing protection, by developing countries. Time is running short and expectations are diminishing, but the historical experience of past Rounds shows that there is always a last-minute positive agreement for reducing the world's trade protection.

Despite all these shortcomings, trade prospects for developing countries are improving. The WTO (2005) annual report on world trade in 2004 and prospects for 2005 shows that developing countries' goods trade share has surged to a 54-year peak. Their share in merchandise world trade has increased sharply, in 2004, to 31 percent of the total, the highest since 1950. Total real merchandise exports have increased by 9 percent, up 9.5, 5.5, and 4 percent, respectively, from 2001, 2002, and 2003 and nominal merchandise exports have increased by 21 percent, the highest in 25 years due to a combination of real growth (9 percent) and a sharp increase in dollar prices (11 percent). The Asian region recorded the highest volume of real merchandise export growth in 2004. China's real exports increased by 14.5 percent, Korea and Singapore in excess of 20 percent, and Japan by 11 percent. South and Central America increased its real exports by 13 percent. The CIS countries' real exports increased by 12 percent, North America and Europe by 6.9 and 6.2 percent respectively, and finally, Africa and the Middle East by 4.6 percent.

Real exports earnings stimulated world imports of merchandise in developing countries. Asian real merchandise imports grew by 14.2 percent, South and Central America by 18.2 percent, the CIS by 16.2 percent, Africa and the Middle East by 12 percent, North America by 10 percent and Europe by 6 percent, showing their relative growth rates, price developments, and exchange rate changes. Finally, commercial services exports increased in nominal terms by 16 percent, 5 percent less than nominal merchandise exports. Within the top 30 leading exporters of merchandise trade 13 are developing countries and among the top 30 importers 14 are developing countries. If intra-European Union at 25 is excluded, the number of developing countries in the top 30 increases to 22 in both cases.

Chapter 8

More Foreign Direct Investment to Developing Countries

One major puzzle in globalization is why capital does not flow sufficiently between countries (the Feldstein–Horioka puzzle, 1980) or from rich to poor countries (the Lucas paradox, 1990). According to the standard neoclassical theory, capital should flow from countries with a lower marginal product of capital (MPK) to those with a higher marginal product of capital or, what is the same, from countries where capital is abundant and, therefore, cheap to countries where it is scarce and expensive. As a result, differences in income per capita reflect differences in capital per capita. If capital were allowed to flow freely, new investments would flow into the poorer countries until the return on investments were equalized in all countries. Why is this not happening effectively enough in some developing countries and not at all in certain others?

There are different explanations. First, because the usual assumptions of the neoclassical model (countries producing the same good, with the same constant returns to scale in production technology using capital and labor as factors of production) do not hold in the real world (Krugman, 2001a). If capital accumulation is subject to external economies and increasing returns to scale, those countries with greater capital endowments may enjoy comparative advantage in those sectors which are capital intensive and highly productive, thus, the profitability of capital (or MPK) may be greater in countries with a greater capital stock and, conversely to the model, they will be able to attract flows from countries with a lower capital stock.

Second, it may be due to differences in the economic "fundamentals" such as the productive structure of the economy, to its technological differences, to missing factors of production, to different government policies and to different institutional structures (Alfaro, Kalemli-Ozcan, and Volosovych, 2005). Lucas (1990) thinks that poor countries have also lower endowments of factors complementary with physical capital, such as human capital and lower total factor productivity (TFP). Lucas finds out that accounting for the differences in human capital quality across countries significantly reduces the return differentials and considering the role of human capital externalities eliminates the return differentials; thus, large differences in capital–labor ratios may coexist with MPK equalization. However his calculations assume that the externalities from the stock of human capital accrue entirely to the local producers, that is, all knowledge spillovers are local. This assumption is at odds with the evidence of large international knowledge spillovers (Helpman, 2004).

Third, it may be the result of international capital market imperfections, mainly sovereign risk and asymmetric information (see more in chapter 9). The reason is that, although capital has a higher return in developing countries, there are market failures or political risks that impede capital flow to them. It can be a taxation issue (Gordon and Bovenberg, 1996) or market inefficiencies (Gertler and Rogoff, 1990; Caselli and Feyrer, 2005) or world capital markets segmentation (Lucas, 1990) or credit frictions (Stulz, 2005) or developing countries' history of serial defaults (Reinhart and Rogoff, 2004) or overborrowing (Uribe, 2006), etc.

Recent empirical evidence is rather split. On the one side, Alfaro, Kalemli-Ozcan, and Volosovych (2005) have found out that the quality of institutions is a key explanatory factor for these puzzles. Using ordinary least squares (OLS) they estimate that improving the quality of institutions to the UK's level from that of Turkey's implies a 60 percent increase in foreign investment and that improving Peru's institutional quality to Australia's level implies a quadrupling of foreign investment.

On the other hand, Caselli and Feyrer (2005) find out: first, the MPK differences are so high that different endowments of complementary production factors or of TPF levels are not the only cause of differences in capital intensity. Second, MKP differences can be sustained even in a world unencumbered by any form of segmentation, discrimination or agency cost, because even if poor-country agents have access to unlimited borrowing and lending at the same conditions offered to rich country agents, the MPK will be higher in poor countries if the relative price of capital goods (relative to output) is higher there.

Third, the cost of credit frictions has been declining over time, as a result of higher integration of financial markets world-wide. As a matter of fact, differences in the rate of return on investing in physical capital are only slightly higher in the developing sample and the cost of these differences in terms of forgone world GPD drops to about one-third of the cost implied by MPK differences. As a conclusion, they find that the world allocation of physical capital is inefficient and that the reason why poor countries have higher MPK, even in the presence of fairly free capital flows, is that they face higher costs of installing capital in terms of forgone consumption and that as financial rates of return are fairly similar in rich and poor countries, additional development aid flows to developing countries are likely to be offset by private flows in the opposite direction to restore the rate of return equalization.

Despite this theory and evidence, one of the most important new features in international capital markets in recent years has been the sharp increase in the influx of foreign direct investment (FDI) into developed and, particularly, developing countries. Maybe this fact makes FDI a different capital flow to others.

FDI inflows to developing countries started to increase from $25 billion in 1990 to $180 billion in 1999; since then they have slowly declined to $150 billion in 2003 but have risen again to $233 billion in 2004 and to $274 billion in 2005, the highest ever (World Investment Report, UNCTAD, 2005). In 1990, FDI flows to developing countries were smaller than official flows, but in 2005, they were four times larger than official flows and three times bigger than portfolio flows. In relative terms, total FDI flows are very important since, while they represent today 8 percent of total domestic investment worldwide, they are relatively more important for developing countries, where they reach 11 percent of domestic investment, and they are essential for the least developed countries, where they represent 17 percent of domestic investment (World Investment Report, UNCTAD, 2005). Finally, although the ratio of the stock of FDI to world output rose from 5.3 percent in 1980 to 7.8 percent in 1990 and to 21.9 percent in 2004, in the case of developing countries, FDI has increased relatively further, from 10 percent of their GDP in 1980 to 33 percent of their GDP in 2004.

Total gross FDI inflows grew from approximately $180 billion in 1991 to $1.4 trillion in 2000, although they fell by 41 percent in 2001 to around $818 billion, affecting developed more than developing countries and continued to fall in 2002 to $679 billion, in 2003 to $637 billion, but they have recovered again in 2004 going up to $695 billion, in 2005 where they have reached $897 billion, and in 2006 when they amounted to $1.2 trillion. Nevertheless, if we ignore 2000 as a very atypical year, total FDI inflows have multiplied by five between 1991 and 2006 while inflows in developing countries multiplied by five and a half in the same period. After 2000, FDI inflows in developed countries have fallen much more than those in developing countries because the big jump in FDI flows in the second half of the 1990s was mainly directed to developed countries through a huge increase in M&As.

Total FDI inflows to emerging countries are much lower than those to developed countries but their share of the total has been increasing since 2000 from 18 percent in 2000 to 31 percent of the total in 2005. Nevertheless, it should be recalled that in 1914 the developing countries received 62.8 percent of all FDI and in 1938 they received 65.7 percent (UNCTAD, 2001). In other words, they are still far from historic levels but their prospects are very positive.

In 2005 FDI flows to developing economies reached $274 billion, up 13 percent from 2004 and 53 percent from 2000. Asia received 63 percent of the total ($173 billion), where China plus Hong Kong represented 37 percent of the total ($100 billion). Latin America and the Caribbean got 26.3 percent of the total ($72 billion), where Mexico reached 6.3 percent of the total ($17.2 billion) and Brazil 5.7 percent ($15.5 billion). Africa received only 10.5 percent of that figure

($29 billion). Not included as developing country, Russia received $26.1 billion, almost as much as Africa.

That is, FDI flows continue to be concentrated in a handful of developing countries, notably China, followed by Russia, Mexico, Singapore, and Brazil, making 64 percent of the total flows to developing countries. According to the OECD, the FDI flows from the 30 OECD countries into developing countries in 2004 have almost doubled from $134 billion in 2003 to $261 billion in 2004 (OECD, 2005). The developing countries with the largest OECD FDI flows were China with $55 billion, the Asian financial centers of Singapore and Hong Kong with $50 billion and Brazil with $18 billion. By contrast, India only received $5.3 billion. These figures show a similar concentration since five emerging market economies account for 60 percent of FDI and 88 percent of the increase.

In terms of stocks, Latin America has the highest stock of FDI coming from OECD countries with $391 billion, followed by Asia with $328 billion and Africa with $73.3 billion. It is also interesting to see that OECD FDI stocks are very much determined by ex-colonial heritage, cultural affinity, or proximity. The US invests mainly in Latin America, followed by Asia and very little in Africa, Japan invests 90 percent of its total in Asia and western Europe invests mainly in eastern Europe and Russia (Germany and Italy) but also in Latin America (Spain, Switzerland, and the UK) and Africa (France and the UK).

There are two clear trends in FDI worth mentioning. The first is the increase in South–South FDI flows, which represent already one-third of the total in spite of the heavy toll that the Asian financial crises in 1997 and the Latin American financial crises later, due to their faster increase than FDI by developed countries since the early 1990s (UNCTAD, 2004). China, for instance is a major investor in other developing countries in commodities and energy but also in manufacturing. Other medium- and high-income developing economies such as Malaysia, South Korea, Taiwan, Hong Kong, Singapore, Chile, Mexico, South Africa, and lately Brazil and India, are investing in other developing economies. If their FDI outflows are viewed in relation to their gross fixed capital formation a number of developing economies such as Singapore, Hong Kong (China), Taiwan, and Chile rank higher than a number of developed countries such as Germany, Japan, and the US.

The second important trend is the increasing FDI in services. Although FDI has grown over time in all three sectors – primary, manufacturing, and services – its composition by sector has shifted toward services. FDI in the primary sector is driven by natural resource-rich areas; manufacturing is increasingly geared to capital and technology-intensive activities although offshoring of labor-intensive manufacturing is still quite high, while FDI in services has generally been growing in both capital-intensive and labor-intensive industries.

The inward and outward FDI stocks in the primary sector more than doubled between 1990 and 2002, driven almost totally by outflows coming from developed countries, although its share of the total fell from 9 percent to 6 percent because of the higher growth in manufacturing and services. The FDI stocks in manufacturing rose nearly three-fold during the same period, but they also fell from 42 percent to 34 percent over the said period, given the higher growth in services. Finally, the FDI stocks in services more than quadrupled during the same period increasing its share to 60 percent compared to 50 percent a decade earlier. In 2004, 63 percent of total M&As were concluded in services. According to the *McKinsey Quarterly* (2005) service workers offshoring by multinational corporations has jumped in the last 5 years from 250,000 in 2000, to 1.5 million in 2004 and it is expected to be 4.1 million in 2008. McKinsey calculates that, at present, only up to 11 percent of all services would be able to be outsourced to a distant place, either in the same country or abroad.

Nevertheless, although FDI flows to developing countries are still highly concentrated in a relatively small number of them, this trend is starting to abate since there are other new developing countries attracting increasing volumes of FDI flows, thanks to the liberalization of their FDI regimes. Since the late 1990s, 394 countries have introduced 1,121 changes in laws and regulations affecting FDI, 1,031 of which were in the direction of more liberalization. During the same period, there has also been a proliferation of bilateral investment treaties (BITs) and double taxation treaties (DTTs) concluded among developed and developing countries and between developing countries as well, bringing the totals to 2,392 and 2,559 respectively. BITs between developing and emerging countries account for 35 percent and between developed and developing countries for 40 percent. DTTs, between developing countries and between emerging countries have reached 19 percent of the total and between developed and developing countries 39 percent of the total.

Another reason why the future for FDI flows to developing countries looks brighter is demographic shifts. According to the United Nations (2005) by 2050 developed countries are going to have a very small proportion of the world's population (13.6 percent of the total) when in 1950 it was 32.3 percent, and, in 2005, 18.7 percent of the world's total, and their population is going to get older (their median age is going to go up from 38 in 2005 to 48 in 2050), which means with a low rate of consumption in relation to their income. Thus, the future large markets in the world are going to be in Asia, Africa, and Latin America, not in the US or the EU and even less in Japan. The recent increasing trend of offshoring and outsourcing manufacturing and services to developing countries is not only based on looking for cheaper labor but mainly on looking for future markets.

The main drivers of FDI are multinational corporations (MNCs) that are now around 70,000 with 700,000 foreign affiliates, representing an FDI stock of $9.0 trillion, a total employment of 60 million people and total sales by foreign affiliates reaching $19.0 trillion. International production within them remains also fairly concentrated: in 2002, the world's 100 largest MNCs (0.14 percent of the total) of which only 4 are based in developing countries, accounted for 14 percent of sales by foreign affiliates world-wide, 12 percent of their total assets and 13 percent of the total employment. Thus, MNCs from developed countries will continue to drive FDI flows, but increasingly, MNCs from developing countries are also contributing to FDI growth. Their share in the global FDI flows rose, from less than 6 percent of the total in the mid-1990s, to 11 percent in the latter half of the 1990s, and later fell to 7 percent in 2003. They account now for about one-tenth of the global outward FDI stock ($900 billion) and they are growing abroad at a faster rate than their developed country counterparts. Nevertheless, in the not too distant future China, India, Russia, Brazil, and Mexico, among other developing countries, are going to have very large MNCs investing in the rest of the world and competing fiercely with those of developed countries (UNCTAD, 2004).

Types of Foreign Direct Investment

Although many critics of globalization argue that FDI decreases exports and depresses salaries in home countries by transferring production to developing countries, and that it also depresses salaries in host countries due to exploitation of disenfranchised workers and minors and by displacing less competitive local companies, most empirical evidence proves the contrary.

First, there are two ways of looking at FDI. The first is to see FDI as an international capital flow from the home to the host country. This item appears in the capital account of the balance of payments as an inflow and outflow in the respective country. The second aspect is the activity and operations undertaken in the host country by companies which are partly or fully controlled by home country companies. These activities include production, employment, sales, capital goods and intermediate products purchases, and research, whose impact does not appear in balance of payments statistics. These activities are frequently not undertaken in the same sector as the home country company or in the same host country, and they may not be performed in the same home country, with the result that the balance of payments figures do not sufficiently reflect the final extent of the FDI. For example, the production derived from FDI, i.e. production by companies located outside their owners' country of residence, represented 6 percent of world GDP in 1990 and 10 percent in 2000, which is more than $3 trillion, equivalent to nearly 30 percent of the US GDP (Lipsey, 2001 and 2002a; UNCTAD, 2001).

Second, if country A invests directly in country B, this does not always mean that new physical capital and production are added to country B at the expense of reducing country A's capital and production. In fact, it often happens in developed countries that country A invests in country B, but the stock of physical capital and the production levels remain unaltered in both countries. For example, the owners and executives of industry X in country A, based on the knowledge and skill acquired there, buy companies from less skilled proprietors in industry X in country B and operate those companies' plants much more efficiently than before. The former proprietors in country B invest the proceeds of the sale or lend it to other executives in country B who are experts in industry Y, enabling them to buy out other less-skilled entrepreneurs in industry Y in country A (Markusen and Maskus, 2001).

Consequently, there are two fundamental types of FDI. The first is based on the comparative advantages of countries for the location of production which is acceptably reflected in capital flows in the balance of payments since there is a net transfer of financial and production resources from one country to another. The second type is determined by the comparative advantages of companies and their executives where there might not even be capital flows between the two countries, as in the case of mergers and acquisitions paid for with the buyer's own stock.

The first type of FDI implies changes in the industrial structure of production and employment in the home and host countries. Normally, these changes consist of a transfer of the production of labor-intensive or natural resource-intensive goods and services from developed to developing countries. The second type of FDI has implications for the ownership of production but not necessarily for its location. The proof is that in the US the percentage of production and employment of US-owned manufacturing companies has fallen since the 1980s by the same proportion as the increase of foreign-owned subsidiaries. The first type of FDI is generally a new investment, typically made from a developed country in a developing country, while the second type is usually an acquisition or a merger between existing companies, taking place between developing countries. This second type has been much more important in the last decade due to the internationalization of large companies from OECD countries, primarily through the boom of mergers and acquisitions (Lipsey, 2002a).

Benefits of Foreign Direct Investment

Contrary to what globalization critics assert both home and host countries tend to benefit from the economic effects of FDI. Below there is a discussion about the empirical research into those effects on home countries and host countries, following the seminal survey by Richard Lipsey (2002b).

Home country benefits

Home countries benefit, first, from specialization in the production of goods and services that are more intensive in capital, technology, and skilled labor, thus greatly increasing their productivity and, therefore, their income and GDP. They achieved this unquestionable advantage by transferring the production of goods and services that are more intensive in labor (or in less-skilled labor) to their subsidiaries in developing countries, i.e. through the internationalization or globalization of most of their production or the phases of production which are less intensive in capital, technology, and lower-skilled labor.

Second, all the studies undertaken to ascertain whether FDI tends to reduce home country exports show that their relationship is complementary and not substitutive, contrary to conventional theory (Markusen, 1997) that horizontal FDI (i.e. when a multinational company decides to produce its final goods in different countries) tends to reduce exports from the parent company's country, whereas vertical FDI (when a multinational company locates different phases of the production of the final product in different countries based on each one's comparative advantages) tends to increase exports between the parent company and its subsidiaries and, consequently, total exports between the host and home countries. The studies performed for the US, Japan, and Sweden (Lipsey, Ramstetter, and Blomstrom, 2000) show that the relationship between FDI and home country exports is positive and the substitution effects which arise are actually small. Even when it was thought that higher unemployment rates in the European Union must be related to the delocalization of production through FDI outflows and lower exports from EU home countries, Fontagné and Pajot (2002), Chedór and Mucchielli (1998), and Chedór, Mucchielli, and Soubaya (2002) show that there was no relationship between the two phenomena in the case of France and that there was a positive correlation between FDI flows and net French exports as a whole and by individual industry.

It is very important to point out in this connection that, though theoretically feasible, it is actually very difficult in practice to differentiate between horizontal and vertical FDI. A multinational's foreign operations include similar activities to those of the parent company, and it is also very difficult to identify all the segments of production in an industry. The operation in the host country may omit certain activities of the parent company because they are performed by a subsidiary and may include some activities which are not carried out by the parent company because they are undertaken by local companies other than the subsidiary or by foreign suppliers which do not exist in the parent company's home country. Likewise, substitution between FDI and the home country's exports only arose prior to globalization, when many countries had high barriers to imports and, since it was not possible to export to countries whose markets were large enough to be attractive, the decision was taken to produce the goods in question in that country as it was less expensive than paying high duties or avoiding the stringent contingencies or quotas which made exporting impossible. Today the situation is very different. Trade is determined by other factors such as comparative advantages in production, transport costs, factor endowments, exchange rates, etc. FDI is closely related not so much to location as to ownership. What moves between countries is not so much physical as intellectual capital or production techniques, which are not easy to see.

Lastly, a distinction must be made between the home country's exports and its multinationals' exports. The US and Japan's exports of manufactures have steadily lost market share, whereas the market share of their multinationals' exports have increased or remained the same, offsetting most of the fall in their country's market share (Lipsey, 1995). This phenomenon is clearly positive since those multinationals not only exploited their production assets in foreign markets but they have also protected their market shares against unfavorable events in their country of origin, such as currency appreciation or increases in unit labor costs or taxes. This means that market shares must be analyzed more in terms of company ownership than in terms of the traditional account of exports between residents and non-residents in the balance of payments. For example, although the US has a large trade deficit, the sales by subsidiaries of its multinational companies in the countries where they are located triple the amount of exports from the US to the rest of the world. A similar phenomenon is observed in connection with the sales by subsidiaries of European Union or Japanese multinationals in comparison with exports (UNCTAD, 2001).

Another important impact of FDI is that, although it has no major effect on its home countries' exports, it may affect demand for that country's production factors and their prices (Lipsey, 2002b). For example, when its multinationals transfer the production of goods and services that are more intensive in labor, or in low-skilled labor, to developing countries, the parent company's demand for this type of labor in the home country tends to fall and may cause higher unemployment or lower salaries, although it tends to increase its demand for more skilled labor since the skilled labor-intensive production phases are concentrated in the home country.

Studies show that, where multinationals transfer more labor-intensive production to developing countries, the total demand for labor in their home country tends to increase per unit of production since more employees are hired for management, supervision, oversight, design, human resources, and R&D tasks, i.e. skilled labor not directly related to production that tends to offset lower demand for less skilled labor directly involved in production, which has been relocated abroad (Head and Ries, 2002).

However, less skilled labor bears the brunt in many cases since its demand decreases. In any event, this effect also occurs through imports from developing countries of goods and services that are intensive in unskilled labor, even if there is no outward FDI (Slaughter, 2000). It is a relentless natural process of the internationalization of economies that makes more developed countries generally focus on the production of goods and services that are less intensive in labor, particularly lower-skilled labor, and more intensive in capital, technology, and skilled labor, allowing developing countries to cover these types of products and export them to developed countries. Nevertheless, the impact of total demand for imports or of outward FDI on labor has been relatively small to date (Borjas, Freeman, and Katz, 1992 and 1997; Lawrence and Slaughter, 1993; Sachs and Shatz, 1994; Krugman, 1995; Slaughter, 1999).

Recent evidence found by Scheve and Slaughter (2002), using panel data from the UK from 1991 to 1999, claims that FDI may be a key factor contributing to the recent increase of individual worker insecurity. They find that FDI activity in industries in which individuals work is positively correlated with individual perception of economic insecurity. The reason seems to be that risk-averse workers are concerned not only about the level but also about the volatility of their earnings, in particular, volatility from risk of unemployment.

This kind of economic insecurity could eventually contribute to the globalization backlash in at least two ways: first, individuals that perceive globalization contributing to their own economic insecurity are much more likely to develop policy attitudes hostile toward world economic integration. Second, increases in economic insecurity from globalization may generate demands for more generous social insurance that compensates workers for a riskier environment (Rodrik, 1997; Garrett, 1998; Boix, 2002). However, at the same time, globalization tends to limit the capacities of governments to provide for such compensation, given that tax bases are more mobile (Rodrik, 1997; Garrett and Mitchell, 2001; Besley, Griffith, and Klemm, 2001). Thus, individuals may develop concerns about globalization because they believe it reduces the insurance provided by the state for all labor market risks, including those derived from global integration.

Nevertheless, these arguments are highly contested by other empirical evidence. Iversen and Cusack (2000) argue that it is not sufficient to show that international price volatility is correlated with growth volatility and government spending as Rodrik does. Rather, they claim it is necessary either that the price volatility of international markets be greater than in domestic markets or that trade concentrates more than it diversifies economic risks. They present evidence that, at least for advanced economies, there is no correlation between trade or capital markets' openness and volatility of output, earnings, or employment. Thus globalization does not increase insecurity or lead to demands for welfare-state growth. In any case, what developed countries must do is help their displaced workers, increase their level of training and education to help them find other jobs, or, as a last resort, provide for them suitable social benefits in order to prevent them acquiring a pessimistic individual perception of the situation and potentially rejecting the globalization process.

Host country benefits

One of the criticisms leveled at FDI inflows by anti-globalization groups is that multinationals which locate certain phases of their production in developing countries either pay low salaries (taking advantage of the lack of workers' rights in those countries to exploit local employees and even minors), or they pay salaries which are too high and drive up wages in the host country, causing it to lose its comparative advantage in labor costs. Another criticism is that multinationals are "footloose" and they can easily leave one country and move to another one abandoning their domestic workers.

All studies on multinationals' labor processes, not only in developing but also in developed countries, have found that they pay higher wages for similar workers than local private companies (even those of a similar size) in the country in question and they increase them annually to a greater extent than local companies. There are many reasons for this: sometimes because they provide superior technology which allows them to have faster productivity growth, or because the plants are larger and have greater economies of scale, or because they choose the best workers, who are more expensive, or because they buy companies that were already paying high wages, or because they are concentrated in industrial activities or regions where wages are higher. Other reasons are because they seek good public relations, or because it is a requirement of the host country's authorities, or because it is established in the wage policy of the multinational that invests in the said countries – since it does not know the local labor market it pays higher wages to attract the best workers. Finally, it is the case also because they want to have a very low labor turnover after investing in training and education to obtain higher productivity rates or because they are introducing the latest technology and they do not want their workers to transfer it to other local competitors (Haddad and Harrison, 1993; Lipsey, 1994; Harrison, 1996; Ramstetter, 1999; Feliciano and Lipsey, 1999; Griffith and Simpson, 2001; Brown, Deardoff, and Stern, 2003).

The potential "spill-over" effects of these higher salaries on the wages paid by other locally owned domestic companies in the same sector and the effects on the host country's average salaries, either through higher wages at the foreign company or through the foreign company's impact on aggregate demand for labor in the country, have also been studied. The evidence in this case is scant and not very conclusive. According to Lipsey (2002b), it can generally be said that the positive effects of FDI "spill-over" are greater than the negative ones, which, if any, are not high enough to offset the former.

The idea that multinationals exploit child labor does not meet the reality. Edmonds and Pavcnik (2002 and 2004) have carried out extensive cross-country empirical work showing that openness to trade and FDI do not play any significant role in perpetuating the levels of child labor that pervade low-income countries. Foreign companies do not engage children to work in their plants and children working in companies which export to developed countries pay higher wages than those selling only in the domestic market. Flanagan (2002) shows that superior labor standards for children were associated with higher labor costs, but were not affecting exports and that US FDI was greater in countries with better child labor standards.

Child labor is mainly related to two main domestic factors: the imperfection of the local capital markets and the inability of their parents to make negative bequests to their children (Baland and Robinson, 2000). First, due to the low level of development in local capital markets they are unable to borrow today against the earnings that education will bring tomorrow, thus they are forced to work instead of going to school or play. They are not poor in terms of their whole lifecycles but they are unable to borrow on their future earnings. Second, if parents were able to bequeath debts to their children, they could in effect borrow against their offspring's future earnings in order to pay for their present education as happens in most developed countries. Another interesting analysis of child labor versus education is that of Moav (2001) who demonstrates that the persistence of poverty is based on the joint determination of the quantity of children (fertility) and the quality of education in the household under the assumption that individuals' productivity as teachers increases with their own human capital and that the minimum time cost associated with raising a child regardless of the child quality – the quantity cost – is not affected by parental education. As a result, the poor choose high fertility rates with low education investment and therefore, their offspring are poor as well.

The solution of simply banning child labor can only be successful if, by banning it, the demand for adult workers (their parents') increases enough to strongly augment their wages so they can use the extra wage to pay for the education of their children. Otherwise the children will be forced to find informal or illegal jobs with even lower wages and longer hours or what is worse, joining a militia or prostitution (Basu and Van, 1998). The other radical solution of banning by developed countries imports of goods manufactured by children can also be counterproductive. The number of children working for exporting companies is less than 7 percent in poor countries (Fallon and Tzannatos, 1998); therefore this low percentage will not permit a sufficient increase in wages of adult workers to replace them and their situation will deteriorate even more, since their wages in exporting companies are higher than in local selling companies or in the informal sector. Finally, the idea that working children have more difficulty in going to school or that they leave school earlier is not proved by empirical research. Ravallion and Wodon (2000) have shown that, in the case of Bangladesh, child work has not had any significant influence in its participation in primary education. In any case International Labor Organization (ILO) Convention 182, against the worst forms of child labor, was signed by 74 countries in just two years and has continued to be signed by most developing countries.

The idea of "footloose" multinationals is not proven either by empirical evidence. Gorg and Strobl (2002) show that multinational plants abroad tend to have longer survival rates than local plants and that jobs created by them do actually last longer in multinational affiliates than in indigenous companies and that they are no more or less likely than indigenous plants to recover lost jobs.

It is also important to observe FDI effects on the host country's productivity since foreign companies are more efficient than domestic ones. First, it is necessary to analyze whether or not this is the case and, second, whether this increased efficiency has "spill-over" effects on local companies in the same sector or region or in other related industries, through copying the foreign company's production systems to improve efficiency or to compete with it, which would finally result in an improvement in the country's average productivity (Lipsey, 2002b).

The vast majority of empirical studies undertaken in developing countries show that, in the manufacturing sector, foreign-owned plants have higher productivity than domestic firms. Sometimes the higher productivity is achieved by foreign firms because they are more capital-intensive per unit product; on other occasions it is because they are more intensive in skilled labor per unit product or more intensive in physical and human capital; in still others, because multinationals invest in the most productive local firms; and, finally, on other occasions it is due to their larger scale of production (Blomstrom and

Wolf, 1994; Kokko, Zejan, and Tansini, 2001; Haddad and Harrison, 1993; Okamoto and Sjoholm, 1999; Ramstetter, 1999; Chuan and Lin, 1999; Erdilek, 2002; Razin, 2002; Mody, Razin, and Sadka, 2002; Kathuria, 2000).

It is also proven that the productivity growth of FDI tends to be higher through greenfield investments, i.e. building a new plant, than through cross-border acquisitions, i.e. trading heterogeneous corporate assets to exploit complementarities. According to Nocke and Yeaple (2004) firms engaging in greenfield investment are systematically more efficient than those engaging in cross-border acquisitions and that most FDI takes the form of cross-border acquisitions when factor price differences between countries are small, while greenfield investment plays a more important role for FDI from high wage into low wage countries, thus in FDI in developing countries.

As for the transfer of technology to other local companies in the same or other sectors, many empirical studies find such transfers in companies in the same industrial sector either because the foreign company compels them to improve the intermediate products purchased from local companies or because the latter compete to improve quality to become the foreign company's supplier (Blomstrom and Kokko, 1998). In other cases the transfer does not occur in the same sector since the foreign company buys its intermediate products from its usual suppliers in other countries, although the evidence is generally positive. This effect has been found by Blomstrom and Wolf (1994) for the case of Mexico, Kathuria (2000) for India, Campos and Kinoshita (2002) for transition economies, and Aitken and Harrison (1999) for Venezuela.

Blomstrom and Kokko (1998) and Kokko (1996) state that the higher the productivity spill-over effect from the foreign company, the greater the level of local learning ability, the higher the level of local competition and the lower the percentage of foreign ownership of the company in question. Gorg and Strobl (2000) find that the wider the technology gap between the foreign company and domestic companies and the greater the host country's trade restrictions, the lower the spill-over effect. Finally, without differentiating between industries, de Mello

(1997) found that FDI inflows tended to increase total factor productivity but not fixed investment in developed countries, and the opposite in developing countries. As a result of the difficulties in measuring productivity in many developing countries, the evidence is not definitive, but most of it is positive for them.

In any event, as Eaton and Kortum (1999) and Keller (2001a and 2001b) demonstrated, the biggest sources of technological change, which lead to higher productivity growth, both in developed and in developing countries, are nearly always external and not domestic since the new technology is initially discovered in a specific country and then spreads to other countries. As a result, the international dissemination of technology is one of the key factors underlying per capita income worldwide, as observed in the first two chapters of this book.

Consequently, developing countries are even more dependent on external sources to increase their productivity than developed countries. These sources are determined to a large extent by FDI inflows since it is multinationals that do the most to disseminate technology by locating in a specific country or entering into an agreement to transfer technology to a local company. In other words, dissemination of technology is an essential element in the convergence of productivity and per capita income worldwide, and this is achieved fundamentally through the ability to attract FDI (Keller, 2002).

Another very important advantage for the host country, especially if it is a developing country, is the positive effect on its exports. The main reason, according to Dobson and Siow Yue (1997), is that foreign companies integrate these countries into the international production networks. When analyzing the impact of the location of US companies' subsidiaries in the electronic industry in south-east Asia, Robert Lipsey (2000) found that they accounted for up to three-quarters of exports in some cases, and that exports by labor-intensive industries, such as food, textiles, and garments, declined over time, whereas those from the chemical and capital goods industries increased over time. Aitken and Harrison (1997) reached the same conclusion about US direct investments in Mexico. Even in countries whose export conditions are worse than in south-east Asia (e.g. Zambia, the Ivory Coast, Indonesia, and

China), the long-term effects on exports were very substantial and higher than the initial capital contribution (Rhee and Belot, 1990; Liu, Wang, and Wei, 2001).

Lastly, all the above-mentioned advantages of FDI inflows for developing recipient countries must necessarily have an impact on their growth rate. Romer (1993) has a very optimistic view of the relationship between FDI and growth, as he considers that the biggest obstacle for a developing country in converging with developed countries is its gap in knowledge and ideas rather than a lack of physical capital. FDI entails both, in the form of human, technological, and organizational capital. Consequently, for a developing country to grow more rapidly, it must try to attract foreign companies, which can close that gap by bringing new ideas, knowledge, and human capital with them.

However, empirical analyses, which simply correlate the stocks and flows of FDI, as a percentage of GDP, with GDP growth or GDP per capita do not seem to provide solid or conclusive results. The reason is that a broad range of other factors affect growth, as stated in previous chapters. Nevertheless, some studies showed positive relationships between the two variables. Such is the case of Blomstrom, Lipsey, and Zejan (1994) who performed regressions of FDI flows every five years between 1960 and 1985 against growth in the subsequent five years.

Other studies showed positive relationships, which are only totally conclusive in certain cases or when combining FDI with other factors. For example, using a sample of 69 developing countries between 1970 and 1989, Borensztein, De Gregorio, and Lee (1998) concluded that the relationship is clearly favorable in developing countries with medium and high income per capita and not so favorable for developing countries with lower income per capita, although it is also positive since it helped to improve the workforce's level of education and the technological levels of those countries. Lipsey (2000b) found the same evidence in groups of five subsequent years up to 1998.

In a previous study, Bhagwati (1978) showed that the relationship depended on the trade policy applied by FDI recipient countries. It tended to be very positive in developing countries, which applied export promotion policies, such as those in south-east Asia, and less positive in countries that applied import substitution policies, such as those in Latin America. Balasubramanyam, Salisu, and Sapsford (1996) reached the same conclusions as Bhagwati in a broad sample of developing countries. Countries that applied policies to promote exports managed to increase FDI efficiency in order to raise GDP growth. Another factor which tended to increase that efficiency, according to Alfaro, Chanda, Kalemli-Ozcan, and Sayek (2002), was the development of local financial markets since, if they were very weak or nonexistent, local companies have greater problems in absorbing or copying the knowledge and technology contributed by foreign companies. Some region-specific studies show higher correlations between FDI and growth. For example, Campos and Kinoshita (2002) found that, for a group of 25 central and east European countries, FDI was a crucial variable for explaining their growth rates since, because of the high level of education of their labor force, technology transfer was faster and more productive.

In short, FDI inflows are now a very important factor for developing countries to have access not only to long-term capital flows but also to new ideas, knowledge and technology and to international export markets. Furthermore, they manage to increase their employment and salary levels and improve productivity. Consequently, the greater the FDI inflows, the faster the developing countries can converge with the most developed countries. Nevertheless, in order to attract those flows, they must create the necessary incentives in terms of educating and training the workforce, accompanied with policies that improve the institutional and productive efficiency of their economies.

Multinationals and FDI

There is also very harsh criticism of the behavior of multinationals and their increasing power and size. It is a well-known fact that certain multinationals have taken advantage of their oligopolistic market power or their political power in certain countries or over certain governments; however, this type of behavior is increasingly rare and more difficult to engage in as the growing number of ever-more-powerful anti-trust agencies try to avoid abuses of market power and the formation of monopolies or oligopolies by all means. Nevertheless, as multinational companies grow in size to adapt to increasingly larger and more global markets, there is a growing need for an international competition policy.

Attempts can be made to achieve this new global scale of anti-trust measures in several ways, as indicated by Graham and Richardson (1997). On the one hand, the global efficiency of the aforementioned anti-trust organizations could be improved considerably if they coordinate their decisions and cooperate with other countries either bilaterally or (preferably) regionally or through multilateral organizations, such as the OECD and the WTO. On the other hand, attempts can be made within the WTO to use its consultation and dispute settlement procedure so that the unilateral decisions of each country's competition authority can be coordinated with other countries. This would be a positive step but it would be preferable for the current Millennium Round of the WTO to reach an agreement on anti-monopoly measures related to international trade and foreign direct investment. Such an agreement could make it possible to counter attempts to form monopolies and cartels, create discrimination or make agreements which distort competition in areas beyond national borders.

Criticism about the growing size of multinationals and their power over developing countries is generally unsubstantiated rhetoric. It is a fact that the size of multinationals is increasing because, with spreading globalization, they have to serve broader and more diverse markets that (it should be recalled) demand their products and services because they are more advanced, better, or less expensive – otherwise there would be no such demand. Their size is directly related to market size as Adam Smith showed more than two centuries ago. Nevertheless, that size will not increase indefinitely. As the Nobel prize-winner Robert Lucas (1978) stated, size is related to the amount of management talent available and this increases with per capita income.

Other economists also found restrictions on size. Rosen (1982) showed that size is limited by the capacity of management supervision and control, which is subject to the law of diminishing returns as size increases. Kremer (1993) maintains that size is dependent on the availability of human capital: companies are larger in countries where there is more human capital. Grossman and Hart (1986) suggested that size depends on the available amount of physical assets that can be controlled. Pagano, Panetta, and Zingales (1998) showed that multinationals' size depended on the degree of development of the financial system, with the result that most of their parent companies are located in the US and the UK, the two countries with the most developed capital markets. Finally, other economists, such as Caves (1998) and Sutton (1997), consider that size obviously depends on domestic anti-monopoly regulations and also on legislation on barriers to entry.

However, the claim that multinationals' size puts them above the governments of many countries is not corroborated by recent experience. It is true that there has been abuse of dominant position, sometimes with the acquiescence of the home or host country and other times not (there have been well-known cases particularly in Africa and Latin America). However, every day there is more national and international awareness of the need to avoid this. It is also true that global companies are much more difficult for national anti-trust authorities to control, hence the need stated above for an international anti-trust system to control them.

Evidently, there are also corrupt leaders in many developing and developed countries; however, for them to be corrupted there must be a company or an investor which corrupts them. In this connection, the OECD has taken very important steps, ratified by all its member countries, to impose a code of conduct on multinationals, so that the amounts paid as "commissions" or "expenses" to land government contracts are not tax-deductible for the multinational in its home country (which used to be possible in Europe, for example), and so that criminal charges can be brought in both the home and host countries against individuals or executives who engage in corruption.

In conclusion, it is not possible to compare companies with countries. The latter are states, which, in accordance with their constitution, exercise coercive power over their citizens and their companies. They can impose taxes and levies, regulate tariffs and public prices, expropriate or even nationalize (viz. oil companies in the 1970s and banks in the 1980s), they can compel a company to reduce its size (AT&T) or break up a monopoly (Microsoft) or they can conscript their citizens into the military. In contrast, companies, whether multinationals or not, are civil organizations which exercise their power through competition in markets and their only coercive power is over their employees, who they can dismiss subject to compliance with labor legislation (Kay, 2002). If multinational companies are as powerful as critics claim, how were Brazil and South Africa able to make some vaccine-producing multinational pharmaceutical companies change their ways? How was an NGO like Greenpeace able to successfully challenge a large oil company?

Moreover, the size comparison between multinationals and countries is totally fallacious. It true that some multinationals are larger than some countries; this came about because globalization enabled many countries to become independent and survive despite their small size – something which would have been impossible in the first half of the twentieth century, when only highly self-sufficient countries were able to survive because of the enormous protectionism. Nowadays, any country – no matter how small – can survive provided that it produces something which can be sold on international markets, ranging from the environment to its services or products. In fact, in 1946 there were only 74 countries in the world and today there are more than 200, of which 70 have less than 2.5 million inhabitants and 35 have less than 500,000 inhabitants. In contrast, very few multinational companies could muster a comparable population, even if they counted their employees' families.

It is certainly not possible to compare countries and companies using the yardsticks of GDP and market capitalization. These two factors are totally different: GDP is an annual flow, whereas market capitalization is the stock at a specific point in time. For a meaningful comparison, we would need to compare a company's market capitalization with a country's total wealth (not just its annual income), which would give a more credible outcome and provide little sustenance for the demagogues who exaggerate the size of multinationals in support of their arguments. Likewise, it is not possible to compare a multinational's annual sales figure (which is a flow) with a country's GDP, because they are radically different. GDP is a measure of the added value on each sale made in a country, net of production and marketing costs; consequently, it cannot be compared directly with a company's gross sales. The comparison would have to be made with a company's pre-tax operating profits and the results would be very different (De Grauwe and Camerman, 2002).

To give an example from the year 2000, which was very favorable for companies since it was a record year for profits, using the last yardstick described above, there would only be two multinationals ranked among the 50 largest countries in the world. In 2001 there was only one, and there were probably none in 2002. Comparing company market capitalization with country GDP, in 2001 (the peak of the largest stock market boom in the last 150 years), 30 companies would have classified among the top 60 countries. In addition to being a fallacious comparison, the figure fell to 10 companies in 2002. If we compare a company's gross sales with a country's GDP, there were 30 companies among the top 80 countries in 2000, but only 15 in 2002. Again, this comparison is totally erroneous.

That said, however, it is the multinational companies that are leading the globalization process, once countries have voluntarily opened up to trade and foreign investment. According to UNCTAD (2004), there are already more than 61,000 multinational or transnational non-financial companies, and they have more than 900,000 subsidiaries located in a different country to the parent company. Through their subsidiaries in the third countries where the latter are located, the US and the EU multinationals sell three times more than the sum of their total exports (to countries outside the EU, in the case of Europe) (UNCTAD, 2004).

These multinationals account for 66 percent of world exports, 14 percent of all domestic sales in the world and almost all global FDI, whose stock reached $7 trillion – 16 percent of total domestic investment in OECD countries. This means that they play an essential role in the development and growth of the world economy, particularly of developing countries.

For all these reasons, it is very interesting to compare the attitude of anti-multinational and anti-globalization groups (which are critical of multinationals), with that of developing or developed countries' authorities, which fight so that multinationals locate in their country because they know that multinationals' direct investments, technology, and employment are an essential complement to national savings, to boost their employment and exports, to improve their human capital, organizational capacity, and level of technology; furthermore, they know that it is the fastest way to integrate into the world's markets and globalize.

In short, the development of multinationals and their investments in emerging countries is absolutely essential for the latter to prosper and not be left behind in the globalization process (which would leave them with no solution for many of their problems of insufficient savings, investment, and employment). This is underpinned by the fact that emerging countries' governments are ones that are most convinced about globalization's advantages and the importance of a multinational's investments in their country and they are usually much more critical of the detractors than are developed countries' governments, which unfortunately have to endure the protesters at every international meeting they attend.

Chapter 9

More Integration of Trade and Finance

The Interrelationship between Trade Openness and Financial Openness

Growing globalization is giving rise to increasing integration between two basic pillars, trade and finance, which are becoming ever more closely interrelated and tend to feed off each other. International trade is always accompanied by international financial flows. Trade flows tend to increase the demand for financial instruments to hedge against the risks arising from such transactions. Financial flows give rise to increased trade, particularly intra-industrial and intra-firm trade. As analyzed in the preceding chapter, international direct investment tends to boost the imports and exports of the host country. If it is a new investment, it increases imports of capital goods and physical capital while new production plants are being built. If it is not, it does so while the company that has been bought develops and improves its production. It also increases exports once the plants have come on stream.

Financial development also facilitates specialization and economies of scale, which are linked to trade as they enable companies in developing countries, which are heavily dependent on external financing, to overcome their liquidity problems and obtain trade financing and longer-term funds to invest in the expansion and upgrading of their production facilities. The International Monetary Fund (2002b) conducted a study on this growing integration. The study includes important analyses and empirical findings that are explained below.

Growing integration is measured by calculating the total trade and financial flows as a percentage of GDP. "Trade openness" is measured by taking the sum of imports and exports of goods and services and dividing it by GDP. "Financial openness" is measured by taking the sum of the external assets and liabilities of foreign direct investment and portfolio investment and dividing it by GDP. Other financial assets, including bank debt, are excluded from this measurement because they are too volatile (IMF, 2002b). Both types of openness have evolved positively, but at different speeds, since the 1970s. Between 1985 and 1997–2001, trade openness increased by 3.9 percentage points of GDP in developed countries and by 15.4 percentage points of GDP in developing countries. Financial openness grew much more quickly between the two periods: by 77.3 percentage points of GDP in developed countries and by only 19.9 percentage points in developing countries.

That is to say, openness has been totally asymmetric; on the one hand, trade openness increased more in developing countries and financial openness increased more in developed countries and, on the other, trade openness increased more than financial openness in developing countries and financial openness increased more than trade openness in developed countries. Greater trade openness in developing countries vis-à-vis developed countries basically reveals the empirical regularity that smaller countries trade more in terms of percentage of GDP than large countries, rather than less restrictive trade policies, which is not the case. It should be recalled that the median GDP of developing countries is half that of developed countries. The strong growth in financial openness in developed countries has enabled the US to become the world's biggest creditor and debtor, while the financial flows to developing countries have remained constant at 4 percent of their GDP (Obstfeld and Taylor, 2002).

These measures reflect not only the trade and restrictive policies of the capital account in the balance of payments, but also: other policies, such as labor and institutional policies; technological factors, such as transport costs and other transaction costs; structural factors, such as geography, cultural heritage, and language; and such events as rising oil prices and falling prices of other raw materials.

Both types of openness have evolved favorably, hand-in-hand, especially in developing countries, and today it can be said that the current level of trade openness (excluding services) is ten GDP points higher than it was in 1914, at the end of the previous phase of globalization, and that the current level of financial openness is 20 GDP points higher than it was then, after having fallen considerably below that level between 1914 and the end of the 1960s. The correlation coefficient between the two since the 1980s is 0.66 in developing countries and 0.38 in developed countries. This correlation is underscored by the fact that developing countries with higher trade ratios are less dependent on domestic saving for investment because their trade openness enables them to obtain more foreign capital, whereas the more closed countries show a high correlation between domestic saving and investment. In other words, trade restrictions are partly responsible for the segmentation of international financial markets and for the more restricted access to international capital markets (Obstfeld and Rogoff, 2000).

Despite the complementary growth of both types of openness, international trade and financial markets continue to be more segmented than domestic ones, even in developed countries. There is much more domestic trade than international trade, even after taking into account the distance factor, the size of economies and other factors (Anderson and Wincoop, 2001). Also, prices of manufactures adjust very slowly to changes in exchange rates, on average 50 percent take more than one year to do so. International financial markets continue to be highly segmented even though there has been a reduction since the 1980s. The correlation between global investment and saving is still very high, which proves there is segmentation, although it has been falling, from 0.9 in the 1980s to 0.6 today. The proportion of foreign shares held by US residents is 11 percent, despite the fact that they account for 50 percent of the world's total market capitalization.

A recent study by Joshua Aizenman and Ilan Noy (2005) has tried to ascertain the bidirectional linkages between financial flows and trade for developing countries with more disaggregated measures of both. They show that the strongest feedback is between FDI and manufacturing trade. Of the linear feedback between trade and FDI of 81 percent,

50 percent can be accounted for by Granger-causality from FDI gross flows to trade openness and 31 percent from trade to FDI; the rest of the total linear feedback is attributable to simultaneous correlation between the two annual series. Similar results are obtained when they instead investigate causality between trade openness and net FDI flows.

Why Do Some Developing Countries Trade Less than Others?

Although the developing countries' integration into world trade markets has generally increased significantly, the distribution is very uneven. This is due primarily to artificial trade barriers created by protectionist policies.

To measure whether a country's degree of trade openness is lower than it should be, "gravity" models of international trade are used (Leamer and Levinson, 1995). These models borrow from Isaac Newton's equation for gravitational force, which states that the gravitational force between two objects is proportional to their mass and inversely proportional to the distance between them. The gravity models of trade state that the magnitude of bilateral trade flows between two countries is positively linked to the combined size of the two countries and negatively linked to the distance between them. This means that trade volume also depends positively on economic mass and negatively on resistance.

The two key variables of mass in the equation are the combined size of the two countries engaging in trade, as measured by GDP, and their level of development, as measured by per capita income. The first variable is important because international trade tends to increase with the size of the economy. The second is important because trade tends to increase, more than proportionally, with the level of development (Frankel, 1997), as demand for product variety increases with income level, which leads to intra-industrial trade of similar goods because the production of differentiated goods is specialized, reflecting increasing returns to scale (Helpman and Krugman, 1985).

The main factor determining resistance in these models is transport costs, which still tend to signify a greater obstacle to trade than tariffs (World Bank, 2002) and for which geographical variables, such as absolute distance between countries, are used. It is a proven fact that neighboring countries tend to trade with each other more than with faraway countries. Relative distance – i.e. the distance between two countries in relation to their distance from other trade partners – is also very important. In fact, it is often a greater disadvantage than absolute distance (Anderson and Wincoop, 2001). The concept of distance used in some models has been the average distance between trade partners (Frankel and Wei, 1998; Soloaga and Winters, 2001; Melitz, 2001). Other geographical variables taken into account are physical geography and whether the country is landlocked or has a navigable river (Limao and Venables, 2001). Historical and/or cultural similarities, such as colonial links and common language, are also generally added to these variables. These similarities tend to reduce transaction costs because of familiarity with customs, institutions, and legal systems.

In addition to these natural resistances, there are also those known as "artificial" resistances. These relate to frictions arising from each country's protectionist trade policies, including tariffs, quotas, and contingencies and the so-called "gray" or internal protection areas. Regional trade agreements and preferential treatment also affect trade flows (Eichengreen, 1996; Frankel, 1997; Soloaga and Winters, 2001). Controls over capital and exchange rates also have an impact on trade, as they increase transaction costs and internal import prices.

In short, gravity models have been most successful in explaining bilateral trade. In the words of Leamer and Levinson (1995), they are "some of the clearest and most robust empirical findings in economics." For the first time, the International Monetary Fund developed a gravity model taking into account both natural and artificial variables (IMF, 2002), showing that a country or region trades below its potential if its current trade with the rest of the world is, on average, less than that

214

predicted by the gravity model. Similarly, a country trades above its potential if its international trade is higher than that predicted by the model. Since the model takes into account the natural causes of trade, the countries or regions that trade less or more than the model predicts they should because they have more or fewer artificial impediments than the median. The IMF results, which match those of Rose (2002a), are as follows.

In line with the results of Al-Atrash and Yousef (2000), the countries with the highest degree of under-trading are those of the Middle East and North Africa, as well as south Asia, although this model does not take into account trade in services, which has increased significantly in these areas as a result of tourism. The degree of under-trading is lower in Latin America. Sub-Saharan Africa trades slightly more than the model would predict which is consistent with Rodrik (1998a) and Coe and Hoffmaister (1999). The countries that trade the furthest above their potential are those of south-east Asia. Under-trading is less prevalent in intra-regional trade than in extra-regional trade, which is not obvious because the model already takes this differential factor into account. One possible explanation for this is the existence of regional preferential trade agreements, such as MERCOSUR. If this factor were included in the model, intra-regional trade in Latin America would not be much higher than the model predicts, especially for the southern cone countries. Regional trade agreements do not appear to divert trade in other developing countries, except in the case of the European Union (Soloaga and Winters, 2001).

The evolution of the extent of under- and over-trading, between 1980 and 1999, mainly reflects the development of artificial barriers to trade. The situation of sub-Saharan Africa and, particularly, of the Middle East and northern Africa worsened during this period, evidencing their increasing marginalization in international trade. Conversely, south-east Asia, South America and, especially, the Caribbean and Central America have been improving their trade levels vis-à-vis the model predictions. Thus, declining trade in certain countries is a very serious problem affecting certain regions of the world, most notably Africa, the Middle East, and south Asia.

The Impact of Trade and Balance of Payment Restrictions on Trade

Although under-trading is an indicator of the existence of artificial barriers to trade, it is not linked to specific policies. To try to ascertain the impact of policies, the IMF (2002) re-estimated the 1995–9 "gravity model" and introduced as variables for artificial restrictions the FMI index of trade restrictiveness, based on average tariffs and other non-tariff barriers, and the index of balance of payment restrictions, which includes current account and capital account balance of payment restrictions.

Both indices suggest that there are less restrictive policies in sub-Saharan Africa, south-east Asia and Latin America than in other developing regions, although these indices have major measurement shortfalls. This means that sub-Saharan Africa's marginalization in international trade is due not so much to restrictive trade policies but to other political and institutional issues in the region. With respect to Latin America, whose trade and balance of payments restrictions are also relatively low, there must be some other type of policies affecting it, because its levels of under-trading, although improving, are still higher than the median.

Both types of restrictions have significantly negative effects on bilateral trade. For each percentage point of increase in these two restrictions, trade volume decreases by half a point. Even the per capita GDP coefficient, which largely explains higher trade volume, becomes smaller when the two restrictive variables are included, suggesting that restrictive policies are inversely linked to the level of economic development. In other words, the two types of policy restrictiveness are greater in developing countries and have a negative effect on their growth. Also interesting is the verification that balance-of-payments restrictions have a highly negative effect on trade. This is consistent with the idea that financial restrictions help to explain the segmentation of global goods markets and parallels the view of Obstfeld and Rogoff (2000) that trade restrictions also help to explain the segmentation of global financial markets. For example, Tamirisa (1999) finds that capital and exchange controls constitute a significant barrier to trade, and Rose (2000) proves that belonging to a monetary union more than triples a country's trade with the other members of such a union.

It is important to make a calculation of the static impact (i.e. without including the subsequently induced effects on income and prices) on trade volume of the full liberalization of these restrictions in developing countries, developed countries, and both groups together. If developed countries were to reduce their restrictions as far as possible, trade between these countries and developing countries would increase by 14 percent. The full liberalization of such restrictions by both groups of countries would boost trade between developed countries by 40 percent, trade between developed and developing countries by 63 percent, and trade among developing countries by 94 percent.

These results show that the higher restrictions in developing countries are part of the reason why these countries trade less per unit of GDP than developed countries. However, geographic and economic development factors clearly play a bigger role in explaining this difference. Per capita income is the biggest reason why adjusted trade between developing countries is much lower than between developed countries, and it is 20 percent of the reason why trade between developing countries and developed countries is lower than among developing countries. Geographical factors, especially distance, are the primary reason for the lower trade between developed and developing countries and they are 40 percent of the reason for lower trade among developing countries. Artificial restrictions are responsible for 10 percent of the lower trade between developed and developing countries and 20 percent of the lower trade among developing countries. The countries that came out on top in this study were those of south-east Asia – not only because they had lower trade and balance of payments restrictions, relatively speaking, than the other developing countries, but because they received more foreign direct investment from multinationals of developed countries through the relocation of labor-intensive production to this region. South-east Asia has thus become an important net exporter of manufactured goods and

217

labor-intensive intermediate products, while sub-Saharan Africa is a net exporter of agricultural products, Latin America a net exporter of agricultural products, raw materials and fuel, and the Middle East and northern Africa net exporters of raw materials and fuels.

Trade and Financial Integration and Macroeconomic Volatility

Macroeconomic volatility is not just a problem in and of itself, but it also reveals a negative correlation with output growth (Ramey and Ramey, 1995; Martin and Rogers, 2000; Hnatkovska and Loayza, 2005). Kose, Prasad, and Terrones (2003) show, for instance, that a 1 percent increase in the standard deviation of output growth is associated with a 0.16 percentage point decline in the average long-term growth of a developing country. Output volatility can have negative effects on growth through different channels: the first is through lowering investment due to the uncertainty of its future returns. Market imperfections associated with credit constraints and/or imperfect access to world financial markets by limiting the financial options could also magnify the negative impact of short-term volatility on long-term growth. The second is through weaker institutions and less developed financial markets, which increase its adverse impact. The third is through a less diversified export base. Economies that are more open to trade and have more diversified export production structures have the ability to withstand higher levels of volatility with fewer adverse effects on growth. The fourth is through excessive fiscal policy. Volatility is strongly associated with discretionary fiscal policy that distorts saving and investment decisions, with adverse consequences on economic growth (Fatás, 2002).

Both trade and financial integration tend to increase economies' exposure to external shocks and output volatility. Trade openness is associated with greater output volatility, while financial openness is associated with higher capital short-term flows and thus short-term volatility (Razin and Rose, 1994). The important thing, however, is to understand how trade integration affects financial vulnerability and vice versa, and how financial integration affects output volatility. To this end, it is advisable to divide developing countries into two groups, depending on whether their trade and financial openness is above or below the median.

On the one hand, the countries of south-east Asia and sub-Saharan Africa have the highest degree of trade openness, while those of Latin America and south Asia have the lowest. On the other hand, the countries of Latin America and south Asia have the highest degree of financial openness. Latin America is the only region that has a much higher proportion of financially open countries than countries open to trade.

There is robust evidence that trade openness has a very positive effect on growth by allocating resources more effectively among countries, disseminating innovation and technology, increasing competition, avoiding rent-seeking, and providing more incentives to implement policies to stimulate growth. The same can be said of the effects of financial openness on growth, in this case by increasing domestic investment and employment – which has a knock-on effect on the dissemination and transfer of technology – and deepening domestic financial markets. However, significant inconsistencies in domestic macroeconomic policies and weak or poorly supervised financial markets can lead to an inefficient allocation of financial flows and even crises, as we have recently seen in Asia and Latin America.

There are two basic types of financial crisis: debt defaults and currency crashes. Detragiache and Spilimbergo (2001) define a debt default as when there are arrears in the payment of external debt to private creditors exceeding 5 percent of total debt or there are agreements with such private creditors to restructure or reschedule the debt. Milesi-Ferretti and Razin (1998) define a currency crisis as when the domestic currency depreciates by 25 percent or more vis-à-vis the dollar or when depreciation at least doubles that of the preceding year, provided that the latter does not exceed 40 percent (to exclude hyperinflationary episodes).

The impact of trade and of the degree of trade openness on a country's vulnerability to external financial crises and their recurrence shows, once again, the growing interrelationship between trade and finance. When correlating the frequency of external crises for developing countries with the total percentage of crises affecting the group of developing countries, based on whether they are more or less open to trade than the median, the results are crystal clear: external financial crises are much more frequent in countries that are less open to trade. Since the 1980s, the countries that are less open to trade have been 20 percent more likely to suffer a debt default and 33 percent more likely to suffer an exchange crisis than the average developing country. The countries of Latin America and the Caribbean have suffered the greatest number of external crises.

This inverse relationship between trade integration and external financial crises has also been statistically significant in empirical econometric studies carried out. Sgherri (2002) shows the same evidence on this relationship after taking into account the more conventional determinants of these crises, such as the country's economic fundamentals, its solvency position, and its currency reserves. The results remain significant, even after introducing two supplementary relationships: the fact that trade openness may be related to the same factors that affect the frequency of financial crises and the fact that financial crises and trade openness may both be affected by factors that are not included in the empirical study. His results ratify earlier analyses by Klein and Marion (1997) and Milesi-Ferretti and Razin (1998).

The reason for these results lies in the fact that trade integration reduces a country's financial fragility by increasing its ability and willingness to service its external financial obligations. A higher percentage of exports relative to GDP means that exchange rate depreciation will provide the country with a greater ability to obtain foreign currencies and, accordingly, enable it to service its debts and reduce the probability of it suffering an unexpected or sudden withdrawal of its previous capital inflows, as the markets will consider that it is abler to pay its debt (Catao and Sutton, 2002). Moreover, trade openness serves as an incentive to meet debt payments by making the country more vulnerable to creditors' sanctions in the event of default (Bulow and Rogoff, 1989).

In other words, greater trade openness creates greater safety against the inherent volatility associated with financial openness. Therefore, countries that are more open financially, as is the case in Latin America, could see the frequency of external financial crises decline by increasing their trade openness.

It is also important to analyze the impact of financial openness on output volatility. Output volatility is defined as the unconditional standard deviation of the growth rate of real GDP per capita over the period 1975–99. This volatility in developing countries is double that of developed countries and, among the former, output volatility in the smaller countries (500,000–1,500,000 inhabitants) is about one-third greater than the average. However, the countries that are more integrated into international capital markets tend to have lower output volatility than less integrated countries, especially toward at the end of the 1990s, when the financial shocks were stronger. This effect is even greater in small countries that are more open as their output volatility is one-third lower than that of less open small countries (Easterly and Kraay, 2000).

Financial openness appears to be also associated with lower output volatility because the magnitude of inflation and exchange rate shocks is lower, thereby cushioning the impact of all external shocks on GDP. The countries that are more open than average financially tend to have higher levels of external debt and tend to suffer bigger external shocks (if measured by the volatility of the real exchange rate, trade flows, and financial flows). However, financially open countries have more stable real exchange rates and inflation rates, generally as a result of the better discipline that international financial markets tend to impose and the greater ability to adopt external best practices in macroeconomic management and institutional development (Rodrik, 2000; Acemoglu, Aghion, and Zilibotti, 2002; Wei, 2000).

This greater stability mitigates the correlation between output volatility and the volatility of external shocks – including the real terms of trade, trade flows, and real exchange rate volatility – in more financially opened countries. Paradoxically, although the more financially closed countries experience less volatile capital flows, the correlation of this lower volatility with output volatility is greater, and the more these countries open up to international financial markets the more they reduce this correlation. This proves that financial openness not only helps to mitigate output volatility in more open countries vis-à-vis more closed countries, but also among more closed countries.

It is also important to distinguish between developing countries that are more open to foreign direct investment and portfolio investment and those that are more open to higher external debt. Higher external debt ordinarily correlates positively with greater output volatility, in financially open and closed countries alike. This occurs because the balance sheet effects exacerbate the impact of external shocks, especially if domestic financial markets are weak or not well developed. However, on average, the indirect impact of greater financial openness on greater output volatility – due to a higher external debt ratio – is generally smaller than the direct mitigating impact and, therefore, the net effect is positive.

The obvious conclusion is that the opening-up of developing countries to trade – which is still at a relatively incipient stage, but growing, and very uneven from one country to the next – has a very positive impact on development, because the biggest barrier these countries face in order to achieve more trade per unit of GDP is their less advanced economic development. That is to say, greater trade openness is not only a source of growth; it is a consequence of it. Moreover, greater trade openness reduces the likelihood of suffering external financial crises, as it improves a country's external financial solvency by enabling it to achieve a larger source of foreign currencies. On the other hand, greater financial openness tends to mitigate external shocks and smooth out output volatility, although the latter also depends on many other factors, such as macroeconomic policy stability and institutional and financial development. It so happens, however, that these factors, in turn, are generally reinforced and developed by financial openness. In short, developing countries that already have a high level of openness to trade (e.g. the smaller countries) could reduce output volatility by increasing their financial openness, and developing countries that are more open financially (e.g. the Latin American countries) could reduce the recurrence and likelihood of external financial crises by opening up more to trade.

A recent study by the IMF (2005) shows that in spite of output volatility being on a downward trend in most developing countries over the past three decades, it remains higher than in developed countries. The main reasons are country-specific factors, underscoring the key role of domestic policies. Such an analysis shows that the large fall in output volatility in developing countries between the periods 1970–86 and 1987–2004 of 34.2 percent, was due in 24.2 percent to the improvement of domestic policies, in 6.8 percent to regional factors and only 3.2 percent to global factors.

Thus, while developing countries have made important strides in strengthening macroeconomic and structural policies in recent years, further progress is needed. The present favorable global economic environment provides an opportune time to address the sources of their output volatility. First, fiscal policies have tended to reinforce output fluctuations and increase volatility, particularly in sub-Saharan Africa and Latin America. To contain the volatility of fiscal policies, greater expenditure restraint is necessary during cyclical upturns to raise budgetary surpluses and reduce debt (Kaminsky, Reinhart, and Végh, 2004).

Second, developing countries with the least developed financial markets (sub-Saharan Africa and Latin America) have on average higher output volatility. Thus, progress in those countries in developing the financial sector and ensuring that it is appropriately regulated and supervised, would help alleviate financing constraints, particularly during downturns, and thereby provide those countries with additional scope to absorb shocks.

Third, terms of trade volatility is associated with higher volatility of output growth. One way to reduce the incidence of terms-of-trade shocks is through structural reforms that promote diversification of the productive base, though this may also require a long-term policy commitment. Naturally, exchange rate flexibility may cushion the impact of those shocks on output growth volatility.

Liberalization of Capital Movements and Financial Crises

The rapid liberalization of financial systems and capital flows in many developing countries – in some cases voluntarily, in others recommended by the IMF and in a small number of cases forced by a specific IMF program – has played an important role in unleashing the recent financial crises in some of these countries. This problem has once again cast doubts on the urgency of liberalizing developing countries' capital accounts and balance of payments in order to achieve financial integration. On the one hand, such a financial opening is inevitable and necessary if these countries are to integrate into global capital markets, benefit from larger inflows of capital and technology, and develop their trade potential. On the other hand, however, the freedom of capital movements, despite being a freedom, has its dangers, as it gives individuals, companies, and financial institutions greater opportunities to take bigger risks – at times imprudent ones – that could trigger a crisis or even systemic risks. However, these dangers can be reduced substantially by implementing sound, stabilizing macroeconomic policies aimed at avoiding aggregate financial imbalances in conjunction with policies to regulate, monitor, and control the financial institutions that implement adequate incentives to ensure efficient risk management.

These problems have sparked a heated debate between those economists who believe that financial markets are predominantly efficient and those who maintain that they are subject to serious problems of "asymmetric information" – i.e. situations in which one of the parties to a financial transaction has less information than the other. This tends to give rise to an inefficient allocation of financial resources, which leads to "agency problems," "adverse selection," "moral hazard," "herd behavior," and "contagion" (De la Dehesa, 2006). All these problems are applicable to lending banks, investors and fund managers.

"Agency problems," or principal and agent problems, arise when, for example, shareholders entrust one or more executives to run their company for them, or when small shareholders invest in a fund managed by experts. In such situations, the information available to the shareholder or investor is far inferior to that available to the executive or fund manager. As a result, it is very difficult for the former to know whether the latter are performing the task entrusted to them correctly. As long as the preferences of one party differ from those of the other, the result will always be less than the optimum.

"Adverse selection" often occurs when lenders have incomplete information on the quality of borrowers. This can provide the worst, or riskiest, borrowers with more incentive to request loans. When lenders cannot obtain sufficient information on the credit quality of borrowers they try to apply price or interest rate conditions that reflect the average quality of the relevant borrower group as a whole, which can be adverse for higher-quality borrowers and beneficial to higher-risk borrowers. As a result, the higher-quality borrowers may curtail their operations in such markets, and the lenders may end up lending primarily to the worst borrowers, causing the resulting allocation of funds to be inefficient.

"Moral hazard" can occur if a borrower's behavior changes in a way that is undesirable for the lender after the transaction has already taken place. For example, a borrower may be inclined to use a loan for a relatively risky project. If everything works out well, the borrower will be successful, but if it does not, it is the lender who stands to lose. As a result, the lender is inclined to make sure the risk on the project is minimal. To bypass this, the borrower may try to alter the project, making it riskier once the loan has been approved. As a result, the project may turn out to be much riskier than the lender had anticipated making him reluctant to grant loans in future and, consequently, his loan volume will end being less than the optimum.

"Herd behavior" is characterized by an increasing inclination by lenders and investors – due to a lack of information – to follow those who they believe have more information on a certain borrower or investment opportunity. Such behavior can cause markets to experience brusque movements and high volatility if a lender, considered by others to have better information on a borrower, ceases for whatever reason to lend money to the borrower, prompting others to do the same and driving the borrower – whether a company or a country – to default, even though the borrower's solvency situation was not really worrying. Such behavior also arises when investors do not have enough information on the quality of their fund managers. The fund managers with the least quality will have an incentive to emulate the investment decisions of other managers who they consider to be of higher quality, to "hide within the herd" so that it is not so easy to assess their skills. Even good managers could have reasons to follow the market, because if they go against it and lose they could risk losing their job.

The aforementioned behaviors can trigger "contagion problems." If investors suddenly withdraw from a company or a country, causing it to go into receivership or default, it is very likely that they will do the same immediately afterwards with a neighboring company or country (or one in similar economic circumstances), pushing it into a financial crisis, even though that company or country was in better shape than the one that went down before it. Further, a financial crisis in a relatively large country could trigger significant losses for managers' portfolios, leading the managers to sell their assets in other healthier countries to generate gains to offset the losses incurred in an attempt to achieve the minimum return demanded by its investors, thereby bringing even healthier countries into the crisis.

Such behavior tends to increase with the advance of financial globalization, as it provides greater investment and diversification opportunities in both instruments and geographical areas. For cost reasons, this reduces lenders' and investors' motivation to gather information on companies or countries in which they have invested a small part of their portfolio. As a result, they are driven toward "herd behavior" with respect to these countries or companies, which tend to be developing countries or small and medium-size enterprises.

As a consequence, in 2001, George Akerlof, Michael Spence, and Joseph Stiglitz, three of the leading experts on modern information economics, were awarded the Nobel Prize for Economics for their extensive groundbreaking work on the problems arising from "asymmetric information" since the 1970s.

While domestic financial markets are affected by asymmetric information problems, international markets are affected to an even greater degree, as geographic and cultural differences make it more difficult to obtain and analyze information, and the different legal systems make it more difficult to apply and execute financial contracts. At the same time, the revolution in information and telecommunication technologies has drastically reduced financial transaction costs, thereby creating a multiplier effect on the number of such transactions and, consequently, on international capital movements.

The liberalization of balance of payments transactions is defined in the IMF Articles of Agreement as the absence of any prohibition whatsoever on current account transactions from balance of payments. This definition leaves out of the prohibition any capital account restriction, therefore any country can introduce capital account restrictions until one day the IMF changes its statutes. This has enabled countries like Chile or Spain to make short-term inflows of capital more expensive – legally and temporarily – by imposing taxes, withholdings, or deposit requirements, but not directly any quantitative restriction, so they were more palatable to the IMF and the markets. Magud and Reinhart (2006) distinguish between measures to discourage inflows and measures to curb outflows. The first (Spain and Chile) seem not to reduce the volume of net flows and hence the current account balance and, when made in good times, may be effective. The second (Malaysia, Venezuela, and many others) tend to reduce outflows and may give room for a more independent monetary policy, but evidence shows that their effectiveness has been very low or nil, except in the case of Malaysia.

The effects of financial liberalization, domestic or external, are very similar. Since domestic financial liberalization intensifies competition in the financial industry, it reduces the protection financial intermediaries have against mismanagement and bad loans, as it forces banks to assume greater risks – to the point of jeopardizing their ability to control them – in order to compete. It also enables banks to engage in riskier projects and obtain more expensive inter-bank funds. Lastly, it affords banks access to more complex derivative financial instruments, which makes it more difficult to evaluate their balance sheets and reduces supervisors' ability to control, evaluate, and limit risk.

External financial liberalization through parallel channels can lead to a greater tendency to amplify the foregoing effects and exacerbate agency problems and distortions arising from asymmetric information in general. The entry of foreign banks increases competition even more, lowers margins and eliminates or reduces domestic banks' ability to cope with delinquent and bad debtors. It also increases these financial institutions' predisposition to take greater risks by offering them access to a very elastic offer of offshore capital and a broader range of investments in financial instruments involving higher returns, higher country risk and higher exchange rate risk, thus increasing their overall risk level and the probability of them suffering a financial crisis.

What this means is that the mechanisms giving rise to a situation that can jeopardize the institutions' financial stability are the same ones in place in the case of domestic or external financial liberalization; however, in this latter case they can be more accentuated. Also, financial liberalization, per se, is not the root of the problem. The root of the problem is the lack of appropriate prudential regulations and supervision, the consequences of which are magnified by liberalization. The lack of prudential regulations is what makes banks, which are losing market share as a result of greater competition, try to reduce their prudential reserves and provisions and, consequently, their solvency, or try to boost their margins with increasingly riskier investments, thus increasing their likelihood of falling into insolvency. If the bank in question is a large one it can end up dragging other banks down with it, triggering a systemic financial risk for the country.

This is why countries that do not have an appropriately regulated financial system that is regularly monitored and inspected to keep its banks from carrying out activities that are too risky should refrain from liberalizing their domestic and external financial systems until they are fully prepared to do so. To this end, they must have a thorough knowledge of risk management techniques and apply them properly; their audit and accounting practices must be the most appropriate and efficient; there must be an independent central bank that is perfectly familiar with its business as lender of last resort and must conduct it efficiently; they must adequately impose minimum capital requirements, appropriate reserves, limits on open positions, an adequate balance between assets and liabilities and an appropriate level of provisions for insolvency, and they must make sure that the executives in charge of such institutions are knowledgeable. This is the only way a financial system can be prepared to embark on full financial liberalization and freedom of capital movements.

Financial liberalization and freedom of capital movements must also be a gradual, sequential process. The solution does not lie in keeping the financial system closed and repressed until an optimal situation of regulation and supervision has been attained. When such controls are sufficiently advanced, the system must be gradually opened up, following a specific sequence. This process may take more than a decade to complete. It is first necessary to liberalize capital inflows and the outflows that each inflow entails. It is advisable to start with long-term capital inflows, particularly from foreign direct investment, which means that outflows of dividends, profits, invested capital, and capital gains (should the foreign investment activity cease) must also be liberalized. It is preferable to start by liberalizing foreign investment in companies and leave the opening of the banking system until the end to keep it from running into competition problems – in the event that it is still weak or not sufficiently capitalized – and having to opt for a riskier path further on down the road. Once this step has been taken, the second step would be to open the doors to inflows to portfolio investments, which also requires the liberalization of all the related outflows. After monitoring the effects of the foregoing capital inflows over a prudent amount of time, it is time to take the most difficult step: liberalizing short-term inflows of capital.

The reason for leaving short-term inflows of capital until the end is very clear. Experience from recent financial crises has taught us that short-term debt can cause serious problems for the financial stability of many developing countries, as it tends to be generally very volatile, is the first outflow to leave the country and can therefore trigger a crisis. Although all inflows of capital have the potential of being abruptly taken out of the country, it is more difficult for long-term inflows to be made liquid and transferred, especially foreign direct investment and real estate investment. The impact on the banking system of a sudden withdrawal of short-term inflows is particularly harmful because it can trigger a wave of insolvencies among domestic banks by rendering them illiquid.

Conversely, portfolio investment inflows, in shares or debt instruments have a heavy impact on the price of such assets but only an indirect impact on banks' balance sheets, the state budget and the financial position of the business sector. It is therefore necessary when liberalizing such short-term inflows to make certain that the state has not accumulated excessive short-term debt and that the financial system has a sufficient cushion of reserves and provisions to handle an abrupt withdrawal of such debt. One way to avoid incurring excessive short-term debt is, of course, to implement a stable budgetary policy without excessive deficits, except when they become necessary because the country is in a recession and the "automatic stabilizers" function properly. Another way is to have a totally flexible exchange rate, which tends to discourage short-term indebtedness, unlike fixed rates, which, with high nominal interest rates and the belief that the currency will not devaluate, encourages excessive short-term indebtedness. In any case, a flexible exchange rate should always be introduced whenever there are substantial capital inflows.

Lastly, any capital outflows that were not previously liberalized should be liberalized progressively, again beginning with long-term outflows – especially those relating to direct investment – and ending with those relating to portfolio and short-term investments. These outflows should be opened up prudently, as experience tells us that if exchange rates have been kept up artificially by prohibiting capital outflows, and interest rates have been kept artificially low as a result of such restrictions on outflows, rapid liberalization can cause a sharp currency devaluation and a sudden rise in short-term interest rates can trigger a crisis, as the state's (and the companies') debt burden would increase, particularly if their debt was denominated in foreign currencies.

In short, the recent financial crises have shown that a too rapid liberalization of the capital account of the balance of payments, by developing countries, can entail more problems than benefits and even can trigger a crisis. This tends to happen when the country's financial system does not have appropriate corporate governance and is not efficiently regulated and controlled by its economic and monetary authorities. It is for this reason that, following the Asian crisis, the IMF drew up a new report, which requested that capital movements, in developing countries, which do not have sound and experienced institutional, regulatory, and control systems, be liberalized prudently and gradually (Eichengreen and Mussa, 1998). The IMF thus rectified its previous stance, in which it expressed its preference for a rapid liberalization. This rectification was expected from the outset. While it took the OECD countries over three decades to liberalize their capital accounts, yet it was believed that developing countries, which are even less prepared for it, could do so in less than a decade.

An IMF paper (Rogoff, Prassad, Wei, and Kose, 2003) tries to find out empirical evidence about whether financial globalization of developing countries tends to produce a higher rate of growth and higher macroeconomic stability in those countries. In principle, financial integration seems to be associated with higher growth and per capita income, although, once other factors are taken into account such as trade flows and political stability, it becomes more difficult to make the connection between financial integration and economic growth. Moreover, financial globalization tends to be associated with higher instability, although not in all cases.

Nevertheless, the paper shows that countries do enjoy the benefits of financial integration, in terms of higher growth and stability, once they have crossed a certain threshold in terms of the soundness of their domestic monetary and fiscal policies and the quality of their social and economic institutions. The more sound and qualitative are the domestic policies the more the benefits. Countries with pegged currencies, unsound macro policies and poor supervision of financial markets are doomed to suffer costly financial crises when they expose themselves to international capital flows.

The authors of the report ask themselves the question: should a country postpone opening its capital account until it has good institutions? Or should it use financial integration as a tool to improve its institutions? The empirical evidence collected hardly suggests that developing countries should be hastening to carry out rapid account liberalization, and certainly not before trade liberalization: of the empirical research review these IMF economists have made on 14 cases, only 3 studies were found to have a positive effect of financial liberalization on growth of output. The reasons have to do not only with financial markets' behavior but also with wrong domestic policies. Nevertheless, they also make clear that there are limits to the usefulness of capital controls, which cannot protect a country from the effects of reckless policies and which tend to eventually lead to corruption and whose effectiveness tends to erode with time and with the increase of globalization.

Still the key issue is that international capital markets, despite being extremely innovative, have not yet been able to find a way to protect developing countries against the risk of volatile capital flows. As Robert Shiller (2003) puts it: "Instead of providing financial instruments for risk management, the global capital markets are still placing risk on developing countries."

Despite these international financial market shortcomings, private capital flows to developing countries continue to be extremely important for them to compensate for their lack of domestic savings and to achieve higher rates of growth. The strong recovery of capital flows to developing countries that began in 2003 carried over to 2004, albeit at a reduced pace. Total private and official net debt flows totaled a record high of almost $325 billion, up significantly from $200 billion during 2000–2, equaling 4.5 percent of their GDP in 2004, up slightly from 4.3 percent in 2003, but significantly below highs exceeding 6 percent reached in the mid-1990s.

But contrary to previous decades, healthy trade balances combined with expanding capital flows have contributed to generate large current account surpluses and foreign reserves accumulation in developing countries, from $292 billion in 2003 to $374 billion in 2004 and to over

$1 trillion in 2006, which have been invested in a sizeable proportion in US Treasuries, helping to finance the US current account deficit but also indicating the growing stake of developing countries in the global financial system and the importance of these countries to compensate for international imbalances (World Bank, 2005).

Chapter 10

More and Better Development Aid

According to the OECD's Development Assistance Committee (DAC), Official Development Assistance (ODA) is the granting under "concessional terms" of public funds to developing countries in order to improve their economic, social, and political conditions; at least 25 percent of the assistance must have a grant element in order to be deemed to have been provided under "concessional or soft" terms. This definition is very important because it clearly excludes military and intelligence aid as well as aid to fight terrorism, drugs, and the spread of weapons of mass destruction, aid for peace-keeping operations, and cultural aid. Whether consciously or not these latter forms of aid are often added to those which are actually ODA.

There are three types of arguments that have been used to justify ODA. The first is moral or humanitarian, which is based on zero tolerance of poverty and on the fact that as the marginal utility of income tends to fall, then, world well-being will be increased by redistributing income from the rich to the poor. The second argument has been political, which is based on the US need to fight communism before and terrorism now after 9/11, or to keep a strong link with their ex-colonies, as with France and the UK. The third one is economic: if due to balance of payment restrictions, there are resources underutilized in poor countries, it makes sense for the rich countries to give aid to the former because both will win, the poor will be less constrained by finance and foreign currency and the rich will get a higher level of return than that of the interest of their loans.

This type of aid seems to be fundamental, especially for the poorest countries and regions of the world, because direct private investment is never used to improve some basic infrastructures, such as rural roads, drinking water supply or public sewage systems, education, primary healthcare, or the fight against endemic diseases or poverty. In view of the scant financial return it provides, this type of aid, which focuses on providing public goods to poor countries, can only come from the public coffers of wealthy countries, as ODA, and donations from altruistic individuals, companies, and organizations. Foreign direct investment is very important, as we saw in the preceding chapter, but it concentrates mostly on few countries, few sectors and, obviously, is non-existent when it comes to very basic needs.

This is why ODA is perceived as necessary: not only because it is in the rich countries' economic interests not to leave these countries by the wayside, but also because, morally, they cannot stand by while the people of these countries are wallowing in misery, hunger, poverty, and death – often in countries which, in addition to being run by corrupt and incompetent governments, are located in areas where the geographic and climatic conditions make survival very difficult. The extreme poverty affecting nearly one billion people is scandalous, morally intolerable and, moreover, dangerous, because it could be a future breeding ground for disease, violence, and even terrorism.

Although the wealthy countries have experienced strong growth since the 1980s, ODA flows have shrunken in absolute terms and, therefore, in relative terms as well. In constant 1999 dollars (i.e. in real terms), ODA amounted to $70 billion in 1992, or 0.44 percent of the OECD countries' GDP. In 2000 it fell to $45 billion, and in 2002, it increased to $50 billion, or 0.22 percent of the OECD countries' GDP. This means that since the 1990s ODA has fallen 29 percent in absolute terms and 50 percent as a percentage of GDP. This, together with the protection and subsidies wealthy countries provide for their own agricultural and labor intensive productions, is one of the international economic scandals of this turn of the century and of the current globalization process in general. It is yet another display of the wealthy countries' lack of solidarity and stinginess when it comes to the very severe problems the poorest countries are facing.

One needs only to compare the foregoing annual ODA figures with other annual figures from developed countries to appreciate the dimensions of this disgraceful attitude: the annual cost of textile, clothing, and footwear protectionism for developed countries is $110 billion; the cost of agricultural protectionism for the same countries is $150 billion; annual agricultural subsidies total $250 billion; and the world's annual weapons expenditure is nearly $900 billion. While ODA flows were falling both to developing and poor countries, from 0.34 percent in 1992 to 0.22 percent in 2001 of donors' GNI, global military expenditure went up from $700 billion to close to $900 billion in 2004 (World Bank, 2005).

The renowned economist Jeffrey Sachs, who chaired the Millennium Summit's Commission on Macroeconomics and Health, estimates that if just 0.1 percent of the wealthy countries' GDP ($25 billion) were allocated to healthcare, 21,000 lives would be saved each day in the poorest countries. This would pave the way for a decline in the growth of the poor countries' fertility rates, as families would have greater certainty that their children would survive until adulthood. As a result, the environmental and population pressures would subside, and investors would be more attracted by a labor force which has not been decimated by malaria, AIDS, tuberculosis, and diarrhea. Sachs (2002) further estimates that the economic benefits would amount to $360 billion per year between 2015 and 2020. Likewise, he estimates that the reduction of poverty and other Summit objectives could be achieved if wealthy countries allocated an additional 10 to 20 percent of their annual arms expenditure – i.e. $50–100 billion per year – to current ODA flows.

Furthermore, 70 percent of this aid is negotiated bilaterally – i.e. directly between the government of the donor country, through its development agency charged with administering assistance, and the recipient country – rather than transferring the aid through international financial agencies, which have much more expertise in handling this type of aid. Examples of such agencies include the World Bank, the Inter-American, Asian and African Development Banks, or, in the last instance, the NGOs that are more experienced and better organized to handle this kind of aid locally. NGOs channeled $10 billion of aid to developing countries in 2000, of which ODA contributions to NGOs amounted to only $1.2 billion and another $3.8 billion were administered directly by them (World Bank, 2001).

This bilateral negotiation of assistance has made it possible for a substantial part of ODA to be used to finance, through soft loans, the sale of the goods, services, and projects of the donor country's private companies to developing countries. In other words, it has merely become another vehicle for export promotion and not, necessarily, for development assistance. This way countries manage to sell poor countries expensive – but unnecessary – infrastructure projects or goods and services that are not primary needs, when what these countries really need is more – and better – education, healthcare, sewage systems, and drinking water and more vaccines and medicines to eradicate the diseases that are ravaging them, such as malaria, tuberculosis, and AIDS.

Although this is the general panorama, it should also be noted that some countries, such as those of northern Europe, France, and Japan, are allocating their aid better than the rest of the OECD countries, although their assistance is also often linked to foreign policy considerations and not to reducing poverty. Also, some private companies are selling goods and services financed with ODA that really help to palliate the poor countries' extreme shortage of public goods.

The countries that donate the most to ODA in relation to the size of their economies are, in first place, Norway, which donates over 0.92 percent of its GNI (Gross National Income), followed by Denmark with 0.84 percent, Netherlands with 0.80 percent, Luxembourg, 0.81 percent and Sweden, 0.79 percent, all of which exceed the 0.7 percent established as the ODA target. Next come Belgium, with 0.60 percent, France, with 0.41 percent, Switzerland and Ireland with 0.39 percent, and Finland and the United Kingdom with 0.35 and 0.34 percent respectively. Italy and the United States are the two countries with the lowest proportions of GNI, with 0.17 and 0.15 percent respectively, and of the latter, only 0.02 percent of GNI is channeled to the poorest countries, as most of its aid is allocated to Egypt, Turkey, and Israel (OECD, 2004). However, in absolute terms the United States is the biggest donor country with $16.25 billion followed by Japan, with $8.9 billion.

Nevertheless, two important clarifications should be made at this juncture. The first is that, since ODA consists of public budget funds, there is a clear correlation between the amount donated by each country and the fiscal pressure in that country: the greater the fiscal pressure, the higher the ODA flows as a percentage of GNI. The second is that, although the United States is the country that allocates the least ODA in terms of GNI, it is the country with the highest volume of private donations, from both individuals and companies, to developing countries.

Paradoxically, the poorest countries only receive a rather small proportion of the total aid, although this could be due to a lack of absorption capacity, as will be shown later. For example, annual ODA flows to sub-Saharan Africa fell from $20 billion in 1995 to $12 billion in 2000 (26 percent of the total), but they have recovered up to $23.7 billion in 2003 (33 percent of the total). Those ODA flows for the group of the 50 poorest countries fell from 37 percent of the total at the end of the 1980s to 32 percent of the total in 2000, recovering again slightly to 33 percent of the total in 2003 (OECD, 2006).

This percentage is still smaller than that allocated to average-income developing countries where a high percentage of the world's poor also live. In 2000 the net assistance per inhabitant was $23 in the case of Europe and Central Asia, $20 in sub-Saharan Africa, $16 in the Middle East and north Africa, $10 for Latin America and the Caribbean, $5 for south-east Asia and the Pacific, and $3 for south Asia, although this phenomenon has to do with the smaller population of the poorest countries (World Bank, 2001), which will be discussed later.

The Monterrey Conference and ODA

At the Monterrey conference organized by the UN, moves were made to improve this situation, and a new commitment was undertaken to raise ODA to $100 billion by 2006, doubling the current amount of $50 billion, with a view to meeting the Millennium Summit Development Goals. To this end, the European Union has undertaken to increase the proportion of its GDP for ODA from the current 0.33 percent to 0.39 percent in 2006 and the United States has undertaken to increase its ODA from the current 0.10 percent of GDP to 0.15 percent in that same year. These undertakings signify $7 billion more per year from the European Union and $5 billion more from the United States. It was also agreed to convert the $6 billion in soft loans from the International Development Agency (IDA) into donations.

This figure is still, of course, a far cry from the OECD's longed-for contribution of 0.7 percent of GDP to development assistance, which would mean $175 billion per year and would make it easy to reach the ambitious, but necessary, UN Millennium Summit Development Goals approved in September 2000 by the world's leaders. The eight development policy goals for 2015 are: (1) to eradicate extreme poverty and hunger in the world; (2) to achieve universal primary education; (3) to promote gender equality and empower women; (4) to reduce child mortality; (5) to improve maternal health; (6) to combat AIDS, malaria, and other diseases; (7) to ensure environmental sustainability; and (8) to develop a global partnership for development. The Monterrey conference was the forum proposed to discuss how to obtain sufficient financing to achieve the above-mentioned goals. Although it did not produce the results expected, what was achieved was a significant increase – and, indeed, a change in the decreasing trend – in ODA funds.

In any event, it should be noted that ODA is not sufficient in itself to raise developing countries' per capita GDP nor, consequently, to achieve their further development. In fact, in some cases it is not even enough to efficiently eliminate poverty on a long-term basis. In the case of Africa, although external aid as a percentage of GDP increased from 5.5 percent of GDP in 1970 to 18 percent in 1995, the annual per capita GDP growth rate, measured in moving ten-year averages, has fallen since the end of the 1970s, was negative from the mid-1980s to the mid-1990s, and has only recovered since 1995, just when the aid began to decline (Artadi and Sala i Martín, 2003; and Easterly and Levine, 1997).

There are many other factors that affect per capita GDP growth, such as population growth and political and social institutions, which have been addressed in greater detail in the previous chapters. According to World Bank economists Dollar, Burnside, and Dollar (2000), development assistance really boosts growth and reduces poverty when the recipient countries implement reasonable economic policies. Also, the poorer the country is, the more efficiently the aid helps to reduce poverty. The problem is that the aid is not allocated properly, based on efficiency criteria and rewarding the countries with the least corruption and best policies and institutions. In 1990, countries with poor policies and deficient institutions received, on average, $44 per inhabitant, while countries with better policies and institutions received, on average, $39 per inhabitant. Since then, the situation has changed and, although ODA is less than it was in 1990, it is allocated much more efficiently. The countries with the soundest policies receive $29 per inhabitant, versus $16 for the countries with worse policies.

The World Bank is much more careful about the assistance that countries grant bilaterally, and its efficiency rate is higher. It currently allocates three times as many dollars per inhabitant ($6.50) to the best-run countries as it does to the ones with worse policies ($2.30). Depending on the source, the World Bank's efficiency ratio, which measures the success of each aid program, is between 60 percent and 80 percent. This latter percentage was obtained from the World Bank's own internal evaluation (Johnston, 2002).

Even so, heavy criticism has rained down on the World Bank for its loan policy. The World Bank spent nearly $30 billion on education. However, Africa, which received a good part of this aid and has improved its education much more than south-east Asia, has been unable to grow, whereas the countries of south-east Asia have grown. Venezuela received $132 million to improve its educational level and, despite this, its productivity per worker is still where it was two decades ago. Nigeria has received $101 million in capital investments since the 1970s, yet it is poorer now than it was back in 1971. Zambia has received $2 billion since the 1970s to fill the gap between its saving and investment, and yet its per capita income has still not managed to surpass $600.

On the other hand, Bangladesh, one of the most corrupt countries in the world according to Transparency International, has grown with less outside aid than other poor countries at a rate of 4.5 percent per year since 1980 and 5 percent per year since 1990 because it has used what aid it has received more productively to develop its clothing industry. In 1977 it joined into a single association a group of 19 companies; today the association comprises 2,700 companies, employs 1.5 million workers and has sales of $2 billion. Its example has been followed by Mauritius, India, and China (Easterly, 2001).

Four basic issues are currently under discussion regarding ODA. The first is what the annual volume should be and how it could be allocated more efficiently. The second is whether ODA should center on donations rather than more or less soft loans, as is generally the case at present. The third issue is whether ODA should also cover debt forgiveness and the fourth issue is how to obtain enough ODA resources to meet the Millennium Development Goals.

Problems of ODA Absorption by Recipient Countries

The absorption capacity of the ODA recipients is also a factor to be considered when giving aid. Sometimes, increasing assistance over a certain "saturation point or level," aid has decreasing capital returns and has no longer a positive effect on economic growth given that developing countries may fail to create a supporting climate for economic activity. This saturation point varies across countries (Collier and Dollar, 2002). In countries with good policies and institutions the saturation point is about 15–25 percent of GDP, whereas in others it is as low as 5–10 percent of GDP.

Thus, allocating aid is a very complex task in which the key factor is how to know that the country in question is well governed and aid is not going to be wasted. There is then a certain consensus about the fact that well administered countries have a high saturation level and that they can absorb more aid that what they get and that some poorly governed countries are getting more aid than they can absorb, but there is not yet a consensus about the saturation levels. On the one side, World Bank economists Devarajan, Miller, and Swanson (2002) show that increasing ODA by US$40–60 billion and allocating it only to the countries with good policies and institutions, the saturation point is reached in only 4 out of 65. But there is not yet any consensus about the ODA level of saturation.

On the other side the IMF economists Heller and Gupta (2002) highlight the difficulties that the poorest countries would face in trying to absorb massive aid, as would be the case if the OECD's targeted 0.7 percent of GDP – $175 billion – were to be achieved and concentrated exclusively on these countries as some experts believe should be done.

Achieving 0.7 percent of GDP must undoubtedly be a permanent objective of the developed countries in order to meet the development goals that they themselves approved at the Millennium Summit. They should try to achieve this figure as soon as possible, because by the 2020s it will be nearly impossible, once the baby-boom generation retires and begins to collect pensions and other social benefits, thereby placing tremendous budgetary constraints on the OECD countries. However, such an increase must also be accompanied by enhanced ODA efficiency and greater transparency and control over its funds to keep them from ending up in the hands of the companies that provide the public goods and services or in those of the local leaders. The citizens of the donor countries, as taxpayers and ultimate suppliers of these funds, have a right to know how they are invested and whether they are being used for the purpose for which they were granted.

A problem would also arise, however, for the recipient countries of the 0.7 percent, particularly if the funds were concentrated in the poorest countries. Recent experience in Uganda, Burkina Faso, Ghana, Malawi, Senegal, and Togo shows that many of these countries, because of their size, cannot easily absorb such large amounts of aid without suffering problems similar to the so-called "Dutch disease" – such as a sharp rise in exchange rates, excessive internal currency creation, or an inadequate public administration to handle the ODA flows correctly – which can have a very harmful effect on their economies.

According to the two IMF economists, only if ODA were spent entirely on imports would its impact on monetary supply or internal demand be avoided. If a significant part of these funds were spent on domestic non-traded goods, the prices of domestic goods would rise. The conversion into local currency of the foreign currencies received would increase the monetary base. There would also be an increase in domestic demand, some of which would filter through to increased imports, weakening the trade balance. Part of the aid would be spent on non-traded domestic goods and services – i.e. those which are not exported and do not compete with imports – which would increase the prices of such products and the general level of prices in the economy. If the country has a fixed exchange rate, the currency would appreciate in real terms, making its exports less competitive. If the country has a flexible rate, the greater supply of foreign currency, not offset by import demand, would trigger the appreciation of both nominal and real exchange rates. In these conditions, the aid might not be efficient enough to reduce poverty, because if the country has a higher inflation rate the poor will have a lower purchasing power, making them even poorer, and a rise in exchange rates would prevent its products from being competitive, increasing unemployment.

There are also microeconomic effects that should be taken into account. First, massive inflows of aid can be too much for a government's administrative capacity to handle, leading to misspending. Second, such large inflows of aid can reduce a government's incentives to implement reform policies for its institutions and worsen its economic policies. Lastly, it can lead to rent-seeking, corruption, and the weakening of the civil society, as recipient governments are generally more likely to be held accountable by foreign donors than by their own citizens.

These issues could materialize if we make a comparative calculation of the potential size of the aid relative to the size of the potential recipients. Let us assume that the entire 0.7 percent of GDP is distributed to the least developed countries (i.e. those with less than $500 of per capita income). The volume of aid per inhabitant would be a very high percentage of the annual income of "the absolute or extreme poor" of those countries where most of their population lives on less than one dollar per day. Therefore, it would be preferable to also distribute the aid to other highly populated countries, which, despite having a higher average per capita income, have a portion of the population living in absolute poverty, mainly in their rural and remote regions. These would be countries with a per capita GDP of $500–800, and they would include India, Nigeria, Pakistan, and even some other low-income countries with a per capita GDP of over $800, such as China, Indonesia, and the Philippines.

How to Allocate ODA More Efficiently

The effectiveness track record of ODA is really disappointing. Since the end of the 1940s, close to US$ two trillion have been spent on development, and their results have been very poor in terms of poverty reduction and growth enhancing. The answer is very complex, but it seems clear that it has proved to be extremely difficult to find out how to enhance development and how to make aid effective. It is not an issue of political will, but of efficiency. The UN itself declared "freedom from hunger" a major theme from 1960 to 1965 and made the 1960s the decade of development. The Atma Ata Conference on Primary Health Care called for slashing preventable deaths among children and mothers and "health for all" in 2000. In 1980 there was a UN resolution for "clean water for all by 1990."

The development community has been working on malaria, guinea worm eradication, illiteracy, women's rights, and equality for decades, as well as on road and bridge building, governance, institutional change, legal reform, environmental protection, small enterprise development, and raising consciousness. Almost everything has been tried but with small results because there is a general perception that doing something is better than doing nothing but without changing radically the way aid is allocated, monitored, and made accountable.

This is the reason why in the ongoing debate about aid, some development experts are becoming increasingly more skeptical and more critical about it. They show that recipient countries have wasted aid and have not been accountable for it and their levels of corruption and lack of governance. That institutions providing aid, whether bilateral or multilateral agencies or even some NGOs, have become bureaucratic, cumbersome, and awkward, lacking strategic clarity and consistency and they have been judged for the amount of projects and money spent and not for their real results. They show that it took industrial countries more than two hundred years to develop and that it will be a utopia to think that the development targets can be achieved in the next decades, even through a big push to ODA resources. As they show that aid is mainly supply driven, thus, they ask for a reduction on aid and a radical rethinking about how to approach development. They finally think that the main issue is probably how to be able to attack at the same time all the multifaceted problems which affect development and that it is necessary first to agree an integrated approach to development before wasting more aid.

Two World Bank economists, Collier and Dollar (1999), carried out a study based on the allocations of aid in 1996 to see what would happen if the aid, increased to 0.7 percent of GDP, were re-allocated so that the poorest countries (those with per capita income of less than $500) with good policies received all the aid and those countries with poor policies or engaged in civil war or violence were excluded from receiving aid.

Three scenarios were used for this purpose. In the first one, China and India would receive only 11 percent of the total ($19.25 billion of the total $175 billion). The poorest countries would receive an average ratio of aid to GDP of 32 percent, which is twice the amount they currently receive. In some countries the aid would reach even higher ratios of GDP: for Ethiopia it would be 90 percent, for Burundi 60 percent, for Uganda 52 percent, for Vietnam 48 percent, and for Nicaragua 43 percent. These percentages would be very difficult for these countries to absorb. In the second scenario, the allocation to China and India would increase to 66 percent of the total ($116 billion), and Nigeria,

Pakistan, the Philippines, and Vietnam would receive $25 billion. This signifies that the poorest countries would receive a lower average ratio of aid to GDP of 12 percent and Ethiopia's share would fall to 33 percent. In this case, only $30 billion would be allocated to the poorest countries, $10 billion for Bangladesh, and $20 billion for all of sub-Saharan Africa.

In the third scenario, an average per capita income cap of $500 is not used to determine the allocation of ODA, because absolute poverty is not limited to the poorest countries. In the third scenario ODA is distributed to each country in relation to the proportion of the population living on less than one dollar per day. In this case China and India would receive $112 billion, almost the same as in the second scenario, but India would receive $73 billion and China $39 billion, because India has a higher proportion of absolute poor. Sub-Saharan Africa would receive $33 billion. With this allocation, which would undoubtedly be the most efficient, bearing in mind the condition of good policies, the poorest countries would receive a percentage in proportion to their GDP of 32 percent, and the low-income countries, which include the largest countries, would receive 8 percent of their GDP.

In conclusion, both the World Bank and the IMF economists consider that: first, it is more efficient to allocate ODA to the absolute poor of the poorest countries and the low-income countries than just to those countries with per capita income of less than $500. This way ODA could be extended to south and east Asia. Second, the macroeconomic situation of some of these countries should be monitored and incentives should be provided so that, at least in the short term, a significant portion of the aid is used to purchase imported goods and services, such as vaccines and medicines, books and teaching materials, and units of drinking water so as to avoid domestic inflationary problems and rising exchange rates, which could prove to be very costly for the recipient country.

Third, assurances would have to be provided that part of the aid would be used to reinforce public institutions and to improve governance. More aid could be allocated to countries that have taken the appropriate measures to cut down on corruption and improve their transparency and accountability. Fourth, part of the aid should be invested in the domestic research and development of drugs and vaccines for the most widespread diseases, of alternative energies to reduce deforestation and to adapt agricultural production to the local climate and achieve higher productivity, thereby reducing the likelihood of starvation. Lastly, trust funds should be set up so that countries which have difficulties absorbing ODA can accumulate it for later use.

Research done by Rajan and Subramanian (2005) tests the general validity of the aid–growth relationship in a very comprehensive way. They do it across time horizons (medium and long run) and periods (1960s through the 1990s) sources of aid (multilateral and bilateral), types of aid (economic, social, food), timing of impact of aid (short-term versus long-term), specifications (cross-section and panel), and samples. Their results find little evidence of a robust positive impact of aid on growth, even by correcting the bias of conventional estimation procedures (ordinary least squares) against finding a positive impact of aid. Moreover, in the cross-sectional analysis, they find some evidence for a negative relationship in the long run, although not significant. They also find some evidence of a positive relationship for the period 1980–2000, but only when outliers are included. Finally, they cannot find evidence that aid works better in better policy or institutional or geographical environments or that certain kinds of aid work better than others.

They argue that one reason for this surprising lack of evidence may be due to the fact that the impact is so small that it cannot be detected against the background noise. In any case it seems clear that its impact is smaller than suggested by its advocates even if its flows are well utilized. So the strong claims about aid effectiveness are unwarranted and aid policies which rely on such claims should be re-examined. By contrast, the effects of good policies on growth are robust and discernible.

The Millennium Project, coordinated by Jeffrey Sachs with a team of 265 development experts from public, non-governmental and private organizations, has issued recently a final report which recommends concentrating most additional aid, at the beginning, in a dozen of poor countries which are in a situation of progressing fast, given their good governance and their high absorption capacity, so as to show the example to the rest of the countries.

Their report proposes four criteria to be able to access aid: first, that the country has to be admitted or in the process of being admitted to the HIPC (Heavily Indebted Poor Countries) initiative; second, that the country must be considered eligible, or be in the process to becoming eligible, for the US MCA (Millennium Challenge Account) cooperation system; third, that it must have made a submission to the APRM (African Peer Review Mechanism) of NEPAD (New Partnership for African Development); and, finally, that it must be in the process of elaborating a Document of Strategy to Reduce Poverty (DSRP). All these different requisites go in the same direction: mainly to poor African countries with good governance. Thus, these criteria exclude totally developing countries with medium incomes and concentrates mainly on Africa.

Whatever is the system of allocation and conditionality, most probably the development debate is going to go on for some time because it is not only a question of bricks-and-mortar projects or giving funds without any serious accountability, but it is mainly a slow process of changing habits, mentalities, institutions, identities, traditional cultural and religious beliefs, concepts of work and leisure, and many other political, societal, and economic structures which have a negative impact on development.

Nevertheless, something more needs to be done, because world citizens should be aware that the present levels of poverty in a world of increasing prosperity are morally unacceptable, socially dangerous, and economically inefficient. Everybody is losing with the present situation.

Should ODA Be Provided as Grants Rather than Loans?

A debate was opened up in Monterrey by the then US Secretary of the Treasury Paul O'Neill, when he recommended that the proportion of grants in ODA flows be increased substantially and, particularly, when he recommended that 50 percent of the World Bank's International Development Association (IDA) loans be converted into grants. These recommendations were rejected by the European countries and, paradoxically, also by the leaders of some developing countries and, logically, by many private lobbies. However, the US's position, despite being the OECD country that contributes the least to ODA in terms of GDP, makes sense, not only because it increases the Bank's development assistance funds but also because it avoids the embarrassment of having to write off, once again, all the debt that the poorest countries owe and cannot repay.

The European countries' arguments against this recommendation are: first, the switch to grants could jeopardize the World Bank's future finances. However, it would take a decade before this change would be noticeable in the Bank's balance sheet, as most IDA loans have a ten-year grace period and it would take 20 years before the volumes became significant. Meanwhile, the Bank's funds could be increased and the situation improved if the wealthy countries reduced their protectionism vis-à-vis the poor countries trying to sell to them. Also, it should be recalled that the World Bank already used this tool several years ago, channeling transfers from the US and the EU without any problems.

Second, grants reduce the control that taxpaying citizens in the recipient countries have over their governments when it comes time to pay interest on the loans. With grants, the already scant internal control could diminish even more, which could reduce their efficient use, or even lead to corruption. In this connection, it is clear that with grants both multilateral financial organizations and governments (bilaterally) will have to be more selective and disciplined to avoid squandering.

Nevertheless, the arguments in favor are more forceful. First, what the poor countries need is to reduce their poverty levels. To do so, their top priority is basic public goods, such as rural roads, drinking water, sewage systems, education, basic medical assistance and medicines. The short-term social return and long-term economic return on these goods is very high, but the medium-term financial return is very small. Considering that these countries are practically insolvent, taking out loans or assuming debt for investments of this kind is not the most appropriate way to finance them, whereas grants are because they do not increase indebtedness.

Second, grants are much easier to monitor and control because they are paid for each unit of public goods or services supplied or developed and they have lower transaction and bureaucratic expenses, both for the donor and for the recipient. Moreover, the probability of corruption is reduced significantly because grants can be allocated directly to those who need them most, without requiring the intervention of the government or rent-seeking bureaucrats at the expense of the rest of the country's citizens. Grants also help to avoid mega-projects of the type undertaken in many poor countries, which, as experience has shown, are not only utterly useless but lend themselves to corruption.

Third, many of these countries are included in debt forgiveness programs because they cannot possibly repay their debt. Accordingly, it seems illogical to burden them with more debt, which will almost certainly also have to be pardoned in the end.

Lastly, grants make the citizens of the recipient country become more directly involved in the projects to be financed with them, thus increasing their likelihood of success. This argument is supported by the positive experience with donations from altruistic individuals and private companies in the past.

It would therefore be very advisable for grants to take on a bigger role in ODA, especially for the poorest countries and individuals in the world, who are the ones who need it the most and who have no other way of getting rid of their debt trap.

Is Debt Forgiveness Useful for Poor Countries?

The decision taken by the IMF and the World Bank in 1996 to pardon the debts of 26 heavily indebted poor countries that were carrying out social and economic reforms under the HIPC initiative to reduce their levels of poverty gave rise to a heated debate between experts in development policy. The idea underlying the initiative was that the heavily indebted poor countries that were making the effort to reduce their levels of absolute poverty deserved to have their debt burden lightened so as to give them a temporary respite to try to escape poverty while preventing them – once and for all – from restructuring their perpetual debt. The Paris Club also then decided to take the terms set forth in Naples in 1994 one step further and to grant an 80 percent reduction in the net present value of their debt servicing.

Since then, this initiative has been gaining force with the support of the G7. In 1998, it was agreed to reduce poor countries' debt servicing by a further $50 billion, to which the World Bank would contribute $11 billion; in exchange, these countries were to step up their domestic programs to reduce poverty. In 2002, reductions of nearly $40 billion had been achieved, representing $25.7 billion in net present value, and six countries – Bolivia, Burkina Faso, Mauritania, Mozambique, Tanzania, and Uganda – had completed their debt reduction programs. In these countries debt has been reduced by 66 percent, the debt/GDP ratio has been cut by 50 percent, debt servicing has been reduced by 33 percent and the debt/export ratio has declined 40 percent.

A total of 42 countries have now joined this initiative, and negotiations are under way for the Ivory Coast, the Democratic Republic of the Congo, the Comoro Islands, the Republic of Central Africa, Benin, Guyana, Mali, and Senegal. It was also rightly decided to add a long-term debt sustainability condition to that of poverty reduction, as some countries that have completed their programs have once again fallen into excessive debt. To fulfill this condition, these countries are required to continually improve their economic and social policies and earmark part of their savings from the program to ensure that their debt levels do not increase again; for their part, the developed countries have to open up their markets to them further and assure them financing under soft terms.

The criticism against this initiative is, first, that it is not new. It had already been proposed on several occasions: in 1977 with UNCTAD;

in 1987 in Venice; in 1988 in Toronto; in 1990 in Houston; in 1991 in London; and in 1994 in Naples. These countries have never been exonerated of their sizeable debts. Second, since these countries' GDP and export growth rates have been lower since the 1990s, they have not managed to reduce their percentages of debt significantly in relation to these two aggregates, despite the enormous cost this entails. Third, the debt reduction program can create perverse incentives for becoming indebted again in the hope that it will be pardoned again; it could thus become an incentive for other countries without such high levels of indebtedness to try to increase them so that they can avail themselves of the program. In fact, Pakistan, Nigeria, and Indonesia are applying as candidates for the program, and the countries that obtained debt reductions totaling $33 billion in 1996 have accumulated $41 billion of debt since then.

Fourth, the program should have given priority not only to the fight against poverty but also to debt sustainability. This was finally done in 2002. Lastly, there have been recent cases that have severely harmed the reputation and credibility of this initiative. Uganda, which is one of the most reformist countries among the poorest countries, spent $47 million on a presidential aircraft, and Tanzania not only bought a presidential aircraft but it also ordered a military traffic control system for another US$40 million, when debt forgiveness is supposed to be used for poverty reduction programs (Easterly, 2001).

However, there are clear examples of countries making good use of debt forgiveness to reduce poverty. For instance, once again in Uganda, the government used the savings from this initiative to waive school fees for two million children. Other countries, such as Mozambique, Senegal, and Burkina Faso, are using these funds to fight AIDS. The World Bank estimates that 40 percent of the funds freed up through debt forgiveness are used for education and 25 percent for healthcare. The main arguments for debt forgiveness fall into two categories. On the one hand, this initiative is imposed by reality. These countries cannot repay their debt, so it is either restructured so that they can "take a temporary break" and resume dealing with the situation later or, if the leaders and policies are credible, a decision may be taken to pardon their debt, provided that they do not voluntarily accumulate it again.

On the other hand, when accumulated debt reaches a certain level it chokes growth. A recent study by Patillo, Poirson, and Ricci (2002), based on a sample of 93 developing countries, analyzed this problem and found that debt contributes positively to growth until it reaches a threshold, after which it becomes increasingly negative. This threshold is reached when debt hits a relative level of 35 percent to 40 percent of GDP or 160 percent to 170 percent of exports (both in terms of net present value). The study also found that the difference in growth among the developing countries in the broad sample – between the less indebted countries (i.e. with debt levels of less than 25 percent of GDP or 100 percent of exports) and the most indebted countries (i.e. with debt levels of more than 95 percent of GDP or 367 percent of exports) – is 2 percentage points per year. When such high levels are reached, not only does the country's investment activity decrease sharply, but there is a severe distortion in the allocation of funds to very short-term, inefficient projects and, in the end, the economic authorities lose any incentive to maintain orthodox economic policies.

Through this study, the authors show the benefits of the debt forgiveness initiative. By reducing a country's debt level by 50 percent, i.e. from 200 percent of exports to 100 percent of exports, its per capita GDP increases by between 0.5 percent and 1 percent per year. Since most of the debt levels of the countries accepted in this program stood at 300 percent of exports, their reduction by 50 percent, to 150 percent, would mean an increase in per capita GDP of 1 percent per year. In the absence of any internal or external shocks requiring them to increase their debt, this would gradually reduce their level of indebtedness.

In any case, debt forgiveness is fortunately going ahead. The G7 recently has promised to forgive up to 100 percent of debts owed to multilateral financial institutions (MFI) by the world's poorest debtors. But behind the generous pledges are deep divisions about what debt relief is really for. On the one hand are the British, for whom debt relief is primarily a popular way to raise aid flows to poor countries. That is why Gordon Brown insists that the money should be additional. He wants rich countries to pay debt service that poor countries owe to the MFI and for that he wants to sell some of the gold reserves of the IMF to pay for the write-off of its loans.

For the US government, debt forgiveness is more about acknowledging past failures and changing the way ODA is delivered. The US Treasury wants to write off the debts of the poorest countries and to give them only grants in the future. But it sees no need for new resources to pay for this; thus, the World Bank would simply give less aid to those countries in the future. Fretting about new money or gold sales is an unnecessary distraction from getting rid of loans that will never be repaid.

The US Treasury would prefer to test new bilateral aid vehicles such as the US funded Millennium Challenge Account (MCA) to add multilateral resources for aid. The MCA is an institution that promises to give aid out of a fund only to honest governments pursuing sound economic policies following the research done by Craig Bumside and David Dollar (2000) showing that aid only works in countries pursuing sound economic policies. The idea is both reasonable and cautious but until now has been in very little demand. Since it was established in 2002, it has only made its first grant in April 2005 for a sum of $110 million to Madagascar.

In any case, selling the IMF gold is not cost free. The IMF gold reserves of 103 million ounces (worth around $40 billion-plus at market prices, but valued at only $9 billion at IMF books) were given by rich countries to bolster the Fund's balance sheet. Thus, less gold reserves will leave the IMF with fewer resources for use to cope with financial crises and its sale may slightly depress gold prices if it is accompanied with the recurrent and timely sales by central banks. But even with less gold the IMF will not reach a situation of financial fragility. This is the reason why the views of the US and the UK on debt forgiveness at the G8 summit in Gleneagles were going to be divergent. The UK would like to consider it as an additional resource to ODA and not as an alternative instrument to be deducted in the future from ODA, at least partially.

The issue is complex, since very often what donors take in debt repayments they give several times over in aid. Mozambique, for example, has paid $71.8 million on its debts in 2003 but it has received in the same year from bilateral and multilateral donors an amount 14 times higher. This is an extreme case but on average the poorest countries have received in aid the double of their debt service every year. A recent paper by Raghuran Rajan (2005), chief economist of the IMF, has shown the difference between both views. What is the difference between an indebted country that pays $100 million as debt service and receives $200 million in aid and another debt-free country that receives $100 million in aid? The annual net inflow is the same but the stock of liabilities is different. This higher stock of debt in the first case can make foreign investors fear that the government is overtaxing their profits in order to repay their debt and that a reduction in foreign investment will deter growth and the ability of the country to repay its debts. Therefore, debt relief is thus in the interest of both the poor country and its foreign investors. It will increase the real value of its creditor's claims and the country's ability to repay its debts.

But, Rajan has doubts about the real efficiency of debt forgiveness because in these very poor countries there other reasons why foreign investors might be deterred from investing in their economies, such as corruption, insecure property rights, bad infrastructure, and fragmented markets, leaving debt as a marginal concern. If a country's government is thoroughly corrupt, then the status quo – no forgiveness and no additional aid – is best, for it gives the government no official resources to misuse and limits its ability to raise private sector funds. Therefore, aid should be distributed to NGOs. If the country has a reasonably committed government, then it should look at the country's primary need. When social sector projects top the list, then what matters is the extent of official sector funding. Here, the best alternative is for debt not to be forgiven but for official creditors to lend more. But if most projects are commercially viable, the best alternative is some relief but leaving enough outstanding official debt that foreign investors lend responsibly. Finally, substantial debt relief is prudent if the risk of financial distress is a serious problem. Therefore, a one size fits all proposal, while politically convenient, is unlikely to benefit recipient countries as much as a proposal that ties debt relief and additional aid to a country's specific situation.

How to Obtain Additional Resources for ODA

Today, on the way up to the Millennium Development Goals (MDG) and to the Doha Round (DR), there is an increasing demand, at least in Europe, to find new financial resources to help development and reduce the poverty levels of those countries and regions being left out of the globalization process and, at the same time, to allow developing countries to grow faster through trade liberalization. On the one hand, developing countries are demanding both more aid and more trade. On the other, developed countries are reluctant to reduce their agricultural and labor intensive manufacturing protections, but they seem to be readier, mainly in the European Union, to increase their volume of aid flows.

On the aid side, OECD countries have made an important effort in 2005, by increasing Official Development Assistance (ODA) to $107 billion, its highest absolute level ever. This total represents 0.33 percent of the combined gross national income (GNI) of the ODA members, up from 0.25 percent in 2004. Moreover, while bilateral aid grants have risen annually since 2001, net official lending to developing countries, largely multilateral, has declined dramatically, falling from $27 billion net inflows in 2001 to $25 billion net outflows in 2004. The largest factor underlying this shift has been a $30 billion decline in lending by the IMF, reflecting repayment of sizeable crisis-related disbursements made in 2001. Net lending by the World Bank also fell by $9 billion over the period as several countries repaid large structural adjustment loans (World Bank, 2005).

These countries have already met in 2005 their Monterrey commitments to raise ODA to 0.30 percent of GNI by 2006. The EU members have a simple average ODA level above that target: 0.50 percent, while the US and Japan levels are still 0.22 and 0.28 percent of GNI respectively. In 2005, the US was the country giving most aid in absolute terms, $27 billion, followed by Japan, with $13 billion, France, with $10 billion, the UK, with $10.7 billion, and Germany with $10.1 billion. These five countries contribute with 67 percent of the total but only France and the UK go above 0.47 percent of GNI.

But the Monterrey consensus falls short of meeting the MDG agreed at the United Nations in 2000. While the Monterrey Agreement estimates an annual increase of $15 billion a year as of 2006, the Millennium Development Project estimated, at the time, an extra $50 billion a year, a figure that will be now even higher. For this reason, an im-portant number of European initiatives have been put forward to try to "front load" the Monterrey commitments and to meet the MDG through "additional and innovative sources and modalities of financing," and among them: the joint IMF/World Bank paper "Aid effectiveness and financial modalities"; the quadripartite report sponsored by the Presidents of Brazil, Chile, France, and Spain, and later by that of Germany; the Landau Report commissioned by President Chirac, and the UK-sponsored Commission for Africa.

Besides the urgent need to improve the effectiveness and reduce the frequent political, military and domestic exports bias in the use of ODA funds, the additional and innovative sources of financing can arise from either increasing the share of national budgets devoted to development, or further "debt relief" by selling assets of the IMF and the World Bank, such as gold reserves, or through new national or international taxes allocated to this purpose.

It is interesting to see that new global taxes have been preferred to new national taxes by the government and NGO experts. This preference goes against traditional conventional wisdom through the old dictum: "no taxation without representation." That means that in order to introduce a new tax, two steps are needed: first it is necessary to create a strong popular support for it and then it has to be approved by parliament, as the democratic representation of the popular vote or, in some small countries, by a referendum. In the case of global taxes both steps are extremely difficult to achieve because both democratic instances do not exist yet globally.

Moreover, new global taxes need to satisfy the following conditions: they must be easy to collect and difficult to evade, they must be neutral in their impact on market incentives and income distribution unless they are deliberately targeted to influence consumption or redistribute income, and they should discourage inappropriate consumption, excessive control of resources, environmentally damaging activities, and social inequities.

The main three global tax proposals on the table are the following: a currency transactions (or Tobin) tax, global environmental taxes, and a global tax on arm sales (Reisen, 2004). The global currency transactions tax was proposed by Nobel Prize winner James Tobin in 1972, as a way of throwing "sand in the wheels" of international finance and so to combat market volatility. Its attraction to NGOs and some governments comes from the fact that a very small tax rate imposed in a very large tax base can yield very sizeable revenues.

However, tax rates have to be extremely low to avoid the very high mobility of their underlying tax base. A 0.01 percent tax rate would yield around 17 billion euros if the tax was limited to the European Union (Spahn, 2002). Other estimations are lower: for instance Nissanke (2003) finds out that a world-wide 0.01 tax rate would yield $17–19 billion. But the actual end results might be much lower, given that daily currency turnover is actually coming down, that, given that most transactions are due to hedging activities, done for the purposes of avoiding over exposure to currencies accumulated from deal-making, a tax would increase volatility rather than decrease it, and that the foreign exchange market could migrate to tax-free jurisdictions (Kenen, 1996; and Reisen, 2002). Thus, even if a Tobin tax was feasible to operate it would not be economically desirable (Reisen, 2004).

Global environmental taxes make more sense given that environmental problems spill across national boundaries, as with the case of chemicals that deplete the ozone layer, carbon greenhouse gases which lead to global warming, depletion of ocean fish stocks, and habitat destruction that impairs biological diversity. This is the reason why existing national green taxes in OECD countries yielded on average 2.5 percent of GDP in 2000.

A global tax on carbon emissions will yield "triple dividends" to the world in the sense that not only will it contribute to improving the global environment, but also that its revenue can allow a reduction of other taxes, such as taxes on labor and employment and that it enhances additional resources for ODA (Sandmo, 2003). A rough estimation shows that a uniform tax of 0.01 percent per liter would correspond to a tax of $21 per metric ton of carbon and yield annual revenue of US$130 billion.

But there are also some serious difficulties in introducing them globally. For instance, the US Congress has passed legislation that makes it illegal for the US to participate in any global tax, and carbon taxes have been opposed because they are regressive and hurt lower income families in spite of the very low rate of taxes on gasoline and other carbon products. Eventually, a global carbon emission tax will be unavoidable but it seems very difficult today to find a world consensus.

Finally, in early 2004, a few heads of state and government (Lula, Lagos, Chirac, and Zapatero) backed by Kofi Annan, re-launched the idea of an international tax on arms sales to revitalize the flagging global drive against hunger and poverty. Although it is a very welcome tax, the problem with it is that it has very low revenue capacity. The annual value of arms trade (imports or exports) was $51.5 billion; therefore a 5 percent tax would not yield more than $2.5 billion annually. Moreover, the biggest obstacle for collecting the tax is that many arms sales, mainly small arms and light weapons, are done through illicit trade and the majority of the countries involved in this kind of arms sales fail to provide annual reports on their imports or exports. Naturally, if a tax is introduced, the illicit arms trade will further rise as a consequence. Even countries under embargo are able to circumvent this and get arms illicitly.

On the trade side, the market access of developing-country exports to ODA member markets still faces very high barriers. While the effective average imports "ad valorem" tariff of developed countries is around 5 percent, that facing developing country exports is higher. The developed countries' tariffs on agriculture and food products coming from developing countries show not only higher average levels of around 15 percent but also huge tariff peaks for many products out of tariff quotas, going up to 500 percent in the EU, up to 350 percent in the US, and up to 50 percent in Japan. For manufactured goods coming from developing countries, developed countries' average tariff rates are lower: around 4 percent, but close to 28 percent of the tariffs show peaks in excess of 15 percent, some reaching up to 100 percent, all of them concentrated on the imports of labor-intensive manufactures, such as textiles, clothing, and shoes. Moreover, tariff escalation, whereby tariff rates increase according to the degree of processing, are common. These effective average tariffs do not take into account other means of protection through specific (not ad valorem) tariffs and non-tariff barriers. The latter affect almost 40 percent of agricultural imports.

Thus, a sensible proposal would be one which tries to tie up additional sources for development financing with enhancing, at the same time, international trade by lowering the impact of developed country trade protection on exports by developing countries. This simple proposal consists in an agreement, among all ODA member countries or at least among those countries that seem to be ready to increase aid, to use the full proceeds extracted out of tariffs and other quantifiable protective measures, charged to developing country imports, to increase ODA to the least developed countries or regions. To give an extreme example: the total US tariff revenue out of Bangladesh imports was, before the expired Multi-fiber Agreement, almost equal to that out of its total imports coming from France, $331 million, and after this agreement, tariffs will go up by replacing quotas.

Some recent rough estimates show that the developed countries' import tariff revenue coming out of developing countries' manufactured and agricultural imports could be in excess of $25 billion every year, which added to the additional $15 billion of ODA per year, approved at Monterrey, would get a total figure in excess of US$40 billion, much closer to the Millennium development goals of an extra $50 billion.

This proposal is simple and transparent, easy to implement, avoids levying new and difficult to introduce global taxes and, at the same time, gives an incentive to ODA member countries to reduce their protection against developing country imports, which will also help their own citizens to increase their disposable income. Thus, almost everybody wins. For instance, EU agricultural protection from developing country imports makes the average EU family pay almost double the international price for its basic foodstuff basket. Thus, if some ODA member countries' governments prefer to maintain their protection, because of political or electoral "sensitivities," they will have to give a higher volume of ODA and vice versa, but eventually they may feel the pressure from the majority of their own citizens to opt for a reduction of their import protection. Moreover, the agreement does not need to wait for the Doha Round to be completed, but it can be done immediately, irrespectively of its uncertain future outcome.

This proposal could eventually produce a "demonstration effect" in other middle income developing countries, which have even higher tariff protection to goods coming from the least developed countries which need more aid, and gives them the opportunity to initiate an ODA program, even if they only start applying it to their own tariff peaks.

Another additional proposal which makes a lot of sense is to enhance the amount of aid that private donors give to these countries. Private aid is by definition more accountable than public aid, because it is not "other people's money" and therefore can be an efficient addition to ODA. For instance, the US allows donors to deduct up to 50 percent of their income from personal income taxes if they are allocated to all kinds of charities, national or foreign. This is why rich American people complement the very low percentages of ODA given by the US. The amount of private donations by US philanthropic individuals was estimated, in 2002, to be 2 percent of GDP, or $220 billion. By contrast, in OECD countries the annual expenditure of philanthropic foundations is estimated only at $3 billion. In the EU countries, their income tax deduction is half that of the US in the best of the cases.

The most important issue is how to give special incentives to private individuals to increase their donations to poor countries, given that most of them are spent nationally or locally. Thus, a special tax agreement by the G7 countries to have above the average income tax deductions for aid to the poorest countries and regions of the world would generate large additional aid flows to reduce the still existing huge levels of poverty and finally be able to meet the UN MDG in 2015, and break from the lack of credibility that previous targets have accumulated through decades of failure.

A recent poll of 26 US-based small charitable organizations sheds some light on the difficulty of transferring donations to poor countries: first, they have very little knowledge and understanding about global issues; second is the widespread perception that their government provides a significant amount of money to the outside world, so that there is no need for foundations to become involved; and third, the fear of funding terrorism and coping with the requirements of the Patriot Act since September 2001. Thus a massive awareness campaign should help to remove these perceptions and increase donations to poor countries. The example of the Melinda and William Gates Foundation raising several billion dollars to get vaccines and treatment for malaria and other diseases in poor countries should be a major example to follow for other rich Americans.

Chapter 11

More Migration

Globalization is not just the process whereby trade flows of goods and services between countries increases. It is also the process whereby movements of capital, technology, and labor among all the countries of the world increase. That is to say, it is not merely the growth in trade in goods and services that gives rise to the phenomenon of globalization but, more specifically, movements between countries of the production factors (labor, capital, and technology) underlying those goods and services. According to the Heckscher–Ohlin model, the two processes will gradually lead to the convergence in all countries of the prices of goods and services, the prices of capital (i.e. interest rates) and the remuneration or the price of labor (i.e. wages), provided that such products, services, capital, and workers are fully homogeneous and excluding the costs of transport and insurance on goods and services.

Such is the case, for example, of workers, as long as they have similar levels of education, training, and experience. Of course, labor is with merit the least mobile production factor. In addition to the difficulty of leaving a family behind, there is also the issue of adapting to different roots, language, culture, beliefs, and lifestyles that logically make it the least flexible and mobile production factor by far.

Despite this, migratory movements are one of the pillars of globalization – they are the "human aspect" of it. Although, owing to labor's inherent lack of mobility, the current process of labor globalization is well behind (indeed, it has only just begun but already starting to accelerate) that of the other two production factors, capital and technology, this does not mean that it will not be very significant in the coming decades. The twenty-first century could very well become another century of great migrations, just as the second half of the nineteenth century was. To explain this, the population trends in the coming years must be analyzed first.

Population Trends in the Twenty-first Century

The United Nations recently revised its population forecasts for the first half of the twenty-first century (UN, 2005). According to this new revision, the world's population is up to 6.4 billion inhabitants in 2005 from 2.5 billion in 1950 growing almost by 2.6 times in 55 years. The future growth of population is going to slow down substantially by the 2050s from 6.4 billion to 9.1 billion, an increase of only 40 percent. The annual population growth rate has been growing very fast during the twentieth century reaching a peak of 2 percent in 1965–70; since then it has been declining, largely as a result of the reduction in fertility rates in the developing world. The current annual population growth rate is 1.21 percent over the period 2000–5 and it will continue to fall further to 0.37 percent by 2045–50. The growth rate dispersion is still high. Developed countries' population growth rate is today 0.3 percent, while developing countries' population is still growing at 1.4 percent, almost five times as fast, and the least developed countries have a population growth rate of 2.4 percent a year, eight times faster than developed countries.

Developed countries represented 32.3 percent of world's population in 1950, but they have come down today to 18.7 percent of the total and they will fall further to only 13.6 percent in 2050. By contrast, developing countries will go up from 81.7 percent of total population today to 86.4 percent in 2050. European population will especially keep falling as a percentage of total population. In 1950, it represented 21.7 percent of the world's total, today only 11.3 percent and it will go down to 7.2 percent of the total in 2050, dropping from 728 million now, to 653 million in 2050, with a loss of 75 million people. Although the

North American share will also go down from 5.1 percent of the total today to 4.8 percent in 2050, its population will go up from 331 million now to 438 million in 2050.

Asian population will also go slightly down from 60.4 percent of the total today to 57.5 in 2050, while growing in absolute terms from 3.9 billion today to 5.21 billion in 2050 and African population will go up from 14.0 percent to 21.3 percent in 2050, growing from 906 million today to 1,937 million in 2050, more than one billion increase. Finally, Latin America and Caribbean and Oceania populations will keep almost constant at 8.6 percent and 0.5 percent respectively in 2050, gaining in absolute terms from 561 million to 783 million and from 33 million to 48 million respectively.

Therefore, the largest markets for future consumption will be Asia, Africa, and Latin America, all of them in the developing world. Only six developing countries account for 50 percent of this population growth to 2050: India, 21 percent; China, 12 percent; Pakistan, 5 percent; Nigeria and Bangladesh, 4 percent each; and Indonesia, 3 percent. It is estimated that the world's population could reach at least 7.7 billion in the low scenario and possibly as much as 10.6 billion in 2050 in the high forecast. But the medium variant scenario of 9.1 billion is considered to have the highest probability and it should be used as the benchmark. If the current fertility and mortality rates were to be maintained over the next 50 years, the world's population would reach the considerable figure of 11.66 billion in 2050. This slowdown of fertility and population growth is based essentially on the growing rates of education levels and on the increasing urbanization of the population in developing countries.

The medium variant scenario, of 9.1 billion inhabitants by 2050, is based on the following assumptions: first, the world fertility rate is expected to fall from 2.65 children per woman in 2000–5 to 2.05 children per woman in 2045–50, just below the replacement rate. It will go up in developed countries from 1.56 children per woman today to 1.84 children in 2050 and it will go down in developing countries from 2.90 children today to 2.07 children in 2050. Nevertheless, the dispersion will be high. European fertility will come up from 1.40 children today to 1.83 in 2050. The North American fertility rate will go down from 1.99 today to 1.85 in 2050. The largest falls will be in Africa, coming down from 4.97 children today to 2.52 in 2050, in Asia from 2.47 children today to 1.91 in 2050, and in Latin America from 2.55 to 1.86. Therefore there is going to be a large convergence in fertility rates among developed and developing countries.

Second, the life expectancy at birth is forecast to increase from 64.7 years to 74.7 years in the same period. Male life expectancy will go up from 62.5 years to 72.4 years and female life expectancy will go up from 67 to 77 years. There will also be a convergence in life expectancy in the developed and developing world. The developed countries' life expectancy will go up from 74.6 now to 81.7 years in 2050 and developing countries' life expectancy will go up faster, from 62.8 years today to 73.6 years in 2050, and even faster will be that of the least developed countries going up from 49.9 years today to 66.1 years in 2050.

The twentieth century witnessed the most rapid decline in child mortality of human history, which is an important indicator of development and of the well-being of children and this trend is going to continue until around the 2050s in spite of the huge pandemics of malaria and AIDS. Child mortality is measured as the proportion of children born alive surviving to the age of five. In 1950–5 almost a quarter of all children born worldwide did not reach their fifth birthday, 224 children per 1,000 did not survive beyond the age of 5. By 2000–5 this rate has fallen to 86 per 1,000. Although child mortality has fallen in all regions in the world, sub-Saharan Africa has lagged behind other major areas in transition to low mortality. While in 2000–5 the mortality rate had reached 98 per 1,000 in south and central Asia, in sub-Saharan Africa it was still 173 per 1,000.

The relative good news is that the demographic impact of the deadly pandemic HIV-AIDS is expected to be somewhat less severe in the future. In the United Nations 2002 population forecast revision the 60 highly infected countries of which 40 were in sub-Saharan Africa, 5 in Asia, 12 in Latin America and Caribbean, and 2 in Europe, amounted to 98 percent of the world total: 33.6 million out of 35.7 million. In the 2004 revision in 49 of the 60 countries HIV prevalence is expected to be lower in 2015 than in 2003, because it is expected that the population being covered by antiretroviral therapy (ART) is going to increase. Nevertheless the epidemic is still expanding and some countries are expecting to see increasing levels of HIV prevalence for several more years.

Life expectancy in the most affected countries already shows dramatic declines. In Botswana, where HIV prevalence was estimated at 36 percent of the adult population in 2003, life expectancy has fallen from 65 years in the 1980s to 37 years in 2003. In southern Africa as a whole, where most of the worst affected countries are, life expectancy has fallen in the same period from 61 years to 48 years. The toll of HIV/AIDS is still huge for child mortality. Thirty-three percent of children infected through mother-to-child transmission are estimated to die before their first birthday and 61 percent die before the age of 5; and it is also very important in female life expectancy where in some sub-Saharan countries female is now below male life expectancy. But the expected improvement in most of the 60 countries is still contingent on a much larger amount of financial resources allocated to fight this terrible pandemic.

International Migration Prospects until the 2050s

There is a long-term trend toward ageing in the world population. According to the United Nations (2004), the world's median age (that is, the age at which 50 percent of the population is older and another 50 percent is younger than that age) is going to increase from 28.1 in 2005 to 37.8 in 2050. In 2005, world's older population (aged 60 and over) was 10 percent and it will reach 22 percent in 2050. In developed countries, the ageing trend is still faster than in the developing world (with the main exception of China). Median age is going to increase from 38 today to 48 in 2050, more than 10 years older than that of the world's total. Population aged 60 and over is going to increase from 20 percent in 2005 to 32 percent in 2050, 10 percentage points higher than the world's average. As a consequence, developed countries' working age population (aged 15–59) is going to shrink in the next 45 years from

63 percent of the total in 2005 to 52 percent of the total by 2050 and there will be an urgent need to avoid a strong decrease in their labor force, given that not only will it make unsustainable their "pay as you go" pension systems but also it will reduce their potential growth rate, given that it is the young who consume more, invest more, innovate more and have more entrepreneurship.

Estimates of net migration between the major development groups has shown that, since 1960, the more developed regions have been net gainers of migrants from the developing countries. In the decade of 1960–1970, annual net inflows of migrants in developed countries reached 431,000, in the decade 1990–2000 annual net flows increased to 2.57 million and the UN 2004 annual net inflow assumption for the future is expected to be of 2.46 million in the decade 2000–2010 and 2.16 million in the decade 2040–50 a slightly slowing trend. The total net inflow until the 2050s is expected to be over 100 million. Asia will be the largest annual net supplier of migrants with 1.24 million a year in the decade 2000–10 and 1.2 million in the decade 2040–50, followed by Latin America and the Caribbean with 740 million and 567 million respectively and Africa will be the third supplier with 410 million and 322 million per year in both decades.

The most striking estimate of the UN demographers is that the least developed countries will be net receivers of migration during the decade 2000–10 and not net suppliers with an annual rate of inflows of 81,000, turning in the last decade of the first half of the century to 270,000 net outflows per year. Among the regions expected to receive the largest annual net inflows are North America with 1.36 million a year in 2000–10 and 1.3 million a year in 2040–50, followed by Europe with 937,000 a year in the first decade and 700,000 in the last decade of the projection and by Oceania with 98,000 in the first and 94,000 a year in the last.

By countries, net inflows will not only be received by North America, Australia, Japan, and western European developed countries but also by Russia, Hong Kong, Israel, Kuwait, Malaysia, Qatar, Saudi Arabia, Singapore, South Africa, and the United Arab Emirates. Net outflows will come mainly from China, India, Indonesia, Mexico, and the

Philippines. Pakistan and Iran will experience net inflows because of the repatriation of Afghan refugees. It is very important to mention that the UN makes explicit that its migration projections are the least robust and are subject to high volatility, therefore mainly reflect a continuation of recent levels of net migration.

These projections seem to me much lower than should be expected out of the demand (pull factors) from developed countries' declining and ageing populations and the supply (push factors) from developing countries' growing and young populations. Let's have a look first at the demand "pull" factors.

Another report by the United Nations (2000) has investigated the level of migration required to achieve population objectives in selected developed countries between 1995 and 2050. Maintaining the size of the population or that of the working-age population (15 to 64 years) at the highest levels reached in the absence of migration after 1995 would imply large inflows of foreign migrants. It estimates at least 1 million immigrants a year in the European Union at 15 countries to keep the total population stable and at least 1.5 million a year to keep the working-age population constant at present levels, figures which are not far from actual migrant inflows. In the case of the United States the inflows needed are lower than the present ones and in the case of Japan the opposite.

But in order to keep constant the old-age dependency ratio, that is, the number of people 65 and over as a proportion of the number of people at working age (15–64), the immigrant inflows needed are expected to be huge. The EU at 15 will start needing 5 million a year and will end needing 17 million a year in 2050 (around 12 million a year on average), the same will happen to Japan, which will need, on average, around 12 million a year as well. The United States will need zero at the beginning and end up needing 30 million a year in 2050, on average 11.5 million per year. As a consequence of that the population of the EU at 15 will need to go up from close to 400 million in 2000 to just over 1 billion in 2050. Japan's population will need to grow from 130 million today to close to 800 million in 2050 and the US from 270 million today to 900 million in 2050.

Even if these very large increases in immigrants could be attracted to countries with ageing populations, immigration policy cannot easily be fine-tuned to reach precise demographic objectives. A policy to control legal immigration is relatively easy, but tackling illegal immigration is very hard and there is no control over emigration, therefore the net result is very difficult to achieve. Moreover, there is the issue of asylum seekers and people displaced as a consequence of natural disasters or wars for humanitarian reasons.

Another report (Goldman Sachs, 2004) estimates the annual migration inflows needed to maintain the labor force share of the population at current levels and shows that annual inflows will have to increase from 30 percent in the case of the US, to over 100 percent in the case of the EU at 15 member countries and up to 700 percent in the case of Japan. For instance, working-age population in Japan which was 68.2 percent of the total in 2000 will go down to 50 percent in 2050. As in 2000 annual migration inflows were only 55,000, that will add, by 2050, 2.7 million immigrants, to its population but, in order to keep working age constant, immigrant population will need to go up to close to 20 million by 2050; that is, the stock of migrants will need to go up from 1.3 percent of the total population in 2000 to 20.2 percent of the total by 2050.

The EU at 15 members had an annual inflow of 1.4 million in 2000, which will add 70 million more migrants in 2050, but in order to keep its labor force at current levels will need to go up to 140 million by 2050. Thus, its stock of foreign population will go up from 5 percent in 2000 to close to 20 percent in 2050. The US had in 2000 an annual inflow of 1.22 million immigrants; that inflow will add 56 million to the US population by 2050, but to maintain its present labor force it will need an extra 15.5 million by 2050. Thus its 2000 foreign-born stock of population of 12.4 percent will need to go up to 17.4 percent by 2050.

The big question then is how Japanese and European citizens who, by contrast to the US citizens, have traditionally been used to being migrants and of whom many are today already opposed to more migration when the stock of foreign-born is still low, would react to such an increase in immigrants to their countries. Thus, it is very clear that it will be very difficult for them to accept such a large increase and thus they may vote against more immigrants after their stock has reached a certain limit of around 10 percent. Today, there are EU countries which have large immigrant stocks, such as Luxembourg with 37.5 percent or Switzerland with 19.7 percent, but they are small nations which have been used to large net immigration for many years, first of migrants coming from the rest of Europe and later from non-European countries. Of the large countries only Germany has a foreign-born stock close to 10 percent and their citizens have increasing difficulties accepting it. The same can be said about France with 7.5 percent or even the UK with 5.5 percent.

Let's now look at the supply "push" factors: the first conclusion that can be drawn from the UN's population projections is that the population of developed countries, at the current immigration rate, is going to increase by 25 million, between 2005 and 2050, while that of developing countries is going to grow by 2.6 billion. Such an enormous imbalance clearly indicates that migratory flows will be very significant in the next fifty or so years. The ultimate volume of such flows will depend, first, on these projections being fulfilled. While projections, as such, are rarely fulfilled, those of the United Nations are prepared with the highest degree of rigor and experience. Indeed, in recent years its projections have always been close to their mark.

The second conclusion is that the ultimate volume of these flows will depend on how globalization progresses. The greater the growth in trade of goods and services, foreign direct investment, technology and development assistance, the smaller the migratory flows from poor countries to wealthy ones. The reason behind this is that trade is substitutive for the movement of persons. If a worker from a developing country can work and export the goods and services he produces, he will not be forced to emigrate, as he will be able to keep his job and collect a salary. If trade becomes increasingly freer, inter-country movement of production factors, labor, capital, and technology can be substituted for trade in the goods and services produced with them, as was brilliantly explained by the Nobel laureate in economics, Robert Mundell (1957).

According to him if a country restricts immigration, this induces trade flows; if the country raises tariffs, this induces immigration. In the newer trade models that base trade on increasing returns and differences in technology across countries, immigration plays a still larger and more distinct role. Technology transfers through persons trained in advanced economies to developing countries can greatly improve their well-being. Immigration from developing to developed countries tends to reduce the terms of trade of the host countries, unless the immigration flows are of highly educated workers, in which case it is more negative for developing countries.

Wealthy countries will tend to specialize in goods intensive in capital, technology, and skilled labor, which they will export to poorer countries. These countries, in turn, will specialize in unskilled labor-intensive goods, primary and intermediate technology, and fewer capital-intensive goods, which they will export to wealthy countries. Each good or service will incorporate the volume of work, capital, and technology involved in producing it, depending on its degree of specialization and comparative advantages, and will be transferred from one country to another, without requiring the direct movement of these production factors. The prices of such production factors will thus tend to equalize over the long term, without requiring movements from one country to another.

This is what has been happening in the world in recent decades. The evolution of the comparative advantages between countries has led developing countries to increase their market shares in international industrial production and trade, especially in manufacturing, while developed countries have become increasingly specialized in services, particularly added-value services. In 1950, industrial employment averaged 41 percent of total employment in Europe. In 2004, it had fallen to 24 percent. The newly industrialized developing countries of Asia and Latin America have done just the opposite and have increased their industrial levels from 14 percent to 35 percent. The large developing countries, such as China and India, have also become more industrialized and their industrial employment now stands at about 30 percent. As globalization has accelerated since the 1980s, trade between developing and developed countries has concentrated on manufactured goods. Today, 60 percent of what developed countries export to developing countries relates to manufactured goods and vice versa. A significant portion of such trade is intra-industrial or intra-firm and is due to multinational firms from developed countries setting up subsidiaries in developing countries, which trade with the parent company or with subsidiaries in other countries.

The same trade-off can be applied to foreign direct investment. The greater the flows of FDI to developing countries, the greater these countries' levels of investment, employment, technology, productivity, salaries, and exports will eventually be, as explained in the preceding chapter. It therefore follows that their growth levels will also be higher and there will be less need for the workers of these countries to seek work abroad.

It is very likely, however, that an increase in trade and foreign direct investment flows in these countries would not be enough, as some, especially the poorest among them, have been left out of the growing trade and financial integration in recent decades. That is why it is very important to increase official development assistance (ODA) as well as private, altruistic aid to help in the development of these countries that have been left out and that need, above all, to improve their basic levels of education, healthcare, drinking water, and media so that they can begin to reduce their population growth rates, attract foreign investment and become sufficiently competitive with their exportable goods and services.

Even if the trade, foreign investment, and development assistance these countries receive were sufficient, the future imbalances caused by demographic trends are so great that migratory flows will probably continue to grow until around the 2050s. For example, whereas Europe as a continent is going to lose 75 million inhabitants between 2005 and 2050, Africa's population is going to increase by 1.03 billion inhabitants. Whereas the European countries bordering the Mediterranean are going to lose 25 million inhabitants, the northern African countries bordering it are going to grow by 123 million. While Italy is going to lose 14.4 million and Spain 8.6 million, Algeria is going to gain 19.8

million, Libya and Tunisia are going to add 5 million each, and Morocco is going to grow by 19.4 million. Spain's southernmost coast is just 15 kilometers from Morocco and the Italian coast is 60 kilometers from Tunisia, which could mean massive flows of immigrants, controlled or otherwise, in the coming decades.

So far, none of these massive movements has taken place, although there have been substantial flows between Mexico and the United States, between the Balkan republics (mainly Albania) and Italy, between the CIS and Russia and between the eastern European countries and Austria and Germany. Nevertheless, they may come in the future. While the migratory flows in recent decades have not been massive, probably due to the acceleration of trade and financial globalization, they have been steadily on the rise. According to UN estimates, in 2000 the number of inhabitants born outside a given country in the world – i.e. the so-called immigration rate – was 2.9 percent of the world's population, or 175 million people. At the end of the 1980s the immigration rate was 1.2 percent, or 60 million people. This means that in a little more than a decade, immigration has increased 290 percent and the immigration rate has almost tripled. This gives us an indication of what could happen in the future. The figures provided by the OECD for all its member states are also significant, as they show that the immigration rate was up to 7 percent in 2000 and that the number of immigrants totaled 60 million (OECD, 2003).

According to these same organizations, the causes of such a rapid increase seem to have been the increase in income and wage differentials between most of the developed countries and the developing countries, the sharp rise in the urban population of developing countries, the rapid drop in the costs of information and transport, and the progressive ageing of the population in the OECD countries.

For Hatton and Williamson (2002), the four main forces behind this rise in emigration since the mid-nineteenth century were: first, the differences in the levels of income and wages between countries. An increase in income, adjusted for education, in one country in relation to the rest of the world and to its neighboring countries tends to increase the net immigration from both. Second is the levels of poverty in the emigrants' source countries. The greater the poverty, the less emigration there will be because emigration, whether legal or illegal, is expensive. Poverty is a clear constraint for emigration.

Third is the proportion of the population aged 15 to 25 as a percentage of the total working-age population in both the country of origin and of destination. The higher the proportion of youth is in the population of the source country and the lower it is in the destination country, the greater the emigration is from the former to the latter. Finally, the other important factor is the proportion of foreign immigrants who have achieved the status of resident in the country of destination. The greater the number of foreign emigrants which are already resident in a country, the higher the probability that emigration will increase, because the emigrants already there always try to bring family and friends and to find work for them.

The distribution of immigrants by destination country has been very uneven. The US's immigration rate reached 6.5 percent in 2000 with an annual inflow of 1.1 million, whereas the immigration rate in the EU was 5 percent with an annual inflow of 1.5 million. There are also major differences in immigration stocks among EU countries. According to the OECD (2003) in 2001, Austria with 9.4 percent, Germany with 9 percent and Belgium with 8.2 percent had the highest rates. The lowest rates were those of Spain and Italy, with close to 3 percent each. By contrast, traditional immigrating countries have much higher stocks: the US had 11.1 percent, Australia 23.1 percent, and Canada 18.2 percent. In 2005, the numbers have increased further in most OECD countries and the immigration rate average for them is now around 8 percent.

An increasing flow of illegal immigration has also been detected. In 2000 the number of illegal immigrants in the US was 0.4 million, while in the EU it was 0.5 million. Today the figures have multiplied by 20 and by 15 respectively in only five years. The number of requests for political asylum have also grown, reaching a historical high in 2001 with over 0.5 million, following the conflicts in the Balkan states. According to the UN High Commission for Refugees, more than 6 million asylum applications were lodged in the high-income countries in the 1990s, against 2.2 million in the 1980s. Although constraints on immigration flows have been tightened recently for internal policy reasons, measures have also been implemented to legalize numerous illegal immigrants.

What will probably happen in the future is that the trends that traditionally move migratory flows will change. As I mentioned earlier, according to George Borjas (1999), there are two types of factors that come into play when deciding to emigrate: the "pull," or attraction, factors and the "push," or expulsion, factors. The first type is determined by the demand for labor and the emigrants already in the destination country. The second type is determined by supply of labor and emigrants in the source country. The first type depends on the destination country's production factors and its specific unfilled labor demands. The second type, on the other hand, depends on the economic, social, and living conditions in the source country and its unfilled labor supply. Attraction factors have dominated in traditional countries of immigration, such as the US, Canada, and Australia, and in the reconstruction of Germany after the Second World War, and now there is a demand for specialists in new information technologies from Asia and central and eastern Europe. Expulsion factors have predominated in the Irish emigration to the United States, Spanish emigration to Latin America, and, more recently, Mexican, Central American, and Caribbean emigration to the US.

Which of the two types of factors will predominate in the coming decades? Taking into account the major demographic imbalances that will occur in the future, or that are occurring now, it would seem logical that both pull and push factors will be large. On the one side, many African countries and some Asian and Latin American countries, for example, are in a critical situation with little or no growth and a very high level of unemployment, not to mention starvation, violence, and civil wars. Some of these explosive situations are already pushing the people of these countries to desperately seek a different country in which to work and live, and they even risk putting themselves in the hands of intermediaries or mafias that take them to Europe or North America in subhuman conditions.

On the other hand, demand "pull" factors are going to increase, as OECD countries are going to increasingly lose labor force and become older societies in the next decades, with very large effects both in living standards and fiscal sustainability. The OECD estimates (Turner, Giorno, De Serres, Vourch, and Richardson, 1998) that the cumulative effect by the mid-twenty-first century could be to reduce living standards – measured by GNP per capita adjusted for terms of trade effects – by 10 percent in the US, by 18 percent in the EU at 15, and by 23 percent in Japan. Welfare systems in OECD countries will also come under increasing pressure as public pensions and public health payments will absorb a growing share of total welfare outlays. Different studies show that by 2050, public expenditure in pensions and health will go up from 13.4 percent of GDP in 2000 to close to 30 percent of GDP by 2050 in the EU and from 10.3 percent of GDP in 2000 to 20.5 percent of GDP in 2050 in the US (De la Dehesa, 2006b).

Both estimates show how difficult it is going to be to maintain the present welfare states in both areas unless there is an increase in taxes, a reduction in welfare services and costs and an increase of the labor forces through large immigration flows. The problem with adding labor force with new immigrants is that later on they are also going to age, to retire and to demand more pensions and more healthcare. Therefore, migration is only a temporary way to improve the very uncertain fiscal situation and increase the living standards until there is a change in their demographic trends.

We are therefore faced with a new migratory paradigm that demands a new analysis to add to the traditional ones, based on the theories of human capital developed by Sjaastad (1962) or on the self-selection and wage differential models postulated by Borjas (1987 and 1994). On the one hand, the human capital model – in which the decision to emigrate is determined by calculating the value of employment opportunities, net of transport costs, alternative labor markets, and by the choice of the one that maximizes the net present value of the emigrant's future expected earnings – is too complex for a desperate worker from a poor country to consider. The self-selection model, based on the wage differences within the source country vis-à-vis those in the destination country, is very difficult to apply in situations where the expulsion factors are overwhelming and the wage differences – not so much within the source country, but between the source and destination countries – are so enormous. In view of the situation that is brewing, the model developed by Faini (1994) might be the most appropriate. This model only takes into account the absolute wage level of each potential emigrant in his country of origin.

How Big Could Migration Flows Be until the 2050s?

The International Organization for Migration (IOM, 2003) has released its latest report on the present migration trends, given that the IOM finds that they are the most reliable indicator of the intensity of globalization. At the start of the twenty-first century, one out of every 35 human beings was an international migrant. This means 175 million people or 2.9 percent of the world's population. These figures do not take into account irregular or illegal migrants. All 190 plus countries in the world are either countries of origin, transit, or destination for migrants, and increasingly are all three simultaneously.

The largest source of migrants has been Mexico, with a net outflow of 6 million between 1975 and 1995. There are at present 24 million Mexicans living in the US. The other larger sources are Bangladesh with 4.1 million, Afghanistan with 4.1 million, and the Philippines with 2.9 million. The largest recipient of migrants is the United States with a net inflow, in the same period, of 16.7 million, followed by Russia with 4.1 million, Saudi Arabia with 3.4 million, India and Canada with 3.3 million each, Germany with 2.7 million, and France with 1.4 million.

By the year 2000, the gross migrant stock, that is, those foreign-born, was 35 million in the US, followed by 13.3 million in Russia, 7.3 million in Germany, 6.9 million in Ukraine, 6.3 million in France and India, 5.8 million in Canada, 5.3 million in Saudi Arabia, 4.7 million in Australia, 4.2 million in Pakistan, and 4 million in the UK. If we take this migrant stock as a proportion of the size of the population of the country, the largest stock is in the United Arab Emirates, with 74 percent of the population, followed by Kuwait: 58 percent, Jordan: 40 percent, Israel: 37 percent, Singapore: 34 percent, Saudi Arabia: 26 percent, Australia and Switzerland: 25 percent each, New Zealand: 23 percent, and Canada: 19 percent. Finally, the relative stock by continent puts Oceania in the first place with 19.1 percent of the total population, followed by North America, with 13 percent, and Europe, with 7 percent.

Nevertheless, these apparently huge flows of international migrants must be kept in proportion. Migration was far bigger in the second half of the nineteenth century. Then, about 7 percent of the world's population were migrants against fewer than 3 percent in 2000. During the first wave of globalization, between 1870 and 1913, migration raised the New World's labor force by a third and lowered the European labor force by one-eighth, figures that have not been exceeded even by California and Mexico since the 1960s (Wolf, 2003).

It is really very difficult to predict future migration trends as they also depend on other endogenous and exogenous factors. From an economic point of view, there is no doubt that the liberalization of immigration is logical and sensible and would be very positive for source countries and destination countries alike (Wolf, 2003; Rodrik, 2001). The reasons are clear. On the one hand, the wealthy countries are losing inhabitants and, therefore, imperatively need to find labor of varying skill levels to keep up their production and consumption activity. Moreover, as their population is rapidly ageing, they are faced with a serious fiscal problem in how to meet future pension commitments; there will be an excess of pensioners drawing a pension and a deficit of workers paying into the system.

On the other hand, poor countries have a growing surplus population in relation to their productive capacity and neither work nor means of survival can be found. Thus, both groups of countries benefit, especially considering that the real wage differential between workers with the same skills in wealthy countries and poor countries is as much as ten to one. At the same time, the differences in the prices of similar traded products or services and in the prices of similar financial assets competing in the market generally do not exceed two to one. The bigger the price differentials between them, the bigger the earnings will be.

This means that the earnings potential arising from the liberalization of movements of persons in the world would be much greater than that arising from the full liberalization of financial and trade flows. For example, an increase in temporary immigration permits for skilled and unskilled workers from developing countries equivalent to 3 percent of the population of wealthy countries would generate US$200 billion of earnings for developing countries. And this is without taking into account other benefits of the so-called "spill-over" effects that these workers would generate upon returning to their countries of origin with their newly acquired knowledge and skills. This figure would be greater than that which would be achieved by sharply lowering the barriers to entry that the wealthy countries still impose on the trade of poor countries' agricultural products, textiles, and footwear, which would not exceed US$150 billion per year (Rodrik, 2001).

Flows of migrant workers' remittances to developing countries have grown steadily since the 1970s and currently amount to $100 billion a year (IMF, 2005). This is more than poor countries receive from aid or capital markets. Given the difficulty in measuring them because of their small size, the real number may be twice as high making remittances for some developing countries greater than ODA flows, than foreign direct investment, and than export revenues. This rising trend is going to persist as population ageing in developed countries continues and pressures to migration in developing countries increase.

These remittances from migrants are also a very important source of income for developing countries. In 2000, of the large countries, India received more than 11.5 billion US dollars, 2.5 percent of its GDP, Mexico, 6.5 billion, 1.1 percent of its GDP, Turkey, 4.8 billion, 2.3 percent of its GDP, Egypt, 3.9 billion, 3.8 percent of its GDP, and Bangladesh 2 billion, 4.3 percent of its GDP. Of the small countries, Morocco got 6.5 percent of its GDP from remittances, Jordan, 21.8 percent, El Salvador, 13.3 percent, Dominican Republic, 8.6 percent, and Ecuador, 8.3 percent (IOM, 2003).

Poor migrant workers earn little money and less respect, they fill the meanest jobs, often with very little or no legal protection. Yet they are able to save remarkable amounts of money: some might put aside up to half their pay or even more. Despite this, governments and financial institutions have usually paid them very little attention because they send home small amounts – no more than a few hundred dollars at a time. That is changing, however, for three reasons: though individually small, remittances are huge in aggregate; they are essential to the economies of migrant home countries and they are now a possible means of money laundering and a source of finance for terrorism.

These payments provide more than 25 percent of GDP in Jordan, Lesotho, Nicaragua, Haiti, or Tonga, and more than 5 percent of GDP for many more countries. In 36 countries remittances exceed all other imports of capital, whether public or private. Remittances reduce poverty, increase the probability of children staying in school, help to finance the start-up of small businesses, education, and housing, and increase growth in recipient countries. As a source of finance remittances have several advantages. Unlike development loans, they do not come with a liability or an obligation to pay interest. They are sent directly to the people for whom they are intended and thus cannot be squandered by governments. They are a more stable funding source than foreign direct investment and even more so than portfolio flows (Rapoport and Docquier, 2005).

Seeing the importance of remittances, governments in receiving countries have been encouraging them. India, the largest recipient, abolished taxes on remittances several years ago. Colombia did the same. Mexico, the second largest, has made sending money home far easier for its many citizens working in the US by issuing an identification card that even illegal immigrants can use to open bank accounts in American banks. Brazil and Guatemala are also introducing them.

Banks and commercial companies have entered into the business of providing the means of sending money home. As a result, many migrants have seen the cost of remittances fall by half in the past few years, although the cost is still high, around 4 percent of the sum sent to Mexico and much more if it is sent to Venezuela or Cuba. They serve now also for obtaining credit, helping the development of small business.

Despite their virtues, remittances can also be a source of trouble, because not knowing the size of their flows and being cash, they can be used for money laundering or financing other illegal activities. There can be also economic costs associated with reliance on remittances. Like any unearned wealth they may foster idleness in those who benefit from them. Finally, they may also result in what the economists call a "Dutch disease," pushing up the value of the currency of the country of destination.

The only disadvantage that emigration has for developing countries is that they lose a section of their more skilled workers. That is to say, they could suffer what is known as a "brain drain," whereby people educated domestically, at the expense of the source country, transfer out their knowledge, working in the destination country. It should be borne in mind, however, that the greater an individual's level of education is, the higher her wages tend to be – well above what she could expect to receive in her home country – while the remittances sent from abroad easily offset the effects of the individual's emigration.

To deal with this problem, the source country can try to require the individual to pay a tax of some sort in the source country to recover the cost of her education, and the destination country can try to ensure that the immigrant who is much more skilled only stays temporarily, which is not easy because destination countries are finding that the immigrants who come to their country increasingly wish to settle down permanently with their families, ultimately adopting the nationality of the destination country. Nevertheless, the fact is that many skilled workers who have migrated end up returning to their home country, either because the domestic situation there has improved or because they wish to retire in the country in which they were born.

Developed countries also benefit from such liberalization. First, immigrants boost the size of the economy and its growth potential. Second, they contribute to the state coffers with their taxes and help to improve the very precarious situation (especially in Spain, Italy, and Japan) of the public pension system. By contributing to the pension system, they increase the asset base, which offsets the excess liabilities and helps to resolve at least temporarily the growing problem of debt issuance to pay the growing number of pensioners resulting from the ageing of the population. Third, they have an education and have shown that they have significant initiative, and they bring these qualities to the economy, enhancing its growth capacity. Fourth, they generally have a higher fertility rate and help to offset the ageing of the population. Finally, only some unskilled domestic workers and a small number of skilled workers of the countries of destination may be negatively affected, either by reducing slightly their wages or by losing their employment.

However, they would also be negatively affected if the barriers to imports from developing countries were fully liberalized, as the unskilled workers from developed and developing countries would be competing with each other indirectly through the work that goes into the products and services traded. But wages depend not only on the supply of labor but also on the supply of capital. George Borjas (1994) estimates that, although immigrants may depress the wages of domestic workers with which they compete, their losses will be more than offset by the increase the immigrants trigger in the return on capital for entrepreneurs, which boosts investment and the economy's aggregate income. In other words, the greater the impact on domestic wages is, the greater the impact on domestic income through capital income will be, given that cheaper labor increases the potential return to employers of building new factories or opening new service companies specialized in labor-intensive products or services and they will hire more natives or other workers.

Empirical evidence is not at all conclusive about the idea that immigrants depress wages of unskilled native workers. David Card (2005) does not find any conclusive evidence about immigration displacing low-skilled natives or reducing their relative wages in the US cities. The reasons may be that immigrants are taking jobs that natives are unwilling to do or that unskilled native workers have shifted to non-tradable activities. George Borjas (2004) finds out that, between 1980 and 2000, immigration caused average workers' wages, of the same categories of education and experience, to be 3 percent lower and high-school-dropouts' wages to be 8 percent lower than they would otherwise have been. But once capital stock is assumed to adjust and increase as a reaction to its higher return, overall wages are unaffected and the loss of wages for high-school-drop-outs is cut to below 5 percent.

Emigration has also historically been the main tool in trying to level out or reduce income differences between people in the world. And it will continue to be the main tool in the future, because the other two factors in equalizing the price of production factors and per capita income – trade and foreign direct and portfolio investment – also have their drawbacks, in some cases political and in others economic. Trade has its drawbacks in that it involves a slow, but sure, liberalization process, requiring multilateral negotiations and catering for many totally opposing interests. Foreign direct investment has its drawbacks in that, for the time being, it only benefits certain developing countries, particularly the biggest ones and those that have the best economic policies, shunning many other countries. The drawbacks of foreign portfolio investment lie in the fact that since the 1990s the wealthy countries, especially the US, have been the net beneficiaries and very few developing countries have obtained significant flows. This lack of sufficient financial flows from wealthy countries to poor countries is confirmed by the following fact: the investment per inhabitant in wealthy countries is six times greater than that in poor countries.

The problem with liberalizing immigration is eminently political. As Martin Wolf (2001) said: "it is no accident that the democracy of masses, the welfare state and immigration control reached advanced countries at about the same time." In developed countries workers with skills similar to the average of their counterparts in developing countries have privileged access to the stock of physical, human, and social capital and they are not willing to allow immigrants to compete with them to obtain it. Those who possess human and physical capital would be benefited, but others who depend on the safety net provided by their welfare state would not.

According to Rodrik, the political problem lies in the fact that immigrants do not have a sufficiently organized or powerful lobby to support immigration in wealthy countries, although Silicon Valley lobbies and landowner associations have, on certain occasions, managed to get the

US government to open the borders, at least temporarily. Trade and investment liberalization has been politically possible because the biggest beneficiaries from wealthy countries, multinational firms and financial entities have managed to organize themselves better and have gained sufficient influence on the liberalizing agenda. Rodrik proposes that economists, who know the benefits of immigration, should organize a pro-immigration lobby and that the discussion on liberalizing migratory movements should be multilateral, as it is for trade and investment through the WTO, where the absence of discrimination and the most-favored nation clause are the norm and, if this is not observed a price must be paid. The treatment of immigration is still in the hands of countries and the special interests of politicians and is not based on economic logic.

Hanson, Scheve, and Slaughter (2005) argue that, although freer immigration and trade would be supported by similar groups, thanks to similar impact on labor income, government policies that redistribute income may alter the distributional politics. In particular, immigrants pay taxes and receive public services in different quantities, while imports can do neither of these things. Therefore, different political coalitions may organize around trade and immigration. They find that high exposure to immigrant fiscal pressures, as expected in most developed countries, reduces support for freer immigration among locals, especially the more skilled who might not object to freer trade.

A similar analysis is made by Hatton and Williamson (2006) who ask themselves why today's labor scarce economies have open trade and closed immigration policies, while a century ago they had just the opposite: open immigration and closed trade policies. This is a paradox, because after all importing labor-intensive products is pretty much the same as importing labor (Mundell, 1957). Trade and migration policies reinforce each other. They call this the "dual policy paradox" which surprisingly has persisted over two centuries. Simple theory predicts that immigration and import restrictions should go together, but, in fact, never have.

There are some explanations for this paradox. First, trade and migration may be less than perfect substitutes or they might not be substitutes at all (Markusen, 1983; Faini, de Melo, and Zimmermann, 1999). There are specific factors, increasing returns and Ricardian differences in productivity, which make reality deviate from the Heckscher–Ohlin and the Stolper–Samuelson model predictions. Second, the increase in anti-immigration attitudes from the previous to the present globalization waves has to do with two factors: the first one is that the strong decline in the cost of migrating has produced an increase in the volume of migrants and a decrease in their skill levels. The second is the change in the fiscal implications of trade and immigration.

In the nineteenth century, customs duties were a major source of government revenue and therefore high tariff protection was a simple and easy way to get revenue; today they are a tiny part of total tax revenue in labor-scarce OECD countries. By contrast, immigration did not have any fiscal impact on government expenditure in the nineteenth century, since there was no welfare state: immigrants generated no tax revenues and they received no fiscal transfers, while tariffs on trade brought a lot of fiscal revenue. Today most OECD countries have welfare states with a universal coverage of their citizens and residents, thus the fiscal cost of immigration is very important because they have a higher dependency on the welfare state than nationals, while the fiscal revenue of imports is negligible. Immigrants are younger, have more children, need more schooling and training and are more often unemployed. Only because they are do they have less dependency on pensions, but they will also have this in the future.

The third reason has to do with the change in the median voter. In the nineteenth century the median voter was unskilled but there were vey few unskilled workers migrating because they could not afford its cost. As the costs of migrating came down while the gap between the poor sending and the rich receiving countries increased, immigration policy got much tougher. Today, the median voter is skilled, and is thus less worried about imports. He should also be less worried about immigration, but is very worried about its costs for the welfare state.

What volume of immigration would be politically feasible? In the case of Japan, which is set to lose 19 million inhabitants over the next 50 years and which is already one of the countries with the oldest population in the world, the actual maximum volume permitted is tiny. Immigration is politically unfeasible except for some temporary workers and the sons and grandsons of previous Japanese migrants to North and South America. In Europe as a whole continent (including Russia), which is going to lose 75 million inhabitants, the attitude toward immigration is more open, and although not beyond what is necessary to maintain the population at current levels, it is not enough to reach the levels needed to maintain the current working-age population, let alone to accept a sufficient number of immigrants to stabilize its dependence ratio, i.e. the number of actively working persons needed to support the pension of each retired person.

The problem of the ageing population is so serious in the EU that it has been calculated that it would take 20 million immigrants per year from 2030 to overcome it. If this happened, the population of the EU, which would probably by then comprise 40 countries (all the European Council countries), would reach 1.0 billion in 2050, i.e. 275 million inhabitants more than in 2000, which would be very positive for the future of the EU but would be politically unacceptable (Wolf, 2001).

To solve the problem of the income gap and try to reduce the income differential between wealthy countries and poor countries, the future migratory flows would have to be huge. One needs only to consider that the population of the developing countries is going to increase by more than 2.6 billion over the next 50 years, whereas that of the developed countries is going stay put, further widening the gap between them in terms of per capita income. The liberalization of migratory flows would trigger massive outflows of emigrants – hundreds of millions – in search of work in wealthy countries, which would probably be politically unacceptable for both the citizens and the politicians of developed countries.

Nevertheless, emigrating – whether legally or illegally – is expensive. That is why in developing countries there are always more people with a higher level of income and education who manage to emigrate than those who are poor and poorly educated who stay put. What this means is that as the income of many of these people rises, they will have greater chances of emigrating, that if they are not emigrating now it is because they do not have the minimum amount of funds needed to do so, and that emigration will be on the rise in the future. The destitute do not emigrate. Most of the emigrants from developing countries have relatively high levels of education.

If we make a simple extrapolation of the migration flows (excluding irregular migrants) over the next 45 years using the present trends, then to maintain the present stock of migrants at 3 percent of the world's population, the total number of migrants will need to increase from 190 million to 280 million by 2050, 90 million more than the present figure. If we extrapolate the migration flows to achieve the level of the stock of migrants at 10 percent of the world's population (the level reached in 1913, at the end of the first wave of globalization) the number of migrants will go up from the present 190 million to 930 million, 740 million more. Most probably, the final number may settle at a figure between these two.

These extrapolations suggest that the pressure to migrate to wealthy countries is going to increase substantially over the next 50 years. But there is still no sign of a political solution from the group of wealthy countries that would give immigration a major boost. On the contrary, at present, new barriers to the flows of immigrants are being raised in most developed countries, so are the pressures from developing countries' migrants to avoid and penetrate them. If a reasonable solution to channel these pressures is not found, the wealthy countries could find themselves being invaded by huge floods of illegal immigrants. This would give rise to a tremendous expense in police and security and an international political panorama highly exposed to conflict, violence, and war. The only way to reduce these huge migration pressures is through directing more trade and investment flows, more technological transfers, more aid to these developing countries, and more selected immigrants, that is, through more economic globalization.

What alternatives have developed countries to immigration if they do not accept much higher levels of foreigners working in their countries? The only alternatives to tackle the increasing public expenditure derived from the ageing of their populations are as follows (De la Dehesa, 2006). On the one hand, to reform and reduce the size and generosity of their welfare states until they are able to increase their fertility rates again, because life expectancy at birth is going to go up further. This alternative is going to take a long time because today immigrants are the only ones adding population to the OECD countries by having higher fertility rates.

This fact explains today the better position of the US in terms of ageing population when compared to Europe. American WASPs have the same fertility rates as Europeans; the difference in fertility rates between the two derives from the fact that there are many more immigrants in the US than in the EU. As it takes such a long time, the problems will have to be solved earlier because as the age of the median voter reaches more than 50 years (which will happen in the EU in 2015) he will make sure that his pension and health costs are going to be secured at the expense of the younger generations. Therefore, a generational clash can produce major political conflicts in many OECD countries.

On the other hand, to increase taxes even further and/or issue more debt to be able to sustain their increasing levels of public expenditure in pensions and health. The problem is that it is not a solution. A tax increase when the average fiscal pressure in Europe is the highest in the world, 42 percent of GDP, seems to be very difficult to accept by European citizens who are now demanding lower taxes. It may be less problematic in Japan where taxes are only 28 percent of GDP or in the US where they are 29 percent of GDP. An increase in the debt to GDP ratio is no solution either. It is now 70 percent of GDP in the EU at 15 and over 110 percent of GDP in Japan.

Standard and Poor's has issued a report showing that if European countries increase their debts to finance the increasing public expenditure to finance the ageing population impact their rating will go down from triple A to triple C. Thus, it will produce a large increase in the cost of servicing their debt which may offset part of their effort to finance their increasing expenditure. The US, with a lower debt to GDP ratio of 30 percent may perhaps be able to succeed but it has many implicit liabilities which are not accounted in the budget which will make it also very difficult.

The alternatives available to OECD countries in order to solve the problem of declining labor forces and thus of activity and growth are the following: on the one side they need to increase further their activity and employment rates before it is too late, when the baby boom generation starts to retire after 2010. On the other hand, they need to try to increase their capital/labor ratios to be able to get higher productivity levels. A third solution is to try to mechanize their small agricultural production that would be left and to robotize manufacturing in order to save the available labor force for high value added services that need higher labor inputs. Finally, they need to outsource and offshore all their production of labor intensive manufacturing and services to developing countries. These measures are already being taken by Japan, whose labor force is shrinking faster than in Europe. But, this is not sufficient; they also need to allow further immigration flows to bridge the gap of their declining and ageing populations, which will end in reducing their potential growth.

Globalization is becoming increasingly a process which increasingly integrates all its relevant flows, goods and services, FDI, and migration and should be taken as a whole and not as the sum of its parts. In this sense, in a recent paper, Ricardo Faini (2004) rightly shows that globalization is not only about the rise in trade, FDI, and migration but also about the changing linkages among these flows. First, the experience of the 1990s has shown that import liberalization did foster not only trade but also inward investment, thus confirming that trade and investment are becoming increasingly complementary. Second, the presence of a skilled labor force is a relevant factor to attract FDI. Moreover, trade policies and the stock of FDI have a positive impact on the incentives to invest in education. This set of findings highlights the possibility of a low equilibrium trap, where the lack of human capital discourages FDI and inadequate foreign investment limits domestic incentives to invest in education. But, at the same time, backtracking in trade or FDI feeds negatively in the rest; therefore, there is an increasing need to study globalization in a fully integrated way and not as a sum of its different components, since all of them are very important and feed each other.

A similar view is expressed by Freeman (2003), who thinks that too much more emphasis has been put by both free-traders and protestors on the effects of trade and labor standards than on capital and especially migration, when the effects of these two factors can be even larger than those of trade. Neither side has asked for freer flows of migrants as if immigration policies were not part of the globalization debate.

In sum, developed countries need to adapt to change and to do everything that can help to solve their negative demographic trends. That is, to reduce their protection and open their markets to developing countries' agricultural and labor intensive production of manufactures, to offshore most of their labor intensive manufacturing and services by investing heavily in developing countries with lower labor costs and broadly similar productivity, to transfer technology to those countries, and to allow for further increases of immigration. At the same time they have to help in a generous way their displaced low-skilled workers to adapt to the higher competition coming from the imports from developing countries and from the new waves of immigration to avoid an increasing trend to reject globalization.

Developing countries need to try not to lose the opportunities that globalization offers to them. That means: improving their governance, their legal and social institutions, their education and health levels; further liberalizing trade and FDI in order to become more integrated in the world economy; reaping the potential benefits of access to developed and other developing markets, and of attracting larger flows of FDI and trade; and being able, in the last instance, to allow redundant labor to migrate to developed countries.

Conclusion

Today, in a simplistic way there are three basic opinions on globalization: the straightforward pro-globalization one, the pro-globalization but with some question marks, and the straight anti-globalization one. I belong to the second view. The first position is called the "liberal" or "market led view" and it is supported by many pro-market economists who think that the market will eventually solve its small costs; the second is a pro-market "eclectic view," supported by most academic economists and some NGOs, who see, in general, the positive impact of globalization and economic opening on most of the world economy but they also see some areas of national and global policy improvements to avoid or reduce its negative effects. The third one is called mainly the "anti-capitalist" one, supported by most anti-globalization movements and some radical NGOs, which only see its most negative aspects and extrapolate them to the whole process.

I am very supportive of globalization in general, in the sense that world economic integration and openness (that is: more trade, more FDI, more technological diffusion, more migration, and more international aid) are all beneficial for the world economy as a whole and for the prosperity of its peoples. But I also recognize some problems in the present globalization process: first, I see the lack of global multilateral institutions which try to solve the large global negative externalities due to terrorism, to environmental free-riding by some companies and countries, to people, drugs and arms trafficking and to exploitation of women, poor children, and youths. Second, I note that existing multilateral institutions in the realm of trade and finance are not as efficient as they should to achieve their tasks: world trade protectionism is still very high, some capital flows to developing countries are still highly volatile and, as a result, help to increase the number of financial crises in developing countries, with devastating consequences for their populations.

Third, I observe the terrible fate of those poor regions and countries which are left behind in the globalization process without hope, because they do not have the minimum requirements, in terms of domestic institutions, human capital, infrastructures and savings to be able to integrate in world markets, either because of national political reasons or because of very high protection, by the rich countries and other developing countries, against their more competitive potential exports of goods, services or against migration. Fourth, I see the greed and lack of solidarity in the rich countries toward those poor regions and countries which are still kept out of the globalization process.

I also understand that the individual attitudes in developed countries against globalization and mainly against competition from developing countries' imports and migrants have a rationale and some of them depend on the skills of the person concerned and his worries about losing his job or a drop in his wage, while the contrary happens in developing countries. As O'Rourke (2003) has shown, as the Heckscher–Ohlin model predicts, being highly skilled is associated with more pro-globalization attitudes in rich countries and vice versa, while in some of the very poorest countries, being highly skilled has a negative, although smaller, impact on pro-globalization sentiment and vice versa. Moreover, individuals view protectionism and anti-immigrant policies as complements rather than substitutes, as the same model establishes.

Something similar happens with the understandable perceptions of many globalization critics who tend to think that globalization is bad for the poor, contrary to most empirical evidence. As Aisbett (2005) has shown, many critics believe that globalization favors concentrating power in corporations and that they are using it for their own benefit, thus harming the poor. They tend to be concerned about absolute non-monetary as well as monetary dimensions of poverty and more concerned about the total number of the poor than about the incidence of poverty, as economists do. In regard to inequality, those critics tend to refer more to changes in absolute inequality and income polarization than to the inequality measures preferred by economists. Thus, their perceptions may not change by reading this book, but I hope that they will understand that economists do not have predetermined perceptions but they merely try to elaborate theories and try contrasting them with reality to prove their validity.

Throughout the pages of this book I have tried to clarify and respond to some of the wrong and right accusations that are currently being leveled against globalization. I have based my rebuttal or my acceptance of them by trying to use the scientific theories and knowledge and the empirical evidence available. Let us review summarily the charges against globalization and my tentative answers.

First, globalization has been accused of increasing the world's poverty level. Throughout this book I have tried to provide a large sample of analyses and empirical evidence which tend to demonstrate how the world's absolute and relative poverty has been reduced significantly since the 1980s, while globalization has gathered momentum. I recognize that this empirical evidence is always debatable, given the poor quality of the data available in some developing countries and the difficulty of its measurement, being based both on national income statistics or direct surveys. A recent poverty measurement, made by Sala i Martín, shows that the number of individuals living on less than one dollar a day has decreased by 234 million since the 1980s, in which time globalization has accelerated, to reach a level of 350 million, in 1998, and that the number of individuals living on less than two dollars a day has fallen by more than 450 million to a level of around one billion, in 1998.

Another empirical work, by Bhalla, shows, as well, that these two levels of absolute poverty have fallen by 615 million and 484 million, respectively. In view of the population boom since the 1980s, the reduction in relative terms has been spectacular: 60 percent and 69 percent, respectively, in the first case and 51 percent and 70 percent, respectively, in the second. However, it should be stressed that its measurement is still under debate and that, unfortunately, this reduction did not take place evenly among countries. Poverty was reduced substantially in Asia, it was reduced slightly in Latin America as a whole (although not in all countries) and it increased in Africa. In any event, I must admit that the current levels of absolute and relative poverty are still economically scandalous and morally unacceptable, even more in light of the huge progress and prosperity achieved by most of the global economy in the past century.

Second, globalization has been accused of significantly increasing the world's level of inequality. Again the measurement of inequality is difficult and under permanent debate, but there is a considerable amount of empirical evidence demonstrating that inequality among the citizens of the world has been reduced, albeit quite modestly, in recent decades of the globalization surge. The Gini coefficient fell from 0.662 in 1980 to 0.633 in 1998, according to Sala i Martín, and from 0.685 to 0.651 between both years, according to Bhalla. The ratio between the richest 20 percent and the poorest 20 percent has also decreased, albeit only very slightly, from 40 times higher in 1970 to 39 times higher in 1998, but I fully recognize that this is still a huge gap. Moreover, although personal world inequality has been reduced slightly, its distribution by countries is uneven. It has increased significantly in many former communist countries as a result of their transition to a market economy, it has increased moderately in some countries of south Asia and Latin America, because of their financial crises, and in many countries in sub-Saharan Africa. In any case, there is still a big divergence in income per capita among countries in the world. There was also a slight rise in inequality within countries, particularly in the developing countries that have grown the most, such as China and India. This is an absolutely natural process, as urban areas and regions with an outlet to the sea are generally the first to benefit from globalization, much before rural and land-locked areas. It has also increased in some countries of Asia, Latin America, and Africa which have been hit by financial crises.

Third, it is argued that globalization has enabled multinationals to acquire more power than states and governments and that they have even become bigger than most countries. Neither of these two arguments is substantiated by available empirical evidence. On the one hand, multinationals have never been subject to more stringent regulations than they are today, and the anti-trust authorities are stronger than ever when it comes to ensuring that competition continues to thrive in all markets. On the other hand, a serious measurement of the size of multinationals relative to countries shows that their greater relative size is due more to the proliferation of small independent countries that have sprung up in the world than to the bigger size of multinationals. The total number of countries has risen since the mid-twentieth century from 46 to almost 200. In any event, recent experience has provided numerous cases of countries of varying sizes showing their superiority over multinationals whenever there has been a conflict between them, as just happened with the issue of cheaper generic vaccines.

At the same time, NGOs have become the new and efficient watchers of multinationals, being able to denounce those activities which could be damaging to the environment and to local communities as well as some shameful corruption practices; as a result they have been able to force them to improve their corporate social responsibility and their awareness of the heavy costs to their sales of having a negative social reputation.

Fourth, multinationals have been accused of exploiting workers in developing countries, paying them much lower wages and making them work in shameful, undignified conditions. Except for a few very notable cases, fortunately in a diminishing trend, there is extensive empirical evidence that reaches just the opposite conclusion. Foreign companies established in both developed and developing countries tend to pay higher wages than domestic companies and the working conditions they offer tend to be better than the general working conditions in the host country. Additionally, they tend to provide their employees with more training and knowledge as well as better retirement conditions than the domestic companies. Moreover, most multinationals target developed and average-income countries when investing abroad; consequently, they are not now generally seeking lower salaries and looser labor regulations but, on the contrary, macroeconomic and political stability, workers with a certain level of skills, and open economies, so that they can gain easier access to other markets.

The same is true of subcontracting. Subcontractors in developing countries are being monitored increasingly by governments and NGOs to make sure they are offering reasonable wages and working conditions, which, obviously, do not have to be identical to those in developed countries because if they were there would be no incentive to subcontract in those countries. Multinationals are increasingly investing in social issues in the developing countries where they are established to show that they are developing greater social responsibility in the host countries.

In any case, it is an undeniable fact that, despite this criticism, developed and developing countries alike are competing ferociously to attract multinationals to invest in their country, because they know that it means more employment, higher wages, more exports, faster technological dissemination, and thus higher growth.

Fifth, developed countries have been accused of maintaining high levels of protectionism on the goods and services exported by developing countries, such as agricultural and food products, textiles, footwear, and clothing. They have also been accused of generously and absurdly subsidizing their own agricultural production, which is largely inefficient and very uncompetitive vis-à-vis that of developing countries. These subsidies also lead to huge stocks of non-competitive products that are exported to developing countries (also with subsidies) at dumping prices, shattering their domestic agricultural prices and markets.

Throughout the book, I have admitted these accusations. I, too, consider these to be shameful practices from which almost everyone in the world stands to lose. On the one hand, in developed countries, the main losers are the consumers, who have to pay much higher prices due to their high levels of protection, thereby reducing their purchasing power, followed by the taxpayers, who have to pay higher taxes to finance inefficient subsidies. On the other hand, in developing countries, the main losers are those producers and workers who cannot access the bigger potential markets with their more competitive products due to inefficient and damaging subsidies and protection.

However, I also supply much evidence that, on average, developing countries protect their production much more than developed countries, even though their protection is much less widespread. This protection means less South–South trade, which is of vital importance for them to achieve more economic growth. Those who oppose globalization should be reminded that what is necessary for increasing growth and reducing poverty and inequality is a drastic reduction of trade barriers, that is, more and better globalization, not less.

Sixth, developed countries have been accused of reducing rather than increasing Official Development Assistance (ODA). This, too, is viewed as another outrage all through the book. I illustrate with ample evidence the present wealthy countries' stinginess and lack of solidarity, which are totally uncalled for in this century of general prosperity. The fact is that some countries have been left behind in the process of prosperity and globalization enjoyed by others and they urgently need this development assistance to create the minimum conditions necessary to benefit from globalization by being able to improve their institutions, educational levels, healthcare, and basic infrastructures.

Although I recognize that development aid has not been, in general, conducive to growth, nevertheless I also urged that the relative volume of assistance not only be increased to 0.7 percent of the GDP of the OECD countries, but that most of the assistance not be bilateral as it is now with political conditionality. Bilateral aid has been most often used to export their own products and services (via soft loans) to poor countries, even when they do not really need them. ODA should be channeled through international financial organizations and NGOs, which are much more familiar with the realities of the poorer countries.

Empirical evidence has shown that ODA may work at most as a catalyst for these poorer economies and as an incentive for them to improve their institutions and policies. It should be made perfectly clear that these countries are not "victims of globalization" as some poorly informed individuals and institutions erroneously argue without any evidence to support their arguments. On the contrary, these countries are, rather, "victims of *the lack of* globalization." The countries that have been able to avail themselves of globalization and have managed to open up their economies have attained much higher growth rates than those of developed and other developing countries. Nevertheless, it is also true that the poorest countries in general have not been able to integrate yet in the globalization process and this is the reason why they need further help from the advanced economies to build up the necessary conditions to join it.

Seventh, international financial organizations, especially the IMF and the World Bank, have been accused of always acting in the interests of the developed countries, which have a greater say in their governing bodies. This accusation is partly true: they are also "political" institutions and their activities inevitably respond to the national interest of their main shareholders. Faini and Grilli (2004) find out that the lending patterns of the World Bank and the IMF are influenced by the commercial and the financial interests of the US and, to a lesser extent, of the EU. At present, their main problem is that their governing bodies do not reflect the weight of developing countries in the world's GDP and population; therefore, the weighting in their governing councils should be changed as soon as possible to truly represent the present demographic and economic power balance.

They have also been accused of strictly applying the principles established in the "Washington Consensus." The truth of the matter is that in the last few years these agencies have generally been adapting to the changing situations of the developing countries as best they could. It is true that on certain occasions in the past they have made serious errors, but it is also true that they have rectified those errors once they became aware of them. Proof of this is that now, perhaps thanks to the criticism they received from NGO and development experts, they are much more careful with the programs that they design and the measures that they take. Moreover, they are proving to be increasingly essential vehicles for the transfer of more funds to poor countries in an attempt to attract more private funds and investments to those countries left out of the process of globalization.

Most of the principles of the so-called "Washington Consensus" (WC) are still absolutely reasonable and valid. These include the opening-up of the economies, fiscal and monetary macroeconomic stability, and exchange rate flexibility, among others. The main problem is that they date from the late 1980s and development theory and practice has evolved much since then; therefore their principles need to be adapted to the new problems and to the special cultural and economic characteristics of every developing country as has been put forward recently by "Barcelona's New Agenda for Development" (2004).

As Mukand and Rodrik (2005) put it:

> Appropiate policies and institutional arrangements have a large element of specificity and experimentation is required to discover what works locally. Reforms that succeed in one setting may perform poorly or fail completely in other settings. We do not mean that economic principles work differently in different places or that economics itself needs to be tailored to local conditions. We make a distinction between economic principles and their institutional embodiment. Most first-order economic principles come institutions-free. Incentives, competition, hard-budget constraints, sound money, fiscal sustainability and property rights are central to the way that economists think about policy and its reform. But these principles do not map directly into institutional solutions. Property rights can be implemented through common law, civil law or, for that matter, Chinese-type socialism. Competition can be maintained through a combination of free entry and laissez faire or through a well-functioning regulatory authority. Macroeconomic stability can be achieved under a variety of fiscal institutions.

Moreover, it has become clearer, following the experience accumulated through their recent currency and financial crises, that developing countries need to liberalize capital movements (other than foreign direct investment), and mainly short term flows, much more prudently and gradually than was suggested by the WC. Moreover, they should carry out this progressive liberalization in the right sequence: that is, first, to open up, at the same time and with the same speed, goods and services markets, and capital markets. Second, to open up capital markets only once their financial institutions and systems are mature enough to absorb such flows, so as not to trigger instability and the possibility of financial crises, like those we have seen in recent years. It seems awkward that whereas the OECD countries took more than three decades to liberalize their capital movements, developing countries have been recommended – and in some cases even forced – to do it in a much shorter time.

The IMF was subsequently the first organization to back-pedal on this issue. However, it is also not easy to maintain capital controls over short-term flows for many years or decades. On the one hand, as the financial system becomes more developed and sophisticated, it is increasingly difficult to apply them. On the other, in those countries with weak political and institutional governance these controls have become a primary source of corruption. Lastly, it should be recalled that the necessary liberalization of trade should be followed by the liberalization of the capital account in the balance of payments and not the other way round. (It is now clear that some countries have followed the wrong sequencing of liberalization, in part wrongly recommended by multilateral financial institutions.) Otherwise, exporters will have an incentive to declare lower revenues than they actually receive from their exports and importers will tend to declare higher payments than they paid for their imports, thus getting round the capital controls.

Another WC principle that, being objectively very positive, should be carefully reconsidered is that of privatizations. They have often been carried out for the sole purpose of obtaining short-term public funds, which have been squandered instead of being used to get other needed assets or to achieve greater efficiency in production. In other cases, companies have been privatized without any regulated, democratic, and transparent process. This has given rise to corrupt privatizations (not to mention the plundering of state assets, as has been the case in certain former communist countries). As Stiglitz and Hoff (2005) show, although privatizations tend to create a demand for the rule of law and property rights, in the case of post-communist countries, which have suffered from the stealing of state assets the demand for the rule of law and for broadly beneficial legal reforms may not emerge because the expectation of weak legal institutions increases the expected relative return to stripping assets, and strippers may gain from a weak or corrupt state. The final outcome can be inefficient even from the narrow perspective of the asset strippers. Finally, other privatizations have been initiated without first establishing a stable regulatory and enhancing-competition framework. As a result, in some developing countries companies have simply gone from state-run monopolies to private monopolies.

In sum, there is no doubt that the "Washington Consensus" needs some reforms and additions, not just because it dates from 1989 and the situation has changed since then, but also because experience has shown that some of its principles should be adapted to the individual situation and institutions of each country rather than being applied homogeneously to all of them as shown by the New Development Agenda of Barcelona.

Eighth, the World Trade Organization (WTO) has been blamed for working for the benefit of multinationals so that they can impose the traditional patent system in poor countries or block the access of such countries to low-priced vaccines and medicines. The truth is that in recent years it has been demonstrated that the rules established for trade-related intellectual property rights (TRIPS), although very reasonable in theory, do not actually work for some developing countries, particularly in the poorest ones in relation to vaccines and other basic medicines.

A new agreement, within the Millennium Round, both by developed and developing countries and by private companies, has recently been reached to adapt these rules to the special situations in these countries. This new agreement, without forfeiting the always necessary patent system – which is what makes it possible for research to continue improving treatments for diseases throughout the world – allows developing countries to have access to inexpensive medicines and vaccines and try to eradicate their ravaging pandemics.

Moreover, the only way the new Millennium Round can be successful is by trading off the high agriculture and labor intensive manufacturing protection by rich countries against a new agreement on foreign investment and intellectual property. In order to achieve this aim it is clear that developed countries should give in to their, negative for all, wrong protection of agriculture and labor intensive manufactures and specialize in what they can produce more efficiently and competitively.

Ninth, globalization has been blamed for provoking financial crises in developing countries. However, there have always been financial crises in both developed and developing countries, although they have been much less frequent (but much more serious) in the past. Many developing countries, both before and now, have been able to accumulate (with the help of developed countries' banks and investors looking for short term higher returns but being blind about risk) much more internal and external debt than they can actually repay and, in the end, they have failed to repay it or they have been perceived by markets as if they will not be able to pay, thus triggering not only a sharp recession for their own economies, but also causing a severe devaluation of their currencies, leading their poorest citizens to become destitute. What is surprising is that financial markets, being so innovative and efficient, have as yet been able neither to reduce the volatility of their capital flows nor to find the right instruments to reduce their risk management.

What globalization has introduced is a greater limitation to tax collection by countries in general, as it enables production factors to be more mobile, especially capital, skilled workers, individuals with higher incomes or wealth, and large international companies. Since these factors are more mobile, they can move to countries with lower taxes, jeopardizing the collection of taxes in countries with a higher level of debt and, consequently, higher tax rates and brackets to pay that debt. Some governments have defensively opted to issue internal debt indexed to the dollar or to other reserve currencies rather than reduce government spending. As a result, they have made their exchange rates more vulnerable, which often tends to result, not only in receivership but also in a sharp devaluation and an increase in inequality. In any event, these greater constraints to domestic indebtedness imposed by globalization benefit the people of developing countries, as they establish barriers to governments with policies of excessive (and often unproductive) government spending, which they can only keep up if they collect more and more taxes at the expense of their citizens' savings.

Globalization not only reduces the overall tax base of developing countries, but also changes its structure. It introduces a shift from "easy to collect" taxes (tariffs, seignorage, etc.) to "hard to collect" taxes (VAT, income tax, etc.). For instance, the revenue/GDP ratio of the easy to collect taxes declined by 20 percent in developing countries between the early 1980s and the late 1990s, while the revenue/GDP of hard to collect taxes increased by 9 percent, resulting in an overall net drop of 7 percent in their total tax revenue/GDP (Aizenman and Jinjarak, 2006).

This may be one of the reasons for the puzzling tax policies in developing countries (compared with those of developed countries) where taxes on labor income play a minor role, while taxes on consumption are important, where effective tax rates vary dramatically by firm, with many firms avoiding taxes entirely by operating through cash in the informal economy and others facing very high taxes. Taxes on capital are also an important source of revenue, because they are collected through the financial sector, so disintermediation limits how much can be collected in taxes. Gordon and Li (2005), showing these differences in company taxation, propose a tariff protection for capital intensive firms, which do pay, and higher inflation as a tax on the cash economy for those that do not pay. In any case, tax revenue is a major issue in developing countries, mainly in Latin America (with the exception of Brazil and Chile) and Africa. A low level of tax revenue not only reduces the possibility of facing debt crises but also reduces the possibility of decreasing the levels of inequality by doing redistribution.

Moreover, I have tried to explain throughout this book that, in order for this new phase of growing globalization to be successful, it is essential for wealthy countries to abstain from incurring excessive current account deficits with developing countries, as is currently the case with the US. The only thing these strong imbalances achieve is to drain what little private savings (now much more mobile) developing countries have, to finance such deficits and not their investment needs.

For the globalization process to work efficiently, wealthy countries, now that their populations are growing older and have more savings, should keep substantial current account surpluses with developing countries to export their higher savings, providing developing countries with financing for their necessary investments. The rationale is very clear, the latter have a younger population, a higher level of consumption, a lower level of savings, more growth potential and the possibility of paying higher interest rates, until in the longer term, these countries bring their population growth rates down. But, in order to be able to attract these savings, developing countries must also try to improve substantially the quality of their laws, institutions, and the soundness of their monetary and fiscal policies. Finally, a new and better contractual system must be achieved for developing countries' debt issues and defaults.

Lastly, I have tried to issue a major warning based on increasing evidence: if the developed does not achieve a higher degree of globalization in the coming years that encompasses all the developing countries through trade, foreign investment, and development assistance so that these countries' living conditions can improve, the huge demographic imbalance between wealthy and poor countries could spark a very severe and unsustainable situation in the long term. If developed countries do not reduce their protection and deepen their flows of trade and foreign investment with developing countries, which are a clear substitute for migratory flows, the expected large increase in the population of developing countries (by close to three billion inhabitants over the next 50 years), while the developed countries as a whole will lose population, may generate massive and likely chaotic migratory flows with very grave consequences for all.

It should not be forgotten that migration is an essential part of globalization and that it has historically resulted in the fastest and most direct way to reduce inequalities between countries. Accordingly, developed countries and their societies must get used to the idea that immigration must necessarily increase at a higher rate over the coming decades and that it would be better if it happens in an orderly fashion by common consent than chaotically. A greater degree of trade, financial, and technological globalization is the only way the world can escape serious migration conflicts in the twenty-first century between severely overpopulated and young countries without sufficient employment and economic opportunities for survival, and aged and rich countries losing their labor force but besieged by the pressure of millions of people trying to get across their borders.

Bibliography

Acemoglu, Daron (2003) "A Historical Approach to Assessing the Role of Institutions on Economic Development," *Finance and Development*, June, IMF, Washington, DC

Acemoglu, Daron (2005) "Politics and Economics in Weak and Strong States," NBER Working Paper 11275

Acemoglu, Daron (2006) "Modelling Inefficient Institutions," NBER Working Paper 11940

Acemoglu, Daron and Johnson, Simon (2003) "Unbundling Institutions," NBER Working Paper 9934

Acemoglu, Daron and Robinson, James A. (2000) "Political Losers as a Barrier to Economic Development," *American Economic Review Papers and Proceedings*, vol. 90

Acemoglu, Daron and Robinson, James A. (2006) *Economic Origins of Dictatorship and Democracy*, Cambridge University Press, New York

Acemoglu, Daron and Ventura, Jaume (2001) "The World Income Distribution," CEPR Discussion Paper 2973

Acemoglu, Daron, Aghion, Philippe, and Zilibotti, Fabrizio (2002) "Distance to Frontier, Selection and Economic Growth," CEPR Discussion Paper 3467

Acemoglu, Daron, Johnson, Simon, and Robinson, James A. (2001) "The Colonial Origins of Comparative Development: An Empirical Investigation," *American Economic Review*, vol. 91, no. 5

Acemoglu, Daron, Johnson, Simon, and Robinson, James (2004) "Institutions as the Fundamental Cause of Long-run Growth," NBER Working Paper 10481

Acemoglu, Daron, Johnson, Simon, Robinson, James, and Thaicharoen, Yunyong (2002) "Institutional Causes, Macroeconomic Symptoms, Volatility Crises and Growth," *Journal of Monetary Economics*, vol. 50

Bibliography

Adams, James D., Clemmons, Roger J., and Stephan, Paula E. (2006) "How Rapidly Does Science Leak Out?," NBER Working Paper 11997

Ades, Alberto and Di Tella, Rafael (1999) "Rents, Competition and Corruption," *American Economic Review*, vol. 89, September

Ades, Alberto and Glaeser, Edward (1999) "Evidence on Growth, Increasing Returns and the Extent of the Market," *Quarterly Journal of Economics*, vol. 114, no. 3

Aghion, Philippe (2002) "Schumpeterian Growth Theory and the Dynamics of Income Inequality," *Econometrica*, vol. 70, no. 3

Aghion, Philippe and Durlauf, Steven (eds.) (2006) *Handbook of Economic Growth*, North Holland, Amsterdam

Aghion, Philippe and Howitt, Peter (1992) "A Model of Growth through Creative Destruction," *Econometrica*, vol. 60

Aghion, Philippe and Howitt, Peter (1998) *Endogenous Growth Theory*, MIT Press, Cambridge, MA

Aghion, Philippe, Caroli, Eve, and Garcia-Peñalosa, Cecilia (1999) "Inequality and Economic Growth: the perspective of the New Growth Theories," *Journal of Economic Literature*, vol. 37, no. 4

Aghion, Philippe, Howitt, Peter, and Violante, Gianlucca L. (2001) "Technology, Knowledge and Inequality," *Journal of Economic Growth*, vol. 7, no. 4

Aghion, Philippe, Bloom, Nicholas, Blundell, Richard, Griffith, Rachel, and Howitt, Peter (2002) "Competition and Innovation: An Inverted U Relationship," NBER Working Paper 9269

Ahluwalia, Montek S. (1976) "Inequality, Poverty and Development," *Journal of Development Economics*, vol. 3, September

Aisbett, Emma (2005) "Why the Critics Are So Convinced That Globalization Is Bad for the Poor," NBER Working Paper 11066

Aitken, Brian J. and Harrison, Ann (1999) "Do Domestic Firms Benefit from FDI?: Evidence from Venezuela," *American Economic Review*, vol. 89, no. 3

Aizenman, Joshua and Jinjarak, Yothin (2006) "Globalization and Developing Countries: A Shrinking Tax Base?," NBER Working Paper 11933

Aizenman, Joshua and Noy, Ilan (2005) "FDI and Trade: Two Way Linkages?," NBER Working Paper 11403

Al-Atrash, Hassan and Yousef, Tarik (2000) "Intra-Arab Trade: Is It Too Little?," IMF Working Paper 00/10, Washington, DC

Alesina, Alberto and Angeletos, George-Marios (2005) "Corruption, Inequality and Fairness," NBER Working Paper 11399

Alesina, Alberto and Rodrik, Dani (1994) "Distributive Politics and Economic Growth" *Quarterly Journal of Economics*, vol. 109, no. 2

Alfaro, Laura, Kalemli-Ozcan, Sebnem, and Volosovycc, Vadym (2005) "Why Does Not Capital Flow from Rich to Poor Countries?: An Empirical Investigation," NBER Working Paper 11901

Alfaro, Laura, Chanda, Areendam, Kalemli-Ozcan, Sebnem, and Sayek, Selin (2002) "FDI and Economic Growth: The Role of Local Financial Markets," Working Paper, University of Houston

Amiti, Mary and Wakelin, Katharine (2002) "Investment Liberalization and International Trade," CEPR Discussion Paper 3492, London

Anand, Subdhir and Kanbur S. M. R. (1993) "The Kuznets Process and the Inequality–Development Relationship," *Journal of Development Economics*, vol. 41, no. 40

Anderson, James E. and Van Wincoop, Eric (2001) "Gravity with Gravitas: A Solution to the Border Puzzle," NBER Working Paper 8079

Anderson, Kym and Valenzuela, Ernesto (2005) "Do Global Trade Distortions Still Harm Developing Country Farmers?," CEPR Discussion Paper 5337

Anderson, Kym, Martin, Will, and van der Mensbrugghe, Dominique (2005) "Doha Merchandise Trade Reform: What's at Stake for Developing Countries?," CEPR Discussion Paper 5156

Anderson, Kym, Dimaran, Betina, Francois, Joseph, Hertel, Thomas, Hoekman, Bernard, and Martin, Will (2000) "Potential Gains from Trade Reform in the New Millennium," paper presented at the Third Annual Conference on Global Economic Analysis, Monash University, Melbourne, Australia, June

Angrist, Joshua D., Lavy, Victor, and Schlosser, Analia (2005) "New Evidence on the Causal Link between the Quantity and Quality of Children," NBER Working Paper 11835

Antrás, Pol, Garicano, Luis, and Rossi-Hansberg, Esteban (2005) "Off-shoring in a Knowledge Economy," NBER Working Paper 11094

Arjona, Ramón, Ladaique, Maxime, and Pearson, Mark (2001) "Growth, Inequality and Social Protection," Labour Market and Social Policy Occasional Paper 51, OECD, Paris

Artadi, Elsa V. and Sala i Martín, Xavier (2003) "The Economic Tragedy of the XXth Century: Growth in Africa," NBER Working Paper 9865

Atkinson, Anthony B. (1999) *The Economic Consequences of Rolling Back the Welfare State*, MIT Press, Cambridge, MA

Auty, Richard M. (2001) *Resource Abundance and Economic Development*, Oxford University Press, Oxford and New York

Bibliography

Bacchetta, Marc and Bora, Bijit (2002) *Market Access for Industrial Products and the Doha Development Agenda*, World Bank, Washington, DC, May

Bairoch, Paul (1988) *Cities and Economic Development*, University of Chicago Press, Chicago

Bairoch, Paul (1992) *Economics and World History, Myths and Paradoxes*, University of Chicago Press, Chicago

Bairoch, Paul and Levy-Boyer, M. (1981) *Disparities in Economic Development since the Industrial Revolution*, Macmillan, London

Baland, Jean-Marie and Robinson, James A. (2000) "Is Child Labour Inefficient?," *Journal of Political Economy*, vol. 108, no. 4

Balasubramanyam, V. N., Salisu, Mohammed, and Sapsford, David (1996) "Foreign Direct Investment and Growth in EP and IS Countries," *Economic Journal*, vol. 106

Baldwin, Richard and Martin, Phillippe (1999) "Two Waves of Globalization: Superficial Similarities, Fundamental Differences," NBER Working Paper 6904

Banerjee, Abhijit V. and Duflo, Esther (2000) "Inequality and Growth: What the Data Say?," NBER Working Paper 7793

Barro, Robert J. (1990) "Government Spending in a Simple Model of Endogenous Growth," *Journal of Political Economy*, vol. 98

Barro, Robert J. (1991) "Economic Growth in a Cross-section of Countries," *Quarterly Journal of Economics*, vol. 106

Barro, Robert J. (1997) *Determinants of Economic Growth: A Cross-country Study*, MIT Press, Cambridge, MA

Barro, Robert J. (1999a) "Inequality, Growth and Investment," NBER Working Paper 7038

Barro, Robert J. (1999b) "Determinants of Democracy," *Journal of Political Economy*, vol. 107, no. 6

Barro, Robert J. (2000) "Education and Economic Growth," Center for International Development Working Paper, Harvard University, Cambridge, MA

Barro, Robert J. and Lee, J. W. (1993) "International Comparisons of Educational Attainment," *Journal of Monetary Economics*, vol. 32

Barro, Robert J. and Lee, J. W. (1996) "International Measures of Schooling Years and Schooling Quality," *American Economic Review*, vol. 86

Barro, Robert J. and Lee, J. W. (2000) "International Data on Educational Attainment: Updates and Implications," NBER Working Paper 7911

Barro, Robert J. and Sala i Martín, Xavier (1990) "Public Finance Models of Economic Growth," *Review of Economic Studies*, vol. 59

Barro, Robert J. and Sala i Martín, Xavier (1995) *Economic Growth*, McGraw-Hill, Inc., New York

Barro, Robert J. and Sala i Martín, Xavier (1997) "Technological Diffusion, Convergence and Growth," *Journal of Economic Growth*, vol. 2

Basu, Kaushik (1999) "Child Labour: Cause, Consequences and Cure with Remarks on International Labour Standards," *Journal of Economic Literature*, vol. 37, September

Basu, Kaushik and Van, Pham Hoang (1998) "The Economics of Child Labour," *American Economic Review*, vol. 88, June

Bauer T. and Zimmermann, Klaus (1999) "Assessment of Possible Migration Pressure and Labour Market Impact Following EU Enlargement to Central and Eastern Europe," IZA Research Report, no. 3, Bonn

Baumol, William (2002) *The Free Market Innovation Machine: Analyzing the Growth Miracle of Capitalism*, Princeton University Press, Princeton, NJ

Beaudry, Paul and Collard, Fabrice (2004) "Globalization, Returns to Accumulations and the World Distribution of Output," NBER Working Paper 10565

Beck, Thorsten, Demirguc-Kunt, Asli, and Levine, Ross (2000) "A New Database of Financial Development and Structure," *World Bank Economic Review*, vol. 14, no. 3

Beck, Thorsten, Levine, Ross, and Loaiza, Norman (2000) "Finance and Sources of Growth," *Journal of Financial Economics*, vol. 58, no. 1–2

Becker, Gary (1982) *Human Capital: A Theoretical and Empirical Analysis with Special Reference to Education*, Chicago University Press, Chicago

Becker, Gary and Lewis H. G (1973) "On the Interaction between the Quantity and Quality of Children," *Journal of Political Economy*, vol. 81, no. 2, part 2

Beegle, Kathleen, Dehejia, Rakeev, and Gatti, Roberta (2004) "Why Should We Care about Child Labour? The Education, Labour Market and Health Consequences," NBER Working Paper 10980

Bell, Charles, Devarajan, Shantayanan, and Gersbach, Hans (2003) "The Long-run Economic Costs of AIDS: Theory and an Application to South Africa," World Bank Report, July

Bertola, Giuseppe (1998) "Macroeconomics of Distribution and Growth," in Anthony Atkinson and François Bourguignon (eds.), *Handbook of Income Distribution*, Elsevier, Amsterdam

Besley, Tim, Griffith, Rachel, and Klemm, Alexander (2001) "Fiscal Reaction Functions," mimeo, Institute of Fiscal Studies, London

Bhagwati, Jagdish (1978) *Anatomy and Consequences of Exchange Control Regimes*, Special Conference Series on Foreign Trade Regimes and Economic Development, vol. 11, Ballinger, Cambridge, MA

Bhagwati, Jagdish (2004) *In Defense of Globalization*, Oxford University Press and Council of Foreign Relations, New York

Bhalla, Surjit (2002) "Imagine There Is No Country: Poverty, Inequality, and Growth in the Era of Globalization," Institute for International Economics, September, Washington, DC

Blomstrom, Magnus and Kokko, Ari (1998) "Multinational Corporations and Spill-overs," *Journal of Economic Surveys*, vol. 12

Blomstrom, Magnus and Wolf, Edward N. (1994) "Multinational Corporations and Productivity Convergence in Mexico," in William Baumol, Richard Nelson, and Edward Wolf (eds.), *Convergence of Productivity: Cross-national Studies and Historical Evidence*, Oxford University Press, Oxford

Boix, Carles (2002) "Globalization and the Egalitarian Backlash: Protectionism versus Compensatory Free Trade," paper prepared for the workshop on Globalization and Egalitarian Redistribution, Santa Fe Institute, New Mexico, May 9

Bonaglia, Federico, Braga de Macedo, Jorge, and Bussolo, Mauricio (2001) "How Globalization Improves Governance," CEPR Discussion Paper 2992

Bordo, Michael D., Eichengreen, Barry, and Kim, Jongwoo (1998) "Was There Really an Earlier Period of International Financial Integration Comparable to Today?," NBER Working Paper 6738

Borensztein, Eduardo, de Gregorio, José, and Lee, Jong-Wha (1998) "How Does Foreign Direct Investment Affect Growth?," *Journal of International Economics*, vol. 45

Borjas, George J. (1987) "Self-selection and the Earnings of Immigrants," *American Economic Review*, vol. 77

Borjas, George J. (1994) "The Economic Benefits from Immigration," NBER Working Paper 4955

Borjas, George J. (1995) "The Economic Benefits from Immigration," *Journal of Economic Perspectives*, vol. 9

Borjas, George J. (1999a) "The Economic Analysis of Immigration," in *Handbook of Labour Economics*, vol. 3-A, Elsevier, Amsterdam

Borjas, George J. (1999b) *Heaven's Door: Immigration Policy and the American Economy*, Princeton University Press, NJ

Borjas, George J. (2003) "The Labour Demand Curve Is Downward Sloping: Re-examining the Impact of Immigration in the Labour Market," NBER Working Paper 9755

Borjas, George J. (2004) "Increasing the Supply of Labour through Immigration: Measuring the Impact on Native Labour Markets," Center for Immigration Studies, May

Borjas, George J., Freeman, Richard, and Katz, Lawrence (1992) "On the Labour Market Effects of Immigration and Trade," in G. Borjas and R. Freeman (eds.), *Immigration and the Work Force: Economic Consequences for the United States and Source Areas*, University of Chicago Press for NBER, Chicago

Borjas, George J., Freeman, Richard B., and Katz, Lawrence F. (1997) "How Much Do Immigration and Trade Affect Labour Market Outcomes," Brookings Papers on Economic Activity, vol. 1

Bouet, Antoine, Bureau, Jean Christophe, Decreux, Yvan, and Jean, Sebastien (2003) "Is Agricultural Liberalization Beneficial to Developing Countries?," *The World Economy*, vol. 28, no. 9

Bourguignon, François and Morrison, Christian (2002) "Inequality among World Citizens: 1820–1992," *American Economic Review*, vol. 92, no. 4

Brown, Drusilla, Deardoff, Alan, and Stern, Robert (2001) "CGE Modeling and Analysis of Multilateral and Regional Negotiating Options," University of Michigan School of Public Policy Research, Discussion Paper 468

Brown, Drusilla, Deardoff, Alan, and Stern, Robert (2003) "The Effects of Multinational Production on Wages and Working Conditions in Developing Countries," NBER Working Paper 9669

Bulow, Jeremy and Rogoff, Kenneth (1989) "Sovereign Debt: Is to Forgive to Forget?," *American Economic Review*, vol. 79, March

Burniaux, Jean Marc, Dang, Thai-Thanh, Fore, Douglas, Forster, Michael, Mira D'Ercole, Marco, and Oxley, Howard (1998) "Income Distribution and Poverty in Selected OECD Countries," OECD Economics Department Working Papers 189, Paris

Burnside, Craig and Dollar, David (2000) "Aid Policies and Growth," *American Economic Review*, vol. 90, no. 4

Campos, Mauro and Kinoshita, Yuko (2002) "FDI as Technology Transferred: Some Panel Evidence from Transition Economies," CEPR Discussion Paper 3417

Card, David (2005) "Is the New Immigration Really So Bad?," NBER Working Paper 11547

Bibliography

Caselli, Francesco and Feyrer, James (2005) "The Marginal Product of Capital," CEPR Discussion Paper 5203

Cashin, Paul A. (1994) "Government Spending, Taxes and Economic Growth," IMF Working Paper WP/94/92

Cass, David and Stiglitz, Joseph E. (1969) "The Implications of Alternative Savings and Expectation Hypothesis for Choices of Technique and Patterns of Growth," *Journal of Political Economy*, vol. 77, no. 4

Castles, Francis G. and Dowrick, Steve (1990) "The Impact of Government Spending Levels on Medium-term Economic Growth in the OECD, 1960–85," *Journal of Theoretical Politics*, vol. 2

Catao, Luis (2002) "Debt Crises: What's Different about Latin America?," *World Economic Outlook*, April, IMF, Washington, DC

Catao, Luis and Sutton, Ben (2002) "Sovereign Defaults: The Role of Volatility," IMF Working Paper 02/149

Caves, Richard (1998) "Industrial Organization and New Findings on the Turnover and Mobility of Firms," *Journal of Economic Literature*, December

Cernat, Lucien, Laird, Sam, and Turrini, Alessandro (2002) *Back to Basics: Market Access Issues in the Doha Agenda*, United Nations Conference on Trade and Development, UNCTAD, New York and Geneva

Chamon, Marcos and Kremer, Michael (2006) "Economic Transformation, Population Growth and the Long-run World Income Distribution," NBER Working Paper 12038

Chedor, Severine and Mucchielli, Jean Louis (1998) "Implantation à l'Etranger et Performance à l'Exportation: un Analyse Empirique sur les Implantations de Firmes Françaises dans les Pays Emergents," *Revue Economique*, May

Chedor, Severine, Mucchielli, Jean Louis, and Soubaya, Isabel (2002) "Intrafirm Trade and Foreign Direct Investment: An Empirical Analysis of French Firms," in Robert E. Lipsey and Jean Louis Mucchielli (eds.), *Multinational Firms and Impacts on Employment, Trade and Technology*, Routledge, London and New York

Chen, Natalie, Imbs, Jean, and Scott, Andrew (2004) "Competition, Globalization and the Decline of Inflation," CEPR Discussion Paper 4495

Chen, Shaohua and Ravallion, Martin (2002) "How Did the World's Poorest Fare in the 1990's?," Development Research Group Working Paper, World Bank, Washington, DC

Chen, Shaohua and Ravallion, Martin (2004) "How Have the World's Poorest Fared Since the Early 1980s," World Bank Working Paper 3341 2004/06

Bibliography

Chinn, Menzie D. and Fairlie, Robert W. (2004) "The Determinants of the Digital Divide: a Cross-country Analysis of Computer and Internet Penetration," NBER Working Paper 10686

Chiswick, Barry R. and Hatton, Timothy J. (2002) "International Migration and the Integration of Labor Markets," in Michael Bordo, Alan Taylor, and Jeffrey Williamson (eds.), *Globalization in Historical Perspective*, Chicago University Press, Chicago

Chuan, Yih-Chyi and Lin, Chi-Mei (1999) "FDI, R&D and Spill-over Efficiency: Evidence from Taiwan's Manufacturing Firms," *Journal of Development Studies*, vol. 35, no. 4

Coe, David T. and Helpman, Elhanan (1995) "International R&D Spill-overs," *European Economic Review*, vol. 39, no. 5

Coe, David T. and Hoffmaister, Alexander W. (1999) "North–South Trade: Is Africa Unusual?," *Journal of African Economies*, vol. 8, July

Coe, David T., Helpman, Elhanan, and Hoffmaister, Alexander W. (1995) "North–South R&D Spill-overs," NBER Working Paper 5048, Cambridge, MA

Cohen, Daniel and Soto, Marcelo (2002) "Why Are Poor Countries Poor? A Message of Hope which Involves the Resolution of a Becker–Lucas Paradox," CEPR Discussion Paper 3528

Cohen, Joel E. and Bloom, David E. (2005) "Cultivating Minds," *Finance and Development*, June, IMF, Washington, DC

Collier, Paul and Dollar, David (2001) "Can the World Cut Poverty in Half? How Policy Reform and Effective Aid Can Meet International Development Goals?," *World Development*, vol. 29, no. 11

Collier, Paul and Dollar, David (2002) "Aid Allocation and Poverty Reduction," *European Economic Review*, vol. 46

Collins, William (1996) "Regional Labour Markets in British India," mimeo, Department of Economics, Harvard University, November

Comin, Diego and Hobijn, Bart (2004) "Cross-country Technology Adoption: Making the Theories Face the Facts," *Journal of Monetary Economics*, vol. 51

Comin, Diego and Hobijn, Bart (2005) "Lobbies and Technology Diffusion," NBER Working Paper 11022

Comin, Diego, Hobijn, Bart, and Rovito, Emilie (2006) "Five Facts You Need to Know about Technology Diffusion," NBER Working Paper 11928

Commission on Macroeconomics and Health (2001) *Macroeconomics and Health: Investing in Health for Economic Development*, World Health Organization, Geneva

315

Bibliography

Coppel, Jonathan and Durand, Martine (1999) "Trends in Market Openness," OECD Economics Department Working Paper 221, Paris

Coppel, Jonathan, Dumont, Jean-Christophe, and Visco, Ignazio (2001) "Trends in Immigration and their Economic Consequences," OECD Economics Department Working Paper 284, Paris

Cornia, Giovanni Andrea and Kiiski, Sampsa (2001) "Trends in Income Distribution in the Post-World War II: Evidence and Interpretation," United Nations University, WIDER Paper no. 2001/89, Helsinki

Crafts, Nicholas F. R. (1983) "British Economic Growth, 1700–1831: A Review of the Evidence," *Economic History Review*, November

Crafts, Nicholas F. R. (1985) *British Economic Growth during the Industrial Revolution*, Oxford University Press, Oxford

Crafts, Nicholas F. R. (1995) "Exogenous or Endogenous Growth?: The Industrial Revolution Reconsidered," *Journal of Economic History*, vol. 55, no. 4

Crafts, Nicholas F. R. (2002) "The Solow Productivity Paradox in Historical Perspective," CEPR Discussion Paper 3142

Crafts, Nicholas F. R. and Harley, C. K. (1992) "Output Growth and the British Industrial Revolution: A Restatement of the Crafts–Harley View," *Economic History Review*, November

Crafts, Nicholas F. R. and Toniolo, Gianni (1996) *Economic Growth in Europe since 1945*, Cambridge University Press for CEPR, Cambridge and London

Crafts, Nicholas F. R. and Venables, Anthony (2001) "Globalization in History: A Geographical Perspective," CEPR Discussion Paper 3079

Cutler, David M., Deaton, Angus S., and Lleras-Muney, Adriana (2006) "The Determinants of Mortality," NBER Working Paper 11963

David, Paul (1991) "Computer and Dynamo: The Modern Productivity Paradox in a Not-Too-Distant Mirror," in *Technology and Productivity: The Challenge for Economic Policy*, OECD, Paris

Deaton, Angus (2005a) "The Great Escape: A Review Essay on Fogel's *The Great Escape from Hunger and Premature Death, 1700–2100*," NBER Working Paper 11308

Deaton, Angus (2005b) "Measuring Poverty in a Growing World or Measuring Growth in a Poor World," *Review of Economics and Statistics*, vol. 87

Deaton, Angus and Subramanian, Shankar (1996) "The Demand for Food and Calories," *Journal of Political Economy*, vol. 104, February

De Grauwe, Paul and Camerman, Filip (2002) "How Big Are Multinational Companies?," *World Economics*, vol. 4, no. 2

Deininger, Klaus and Squire, Lyn (1996) "A New Data Set Measuring Income Inequality," *World Bank Economic Review*, vol. 10

Deininger, Klaus and Squire, Lyn (1998) "New Ways of Looking at Old Issues: Inequality and Growth," *Journal of Development Economics*, vol. 57

De la Dehesa, Guillermo (2000) "Comprender la Globalización," Alianza Editorial, Madrid

De la Dehesa, Guillermo (2002a) *Globalización, Desigualdad y Pobreza*, Alianza Editorial, Madrid

De la Dehesa, Guillermo (2002b) *Venture Capital: The US versus the EU*, The Group of Thirty, Washington, DC

De la Dehesa, Guillermo (2006a) *Europe at the Cross-roads*, McGraw-Hill, New York

De la Dehesa, Guillermo (2006b) *Winners and Losers in Globalization*, Blackwell Publishing, New York and Oxford

De Long, Bradford (2000) "Cornucopia: The Pace of Economic Growth in the Twentieth Century," NBER Working Paper Series 7602, March

De Long, Bradford (2001a) "An Historical Take on the New Economy," j-bradford-delong.net

De Long, Bradford (2001b) "The World's Income Distribution: Turning the Corner?," j-bradford-delong.net

De Melo, Luiz (1997) "Foreign Direct Investment in Developing Countries and Growth: a Selective Survey," *Journal of Development Studies*, vol. 34, no. 1

Desai, Mihir (1999) "Are We Racing to the Bottom?: Evidence on Dynamics of International Tax Competition," *Proceedings of the Annual Conference on Taxation*, National Tax Association, Washington, DC

De Soto, Hernando (2000) *The Mystery of Capital: Why Capitalism Triumphs in the West and Nowhere Else?*, Basic Books, New York

Detragiache, Enrica and Spilimbergo, Antonio (2001) "Crisis and Liquidity: Evidence and Interpretation," IMF Working Paper 01/02, Washington, DC

Devarajan, Shantayanan, Miller, Marcus, and Swanson, E. V. (2002) "Development Goals: History, Prospects and Costs," World Bank Policy Research Working Paper 2189, April, Washington, DC

Diamond, Jared (1997) *Guns, Germs and Steel*, Norton, New York

Dikhanov, Yuri and Ward, Michael (2000) *Measuring the Distribution of Global Income*, World Bank, Washington, DC

Di Mauro, Francesca (2000) "The Impact of Economic Integration on FDI Exports: A Gravity Approach," CEPS Working Document 156, Brussels

Bibliography

Dixit, Avinash (2004) *Lawlessness and Economics: Alternative Models of Governance*, Princeton University Press, Princeton, NJ

Djankov, Simeon, La Porta, Rafael, Lopez de Silanes, Florencio, and Shleifer, Andrei (2002) "Regulation of Entry," *Quarterly Journal of Economics*, vol. 117, no. 1

Djankov, Simeon, La Porta, Rafael, Lopez de Silanes, Florencio, and Shleifer, Andrei (2003) "The New Comparative Economics," *Journal of Comparative Economics*, vol. 31, no. 4

Dobson, Wendy and Siow Yue, Chia (1997) *Multinationals and East Asian Integration*, International Development Research Centre, IDC/ISEAS, Ottawa, Canada

Dollar, David (2001) "Globalization, Inequality and Poverty since 1980," Policy Research Group Working Paper 3333, World Bank, Washington, DC

Dollar, David and Kraay, Art (2000) *Growth is Good for the Poor*, IMF Seminar Series. 2000–35, Washington, DC

Dollar, David and Kraay, Art (2002a) "Spreading the Wealth," *Foreign Affairs*, January–February

Dollar, David and Kraay, Art (2002b) *Institutions, Trade and Growth*, Carnegie Rochester Conference Series on Public Policy

Dowrick, Steve and Akmal, Muhammad (2001) "Contradictory Trends in Global Income Inequality: A Tale of Two Biases," *Australian National University*, March

Dunning, John H. (1993) *Multinational Enterprises and the Global Economy*, Addison-Wesley, New York

Durlauf, Steve (1995) "Multiple Regimes and Cross-Country Growth Behavior," *Journal of Applied Econometrics*, vol. 10

Easterly, William (1999) "Life during Growth," *Journal of Economic Growth*, vol. 4

Easterly, William (2000) "The Middle Class Consensus and Economic Development," Development Research Group Working Paper 2346, World Bank, Washington, DC

Easterly, William (2001) *The Elusive Quest for Growth: Economists' Adventures and Misadventures in the Tropics*, MIT Press, Cambridge, MA

Easterly, William (2002) "The Cartel of Good Intentions," *Foreign Policy*, no. 131, July–August

Easterly, William and Kraay, Aart (2000) "Small States, Small Problems?: Income, Growth and Volatility in Small States," *World Development*, vol. 28, November

Easterly, William and Levine, Ross (1997) "Africa's Growth Tragedy: Policies and Ethnic Divisions," *Quarterly Journal of Economics*, vol. 112, no. 4

Easterly, William and Levine, Ross (2002) "Tropics, Germs and Crops: How Endowments Influence Economic Development," NBER Working Paper 9106

Easterly, William and Rebelo, Sergio (1993) "Fiscal Policy and Economic Growth: An Empirical Investigation," *Journal of Monetary Economics*, vol. 32, no. 3

Eaton, Jonathan and Kortum, Samuel (1997) "Technology and Bilateral Trade," NBER Working Paper 6253

Eaton, Jonathan and Kortum, Samuel (1999) "International Technology Diffusion: Theory and Measurement," *International Economic Review*, vol. 40, no. 3

Economist, The (2001a) "Of Rich and Poor," Economic Focus, April 28

Economist, The (2001b) "Does Inequality Matter?," June 16

Economist, The (2001c) "Patents and the Poor," Special Report, June 23

Economist, The (2001d) "Getting Better All the Time: A Survey of Technology and Development," November 10

Economist, The (2002a) "Aid Effectiveness," March 16

Economist, The (2002b) "Convergence, Period," Economic Focus, July 20

Economist, The (2002c) "For 80 Cents More," Special Report, "Health Care in Poor Countries," August 17

Economist, The (2002d) "The Green Reaper" and "Half a Billion Americans?," Special Report, "Demography and the West," August 24

Economist, The (2002e) "Outward Bound," Special Report on Migration, September 28

Economist, The (2004) "More or Less Equal?," Special Report on Global Economic Inequality, March 13

Economist, The (2005) "Meritocracy in America," Special Report, January 1

Economist Intelligence Unit (2002) "FDI Forecasts," quoted in *The Economist*, April 6

Edison, Hali (2003) "How Strong Are the Links between Institutional Quality and Economic Performance," *Finance and Development*, June, IMF, Washington, DC

Edmonds, Eric and Pavcnik, Nina (2002) "Does Globalization Increase Child Labour?: Evidence from Vietnam," NBER Working Paper 8760

Edmonds, Eric and Pavcnik, Nina (2004) "International Trade and Child Labour: Cross-country Evidence," NBER Working Paper 10317

Bibliography

Eichengreen, Barry J. (1996) *Globalizing Capital: A History of the International Monetary System*, Princeton University Press, Princeton, NJ

Eichengreen, Barry and Mussa, Michael (1998) "Capital Account Liberalization: Theoretical and Practical Issues," IMF Occasional Paper 172, Washington, DC

Engerman, Stanley L. and Sokoloff, Kenneth L. (2005) "Colonialism, Inequality and Long-run Paths of Development," NBER Working Paper 11057

Erdilek, Asim (2003) "A Comparative Analysis of Inward and Outward FDI in Turkey," *Transnational Corporations*, vol. 12, no. 3

Faini, Ricardo (1994) "Migration and Growth: The Experience of Southern Europe," CEPR Discussion Paper 0964, London

Faini, Ricardo (2004) "Trade Liberalization in a Globalizing World," CEPR Discussion Paper 4665, October

Faini, Ricardo and Grilli, Vittorio (2004) "Who Runs the IFIs?," CEPR Discussion Paper 4666

Faini, Ricardo, De Melo, Jaime, and Zimmermann, Klaus (eds.) (1999) *Migration, the Controversies and the Evidence*, Cambridge University Press, Cambridge

Fallon, Peter and Tzannatos, Zafiris (1998) "Child Labour: Issues and Directions for the World Bank," World Bank, Washington, DC

FAO (2001) *Annual Report*, Rome

Fatás, Antonio (2002) "The Effects of Business Cycles on Growth," in Norman Loayza and Raimundo Soto (eds.), *Economic Growth: Sources, Trends and Cycles*, Central Bank of Chile, Santiago

Feenstra, Robert C. and Hanson, Gordon H. (2001) "Global Production Sharing and Rising Inequality: A Survey of Trade and Wages," NBER Working Paper 8372

Feis, Herbert (1930) *Europe: The World's Banker 1870–1914*, Yale University Press, New Haven, CT

Feldstein, Martin and Horioka, Charles (1980) "Domestic Savings and International Capital Flows," *Economic Journal*, vol. 90

Feliciano, Zadia and Lipsey, Robert E. (1999) "Foreign Ownership and Wages in the US 1987–1992," NBER Working Paper 6923

Fischer, Stanley (2003) "Globalization and Its Challenges," AEA Papers and Proceedings, *American Economic Review*, vol. 93, no. 2

Flanagan, Robert J. (2002) "Labour Standards and International Competitive Advantage," prepared for the Conference on Labour Standards, Stanford University, May

Bibliography

Fogel, Robert W. (2000) *The Fourth Great Awakening and the Future of Egalitarianism*, Chicago University Press, Chicago, IL

Fogel, Robert W. (2005) "Changes in the Physiology of Ageing during the Twentieth Century," NBER Working Paper 11233

Fogel, Robert W. and Costa, Dora L. (1997) "A Theory of Techno-physio Evolution with some Implications for Population, Health Care Costs and Pension Costs," *Demography*, vol. 34, no. 1

Fontagné, Lionel (2003) "Market Access and Domestic Support Measures," *CESifo Forum*, vol. 4, no. 3

Fontagné, Lionel and Pajot, Michael (2002) "Relationships between Trade and FDI Flows within Two Panels of US and French Industries," in Robert E. Lipsey and Jean Louis Muccielli (eds.), *Multinational Firms and Impacts on Employment, Trade and Technology*, Routledge, London and New York

Fontagné, Lionel, Guerin, J. L., and Jean, S. (2003) "Multilateral Trade Liberalization: Scenarios for the New Round and Assessment," CEPII Working Paper, Paris

Forbes, Kirstin (2000) "A Reassessment of the Relationship between Inequality and Growth," *American Economic Review*, vol. 90, no. 4

Francois, Joseph (2000) *Assessing the Results of General Equilibrium Studies of Multilateral Trade Negotiations*, UNCTAD Policy Issues in International Trade and Commodities Study Series, no. 3, Geneva

Francois, Joseph and Martin, Will (2003) "Formula Approaches for Market Access Negotiations," *World Economy*, vol. 23, no. 1

Francois, Joseph, Hoekman, Bernard, and Manchin, Miriam (2005) "Preference Erosion and Multilateral Trade Liberalization," CEPR Discussion Paper 5153

Francois, Joseph, van Meijl Hans, and van Tongeren, Frank (2003) *Economic Implications of Trade Liberalization under the Doha Round*, Erasmus University, Rotterdam

Frankel, Jeffrey A. (1997) *Regional Trading Blocs in the World Economic System*, Institute of International Economics, Washington, DC

Frankel, Jeffrey A. (1999) "Proposals Regarding Restrictions on Capital Flows," *African Finance Journal*, vol. 1, no. 1

Frankel, Jeffrey A. and Romer, David (1999) "Does Trade Cause Growth?," *American Economic Review*, vol. 89, no. 3

Frankel, Jeffrey A. and Wei, Shang-Jin (1998) "Regionalization of World Trade and Currencies" in Jeffrey A. Frankel (ed.), *The Regionalization of the World Economy*, University of Chicago Press, Chicago

Bibliography

Fraser Institute (2005) *Economic Freedom of the World*, Vancouver, Calgary and Toronto, Canada

Freeman, Richard (2003) "Trade Wars: The Exaggerated Impact of Trade in Economic Debate," NBER Working Paper 1000

Freeman, Richard, Oostendorp, Remco H., and Rama, Martin (2001) "Globalization and Wages," mimeo, World Bank, Washington, DC

Fujita, Masahisa and Thisse, Jacques-François (2003) "Globalization and the Evolution of the Supply Chain: Who Gains and Who Loses?," CEPR Discussion Paper 4152

Fujita, Masahisa, Krugman, Paul, and Venables, Anthony (1999) *The Spatial Economy: Cities, Regions and International Trade*, MIT Press, Cambridge, MA

Galor, Oded (2004) "From Stagnation to Growth: a Unified Growth Theory," CEPR Discussion Paper 4581

Galor, Oded and Moav, Omer (2002) "Natural Selection and the Origin of Economic Growth," *Quarterly Journal of Economics*, vol. 117

Galor, Oded and Moav, Omer (2003) *Das Human Kapital: A Theory of Demise of the Class Structure*, Brown University, Providence, RI

Galor, Oded and Moav, Omer (2004) "From Physical to Human Capital Accumulation: Inequality and the Process of Development," *Review of Economic Studies*, vol. 71, no. 4

Galor, Oded and Moav, Omer (2005) "Natural Selection and the Evolution of Life Expectancy," CEPR Discussion Paper 5373

Galor, Oded and Mountford, A. (2003) *Trading Population for Productivity*, Brown University, Providence, RI

Galor, Oded and Mountford, Andrew (2006) "Trade and the Great Divergence: The Family Connection," CEPR Discussion Paper 5490

Galor, Oded and Weil, David N. (1999) "From Malthusian Stagnation to Modern Growth," *American Economic Review*, vol. 89

Galor, Oded and Weil, David N. (2000) "Population, Technology and Growth: From the Malthusian Regime to the Demographic Transition," *American Economic Review*, vol. 110

Galor, Oded and Zeira, Joseph (1993) "Income Distribution and Macroeconomics," *Review of Economic Studies*, vol. 60

Gallup, John Luke and Sachs, Jeffrey D. (1998) "The Economic Burden of Malaria: Cross-Country Evidence," in *Health, Health Policy and Health Outcomes*, Final Report, Director General Transition Team, World Health Organization

Bibliography

Gallup, John Luke, Sachs, Jeffrey D., and Mellinger, Andrew D. (1999) "Geography and Economic Development," *International Regional Science Review*, vol. 22, no. 2

Ganslant, Mattias, Maskus, Keith E., and Wong, Eina V. (2001) "Developing and Distributing Essential Medicines to Poor Countries: The Defend Proposal," *World Economy*, vol. 24, no. 6

Garrett, Geoffrey (1998) "Global Markets and National Politics," *International Organization*, vol. 52, no. 4

Garrett, Geoffrey and Mitchell, Deborah (2001) "Globalization, Government Spending and Taxation in the OECD," *European Journal of Political Research*, vol. 39

Gerschenkron, Alexander (1962) *Economic Backwardness in Historical Perspective*, Harvard University Press, Cambridge, MA

Gertler, Mark and Rogoff, Kenneth (1990) "North–South Lending and Endogenous Domestic Capital Market Inefficiencies," *Journal of Monetary Economics*, vol. 26

Giavazzi, Francesco and Tabellini, Guido (2004) "Economic and Political Liberalizations," NBER Working Paper 10657

Glaeser, Edward, Scheinkman, Jose, and Shleifer, Andrei (2002) "The Injustice of Inequality," NBER Working Paper 9150

Glaeser, Edward, La Porta, Rafael, Lopez de Silanes, Florencio, and Shleifer, Andrei (2004) "Do Institutions Cause Growth?," NBER Working Paper 10568

Goldman Sachs (2004) "Making the Most of Global Migration," Global Economics Paper 115

Gordon, Roger H. and Bovenberg, Lans A. (1996) "Why Capital Is so Immobile Internationally? Possible Explanations and Implications for Capital Income Taxation," *American Economic Review*, vol. 86

Gordon, Roger H. and Li, We (2005) "Tax Structure in Developing Countries: Many Puzzles and Possible Explanation," NBER Working Paper 11267

Gorg, Holger and Strobl, Eric (2000) "Multinational Companies, Technology Spillovers and Firm Survival: Evidence from Irish Manufacturing," *Research Paper* 2000–12, Centre for Research on Globalization and Labour Markets, University of Nottingham, UK

Gorg, Holger and Strobl, Eric (2002) "Footloose Multinationals?," CEPR Discussion Paper 3402

Graham, Edward M. (1996) *Global Corporations and National Governments*, Institute for International Economics, Washington, DC

Bibliography

Graham, Edward M. and Richardson, David J. (1997) *Competition Policies for the Global Economy*, Institute for International Economics, Washington, DC

Greenwood, Jeremy (1999) "The Third Industrial Revolution: Technology, Productivity and Income Inequality," *Federal Reserve Bank of Cleveland Review*

Greenwood, Jeremy and Jovanovic, Boyan (1998) "Accounting for Growth," University of Rochester, Center for Economic Research Working Paper 475, New York

Greenwood, Jeremy and Yorukoglu, Mehmet (1997) "1974," Carnegie–Rochester Conference Series on Public Policy, vol. 46, June

Greenwood, Jeremy, Hercowitz, Zvi, and Krusell, Per (1997) "Long Run Implications of Investment-specific Technical Change," *American Economic Review*, vol. 87, no. 3

Gresser, Edward (2002) "America's Hidden Tax on the Poor: The Case for Reforming US Tariff Policy," Progressive Policy Institute Report, March, Washington, DC

Griffith, Rachel and Simpson, Helen (2001) *Characteristics of Foreign-owned Firms in British Manufacturing*, Institute of Fiscal Studies, London

Grossman, Gene and Helpman, Elhanan (1991) *Innovation and Growth in the Global Economy*, MIT Press, Cambridge, MA

Grossman, Gene and Helpman, Elhanan (2002) "Outsourcing versus FDI in Industry Equilibrium," CEPR Discussion Paper 3647

Grossman, Sanford and Hart, Oliver (1986) "The Costs and Benefits of Ownership," *Journal of Political Economy*, vol. 94

Guiso, Luigi, Sapienza, Paola, and Zingales, Luigi (2002) "People's Opium?: Religions and Economic Attitudes," NBER Working Paper 9327, October

Guiso, Luigi, Sapienza, Paola, and Zingales, Luigi (2006) "Does Culture Affect Economic Outcomes?," CEPR Discussion Paper 5505

Gunder Frank, André (1998) *ReOrient: Global Economy in the Asian Age*, University of California Press, Berkeley

Gupta, Sanjeev, Clements, Benedict, and Tionsong, Erwin (1998) "Public Spending on Human Development," *Finance and Development*, no. 3, September, IMF, Washington, DC

Gwartney, James, Lawson, Robert, and Holcombe, Randall G. (1998) "The Size and Functions of Government and Economic Growth," Joint Economic Committee Paper, Washington, DC

Gylfason, Thorvaldur (2001) "Natural Resources, Education and Economic Development," *European Economic Review*, vol. 45, September

Bibliography

Gylfason, Thorvaldur (2004) "Natural Resources and Economic Growth: From Dependence to Diversification," CEPR Discussion Paper 4804

Gylfason, Thorvaldur and Zoega, Gylfi (2001) "Natural Resources and Economic Growth: The Role of Investment," CEPR Discussion Paper 2743

Gylfason, Thorvaldur, Herbertson, Tkyggvi T., and Zoega, Gylfi (1999) "A Mixed Blessing: Natural Resources and Economic Growth," *Macroeconomic Dynamics*, vol. 3

Haddad, Mona and Harrison, Ann (1993) "Are There Positive Spill-overs from Direct Foreign Investment?," *Journal of Development Economics*, vol. 42

Hall, Robert and Jones, Charles I. (1999) "Why Do Some Countries Produce so Much More Output per Worker than Other Countries?," *Quarterly Journal of Economics*, vol. 114, no. 1

Hamilton, Carl (2002) "Globalization and Democracy," CEPR Discussion Paper 3653

Hansen, Gary and Prescott, Edward (2002) "Malthus to Solow," *American Economic Review*, vol. 92

Hanson, Gordon H., Scheve, Kenneth F., and Slaughter, Mathew J. (2005) "Public Finance and Individual Preferences over Globalization Strategies," NBER Working Paper 11028

Hanushek, Eric A. (2005) "Why Quality Matters in Education," *Finance and Development*, June, IMF, Washington, DC

Harley, Knick C. (1980) "Transportation, the World Wheat Trade and the Kuznets Cycle 1850–1913," *Explorations in Economic History*, vol. 17, no. 3

Harrison, Ann (1996) "Determinants and Effects of FDI in Cote D'Ivoire, Morocco and Venezuela," in Mark J. Roberts and James R. Tybout (eds.), *Industrial Evolution in Developing Countries*, Oxford University Press–World Bank, Oxford and New York

Hathaway, Dale and Ingco, Merlinda (1996) "Agricultural Liberalization and the Developing Countries," in Will Martin and Alan Winters (eds.), *The Uruguay Round and the Developing Countries*, Cambridge University Press, Cambridge, MA

Hatton, Timothy J. and Williamson, Jeffrey G. (2001) "Demographic and Economic Pressure on Migration Out of Africa," NBER Working Paper 8124

Hatton, Timothy J. and Williamson, Jeffrey G. (2002) "What Fundamentals Drive World Migration?," CEPR Discussion Paper 3559

Hatton, Timothy J. and Williamson, Jeffrey G. (2006) "A Dual Policy Paradox: Why Have Trade and Immigration Policies always Differed in Labour Scarce Economies?," CEPR Discussion Paper 5443

Head, Keith and Ries, John (2002) "Offshore Production and Skill Upgrading by Japanese Manufacturing Firms," *Journal of International Economics*, vol. 58

Hecksher, Eli F. (1919) *The Effect of Foreign Trade on the Distribution of Income*, Ekonomisk Tidskrift, Stockholm

Heckscher, Eli F. and Ohlin, Bertil (1991) *Heckscher–Ohlin Trade Theory*, translated, edited, and introduced by Harry Flam and June Flanders, MIT Press, Cambridge, MA

Heller, Peter S. and Gupta, Sanjeev (2002) "Challenges in Expanding Aid Flows," *Finance and Development*, IMF, June

Helpman, Elhanan (ed.) (1998) *General Purpose Technologies and Economic Growth*, MIT Press, Cambridge, MA

Helpman, Elhanan (2004) *The Mystery of Economic Growth*, Belknap Press of Harvard University Press, Cambridge, MA, and London

Helpman, Elhanan and Krugman, Paul R. (1985) *Market Structure and Foreign Trade: Increasing Returns, Imperfect Competition and the International Economy*, MIT Press, Cambridge, MA

Henson, S. J., Loader, R. J., Swinbank, A., Bedahl, M., and Lux, N. (2000) *Impact of Sanitary and Phytosanitary Measures on Developing Countries*, Centre for Food Economics Research, University of Reading, Reading

Herbst, Jeffrey I. (2000) *States and Power in Africa: Comparative Lessons in Authority and Control*, Princeton University Press, Princeton, NJ

Herrendorf, Berthold and Valentinyi, Akos (2005) "What Sectors Make the Poor Countries So Unproductive?," CEPR Discussion Paper 5399

Hertel, Thomas W. (ed.) (1997) *Global Trade Analysis: Modeling and Applications*, Cambridge University Press, Cambridge and New York

Hertel, Thomas W. and Keeney, Roman (2006) "What Is at Stake: The Relative Importance of Import Barriers, Export Subsidies and Domestic Support," ch. 2 in Kym Anderson and Will Martin (eds.), *Agricultural Trade Reform and the Doha Development Agenda*, Palgrave Macmillan and the World Bank, Washington, DC

Hertel, Thomas W., Hoekman, Bernard, and Martin, Will (2002) "Developing Countries and a New Round of WTO Negotiations," *World Bank Research Observer*, vol. 17, no. 1

Higgins, Matthew and Williamson, Jeffrey G. (1999) "Explaining Inequality the World Round: Cohort Size, Kuznets Curves and Openness," NBER Working Paper 7224

Bibliography

Hnatkovska, Viktoria and Loayza, Norman (2005) "Volatility and Growth," in Joshua Aizenman and Brian Pinto (eds.), *Managing Economic Volatility and Crises: A Practitioner's Guide*, Cambridge University Press, Cambridge

Hoekman, Bernard (2003) "More Favourable Treatment of Developing Countries: Toward a New Grand Bargain," *Development Outreach*, July, World Bank

Hoekman, Bernard (2004) "Dismantling Discrimination against Developing Countries: Access, Rules and Differential Treatment," CEPR Discussion Paper 4694

Hoekman, Bernard, Ng, Francis, and Olarreaga, Marcelo (2001) "Eliminating Excessive Tariffs on Exports of Least Developed Countries," World Bank Policy Research Working Paper WPS 2604

Hoekman, Bernard, Ng, Francis, and Olarreaga, Marcelo (2002) "Reducing Agricultural Tariffs versus Domestic Support: What's More Important for Developing Countries?," World Bank Policy Research Working Paper 2595

Hornstein, Andreas (1999) "Growth Accounting with Technological Revolutions," *Federal Reserve Bank of Richmond Economics Quarterly*, vol. 85, no. 3

Hornstein, Andreas and Krusell, Per (1996) "Can Technology Improvements Cause Productivity Slowdowns?," in Ben Bernanke and Julio Rothemberg (eds.), *NBER Macroeconomics Annual 1996*, MIT Press, Cambridge, MA

Hornstein, Andreas, Krusell, Per, and Violante, Gianni L. (2000) "Vintage Capital as an Origin of Inequalities," CEPR Discussion Paper 3596

Howitt, Peter (2000) "Endogenous Growth and Cross-country Income Differences," *American Economic Review*, vol. 90

Hummels, David (1999) "Have International Transport Costs Declined?," Economics Department Paper, Purdue University

Humphrey, Rachel (2003) "International Grant Making: a Matter of Will," *Alliance Extra*, June

Ianchovichina, Elena, Mattoo, Aaditya, and Olarreaga, Marcelo (2001) "Unrestricted Market Access for Sub-Saharan Africa: How Much Is It Worth and Who Pays?," CEPR Discussion Paper 2820

IMF (2002a) "Recent Trends in the Transfer of Resources to Developing Countries," Development Committee, August 27, Washington, DC

IMF (2002b) "Trade and Financial Integration," *World Economic Outlook*, "Trade and Finance," September, Washington, DC

IMF (2005) "Two Current Issues Facing Developing Countries," *World Economic Outlook*, April, Washington, DC

IMF and World Bank (2002) "Market Access for Developing Country Exports: Selected Issues," Report Prepared for the International Monetary Fund and the World Bank Annual Meetings, September 26, and World Economic Outlook, October, Washington, DC

Inglehart, Ronald (1999) "Trust, Well-being and Democracy," in Mark Warren (ed.), *Democracy and Trust*, Cambridge University Press, Cambridge, MA

IOM, International Organization for Migration (2003) *World Migration 2003: Managing Migration Challenges and Responses for People on the Move*, Geneva

Irwin, Douglas A. and Tervio, Marko (2000) "Does Trade Raise Income? Evidence from the Twentieth Century," NBER Working Paper 7745

Iversen, Torben and Cusack, Thomas (2000) "The Causes of Welfare State Expansion," *World Politics*, vol. 52

Jain, Shall (1975) *Size Distribution of Income: Compilation Data*, World Bank, Washington, DC

Johnston, Timothy (2002) *2000 Annual Review of Development Effectiveness*, World Bank, Washington, DC

Jones, Charles I. (1994) "Economic Growth and the Relative Price of Capital," *Journal of Monetary Economics*, vol. 34

Jones, Charles I. (1997) "On the Evolution of the World Income Distribution," *Journal of Economic Perspectives*, vol. 11, no. 3

Jones, Charles I. (2001) "Was the Industrial Revolution Inevitable? Economic Growth over the Very Long Run," *Advances in Macroeconomics*, vol. 1

Jones, Charles I. (2004a) "Growth and Ideas," NBER Working Paper 10767

Jones, Charles I. (2004b) "The Shape of Production Functions and the Direction of Technical Change," NBER Working Paper 10457

Kakwani, Nanak (1980) *Income Inequality and Poverty: Methods of Estimation and Policy Applications*, Oxford University Press, Oxford

Kaldor, Nicholas (1956) "Alternative Theories of Distribution," *Review of Economic Studies*, vol. 23, no. 2

Kaldor, Nicholas (1957) "A Model of Economic Growth," *Economic Journal*, vol. 67

Kaldor, Nicholas (1961) "Capital Accumulation and Economic Growth," in F. A. Lutz and D. C. Hague (eds.), *The Theory of Capital*, St Martin's Press, New York

Kaminsky, Graciela, Reinhart, Carmen, and Végh, Carlos (2004) "When It Rains, It Pours: Pro-cyclical Capital Flows and Macroeconomic Policies," NBER Working Paper 10780

Bibliography

Kaplow, Louis (2002) "Why Measure Inequality?," NBER Working Paper 9342, November

Kathuria, Vinish (2000) "Productivity Spill-overs from Technology Transfer to Indian Manufacturing Firms," *Journal of International Development*, vol. 12

Kay, John (2002) "Globalization's Paradox," *Financial Times*, November 14

Keeney, Roman and Hertel, Thomas W. (2005) "GTAP–AGR: A Framework for Assessing the Implications of Multilateral Changes in Agricultural Policies," Global Trade Analysis Technical Paper no. 24, Center for Global Trade Analysis, Purdue University, West Lafayette

Keller, Wolfgang (2001a) "Knowledge Spill-overs at the World's Technology Frontier," CEPR Discussion Paper 2815

Keller, Wolfgang (2001b) "The Geography and Channels of Diffusion at the World's Technology Frontier," NBER Working Paper 8150

Keller, Wolfgang (2002) "International Technology Diffusion," CEPR Discussion Paper 3133, January

Kenen, Peter (1996) "The Feasibility of Taxing Foreign Exchange Transactions," in Mahbub Ul Haq, Inge Kaul, and Isabelle Grunberg (eds.), *The Tobin Tax*, Oxford University Press, Oxford

King, Robert and Rebelo, Sergio (1993) "Transitional Dynamics and Economic Growth in the Neoclassical Model," *American Economic Review*, vol. 83

Klein, Michael W. and Marion, Nancy P. (1997) "Explaining the Duration of Exchange-rate Pegs," *Journal of Development Economics*, vol. 54, December

Kokko, Ari (1996) "Productivity Spill-overs from Competition between Local Firms and Foreign Affiliates," *Journal of International Development*, vol. 8

Kokko, Ari, Zejan, Mario, and Tansini, Ruben (2001) "Trade Regimes and Spill-over Effects of FDI: Evidence from Uruguay," *Weltwirtschaftliches Archiv*, vol. 137, no. 1

Kose, Ayhan M., Prasad, Eswar S., and Terrones, Marco E. (2003) "Financial Integration and Macroeconomic Volatility," IMF Staff Papers, vol. 50, Special Issue, Washington, DC

Kremer, Michael (1993) "Population Growth and Technological Change: One Million B.C. to 1990," *Quarterly Journal of Economics*, vol. 108

Kremer, Michael and Jayachandran, Seema (2002) "Odious Debt," *Finance and Development*, IMF, June

Kristov, Lorenzo, Lindert, Peter, and McLelland, Robert (1992) "Pressure Groups and Redistribution," *Journal of Public Economics*, vol. 48, no. 2

Krugman, Paul R. (1991a) "Increasing Returns and Economic Geography," *Journal of Political Economy*, vol. 49

Bibliography

Krugman, Paul R. (1991b) *Geography and Trade*, MIT Press, Cambridge, MA

Krugman, Paul R. (1995) "Growing World Trade: Causes and Consequences," *Brookings Papers on Economic Activity*, Brookings Institution, Washington, DC

Krugman, Paul R. (1996) "Does Third World Growth Hurt First World Prosperity?," *Harvard Business Review*, vol. 72, Cambridge, MA

Krugman, Paul R. and Venables, Anthony J. (1995) "Globalization and the Inequality of Nations," *Quarterly Journal of Economics*, vol. 110

Krusell, Per and Rios-Rull, Jose Victor (1996) "Vested Interests in a Positive Theory of Stagnation and Growth," *Review of Economic Studies*, vol. 63, no. 2

Krusell, Per, Ohanian, Lee E., Rios-Rull, Jose Victor, and Violante, Giovanni L. (2000) "Capital–skill Complementarity and Inequality: A Macroeconomic Analysis," *Econometrica*, vol. 63, no. 5

Kuznets, Simon (1955) "Economic Growth and Income Inequality," *American Economic Review*, vol. 45, no. 1

Kuznets, Simon (1962) "Quantitative Aspects of the Economic Growth of Nations, vii: The Share and Structures of Consumption," *Economic Development and Cultural Change*, vol. 10, no. 2

Kuznets, Simon (1966) *Modern Economic Growth*, Yale University Press, New Haven, CT

Kuznets, Simon (1967) "Quantitative Aspects of the Economic Growth of nations, x: Level and Structure of Foreign Trade: Long Term Trends," *Economic Development and Technical Change*, vol. 15

Kuznets, Simon (1973) *Population, Capital and Growth: Selected Essays*, Norton, New York

Lall, Sanjaya (1979) "The International Allocation of R&D Activity by US Multinationals," *Oxford Bulletin of Economics and Statistics*, vol. 41, no. 4

Landes, David (1969) *The Unbound Prometheus: Technological Change and Industrial Development in Western Europe from 1750 to the Present*, Cambridge University Press, Cambridge, MA

Landes, David (1998) *The Wealth and Poverty of Nations*, Little, Brown, London

Lane, Phillip (2004) "Empirical Perspectives on Long Term External Debt," *Topics in Macroeconomics*, vol. 4

Lankes, Hans Peter (2002) "Market Access for Developing Countries," *Finance and Development*, vol. 39, no. 3, IMF, Washington, DC

Bibliography

La Porta, Rafael, Lopez de Silanes, Florencio, Shleifer, Andrei, and Vishny, Robert W. (1997) "Trust in Large Organizations," *American Economic Review*, vol. 87, no. 2

La Porta, Rafael, Lopez de Silanes, Florencio, Shleifer, Andrei, and Vishny, Robert W. (1998) "Law and Finance," *Journal of Political Economy*, vol. 106, no. 6

La Porta, Rafael, Lopez de Silanes, Florencio, Shleifer, Andrei, and Vishny, Robert W (2000) "The Quality of Government," *Journal of Law, Economics and Organization*, vol. 15, no. 1

Lawrence, Robert and Slaughter, Matthew (1993) "Trade and US Wages: Great Sucking Sound of Small Hiccup?," Brookings Papers on Economic Activity, no. 2, Washington, DC

Leamer, Edward E. (2000) "What's the Use of Factor Content?," *Journal of International Economics*, vol. 50

Leamer, Edward E. and Levinson, James (1995) "International Trade Theory: The Evidence," in Gene Grossman and Kenneth Rogoff (eds.), *Handbook of International Economics*, vol. 3, Elsevier, Amsterdam

Levine, Ross (1997) "Financial Development and Economic Growth," *Journal of Economic Literature*, vol. 35, no. 2

Levine, Ross (2000) "Bank-based or Market-based Financial Systems: Which Is Better?," NBER Working Paper 9138, September

Levine, Ross and Zervos, Sara (1998) "Stock Markets, Banks and Economic Growth," *American Economic Review*, vol. 88, no. 3

Lewis, Arthur W. (1954) *Economic Development with Unlimited Supply of Labour*, Manchester School Series, vol. 22, Manchester

Li, Hong Yi, Squire, Lyn, and Zou, Hen-Fu "Explaining Inter-temporal Variations in Income Inequality," *Economic Journal*, vol. 108

Limao, Nuno and Venables, Anthony J. (2001) "Infrastructure, Geographical Disadvantage, Transport Costs and Trade," *World Bank Economic Review*, vol. 15, October

Lindbeck, Assar (1975) "Inequality and Redistribution Policy Issues: Principles and Swedish Experience," *Education, Inequality and Life Chances*, vol. 2, OECD, Paris

Lindert, Peter H. (1996) "What Limits Social Spending?," *Explorations in Economic History*, vol. 33

Lindert, Peter H. and Williamson, Jeffrey G. (2001) "Does Globalization Make the World More Equal?," NBER Working Paper 8228, April

Bibliography

Lipset, Seymour M. (1960) *Political Man: The Social Basis of Modern Politics*, Doubleday, New York

Lipsey, Robert E. (1994) "Foreign-owned Firms and US Wages," NBER Working Paper 4927

Lipsey, Robert E. (1995) "Outward Direct Investment and the US Economy," in Martin Feldstein, James Hine, and Glenn Hubbard (eds.), *The Effects of Taxation on Multinational Corporations*, Chicago University Press, Chicago, IL

Lipsey, Robert E. (2000a) "Interpreting Developed Countries' Foreign Direct Investment," NBER Working Paper 7810

Lipsey, Robert E. (2000b) "Affiliates of US and Japanese Multinationals in East Asian Production and Trade," in Takatoshi Ito and Anne Krueger (eds.), *The Role of FDI in East Asian Development and Trade*, University of Chicago Press, Chicago, IL

Lipsey, Robert E. (2001) "Foreign Direct Investment and the Operations of Multinational Firms: Concepts, History and Data," NBER Working Paper 8665

Lipsey, Robert E. (2002a) "Foreign Production of US Firms and Parent Firm Employment," in Robert E. Lipsey and Jean Louis Muccielli (eds.), *Multinational Firms and Impact on Employment Trade and Technology: New Perspectives for a New Century*, Routledge, London

Lipsey, Robert (2002b) "Home and Host Country Effects of FDI," NBER Working Paper 9293, October

Lipsey, Robert E., Ramstetter, Eric, and Blomstrom, Magnus (1999) *Parent Exports and Affiliate Activity in Japanese Multinational Companies: 1986, 1989 and 1992*, Institute for International Trade and Investment, Tokyo

Lipsey, Robert E., Ramstetter, Eric D., and Blomstrom, Magnus (2000) "Outward FDI Parent Exports and Employment: Japan, the United States and Sweden," NBER Working Paper 7623

Liu, Xiaming, Wang, Chenchang, and Wei, Yingqi (2001) "Causal Links between FDI and Trade in China," *China Economic Review*, vol. 12

Logan, Trevor D. (2005) "The Transformation of Hunger: The Demand for Calories Past and Present," NBER Working Paper 11754

Lucas, Robert E. (1978) "On the Size and Distribution of Business Firms," *Bell Journal of Economics*, vol. 9

Lucas, Robert E. (1988) "On the Mechanics of Economic Development," *Journal of Monetary Economics*, vol. 22

Bibliography

Lucas, Robert E. (1990) "Why Doesn't Capital Flow from Rich to Poor Countries?," *American Economic Review Papers and Proceedings*, vol. 80, May

Lucas, Robert E. (2000) "Some Macroeconomics for the 21st Century," *Journal of Economic Perspectives*, vol. 14, no. 1

Lucas, Robert E. (2002) *Lectures on Economic Growth*, Harvard University Press, Cambridge, MA

McArthur, John W. and Sachs, Jeffrey D. (2001) "Institutions and Geography: Comment on Acemoglu and Robinson (2000)," NBER Working Paper 8114

Maddison, Angus (1983) "A Comparison of Levels of GDP Per Capita in Developed and Developing Countries: 1700–1980," *Journal of Economic History*, March

Maddison, Angus (1995a) *The World Economy 1820–1902*, OECD Development Center, Paris

Maddison, Angus (1995b) *Explaining the Economic Performance of Nations: Essays in Time and Space*, Elgar, Aldershot

Maddison, Angus (2001) *The World Economy: A Millennial Perspective*, OECD, Paris

Maddison, Angus (2003) "The World Economy: Historical Statistics," CD-ROM, OECD, Paris

Magud, Nicholas and Reinhart, Carmen M. (2006) "Capital Controls: An Evaluation," NBER Working Paper 11973

Mankiw, Gregory (1995) "The Growth of Nations," Brookings Papers on Economic Activity, Washington, DC

Mankiw, Gregory, Romer, David, and Weil, David (1992) "A Contribution to the Empirics of Economic Growth," *Quarterly Journal of Economics*, vol. 107

Markusen, James R. (1983) "Factor Movements and Commodity Trade as Complements," *Journal of International Economics*, vol. 13

Markusen, James R. (1997) "Trade versus Investment Liberalization," NBER Working Paper 6231

Markusen, James R. and Maskus, Keith E. (2001) "General-equilibrium Approaches to the Multinational Firm: A Review of Theory and Evidence," NBER Working Paper 8334

Marshall, Alfred (1890) *Principles of Economics*, Macmillan, London

Marshall, Alfred (1920) *Principles of Economics*, 8th edn., Macmillan, London

Martin, Will (2001) "Trade Policies and Developing Countries," mimeo, World Bank, Washington, DC

Bibliography

Martin, Will and Winters, Alan (1996) *The Uruguay Round and the Developing Countries*, Cambridge University Press, Cambridge, MA

Maskus, Keith E. (1999) "Should Core Labour Standards be Imposed Through International Trade Policy?," World Bank Policy Research Working Paper 1817

Maskus, Keith E. (2003) "Trade and Competitiveness Aspects of Environmental and Labour Standards in East Asia," ch. 7 in Kathi Krumm and Homi Kharas (eds.), *East Asia Integrates: A Trade Policy Agenda for Shared Growth*, World Bank, Washington, DC

McKinsey Quarterly (2005) "Sizing the Emerging Global Labour Market," no. 3

Melchior, Arne (2001) "Global Income Inequality: Beliefs, Facts and Unresolved Issues," *World Economics*, vol. 2, July–September

Melchior, Arne, Telle, Kjetil, and Wiig, Harald (2000) *Globalization and Inequality: World Income Distribution and Living Standards 1960–1998*, Royal Norwegian Ministry of Foreign Affairs Report 6-b, Oslo

Melitz, Jacques (2001) "Geography, Trade and Currency Union," CEPR Discussion Paper 2987

Milanovic, Branko (1999) *The Median Voter Hypothesis, Income Inequality and Income Redistribution: an Empirical Test with the Required Data*, World Bank, Development Research Group, Washington, DC

Milanovic, Branko (2002) "True World Inequality 1988 and 1993: First Calculations Based on Households Surveys Alone," *Economic Journal*, vol. 112, January

Milessi-Ferretti, Gian Maria and Razin, Asaff (1998) "Current Account Reversals and Currency Crises: Empirical Regularities," IMF Working Paper 98/89, Washington, DC

Mirrlees, James A. (1971) "An Exploration into the Theory of Optimum Income Taxation," *Review of Economic Studies*, vol. 38, no. 114

Moav, Omer (2001) "Cheap Children and the Persistence of Poverty," CEPR Discussion Paper 3059

Mody, Ashoka, Razin, Assaf, and Sadka, Efraim (2002) "The Role of Information Driving FDI: Theory and Empirical Evidence," NBER Working Paper 9255

Mokyr, Joel (1990) *The Lever of Riches: Technological Creativity and Economic Progress*, Oxford University Press, New York

Mokyr, Joel (1993) "The New Economic History and the Industrial Revolution," in J. Mokyr (ed.), *The British Industrial Revolution: An Economic Perspective*, Westview Press, Boulder, CO

Bibliography

Mokyr, Joel (2002) *The Gifts of Athena: Historical Origins of the Knowledge Economy*, Princeton University Press, Princeton, NJ

Moran, Theodore H. (1998) *FDI and Development*, Institute for International Economics, Washington, DC

Mukand, Sharud and Rodrik, Dani (2005) "In Search of the Holy Grail: Policy Convergence, Experimentation and Economic Performance," *American Economic Review*, vol. 95, March

Mundell, Robert (1957) "International Trade and Factor Mobility," *American Economic Review*, vol. 47, June

Mundell, Robert (2000) "A Reconsideration of the Twentieth Century," *American Economic Review*, vol. 90, no. 3

Myrdal, Gunnar (1972) *Against the Stream: Critical Essays in Economics*, Vintage Books, Random House, New York

Naim, Moisés (2002) "The Missing Agenda at Monterrey," *Financial Times*, April 1

Nissanke, Machiko (2003) "Revenue Potential of the Tobin Tax for Development Finance: A Critical Appraisal," WIDER Discussion Paper 81

Nocke, Volker and Yeaple, Stephen (2004) "An Assignment Theory of Foreign Direct Investment," NBER Working Paper 11003

Nogués, Julio (2002) "Comments on the Papers by Andrew Berg and Anne Krueger on 'Trade, Growth and Poverty' and on Alan Winters on 'Doha and World Poverty Targets,'" World Bank, April, Washington, DC

North, Douglass (1981) *Structure and Change in Economic History*, Norton, New York

North, Douglass C. (1990) *Institutions, Institutional Change and Economic Performance*, Cambridge University Press, Cambridge

North, Douglass C. (1991) "Institutions," *Journal of Economic Perspectives*, vol. 5, no. 1

North, Douglass C. (2000) "Big-bang Transformations of Economic Systems: An Introductory Note," *Journal of Institutional and Theoretical Economics*, vol. 156, no. 1, March

North, Douglass and Thomas, Robert P. (1973) *The Rise of the Western World: A New Economic History*, Cambridge University Press, Cambridge

North, Douglass C. and Weingast, Barry R. (1989) "Constitutions and Commitment: The Evolution of Institutions Governing Public Choice in Seventeenth-century England," *Journal of Economic History*, vol. 49

North, Douglass C., Summerhill, William, and Weingast, Barry R. (2000) "Order, Disorder and Economic Change: Latin America versus North

America," in Bruce Bueno de Mesquita and Hilton L. Root (eds.), *Governing for Prosperity*, Yale University Press, New Haven, CT

Obstfeld, Maurice and Rogoff, Kenneth (2000) "The Six Major Puzzles in International Macroeconomics: Is There a Common Cause?," *NBER Macroeconomics Annual 2000*, Ben Bernanke and Kenneth Rogoff (eds.), MIT Press, Cambridge, MA

Obstfeld, Maurice and Taylor, Alan M. (2002) "Globalization and Capital Markets," in "Globalization in Historical Perspective," NBER Working Paper 8846

OECD (2001a) *Market Effects of Crop Support Measures*, Paris

OECD (2001b) *State Trading Enterprises in Agriculture*, Paris

OECD (2001c) *Agricultural Policies in Emerging and Transition Economies: Special Focus on Non-tariff Measures*, Paris

OECD (2001d) "Agricultural Policy Reform: The Need for Further Progress," OECD Economic Outlook 70, December

OECD (2002a) *Agricultural Policies in OECD Countries: Monitoring and Evaluation*, Paris

OECD (2002b) *Agriculture and Trade Liberalization: Extending the Uruguay Round Agreement*, Paris

OECD (2003) *Trends in International Migration 2002*, Paris

OECD (2006) *Official Development Assistance Tops $100 Billion in 2005*, Development Assistance Committee Annual Report, Paris

Ohlin, Bertil (1933) *Interregional and International Trade*, Harvard University Press, Cambridge, MA

Okamoto, Yumiko and Sjoholm, Fredrik (1999) "FDI and the Dynamics of Productivity: Microeconomic Evidence," Working Paper Series in Economics and Finance, no. 348, Stockholm School of Economics

Olson, Mancur (1982) *The Rise and Decline of Nations: Economic Growth, Stagflation and Economic Rigidities*, Yale University Press, New Haven and London

Olson, Mancur (2000) *Power and Prosperity: Outgrowing Communist and Capitalist Dictatorships*, Basic Books, New York

O'Rourke, Kevin H. (2001) "Globalization and Inequality: Historical Trends," NBER Working Paper 8339, June, Cambridge, MA

O'Rourke, Kevin H. (2003) "Heckscher–Ohlin Theory and Individual Attitudes Towards Globalization," NBER Working Paper 9872

O'Rourke, Kevin H. and Williamson, Jeffrey G. (1996) "Factor Price Convergence in the Late Nineteenth Century," *International Economic Review*, vol. 37, no. 3

Bibliography

O'Rourke, Kevin H. and Williamson, Jeffrey G. (1999) *Globalization and History: The Evolution of a Nineteenth Century Atlantic Economy*, MIT Press, Cambridge, MA

O'Rourke, Kevin H. and Williamson, Jeffrey G. (2001) "After Columbus: Explaining the Global Trade Boom 1500–1800," NBER Working Paper 8186

Özden, Çaglar and Reinhart, Eric (2002) *The Perversity of Preferences: GSP and Developing Country Trade Policies 1976–2000*, Emory University, Atlanta, GA

Pagano, Marco, Panetta, Francesco, and Zingales, Luigi (1998) "Why Companies Go Public?," *Journal of Finance*, vol. 50

Parente, Stephen and Prescott, Edward (1994) "Barriers to Technology Adoption and Development," *Journal of Political Economy*, vol. 102

Parente, Stephen and Prescott, Edward (1999) "Monopoly Rights and Barriers to Riches," *American Economic Review*, vol. 89

Parente, Stephen and Prescott, Edward (2002) *Barriers to Riches*, MIT Press, Cambridge, MA

Patel, Parimal and Pavitt, Keith (2000) "National Systems of Innovation under Strain: The Internationalization of R&D," in Ray Barrel, G. Mason, and Mary O'Mahony (eds.), *Productivity, Innovation and Economic Performance*, Cambridge University Press, Cambridge, MA

Patillo, Catherine, Poirson, Helene, and Ricci, Luca (2002) "External Debt and Growth," *Finance and Development*, IMF, June

Perotti, Roberto (1992) "Fiscal Policy, Income Distribution and Growth," Columbia University Working Paper 636

Perotti, Roberto (1993) "Political Equilibrium, Income Distribution and Growth," *Review of Economic Studies*, vol. 60

Perotti, Roberto (1994) "Income Distribution and Investment," *European Economic Review*, vol. 38

Perotti, Roberto (1996) "Growth, Income Distribution and Democracy: What the Data Say," *Journal of Economic Growth*, vol. 1, no. 2

Persson, Thorsten and Tabellini, Guido (1994) "Is Inequality Harmful for Growth?," *American Economic Review*, vol. 84, no. 3

Persson, Thorsten and Tabellini, Guido (2006) "Democracy and Development: The Devil in the Details," NBER Working Paper 11993

Piketty, Thomas (1995) "Social Mobility and Redistributive Politics," *Quarterly Journal of Economics*, vol. 100

Piketty, Thomas (1997) "The Dynamics of Wealth Distribution and the Interest Rate with Credit Rationing," *Review of Economic Studies*, vol. 64

Bibliography

Portes, Richard and Rey, Helene (1999) "The Determinants of Cross-border Equity Flows," NBER Working Paper 7336

Pritchett, Lan (1997) "Divergence, Big Time," *Journal of Economic Perspectives*, vol. 11, no. 3

Puga, Diego and Venables, Anthony J. (1996) "The Spread of Industry: Agglomeration in Economic Development," *Journal of Japanese and International Economies*, vol. 10

Putnam, Robert (1993) *Making Democracy Work: Civic Traditions in Modern Italy*, Princeton University Press, Princeton, NJ

Quah, Danny T. (1996) "Twin Peaks: Growth and Convergence in Models of Distribution Dynamics," *Economic Journal*, July

Quah, Danny T. (1997) "Empirics for Growth and Distribution: Stratification, Polarization and Convergence Cubs," *Journal of Economic Growth*, vol. 2

Quah, Danny T. (2002) "One Third of the World's Growth and Inequality," CEPR Discussion Paper 3316

Radelet, Steve (2005) "Grants for the World's Poorest: How the World Bank Should Distribute its Funds," *Centre for Global Development Notes*, June

Rajan, Rhaguran G. (2005) "Debt Relief and Growth: How to Craft an Optimal Debt Relief Proposal," *Finance and Development*, June, IMF, Washington, DC

Rajan, Rhaguram G. and Subramanian, Arvind (2005) "Aid and Growth: What Does the Cross-country Evidence Really Show?," NBER Working Paper 11513

Ramey, Gary and Ramey, Valerie A. (1995) "Cross-country Evidence on the Link Between Volatility and Growth," *American Economic Review*, vol. 85, December

Ramstetter, Eric D. (1999) "Comparisons of Foreign Multinationals and Local Firms in Asian Manufacturing over Time," *Asian Economic Journal*, vol. 13, no. 2

Rapoport, Hillel and Docquier, Frédéric (2005) "The Economics of Migrants' Remittances," in Gerard-Varet, Luis-André, Kolm, Serge-Christophe, and Ythier, Jean Mercier (eds.), *Handbook of Economics of Reciprocity, Giving and Altruism*, North Holland, Amsterdam

Ravallion, Martin (2001) "Growth, Inequality and Poverty: Looking beyond the Averages," *World Development*, vol. 29, no. 4

Ravallion, Martin (2003) "Measuring Aggregate Welfare in Developing Countries: How Well Do National Accounts and Surveys Agree," *Review of Economics and Statistics*, vol. 85, no. 3

Ravallion, Martin and Wodon, Quentin (2000) "Does Child Labour Displace Schooling?: Evidence on Behavioural Responses to an Enrolment Subsidy," *Economic Journal*, vol. 110, March

Razin, Assaf (2002) "FDI Contribution to Capital Flows and Investment in Capacity," NBER Working Paper 9204

Razin, Assaf and Loungani, Prakash (2005) "Globalization and Disinflation: The Efficiency Channel," CEPR Discussion Paper 4895

Razin, Assaf and Rose, Andrew K. (1994) "Business Cycle Volatility and Openness: An Exploratory Cross-sectional Analysis" in Leonardo Leiderman and Assaf Razin (eds.), *Capital Mobility: The Impact on Consumption, Investment and Growth*, Cambridge University Press, Cambridge, MA

Rebelo, Sergio T. (1991) "Long-run Policy Analysis and Long-run Growth," *Journal of Political Economy*, vol. 99, no. 3

Reinhart, Carmen and Rogoff, Kenneth (2004) "Serial Default and the Paradox of Rich to Poor Countries Capital Flows," NBER Working Paper 10296

Reisen, Helmut (2002) "The Tobin Tax: Can It Work?," *OECD Observer*, May

Reisen, Helmut (2004) "Innovative Approaches to Funding the Millennium Development Goals," Policy Brief 24, OECD Development Center, OECD, Paris

Rhee, Yung and Belot, Therese (1990) "Export Catalysts in Low Income Countries," World Bank Discussion Papers 72

Rigobon, Roberto and Rodrik, Dani (2004) "Rule of Law, Democracy, Openness and Income: Estimating their Interrelationships," CEPR Discussion Paper 4653

Rodriguez, Francisco and Rodrik, Dani (2000) "Trade Policy and Economic Growth: A Skeptic's Guide to the Cross-national Evidence," *NBER Macroeconomic Annual*, vol. 15

Rodrik, Dani (1997) *Has Globalization Gone Too Far?*, Institute for International Economics, Washington, DC

Rodrik, Dani (1998a) "Trade Policy and Economic Performance in Sub Saharan Africa," NBER Working Paper 6562

Rodrik, Dani (1998b) "Comment on 'Equity and Growth in Developing Countries: Old and New Perspectives on Policy Issues,'" by Michael Bruno, Martin Ravallion, and Lyn Squire, in Vito Tanzi and K. Chu (eds.), *Income Distribution and High-quality Growth*, MIT Press, Cambridge, MA

Rodrik, Dani (2000) "Institutions for High Quality Growth: What They Are and How to Acquire Them," *Studies in Comparative International Development*, vol. 35, fall

Rodrik, Dani (2001) "Mobilising the World's Labour Assets," *Financial Times*, November 27

Rodrik, Dani and Subramanian, Arvind (2003) "The Primacy of Institutions," *Finance and Development*, June, IMF, Washington, DC

Rodrik, Dani, Subramanian, Arvind, and Trebbi, Francesco (2002) "Institutions Rule: The Primacy of Institutions over Geography and Integration in Economic Development," NBER Working Paper 9305

Rogoff, Kenneth S. (2003) "Disinflation: an Unsung Benefit of Globalization?," *Finance and Development*, vol. 40, no. 4

Rogoff, Kenneth S. (2004) "Globalization and Global Disinflation," *Monetary Policy and Uncertainty: Adapting to a Changing Economy, Proceedings of the 2003 Jackson Hole Symposium*, Federal Reserve Bank of Kansas City

Rogoff, Kenneth S. and Reinhart, Carmen M. (2004) "Serial Default and the Paradox of Rich-to-Poor Capital Flows," *American Economic Review*, vol. 94, no. 2

Rogoff, Kenneth S., Prassad, Eswar, Wei, Shang-Jin, and Kose, Ayhan (2003) *The Effects of Financial Globalization on Developing Countries: Some Empirical Evidence*, IMF, Washington, DC

Romer, Paul M. (1986) "Increasing Returns and Long-Run Growth," *Journal of Political Economy*, vol. 94, no. 5, October

Romer, Paul M. (1993) "Two Strategies of Economic Development: Using Ideas and Producing Ideas," *Proceedings of the World Bank Annual Conference on Development Economics*, Supplement to the World Bank Review and the World Bank Research Observer, Washington, DC

Rose, Andrew K. (2000) "One Money, One Market: The Effect of Common Currencies on Trade," *Economic Policy*, no. 30, April

Rose, Andrew K. (2002a) "Estimating Protectionism from the Gravity Model," *Processed*, IMF Research Department, Washington, DC

Rose, Andrew K. (2002b) "Do We Really Know that WTO Increases Trade?," CEPR Discussion Paper 3538

Rose, Andrew K. (2002c) "Do WTO Members Have More Liberal Trade Policy?," CEPR Discussion Paper 3659

Rosen, Sherwin (1982) "Authority, Control and Distribution of Earnings," *Bell Journal of Economics*, fall

Sachs, Jeffrey (2001) "Tropical Underdevelopment," NBER Working Paper 8119, February

Sachs, Jeffrey (2002a) "Health and Economic Development," *Project Syndicate*, January

Sachs, Jeffrey (2002b) "The Rich Should Keep their Word," *Project Syndicate*, March

Sachs, Jeffrey (2002c) "Death of Poor, Responsibility of Rich," *Project Syndicate*, June

Sachs, Jeffrey (2002d) "Weapons of Mass Salvation," *The Economist*, October 26

Sachs, Jeffrey (2003a) "Institutions Don't Rule: Direct Effects of Geography in Per Capita Income," NBER Working Paper 9490, February

Sachs, Jeffrey (2003b) "Institutions Matter But Not for Everything," *Finance and Development*, June, IMF, Washington, DC

Sachs, Jeffrey (2005a) *The Millennium Project Report*, United Nations, New York, January

Sachs, Jeffrey (2005b) *The End of Poverty: How We Can Make It Happen in Our Lifetime*, Penguin, New York

Sachs, Jeffrey and Shatz, Howard (1994) "Trade and Jobs in US Manufacturing," Brookings Papers on Economic Activity 1, Washington, DC

Sachs, Jeffrey and Warner, Andrew (1995) "Economic Reform and the Progress of Global Integration," Brookings Papers on Economic Activity 1

Sachs, Jeffrey, Mellinger, Andrew, and Gallup, John Luke (2001) "The Geography of Poverty and Wealth," *Scientific American*, 284

Saint-Paul, Gilles and Verdier, Tierry (1992) "Historical Accidents and the Persistence of Distributional Conflicts," *Journal of Japanese and International Economics*, vol. 6

Sala i Martín, Xavier (2002a) "The Disturbing 'Rise' of Global Income Inequality," NBER Working Paper 8904, April

Sala i Martín, Xavier (2002b) "The World Distribution of Income (Estimated from Individual Country Distributions)," NBER Working Paper 8933, April

Sala i Martín, Xavier and Subramanian, Arvind (2003) "Addressing the Natural Resource Curse: Nigeria," mimeo, Columbia University

Sala i Martín, Xavier, Doppelhoffer, Gernot, and Miller, Ronald (2003) "The Empirical Determinants of Growth: A Bayesian Average of Classical Estimates Approach," *American Economic Review*, vol. 95

Sandmo, Agnar (2003) "Environmental Taxation and Revenue for Development," WIDER Discussion Paper, 86, Helsinki

Scheve, Kenneth and Slaughter, Matthew J. (2002) "Economic Insecurity and the Globalization of Production," NBER Working Paper 9339

Schmuckler, Sergio and Zoido-Lobaton, Pablo (2001) "Financial Globalization: Opportunities and Challenges for Developing Countries," *Processed*, World Bank, Washington, DC

Bibliography

Schultz, Paul T. (1989) "Education Investments and Returns," in H. Chenery and T. N. Srinivasan (eds.), *Handbook of Development Economics*, vol. 1, Elsevier, Amsterdam

Schultz, Paul T. (1998) "Inequality and the Distribution of Personal Income in the World: How it is Changing and Why," *Journal of Population Economics*, vol. 11, no. 3

Sen, Amartya (1999) *Development as Freedom*, Oxford University Press, Oxford

Sen, Amartya (2000) "Social Exclusion: Concept, Application and Scrutiny," Social Development Papers 1, Asian Development Bank

Sgherry, Silvia (2002) "Trade, Financial Openness and Volatility: Some Interactions," IMF Working Paper, Washington, DC

Shiller, Robert (2003) *The New Financial Order: Risk in the 21st Century*, Princeton University Press, Princeton, NJ

Shleifer, Andrei (1993) "Corruption," *Quarterly Journal of Economics*, vol. 108, no. 3

Sjaastad, Lawrence (1962) "The Costs and Returns of Human Migration," *Journal of Political Economy*, vol. 70

Slaughter, Matthew J. (1999) *Globalization and Wages: A Tale of Two Perspectives*, Blackwell, Oxford

Slaughter, Matthew J. (2000) "Production Transfer within Multinational Enterprises and American Wages," *Journal of International Economics*, vol. 50, no. 2

Smith, Adam (1776) *An Inquiry into the Nature and Causes of the Wealth of Nations*, Clarendon Press, Oxford, 1976 and 1983

Soloaga, Isidro and Winters, Alan L. (2001) "Regionalism in the Nineties: What Effect on Trade?," *North American Journal of Economics and Finance*, vol. 12, March

Solow, Robert (1956) "A Contribution to the Theory of Economic Growth," *Quarterly Journal of Economics*, vol. 70, no. 1

Soto, Marcelo (2002) "Rediscovering Education in Growth Regressions," OECD Development Centre. T.P. 202

Spahn, Paul Bernd (2002) *On the Feasibility of a Tax on Foreign Exchange Transactions*, Federal Ministry for Cooperation and Development, Germany

Spilimbergo, Antonio, Londoño, Juan Luis, and Szekely, Miguel (1999) "Income Distribution, Factor Endowments and Trade Openness," *Journal of Development Economics*, vol. 59, no. 1

Stiglitz, Joseph E. (1998) "Towards a New Paradigm for Development: Strategies, Policies and Processes," Prebisch Lecture, October, UNCTAD, Geneva

Stiglitz, Joseph E. (2003) *Globalization and Its Discontents*, Norton, New York

Stiglitz, Joseph E. and Hoff, Karla (2005) "The Creation of the Rule and the Legitimacy of Property Rights: The Political and Economic Consequences of a Corrupt Privatization," NBER Working Paper 11772

Storesletten, Keith (2000) "Sustaining Fiscal Policy through Immigration," *Journal of Political Economy*, vol. 108

Straubhaar, Thomas (1988) *On the Economics of International Labour Migration*, Paul Haupt, Stuttgart

Stulz, Renee (2005) "The Limits to Financial Globalization," NBER Working Paper 11070

Stulz, Renee and Williamson, Rohan (2001) "Culture, Openness and Finance," NBER Working Paper 8222

Subramanian, Arvind and Wei, Shang-Jin (2003) "The WTO Promotes Trade, Strongly but Unevenly," NBER Working Paper 10024

Summers, Robert and Heston, Alan (1998) "A New Set of International Comparisons of Real Product and Price Levels Estimates for 130 Countries 1950–1985," *Review of Income and Wealth*, vol. 34, no. 1

Sutton, John (1997) "Gibrat's Legacy," *Journal of Economic Literature*, vol. 35

Swan, Trevor (1956) "Economic Growth and Capital Accumulation," *Economic Record*, vol. 32, November

Tabellini, Guido (2000) "A Positive Theory of Social Security," *Scandinavian Journal of Economics*, vol. 102, no. 3

Tabellini, Guido (2005) "Culture and Institutions: Economic Development in the Regions of Europe," Working Paper IGIER, Milan

Tamirisa, Natalia (1999) "Exchange and Capital Controls as Barriers to Trade," IMF Staff Papers, vol. 46, March

Tamura, Robert (1996) "From Decay to Growth: A Demographic Transition to Economic Growth," *Journal of Economic Dynamics and Control*, vol. 20

Tavares, José and Wacziarg, Romain (2001) "How Democracy Affects Growth," *European Economic Review*, vol. 45

Taylor, Alan M. and Williamson, Jeffrey G. (1997) "Convergence in the Age of Mass Migration," *European Review of Economic History*, vol. 1, no. 1

Temple, Jonathan (2000) "Inflation and Growth: Stories Short and Tall," *Journal of Economic Surveys*, vol. 14, September

Turner, Dave, Giorno, Claude, De Serres, Alain, Vourch, Anne, and Richardson, Pete (1998) "The Macroeconomic Implications of Ageing in a Global Context," OECD Economics Department Working Paper 193

Tyers, Rod and Anderson, Kym (1992) *Disarray in World Food Markets: A Quantitative Assessment*, Cambridge University Press, Hong Kong

UK DTI Department of Trade and Industry (2004) *The 2004 Scoreboard: Top 700 UK and Top 700 International Companies by R&D Investment*, London

UNCTAD (2001) *World Investment Report*, Geneva

UNCTAD (2002a) *World Investment Report*, Geneva

UNCTAD (2002b) *The Least Developed Countries Report 2002: Escaping the Poverty Trap*, Geneva

UNCTAD (2004) *World Investment Report*, Geneva

UNCTAD (2005) *World Investment Report*, Geneva

UNDP (1999) *World Human Development Report*, United Nations, New York

UNESCO (2000) "Education for All," *(EFA) Global Monitoring Report*, Paris

United Nations (2001) *World Population Prospects: The 2000 Revision*, New York

United Nations (2002) "Population Ageing and Development: Operational Challenges in Developing Countries," *UNFPA*, no. 5, New York

United Nations (2005) *World Population Prospects: The 2004 Revision*, New York

Uribe, Martin (2006) "On Overborrowing," NBER Working Paper 11913

Venables, Anthony J. (1996) "Equilibrium Locations of Vertically Linked Industries," *International Economic Review*, vol. 37, no. 2, May

Venables, Anthony J. (1999) "Trade Liberalization and Factor Mobility: an Overview" in Ricardo Faini, J. de Mello and Klaus Zimmerman (eds.), *Migration: The Controversies and the Evidence*, Cambridge University Press, Cambridge

Venables, Anthony J. (2001) "Geography and International Inequalities: The Impact of New Technologies," 13th Annual Bank Conference on Development Economics, May, World Bank, Washington, DC

Ventura, Jaume (1997) "Growth and Interdependence," *Quarterly Journal of Economics*, vol. 112, no. 1

Ventura, Jaume (2005) "A Global View of Economic Growth," NBER Working Paper 11296

Wacziarg, Romain (1998) "Measuring the Dynamic Gains from Trade," Policy Research Working Paper 2001, World Bank, Washington, DC

Wade, Robert (2001a) "The Rising Inequality of World Income Distribution," *Finance and Development*, December, IMF, Washington, DC

Wade, Robert (2001b) "Winners and Losers," *The Economist*, April 28

Bibliography

Watkins, Keith (2003) "Farm Fallacies that Hurt the Poor," *Development Outreach*, World Bank, July

Weber, Max (1905 and 1956) *The Protestant Ethic and the Spirit of Capitalism*, Allen and Unwin, London

Wei, Shang-Jin (1996) "Intra-national versus International Trade: How Stubborn Are Nations in Global Integration?," NBER Working Paper 5531

Wei, Shang-Jin (2000) "Natural Openness and Good Government," NBER Working Paper 7765

Williamson, Jeffrey G. (1997) "Globalization and Inequality: Past and Present," *World Bank Research Observer*, vol. 12, no. 2

Williamson, Jeffrey G. (2000) "Land, Labour and Globalization in the Preindustrial Third World," NBER Working Paper 7784

Wolf, Martin (2002) "Fighting for Economic Equality," *Financial Times*, November 28

Wolf, Martin (2003) "Humanity on the Move: The Myths and Realities of International Migration," *Financial Times*, July 30

Wolf, Martin (2004) "A Matter of More than Economics," *Financial Times*, April 13

World Bank (1991) *The Pressing Task of Development*, World Development Report, Washington, DC

World Bank (2000) *Entering the 21st Century*, World Development Report, Washington, DC

World Bank (2001) *Attacking Poverty*, World Development Report, Washington, DC

World Bank (2002) *Institutions for the Markets*, World Development Report, Washington, DC

World Bank (2002a) *Global Economic Prospects 2002: Making Trade Work for the Poor*, Washington, DC

World Bank (2002b) *Development, Trade and WTO: A Hand Book*, Washington, DC

World Bank (2002c) *The HIPC Initiative: Background and Update*, Issue Brief, Washington, DC

World Bank (2002d) *Globalization, Growth and Poverty: Building an Inclusive World Economy*, World Bank, Washington, DC

World Bank (2005) "Mobilizing Finance and Managing Vulnerability," *Global Development Finance*, Washington, DC

World Competitiveness Yearbook (2000), IMD, Lausanne

Bibliography

World Trade Organization (2005) "World Trade 2004, Prospects for 2005," April, Geneva

Young, Alwyn (1991) "Learning by Doing and the Dynamic Effects of International Trade," *Quarterly Journal of Economics*, vol. 106, no. 2

Index